The Smoothies Bible Second Edition

Pat Crocker

Robert
ROSE

The Smoothies Bible, Second Edition
Text copyright © 2003, 2010 Pat Crocker
Photographs and illustrations copyright © 2003, 2010 Robert Rose Inc.
Cover and text design copyright © 2010 Robert Rose Inc.

This is a revised and expanded edition of *The Smoothies Bible*, published by Robert Rose Inc. in 2003.

For complete cataloguing information, see page 371.

Disclaimer
The Smoothies Bible is intended to provide information about the preparation and use of juices containing whole foods and medicinal herbs. It is not intended as a substitute for professional medical care. The publisher and author do not represent or warrant that the use of recipes or other information contained in this book will necessarily aid in the prevention or treatment of any disease, and specifically disclaim any liability, loss or risk, personal or otherwise, incurred as a consequence, directly or indirectly, of the use and application of any of the contents of this book. Readers must assume sole responsibility for any diet, lifestyle and/or treatment program that they choose to follow. If you have questions regarding the impact of diet and health, speak to a healthcare professional.

The recipes in this book have been carefully tested by our kitchen and our tasters. To the best of our knowledge, they are safe and nutritious for ordinary use and users. For those people with food or other allergies, or who have special food requirements or health issues, please read the suggested contents of each recipe carefully and determine whether or not they may create a problem for you. All recipes are used at the risk of the consumer.

We cannot be responsible for any hazards, loss or damage that may occur as a result of any recipe use.

For those with special needs, allergies, requirements or health problems, in the event of any doubt, please contact your medical adviser prior to the use of any recipe.

Design and Production: PageWave Graphics Inc.
Editor: Carol Sherman
Recipe Editor: Jennifer MacKenzie
Copy Editor: Christina Anson Mine
Indexer: Gillian Watts
Photography: Colin Erricson
Photograph on chapter openers: istockphoto.com/arsat
Food Styling: Kathryn Robertson
Prop Styling: Charlene Erricson
Illustrations: Kveta/Three In A Box

Cover image: Orange Pom (page 195), Mango Marvel (page 189) and Blueberry Banana (page 285)

We acknowledge the financial support of the Government of Canada through the Book Publishing Industry Development Program (BPIDP) for our publishing activities.

Published by Robert Rose Inc.
120 Eglinton Avenue East, Suite 800, Toronto, Ontario, Canada M4P 1E2
Tel: (416) 322-6552 Fax: (416) 322-6936
www.robertrose.ca

Printed and bound in Canada

5 6 7 8 9 MI 18 17 16 15 14 13 12

Contents

To my beautiful daughter, Shannon Alexandra,
may you always be blessed with good friends
whom you toast in good health.

Acknowledgments

Writers work alone and yet they are able to communicate with so many people. I am told that I now have 400,000 books in print with Robert Rose, and that means that from my second-floor studio office in the village of Neustadt, Ontario, I am able to reach out to a vast number of people. Just the thought of it humbles me. My thanks to Bob Dees and Marian Jarkovich and all the other members of the Robert Rose team: first, for your continued belief in my books, and second, for working to publish and market them. And thanks to the almost half a million people who own my books and enjoy my recipes.

We all live and work for positive recognition, and one of the greatest honors that a culinary herbalist and author can receive is the Gertrude Foster Award for Excellence in Herbal Literature. In 2009, the Herb Society of America bestowed that special honor on me. I am proud to join the list of distinguished herbal authors who have been recognized in this special way.

The challenges of writing this book were made easier with the support of the small-appliance industry. I thank the following blender manufacturers for providing the machines that tested the recipes in this book.

- Braun (www.braun.com)
- Cuisinart (www.cuisinart.com)
- Hamilton Beach/Proctor Silex (www.hamiltonbeach.com)
- KitchenAid (www.kitchenaid.com)
- Krups (www.krups.com)
- Vita-Mix (www.vitamix.com)
- Waring (www.waringproducts.com)

The people who support creative endeavors are the true heroes in book publishing. Thanks to my brilliant editor, Carol Sherman, recipe tester Jennifer MacKenzie, copy editor Tina Anson Mine, indexer Gillian Watts, designers Kevin Cockburn and Joseph Gisini at PageWave Graphics, photographer Colin Erricson and food stylist Kathy Robertson, without whose great work my books would not shine as brightly as they do.

Of course, my family continues to be my font of creative energy, sharing ideas, helping with kitchen chores and cheering me on to great-tasting dishes.

Preface

It is very exciting to be updating a book that was so favorably embraced upon its release almost seven years ago. In this new edition, I welcome more antioxidant fruits and vegetables into the smoothies mix; I serve classic cocktails — with and without the alcohol; and I remain true to the premise of the book, which is that smoothies are a delicious part of a healthy diet and lifestyle.

It's true, now more than ever, that homemade smoothies add vital vitamins and minerals, and a host of enzymes and other nutrients, to our not-so-perfect diets. By consuming as few as one or two smoothies a week, we do our bodies the favor of getting close to three of the five daily servings of fruits and vegetables recommended by all health professionals. But why stop at one or two?

This second edition includes the 300+ original smoothie recipes, plus more than 100 fresh new ways to slurp, sip and spoon your way to a healthier body. Don't delay. Start today with Pomegranate Perfect or Berry Yogurt Flip!

Drink to your health, Pat Crocker
www.foodwedsherbs.blogspot.com
www.riversongherbals.com

Introduction

Smoothies came to us via the beaches of California, where warm weather and cool, healthy drinks are part of the culture. With the introduction of blenders, Californians could buy blended thirst-quenching drinks made with orange juice, bananas and strawberries (with or without ice) right on the beach. Soon these coolers were known simply as "smoothies." It wasn't long before other combinations were created and a whole new category of beverages was invented. In 1961, Ann Seranne and Eileen Gaden included recipes for what they called "smoothees" in their *Blender Cookbook* (Doubleday & Co., Inc.). Even then, experimentation was spawning drinks such as their "Mocha Smoothee," "Orange-Pineapple Smoothee" and "Pineapple-Banana Smoothee" — all made with fruit juices and fresh bananas and enhanced with ice cream.

Types of Smoothies

Smoothies can be made from fruits, vegetables, herbs and/or a variety of other healthy ingredients. Smoothies require a liquid base — from juice to milk to stocks and broth to herbal tea. They can be served hot, cold, at room temperature — even frozen — and you will find them all in this book.

Smoothies as Part of a Healthy Diet

A nutritious diet includes protein, carbohydrates, fat, vitamins, minerals, enzymes, phytochemicals, fiber and water in proportions that promote growth and maintain healthy cells. It also includes ample quantities of vegetables and fruits. In fact, the phytochemicals in fruits and vegetables hold the key to preventing many diseases, such as cancer and heart disease, and debilitating conditions, such as asthma, arthritis and allergies. The problem is, even the most disciplined person can find it difficult to consume the quantities of fruits and vegetables that health professionals recommend. Adding a daily smoothie — or two — to your diet is one of the easiest ways to ensure that you eat enough fruits and vegetables to promote good health.

Smoothies can contribute in a significant way to ensuring a healthy diet by making it easier to consume the recommended five to eight daily servings of fruits and vegetables. One large glass of pure, raw or lightly cooked, blended fruits or vegetables will help improve the immune system, increase energy, strengthen bones, clear skin and lower the risk of disease. For maximum benefit, it is wise to consume a wide variety of organic fruits and vegetables and include some herbs and other nutritional ingredients, such as flax seeds or sea herbs.

Be sure to use the front sections of this book to determine the ingredients that will maximize health wellness for you and your specific health issues.

How Big Is One Serving?

One whole orange, apple or carrot represents one serving of fruits or vegetables. For larger fruits, such as melons or pineapples, about one slice or wedge (about 1/2 cup/125 mL chopped) equals one serving, as does the same amount of a chopped vegetable. Calculate the total number of servings of fruits and vegetables you're getting in a smoothie by adding the amounts of fruits and vegetables in the recipe and dividing by the number of people who are sharing it.

Added Nutrition

Because smoothies are made in a powerful grinding machine and are thickly textured, it is easy to include nuts, grains, herbs and other supplements that you likely wouldn't add to milk or plain juice. This means that smoothies are a perfect base to which you can add nutrient-rich ingredients such as flax seeds, wheat and barley grass, organic soy protein powder, psyllium seeds and wheat germ. See Other Ingredients, page 146, for information on the dietary value of these and other nutritious additions.

Tips for Making Smoothies Part of Your Daily Routine

- Position the blender in a convenient place on the counter.
- Always keep fresh bananas and seasonal fruit on hand.
- Stock the cupboards and freezer with favorite ingredients.
- Teach school-age children how to use the blender safely and clean it afterward.
- Write favorite recipes and ingredient combinations on cards and keep them in a place that is easily accessible.
- Introduce elders in your family and circle of friends to smoothies and show them how to add medicines or herbal remedies.
- Take a blender to work.

Benefits of Smoothies

Fruit or vegetable smoothies are an excellent way to enhance your health, because they provide vitamins, minerals, phytochemicals and most importantly, fiber. Smoothies make use of the whole fruit or vegetable and thus provide a valuable source of bulk: complex carbohydrates and their cleansing fiber. Smoothies made with milk, cheese, yogurt or tofu deliver the goodness of protein and calcium. Depending upon the smoothie, here are some of the healthful nutrients that may be added to your diet.

- **Antioxidants** are phytochemicals that counteract aging and reduce your susceptibility to cancers caused by cell-damaging free radicals that form in the body and initiate disease processes. Herbs, fruits and vegetables are high in antioxidants.
- **Calcium** is necessary to keep your heart, skin, teeth, bones and muscles healthy, and for proper blood clotting. Dairy-based smoothies and those rich in parsley, leafy greens, broccoli, prunes, almonds and pumpkin seeds are good sources of calcium.
- **Chlorophyll** has a unique structure that allows it to enhance the body's ability to produce hemoglobin and, therefore, increase the delivery of oxygen to cells. It is found only in plants.
- **Enzymes** are elements in fruits and vegetables that act as catalysts for chemical reactions in the body. They allow efficient digestion and absorption of food and support the metabolic processes involved in tissue growth. Enzymes give you a high energy level and promote good health. They are destroyed by heat, but smoothies made from fresh, raw fruits and vegetables leave them intact and readily absorbable.
- **Fiber** in the forms of cellulose, pectin, lignin and hemicellulose is found in fruits and vegetables and is essential to a healthy body. Fiber slows the absorption of food (increasing the absorption of nutrients), helps lower cholesterol and reduces the risk of heart disease. It also helps you eliminate toxins and carcinogens and prevents hemorrhoids, varicose veins, constipation, colitis and gallstones. Since toxins and bacteria are not given the chance to multiply when adequate fiber is present in the diet, the growth of diseases such as cancer is prevented. Along with all the vitamins, minerals, enzymes and phytochemicals, fiber in whole fruits and vegetables is retained when they are blended or pulped. Pulped fruit has a better cleansing effect on the body than juices because of its higher fiber content. Fiber in smoothies cleanses the body in a manner that's different from that of the fiber found in extracted juices. Insoluble fiber adds bulk to fecal matter, facilitating its rapid elimination through the colon. As a result, there is no undue multiplication of bacteria and production of toxins.

- **Iron** is a mineral that is present in the body, mostly in the blood. It carries oxygen, which is necessary for life itself, in the blood to organs and muscles. The best plant sources of iron are parsley, dates, some nuts (including Brazil nuts and almonds), sesame seeds and pumpkin seeds.
- **Long-lasting satisfaction** is a benefit of including smoothies in your diet. Pulping different fruit-and-vegetable combinations and mixing them with herbs, nuts, seeds and whole grains nourishes the body and leaves you feeling fuller longer than fast foods, soft drinks or coffee.
- **Magnesium** is essential for strong bones and teeth, healthy muscles and abundant energy. The best plant sources are raisins, spinach and other dark green vegetables, garlic, nuts and wheat germ.
- **Manganese** benefits bones, nerves and cell tissue. Animals that are deficient in manganese develop severe osteoporosis, and some doctors think the same may apply to humans. The best plant sources of manganese are grapes, pineapples, raspberries, strawberries, blackberries, watercress, beets, celery and oats.
- **Phosphorus** assists in energy production and helps build bones, teeth and muscle tissue. All fresh fruits and vegetables deliver phosphorus.
- **Phytonutrients**, or **phytochemicals**, come in hundreds of forms and are found in fresh, whole foods. They are important to the growth and maintenance of healthy bodies. New nutrients or chemicals in food are constantly being discovered and researched. Adding smoothies to your diet is one way of ensuring that you consume the variety of fruits, herbs and vegetables necessary to guarantee that you're getting the full range of nutrients.
- **Potassium** keeps nerves and muscles healthy, and regulates bodily fluids, insulin secretion and metabolism. It also helps the body make use of nutrients. Diets high in potassium have been found to lower blood pressure. The best plant sources of potassium are cantaloupes, avocados, dried peaches, apricots, bananas, celery, parsley and watercress.
- **Sodium** is vital in our bodies because it assists in nerve activity and heart function. Processed foods contain large amounts of sodium — more than is needed by, or even safe for, the body. However, small amounts of sodium are found naturally in celery, beets and watercress and are enough to do the job in the body and lend a light, pleasant, salty taste.
- **The spark of life**, or the living "green power" that is present in all living plants is available to the body when you consume fresh, raw fruits and vegetables. This "life force" is a natural, vital component that is lost in processing.
- **Sugar** in its natural form in fruits and vegetables comes bundled with vitamins, minerals, enzymes and other phytochemicals that refined sugar lacks. Fruit and vegetable sugars are carbohydrates

and, as such, deliver the same energy as pastries, candies and soft drinks, but without the chemicals and fat.

Caution: People with diabetes and those who are prone to yeast infections and hypoglycemia must watch how and when they use fruits because they cause a rapid rise in blood sugar.

- **Vitamin A** is found in bright orange fruits and vegetables, such as apricots, mangos, melons, papayas, tangerines, carrots and tomatoes. It is important for healthy skin and tissue, improves night vision and acts as an antioxidant.
- **B Vitamins** are essential for brain function; conversion of protein, fat and carbohydrates to energy; glowing skin and hair; and nerve function. Watercress, peppers, tomatoes, strawberries, avocados, bananas, nuts and seeds all contain large doses of B vitamins.
- **Vitamin C** is present in citrus fruits, papayas, mangos, pineapples, melons, kiwis, tomatoes and peppers, is a powerful antioxidant that fights infection and builds strong bones and joints.
- **Vitamin E** is a powerful antioxidant that promotes healing. It is found in large amounts in seeds, nuts and wheat germ.
- **Vitamin K** is important for blood clotting. Broccoli, lettuce and watercress are high in vitamin K.
- **Water** is essential because human cells are made of at least 65% water, and the body requires water to perform many functions. Drinking a minimum of eight large glasses of water a day is essential. Unlike coffee, soft drinks and alcohol, which remove water from the body as they are metabolized, smoothies are high in water, which replenishes lost fluids while supplying all the vitamins, minerals, enzymes and phytochemicals we need for life. In addition, fresh fruit-and-vegetable smoothies maintain the alkalinity of bodily fluids, which is vital for proper immune-system and metabolic function.
- **Zinc** is necessary for hormone control, growth, healing, and heart and nerve activity. The best plant sources of it are ginger, nuts and oats.

Equipment for Smoothies

Blenders are better at pulping and blending than food processors. The Vita-Mix is the best machine to use for smoothies and blended drinks since it reduces foods (even seeds) to minuscule particles. Most blended drinks or smoothies call for some juice, and it is best if fresh, raw fruits or vegetables are first juiced using a juice extractor, then added to a blending/pulping machine.

Blenders

The recipes in this book are best made in a traditional blender that has a jar or jug with rotating blades set on a motor. Today, all blenders come with tight-fitting lids and openings that allow you to add ingredients while the motor is running. A food processor may be used for drinks that do not require ice. Today, many makes and models of blenders are available, in a wide range of prices.

Cleaning Your Blender

Disconnect the power cord before cleaning. Never immerse the motorized base in water; wipe it clean with a damp cloth. Drop $\frac{1}{2}$ tsp (2 mL) liquid dishwashing soap into the jug and fill to the halfway mark with hot water. Replace the lid securely and turn the switch to pulse-clean, mix or low. Run for several seconds. Pour soapy water out and rinse the jug and lid with hot water. From time to time, the jug can be disassembled and thoroughly cleaned in hot soapy water or in the dishwasher, according to the manufacturer's instructions.

Buying a Blender?

Consider the following when determining which blender to purchase.

- **Base:** A heavy base stabilizes the machine and keeps it from vibrating or moving around on the counter. Washable heavy-duty stainless steel or heavy-gauge plastic are practical. Flat touch-pad buttons do not collect food debris and are easy to keep clean.
- **Motor:** Heavy-duty motors (120 volts, 60 hertz or more) are strong enough to chop ice cubes and the hard ingredients that some of the recipes call for. Less-powerful motors tend to burn out faster and may cause the machine to vibrate or jump around on the counter when ice, frozen fruit or hard vegetables are being processed.
- **Jug size, shape and capacity:** From tall to squat, fat to thin, the shape of blender jugs varies. Today, in response to consumer needs, many brands are moving to a wider jug that can process ice with less liquid. Jugs are usually made to hold between 5 and 6 cups (1.25 and 1.5 L), although some hold as much as 8 cups (2 L). When purchasing, consider the number of servings you will be making at one time to determine what size suits you best.
- **Jug materials:** Jugs are available in plastic, glass or stainless steel. Plastic is usually the least expensive. It is durable (a must if children are using the machine) and lightweight, but it scratches over time and is not recommended for processing ice. Glass is easier to clean, dishwasher-safe and fine for ice, and it doesn't wear out. Glass is more expensive than plastic, however. Stainless steel is top of the line: it is easy to clean and keeps frozen mixtures cold but is the most costly of the three.
- **Settings and speeds:** Some blenders only have two speeds (low and high); others have several (from mix to purée to liquefy and everything in between) Two speeds are essential, but if you plan to use ice in drinks (see Frozen Smoothies, page 326), look for a blender that has a pulse or ice crush setting, which is designed to crush ice evenly without liquefying it.
- **Appearance:** Blenders have become sleeker, with rounded corners, and are available in a variety of colors. While design does not affect performance, it is a consideration if the machine will be kept out on the counter where it is likely to be seen.

Healthy Body Systems

Healthy Living

Today, the big killers in Western societies are the cancers, cardiovascular disease, diabetes and hypertension, most of which are preventable by diet. Immunity and obesity play a role in either reducing or elevating disease, and they in turn are both affected by the foods we eat.

Doctors, scientists, naturopaths, nutritionists and medical herbalists all agree: to be healthy and prevent disease, a healthy lifestyle is essential. Following these guidelines will maintain and help to restore good health:

Guidelines to Good Health

- Limit alcohol consumption — use of alcohol is clearly linked to a slightly increased risk of getting breast cancer. Postmenopausal women who take less than one drink per day can increase the risk of dying from breast cancer by up to 30%.
- Exercise — moderate daily physical activity can lower cancer risk, boost the immune system, help prevent obesity, decrease estrogen and insulin growth factor (IGF), improve overall health and emotional well-being.
- Do not smoke — smoking is related to one-third of all cancers and 80% of all lung cancer.
- Eat well — a healthy diet is the best defense against disease.

Guidelines to Eating Well

- Eat a minimum of five servings of fruit and vegetables every day.
- Focus on the most colorful fruit and vegetables, such as red peppers, dark leafy greens, oranges, carrots, apricots, blueberries.
- Choose whole grains over processed grains and white flours.
- Limit refined carbohydrates, such as pastries, sweetened cereals, soft drinks, candy, salty snacks.
- Cook with olive or organic canola oil.
- Avoid trans fats, found in many margarines and baked and convenience products.
- Limit intake of saturated fats and cholesterol found in meats and dairy products.
- Add avocados, natural nuts, seeds, cold water fish (cod, sardines, salmon) to the diet.
- Control portion sizes.

Smoothies for Health

Smoothies can contribute in a significant way to ensuring a healthy diet by making it easier to consume the recommended five to eight daily servings of fruits and vegetables. One large glass of pure, raw or lightly cooked, blended fruits or vegetables will help improve the immune system, increase energy, strengthen bones, clear skin and lower the risk of disease. For maximum benefit, it is wise to consume a wide variety of organic fruits and vegetables and include some herbs and other nutritional ingredients such as flax seeds or sea vegetables.

Be sure to use the front sections of this book to determine the ingredients that will maximize health for you and your specific health issues.

Healthy Bodies

The body may be characterized by seven major systems: Cardiovascular (the heart and its components), Nervous (the brain, spinal cord and nerves), Endocrine (glands and hormones), Digestive (mucous membranes, stomach, pancreas, bladder, bowel), Musculoskeletal (muscles, bones, joints, connective tissue), Respiratory (nose, trachea, bronchial tubes, lungs) and Immune (protective cells). Each system has a role to play in keeping the body disease-free. And each system responds positively to specific whole foods.

In the following pages, you will find information on each system, including its importance to our health, what kinds of problems we develop when the systems break down and the diet and lifestyle changes we need to make to keep each system working as well as it can. As always, check with a health-care specialist if you are experiencing health problems.

Cardiovascular System

Healthy Cardiovascular System

The cardiovascular system consists of the heart, the arteries and veins, and the blood that runs through them. The heart is a muscular organ responsible for pumping oxygenated blood that has just come from the lungs, and for delivering it via the arteries to all body tissues and organs. The body's tissues and organs depend on this oxygen and other nutrients to function. The heart is also responsible for bringing de-oxygenated blood back from the body via the veins to the heart so this blood can be sent to the lungs to get more oxygen.

See details on the following Cardiovascular Health Conditions:

- Anemia, page 31
- High Cholesterol, High Blood Pressure, Cardiovascular Disease, Heart Failure and Stroke, page 53

Cardiovascular Problems

Atherosclerosis, high cholesterol, high blood pressure

Cardiovascular disease — or heart disease, as it is most commonly called — is an illness that pertains to the heart and the blood vessels. Atherosclerosis is the most common precursor to heart disease.

Atherosclerosis occurs when fatty deposits build up on the inside of the arteries, restricting blood flow to the organs supplied by the arteries. If this narrowing and decreased blood flow happens in the coronary arteries, the arteries that supply the heart muscle itself, coronary heart disease occurs. Coronary heart disease has few signs or symptoms, until the arteries become severely occluded, resulting in tissue death and a heart attack.

Digestive System

Healthy Digestive System

The digestive system is responsible for mixing the food we eat and breaking it down into smaller molecules that our body can absorb and use. Digestion starts at the mouth with chewing and breaking carbohydrate molecules down with the aid of enzymes found in saliva. Food then travels down the esophagus into the stomach, where hydrochloric acid, also known as HCl, and digestive enzymes break down proteins and allow for the absorption of some substances. Most digestion and absorption of nutrients takes place in the small intestine, with the help of the liver and gall bladder, which provide bile, and the pancreas, which provides digestive enzymes. Food molecules, such as monosaccharides (carbohydrate units), amino acids (protein units) and fatty acids, as well as vitamins, minerals and water are absorbed into the bloodstream and lymphatic system, while indigestible foods (mostly fiber) continue down to the large intestine and eventually get eliminated.

The entire digestive system is lined with mucous membranes. Mucous membranes act as a barrier and are responsible for mucous secretions that aid in the digestive process. A smooth muscle layer also exists in the entire digestive tract, and is responsible for mixing and breaking food down, as well as propelling food downwards through the digestive tract.

Food Combining

Food combining is a disciplined method of eating foods in a specific order or combination. It is used as a short-term aid to digestive problems and, in simple terms, requires eating protein foods, carbohydrate foods and fruit at different times, thus allowing for complete and efficient digestion of these foods.

Protein foods — meat, poultry, fish, eggs, nuts, seeds, dairy products, soy products — require the most time and energy for the body to digest.

Carbohydrates are the starches and sugars found in foods that furnish most of the energy needed for the body's activities. Squash, legumes, grains (wheat, oats, rice, rye, etc.), pasta, beets, parsnips, carrots, sweet potato and pumpkin are starchy carbohydrate foods that break down faster than protein but not as quickly as fruit. Fruits are the high-sugar carbohydrate foods that are digested very quickly, and are thus considered separately in food combining

Fruit requires the least time and energy for digestion and should be eaten before a meal or at least 2 hours after a meal. When taken this way, fruit acts as a digestive cleanser, promoting digestive function. Fruit taken with a meal causes digestive problems. Melons and bananas should be eaten separately from other fruit.

Health conditions that may benefit from food combining are food allergies and intolerances, indigestion, inflammatory bowel, flatulence, fatigue and peptic ulcer.

The best food combination meals

- Fruit alone. This is best taken as a variety of fruits at breakfast.
- Proteins with non-starchy vegetables: leafy green vegetables, asparagus, broccoli, cabbage, celery, cucumber, onion, peppers, sea vegetables, tomatoes, zucchini.
- Grains with non-starchy vegetables.

Digestive Problems

Heartburn, constipation, IBS and IBD, colon cancer

Heartburn is one of the most common digestive complaints. It can be a symptom of gastric reflux, a hiatal hernia or a gastric or duodenal ulcer. Determining the cause of heartburn is important because these conditions can be easily treated but can become serious if not attended to.

Constipation occurs when bowel movements are infrequent or difficult, causing bloating, headaches or hemorrhoids, to name a few symptoms. Constipation can be caused by a lack of fiber or water in the diet, stress, or perhaps disease.

Constipation can be an indicator of other digestive system diseases. For example, constipation alternating with diarrhea can be one of the symptoms of irritable bowel syndrome (IBS). Other symptoms of IBS include abdominal pain and cramps, excess gas and bloating. IBS can be caused by sensitivity to foods and is often associated with emotional stress — and it can be extremely disabling.

Inflammatory bowel disease (IBD) includes two conditions with chronic inflammation of the bowels: Crohn's disease and ulcerative colitis. In these conditions, inflammation of the bowel can result in such symptoms as diarrhea, bleeding, cramping and a feeling of urgency. The cause of these conditions is not known. Consult a physician if you are suffering from any of the above symptoms.

The digestive system is also susceptible to cancer. Colon cancer is the second most common form of cancer, and one that can be easily prevented with a healthy lifestyle and regular bowel movements. Colon cancer is treatable, but early detection and treatment are crucial. If you experience a change in bowel habits, blood in the stool, unexplained weight loss or fatigue, consult your physician.

See details on the following Digestive Conditions:

- Constipation, page 41
- Diarrhea, page 44
- Diverticular Disease, page 45
- Heartburn, page 55
- Indigestion, page 60
- Inflammatory Bowel Disease, page 64
- Irritable Bowel Syndrome, page 66
- Peptic Ulcers, page 78

Endocrine System

Healthy Endocrine System

The endocrine system consists of the endocrine glands and the hormones produced by these glands, which work together to serve as one of the body's main control systems. Hormones are chemicals that carry messages through the blood. To do this, hormones travel from the endocrine glands in which they are produced to the target cells where they will perform their function. For example, the thyroid gland produces and secretes thyroid hormones (thyroxine or T4, and triiodothyronine or T3), which control the body's metabolic rate. The pancreas, which secretes digestive enzymes as part of the digestive system, also performs an endocrine function by releasing the insulin and glucagon responsible for balancing blood sugar.

The reproductive organs are also part of the endocrine system. In females, the ovaries manage the functioning, growth and development of the female reproductive system, including the breasts, via hormones such as estrogen and progesterone. In males, the testes produce testosterone, which is responsible for the functioning, growth and development of the male reproductive system.

Many other glands and organs are part of the endocrine system, including the hypothalamus in the brain and the pituitary gland just below it. Both control many glands through the hormones they secrete. Hormonal feedback can signal to these glands to produce more or less hormones that help keep the body's functions in balance.

See details on the following Endocrine Conditions:

- Diabetes, page 43
- Hypoglycemia, page 57
- Menopause, page 71
- Menstrual Disorders, page 72

Endocrine Disorders

Hormone imbalance, hyperthyroidism, hypothyroidism, diabetes

Most endocrine disorders occur when too much or too little of a hormone is produced by an endocrine gland, when the target cell exerts a reduced response or, in some cases, when our body cannot properly eliminate excess hormones.

Immune System

Healthy Immune System

The immune system consists of a complex collection of cells found throughout the body. These cells are responsible for protecting the body against infection, as well as for constant surveillance and destruction of the cancer cells.

The skin and mucous membranes, along with chemical substances like mucus, tears and stomach acid, are also an important part of the immune system, acting as frontline barriers that prevent foreign materials and pathogenic organisms from entering and harming the body.

When the immune system does not work optimally, we see an increased risk for infections and cancers, as well as the development of allergies and inflammatory diseases.

Support and enhancement of the immune system through consumption of whole foods, proper intake of water, regular moderate exercise and mental relaxation can increase the body's resistance to colds, influenza and cancers, and keep allergies and inflammation in check.

See details on the following Immune Conditions:

- AIDS + HIV, page 26
- Allergies, page 28
- Cancer Prevention, page 37
- Chronic Fatigue Syndrome, page 39
- Common Cold, page 40
- Herpes Simplex, page 55
- Immune Deficiency, page 57
- Influenza, page 64
- Lupus, page 70

Immune System Disorders

Frequent and chronic infections, cancer, inflammation, allergies

Frequent and chronic infections may include anything from a common cold, flu, ear infections and urinary tract infections to more serious illnesses, such as herpes virus infections, bronchitis and pneumonia. Viruses, bacteria, fungi and parasites can all cause infections, especially when they do not meet adequate resistance from a weakened immune system.

Similarly, cancer risk increases when there is damage to a cell's DNA and the immune system's DNA repair or cancer surveillance systems are not functioning at an optimal level. DNA can be damaged by free radicals produced inside the body or by elements from the external environment, such as chemicals, radiation or viruses.

See also
• Garlic, page 127

Musculoskeletal System

Healthy Musculoskeletal System

Muscles, bones, joints and connective tissues make up the musculoskeletal system, responsible for the movement of the human body and its individual parts. The musculoskeletal system also gives structure to the body and physically protects the internal organs.

Nutrition is very important in the management of this system; for example, muscle contraction and relaxation depend on minerals such as calcium and magnesium to perform movements and maintain an upright posture and balance. Bones also need minerals to maintain their density and withstand the pulling forces created by the muscles and the impact of accidents and falls.

Another important part of the musculoskeletal system is the joints, such as the hips, knees and elbows. Within the joints, the ends of the bones are covered with cartilage and are surrounded by synovial fluid, a lubricating fluid, which allows smooth and frictionless motion where two bones meet.

Musculoskeletal Disorders

Arthritis, osteoporosis, low back pain, muscle spasms and cramps, sprains and strains

Muscle cramping and spasms can occur with dehydration and if minerals such as calcium, sodium, potassium and magnesium are not in the proper balance. This can cause simple cramping of the calf muscle or more aggravate existing conditions, such as low back pain. Low back pain can also be due to misalignment of the spine or other parts of the skeleton, nerve impingement, injury and chronic inflammation.

See details on the following Musculoskeletal Conditions:

- Arthritis, page 32
- Osteoporosis, page 75

Inflammation also occurs during arthritis. There are many types of arthritis, some with more inflammation than others. For example, osteoarthritis, the most common type, is characterized by wear and tear at the joints, wearing down of the joint cartilage, and causing changes in the bone. Although minimal, osteoarthritis consists of some inflammation at the joint and in surrounding tissues. Symptoms can be stiffness and pain at the joint and eventually restricted joint function. On the other hand, rheumatoid arthritis is an autoimmune condition characterized by chronic inflammation that can affect the joints as well as other areas of the body. Rheumatoid arthritis can give symptoms of inflammation at the joint, such as pain, redness, swelling and eventually deformity, but also generalized symptoms of fatigue, weakness and low-grade fever. Regardless of the cause and the differing symptoms and location, nutrition is essential to repair and build cartilage and decrease inflammation.

Unlike arthritis, osteoporosis is mostly symptom-free, which is why people at increased risk must get regular bone-density checks. In osteoporosis, the bone density is diminished and the bones become brittle and susceptible to fractures. The density of the bone depends on many nutrients, such as calcium, magnesium and zinc, for the strength to withstand trauma, perform movement and provide support.

Nervous System

Healthy Nervous System

The nervous system is a highly complex system made up of two main parts, the central and the peripheral nervous systems, which together allow us to respond to our internal and external environments. The central nervous system consists of the brain and the spinal cord, while the peripheral nervous system is made up of nerves (sensory and motor) and connects the central nervous system with other parts of the body.

The peripheral nervous system is responsible for receiving information, such as taste, sound or hormone levels, from the internal and external environments and for relaying that information to the central nervous system via peripheral sensory nerves. The spinal cord and brain integrate this information in the central nervous system and generate a response, which is then sent to other parts of the body via the peripheral motor nerves. For example, the peripheral sensory nerves might relay information about a song on the radio to the spinal cord and the brain. A response would then be sent through the peripheral motor nerves to make a movement to turn up the radio.

Of course, not all responses are conscious. The peripheral nervous system also consists of the autonomic nervous system, which controls internal organs and glands, such as the heart, or the thyroid gland, which is responsible for the body's metabolism. Through this system, consisting of sympathetic and parasympathetic responses, the body can maintain an internal balance and react to different stimuli based on the needed responses. For example a sympathetic or "fight or flight" response is created when you are frightened or stressed. This response causes your heart rate to increase. In contrast, a parasympathetic response allows you to perform such functions as relaxing and digesting your food after a meal. These two parts of the autonomic nervous system act on the same organs and glands, but have opposing effects, helping maintain balance in the body.

Nervous System Disorders

Anxiety, depression, seasonal affective disorder, memory loss and decreased cognitive function

Depression is a condition that occurs when there is an imbalance of neurotransmitters in the brain. It can be characterized by a loss of interest or pleasure in usual activities and a lack of energy. It can also affect appetite, with either a decrease or increase, and subsequent changes in body weight. Depression can be quite debilitating and can trigger feelings of worthlessness or even thoughts of death or suicide.

Seasonal affective disorder (SAD) is a form of depression that occurs with diminished exposure to sunlight in the winter months. This disorder may result in the general symptoms of depression, and also an increase in sleep, appetite and perhaps body weight.

Anxiety is a devastating psychiatric disorder that can consist of feelings of agitation, nervousness, fearfulness, irritability or shyness. Other symptoms may include heart palpitations, flushing of the face, sweating, shallow breathing or even fainting. Both anxiety and depression can be caused by psychological factors; a physical cause, such as trauma or illness; nutrient deficiencies; or the side-effects of medications.

As a result of normal living and aging, the nervous system suffers from oxidation of its cells, improper nutrient status and a decrease in blood circulation. These and other factors can lead to a decline in neurotransmitter levels, a decrease in the number of connections between neurons and an actual decrease in brain size, leading to a decrease in cognitive function and memory loss.

See details on the following Nervous System Conditions:

• Anxiety States, page 32

• Depression, page 42

• Parkinson's Disease, page 77

Respiratory System

Healthy Respiratory System

The respiratory system is responsible for the exchange of oxygen and carbon dioxide between the external environment and the blood. The air that we breathe travels in through the nose, past the pharynx and larynx, down the trachea, into the bronchi and bronchioles and eventually reaches its destination: the lungs. In the lungs, the exchange of gases occurs in tiny air sacs called alveoli, where oxygen from the air enters the bloodstream and carbon dioxide from the bloodstream enters the air to be expelled. Through the actions of inspiration and expiration, the air flows in and out of the lungs providing all body cells with the fresh supply of oxygen essential to them for survival.

The respiratory system is also responsible for protecting the body against microbes, toxic chemicals and foreign matter. This is achieved with the help of cilia, tiny hair-like structures that sweep mucus and foreign materials out of the system. The cilia also work with the immune system to produce mucus and perform phagocytosis (engulfing pathogens and debris).

Respiratory Disorders

Asthma and allergies, respiratory tract infections, lung cancer

Asthma is the most common illness associated with the respiratory system. It is an inflammatory condition of the lungs and airways in which swelling, smooth-muscle contraction and excess mucus production create acute breathing difficulties. Someone who suffers from asthma might experience a feeling of tightness and constriction of the chest, with shortness of breath, wheezing and coughing. It is believed that asthma, like allergies, is a hypersensitivity disorder and therefore greatly linked to the immune system.

The respiratory system is the most susceptible to infection, because it is directly exposed to the external environment. Therefore, respiratory infections, such as colds, sinusitis, bronchitis and pneumonia, also greatly depend on the immune system. Here, the immune system is responsible for protecting the respiratory system by producing mucus, attacking foreign invaders and developing a proper response to fight pathogens once they enter the body.

The respiratory system is also susceptible to cancer. Lung cancer is the most prevalent form of cancer today and can affect one or both lungs. Smoking is the biggest risk factor for lung cancer, so quitting smoking is a valuable method in its prevention. Other methods include eating a vitamin-rich diet, which can help reduce the risk of cancer but also the chance that cancer will come back once treated.

See details on the following Respiratory System Conditions:

• Allergies, page 28
• Bronchitis, page 36
• Cancer Prevention, page 37

Health Conditions

The combined wisdom of common sense, human observation and scientific study all point to the importance of our diet in preventing and controlling disease. General dietary principles are set out on page 14. In this section, you will find recommendations for specific health conditions.

These recommendations are not intended to take the place of consultation with a medical practitioner. For best results, and especially if faced with a serious condition, contact a doctor, medical herbalist or natural health specialist who can provide you with a diet and lifestyle program suited to your needs. For each condition, the best fruits, vegetables, herbs and other foods are recommended.

AIDS & HIV
Acquired Immunodeficiency Syndrome & Human Immunodeficiency Virus

There is no known cure for AIDS, and anyone with HIV should be under a doctor's care. However, dietary therapy can improve immune function, promote resistance to infections associated with AIDS and reduce symptoms associated with HIV and AIDS.

Healing Foods

Fruits and vegetables
citrus fruits, peaches, pears, strawberries, asparagus, avocados, broccoli, carrots, cauliflower, leafy greens, onions, squash

Herbs
aloe vera, astragalus, burdock (leaf, root and seeds), evening primrose oil, garlic, ginseng, licorice*, turmeric

Other
cereal grasses, flax seeds, kelp, pumpkin seeds, soy yogurt, sprouted seeds, sunflower seeds, tofu, whole grains

* Avoid licorice if you have high blood pressure. The prolonged use of licorice is not recommended under any circumstances.

What to Do

Maximize
- Organic fruits and vegetables, which are free of chemicals
- Shiitake mushrooms, which studies have shown to strongly support the immune system
- Garlic — an antibacterial, antiviral and antifungal — which guards against opportunistic infections

Minimize
- Sweet foods, including honey and fruit juices, which encourage the growth of molds and yeast

Eliminate
- Refined flour
- Animal fats in meat and dairy products, as they decrease immunity
- Alcohol, which increases susceptibility to infection
- Food allergies and intolerances (see Appendix A: Food Allergies, page 373)
- Sugar

Other Recommendations
- Exercise daily, according to your fitness level. This helps improve circulation and eliminates toxins through sweating.
- Practice stress-reduction techniques, such as yoga, tai chi and meditation to strengthen the immune system by decreasing stress.

Healing Smoothies

- Allium Antioxidant, page 258
- C-Green, page 231
- Cauliflower Cocktail, page 230
- Cream of Broccoli, page 234
- Green Energy (use ginseng instead of ginkgo), page 265
- Leafy Pear, page 187
- Minestrone, page 241
- Orange Silk, page 195

Aging

Several scientific studies show that eating a diet high in nutrients but low in calories helps reduce signs of aging and increases life span. Recent studies also show that oxidation is one of the most important factors that contributes to aging. Oxidation occurs when cells are damaged by free radicals, by-products produced when the body converts oxygen to energy. The progression of Parkinson's disease and Alzheimer's disease has been linked to oxidative stress. Heart disease, cancer, arthritis and wrinkles are also signs of cell damage, often caused by free radicals. Antioxidants, which are found in many fruits and vegetables, protect the body from free-radical damage.

Healing Foods

Fruits and vegetables
apples, blueberries, grapefruits, oranges, pears, raspberries, strawberries, beets, broccoli, cabbage, carrots, celery, leafy greens, onions, pumpkin, sweet potatoes, tomatoes

Herbs
cayenne, German chamomile, garlic, ginger, ginkgo, green tea, lemon balm, milk thistle, oregano, parsley*, peppermint, rosemary, sage**, spearmint, thyme, turmeric

Other
cereal grasses, extra virgin olive oil, flax seeds, nuts, pumpkin seeds, sea herbs, sesame seeds, soy products, sunflower seeds, yogurt with active bacterial cultures

* If you are pregnant, limit your intake of parsley to ½ tsp (2 mL) dried or one sprig fresh per day. Do not take parsley if you are suffering from kidney inflammation.

** Do not take sage if you have high blood pressure or are pregnant or breastfeeding.

What to Do

Maximize
- Antioxidant-rich fruits and vegetables
- Antioxidant herbal teas (any combination of oregano, rosemary, lemon balm, sage, thyme and peppermint)
- Effective digestion. Remedying digestive problems (see Indigestion, page 60) will improve your body's ability to absorb nutrients

Minimize
- Animal fats in meat and dairy products. Replace some meat meals with fish and vegetable protein

Eliminate
- Unnecessary calories

Healing Smoothies

- Beta Blast, page 169
- Black Pineapple, page 170
- Blueberry, page 171
- Fruit of Life, page 180
- Gingered Beets, page 237
- Smart Smoothie, page 276
- Spa Special, page 277
- Tutti-Fruity, page 219
- Wake up and Shine, page 219

Allergies
Hay Fever, Eczema & Asthma

The symptoms of allergic reactions evidenced in hay fever, eczema and asthma are caused by inflammation, which is the body's normal healing response to injury. Allergies are an example of chronic inflammation, in which factors such as food intolerance, stress and poor digestion allow a toxin to activate the immune system. This causes inappropriate inflammatory responses on the skin or in the eyes, nose or airways. Proper nutrition and the use of appropriate herbs can reduce the severity of the inflammation.

Healing Foods

Fruits and vegetables
apples, blueberries, grapes, mangoes, oranges, raspberries, strawberries, asparagus, beets, carrots, onions, red and green bell peppers, spinach, watercress

Herbs
astragalus, burdock root*, calendula*, cinnamon, dandelion leaf and root*, elderflower, garlic, ginger, licorice**, parsley***, stinging nettle, thyme, turmeric, yarrow*

Other
flax seeds, nuts (except peanuts), pumpkin seeds, rice, soy products, whole grains, yogurt with active bacterial cultures

* People who are allergic to ragweed may also be allergic to herbs in the same botanical family (the *Compositae*, or daisy, family). The herbs in this family include burdock, calendula, chamomile, chicory, dandelion, echinacea, feverfew, milk thistle and yarrow (avoid yarrow if you are pregnant).

** Avoid licorice if you have high blood pressure. The prolonged use of licorice is not recommended under any circumstances.

*** If you are pregnant, limit your intake of parsley to ½ tsp (2 mL) dried or one sprig fresh per day. Do not take parsley if you are suffering from kidney inflammation.

What to Do

Maximize
- Fruits and vegetables that provide flavonoids and antioxidants, which support appropriate immune response
- Essential fatty acids (found in oily fish, flax seeds and sunflower seeds, among other foods), which are anti-inflammatory and reduce the severity of allergies
- Herbs that optimize digestion (dandelion root, as required), boost immunity (astragalus, garlic) and nourish the nervous system (oat straw, skullcap)

Eliminate
- Food allergies and intolerances (see Appendix A: Food Allergies, page 373)
- Sugar, including honey and fruit sugars. Studies have shown that sugars decrease immune function by impairing white-blood-cell activity. Excess sugar also promotes yeast infections, which increase allergic reactions
- Alcohol, which depresses immune function
- Mucus-forming foods (dairy products, bananas)

Other Recommendations
- Reduce stress. Stress and high emotion are factors in lowered immunity, which increases susceptibility to allergies. Sleep and relaxation help to produce immunity-enhancing compounds.
- Improve digestion. Poor digestion keeps the body from eliminating toxins and limits the absorption of nutrients. When food is completely digested, allergic reactions are often eliminated.
- Get adequate protein, which is essential for optimum immune function. The best sources of protein are fish, such as tuna, salmon, sardines, trout, cod and herring.

Healing Smoothies

- Berry Fine Cocktail, page 168
- Blueberry, page 171
- C-Green, page 231
- Citrus Cocktail, page 176
- Detox Delight (use a recommended herb instead of milk thistle), page 179
- Gingered Greens, page 238
- Granate Berry, page 183
- Green Energy (use a recommended herb instead of ginkgo), page 265
- Mango Madness (substitute 1/4 cup/50 mL yogurt for banana), page 188

Alopecia

Healing Foods

Fruits and vegetables
broccoli, cabbage, garlic, onions, spinach

Herbs
ginger, rosemary, stinging nettle

Other
brown rice, eggs, flax seeds, nuts, soy products, sunflower seeds

Alopecia is a partial or complete loss of hair. It can be caused by severe stress; skin diseases; excessive sunlight; thyroid imbalances; excessive sex hormones; or strong chemicals, such as those used for cancer treatment or on the hair, that interfere with the nutrition of the hair follicles.

Hair consists largely of protein, which is made from amino acids and minerals, and is greatly affected by nutrition. Rosemary is traditionally used to treat hair problems. A rosemary tea can be used both internally and externally to stimulate blood flow to the scalp.

What to Do

Include in Your Diet

- High-protein foods (meat, fish, poultry, eggs, cheese, brown rice, nuts, seeds, soybeans)
- Foods that contain sulfur (egg yolks, cauliflower, cabbage, turnips, onions, garlic)
- Calcium-rich foods (dairy products, leafy greens, sea herbs)

Maximize

- Antioxidant-rich fruits and vegetables, especially broccoli, cabbage, garlic, onions and spinach

Minimize

- Stress. Relaxation techniques, such as meditation and yoga, can help alleviate the stresses and tensions of life

Healing Smoothies

- Allium Antioxidant, page 258
- Cabbage Cocktail, page 226
- Green Energy (use a recommended herb instead of ginkgo), page 265
- Green Gift, page 238
- Spinach Salad, page 249

Alzheimer's Disease & Dementia

Healing Foods

Fruits and vegetables
blueberries, citrus fruits, grapes, asparagus, broccoli, beets and beet greens, carrots, green bell peppers, kale, okra, onions, spinach, sweet potatoes, watercress, yams

Herbs
basil, garlic, German chamomile, ginger, ginkgo, ginseng, dandelion leaves and flowers, lemon balm, licorice*, stinging nettle, parsley**, red clover flowers, rosemary, sage, skullcap, turmeric

Other
Brazil nuts, brown rice, cider vinegar, egg yolks, extra virgin olive oil, flax seeds, lecithin, legumes, lentils, nuts, oats, pumpkin seeds, sea herbs, soy products, wheat germ

---

* Avoid licorice if you have high blood pressure. The prolonged use of licorice is not recommended under any circumstances.

** If you are pregnant, limit your intake of parsley to ½ tsp (2 mL) dried or one sprig fresh per day. Do not take parsley if you are suffering from kidney inflammation.

Dementia is characterized by impairment of memory, judgment and abstract thinking. It may be caused by stress, by impaired circulation caused by a buildup of fatty deposits in the blood vessels of the brain or by a degenerative disease, such as Alzheimer's disease. Recognized risk factors for Alzheimer's disease include acetylcholine deficiency, free-radical damage and inflammation of brain tissue. Diet can play a role in the prevention of Alzheimer's by nourishing the brain; by lowering cholesterol, which causes fatty deposits to form in the blood vessels of the brain; and by providing antioxidants to protect against free radicals that cause brain-cell damage. Foods that contain choline, a building block of acetylcholine (a chemical that plays a key role in cognition and reasoning) may help prevent Alzheimer's disease.

What to Do

Maximize

- Fresh fruits and vegetables, which provide vitamins and minerals to feed brain tissue and antioxidants to eliminate free radicals
- Foods that contain choline, a building block of acetylcholine (Brazil nuts, lecithin, dandelion flowers, mung beans, lentils, fava beans)
- Nuts and seeds, which provide essential fatty acids to nourish the brain

Minimize

- Meat and dairy products
- Environmental toxins

Eliminate

- Refined and processed foods
- Alcohol
- Fatty foods, fried foods and oils (except extra virgin olive oil)
- Aluminum in cookware, foil, deodorants and antacids. There is a suspected relationship between aluminum and Alzheimer's disease. Avoid preparing foods with aluminum cooking utensils. Although no direct link has been established between Alzheimer's and aluminum, high concentrations of aluminum have been found when autopsies were performed on Alzheimer's patients. It is probably wise to err on the side of caution.

Other Recommendations

- Eat oily fish (salmon, sardines, mackerel, herring), which provide essential fatty acids to nourish brain and nerve tissue.
- Rosemary and sage traditionally have been used to improve memory. Both herbs are rich in antioxidants. Studies also show that they contain substances that conserve acetylcholine.

- Ginkgo biloba improves blood flow to the brain, which is helpful in cases in which a doctor has diagnosed that insufficient blood flow to the brain is causing dementia. If dementia is not caused by insufficient cerebral blood flow, do not use ginkgo biloba, as it may cause other problems.
- Take anti-inflammatory herbs (German chamomile, ginseng, licorice, turmeric) to reduce the inflammation of brain tissue associated with Alzheimer's disease.

Healing Smoothies

- Beet, page 225
- Black Pineapple, page 170
- Blueberry Smoothie, page 171
- Brocco-Carrot, page 226
- C-Blend, page 174
- Peppered Beet, page 244
- Pomegranate Plus, page 206
- Red Horizon, page 210
- Smart Smoothie, page 276
- Tomato Froth, page 251

Anemia

Healing Foods

Fruits and vegetables
apples, citrus fruits, grapes, peaches, strawberries, beets and beet greens, broccoli, carrots, fennel, green peas, Jerusalem artichokes, leafy greens, watercress

Herbs
burdock root, dandelion leaf and root, stinging nettle, parsley*

Other
almonds, blackstrap molasses, dried apricots, figs, kelp, prunes, raisins

* If you are pregnant, limit your intake of parsley to ½ tsp (2 mL) dried or one sprig fresh per day. Do not take parsley if you are suffering from kidney inflammation.

Anemia is a deficiency of hemoglobin in the blood, which results in fatigue and facial pallor. Other symptoms depend on the type of anemia, which can be determined by a blood test. Iron-deficiency anemia is the most common type and may be precipitated by heavy menstrual flow, internal bleeding, dietary deficiency of iron, pregnancy or rheumatoid arthritis. To treat anemia, you must determine the type, then work to alleviate the underlying cause. For all types of anemia, increasing the body's ability to absorb nutrients is helpful.

What to Do

Maximize
- Iron-rich foods and herbs (sea herbs, beets, dried fruits, almonds, spinach, stinging nettle, parsley*, watercress)
- Foods rich in vitamin C
- Herbal bitters, such as dandelion root, to improve iron absorption

Minimize
- Whole wheat bread, which limits iron absorption

Eliminate
- Foods that limit iron absorption (coffee, tea, chocolate, wheat bran)

Healing Smoothies

- Appled Beet, page 223
- Apricot Peach, page 164
- Beet, page 225
- Orange Pom, page 195
- Orange Slushie, page 196
- Peachy Currant, page 198
- Popeye's Power, page 272
- Sea-Straw, page 212

Anxiety States
Anxiety, Stress & Panic Attacks

Anxiety is characterized by a mood of fear and is often associated with insomnia. Panic disorders are recurrent attacks of severe anxiety. Causes may include fatigue, stress, nervous disorders, depression or hormone imbalance.

Healing Foods

Fruits and vegetables
apricots, bananas, broccoli, carrots, celery, fennel, leafy greens, onions, watercress

Herbs
alfalfa, borage, dandelion leaf, garlic, German chamomile, kava kava, lavender, lemon balm, parsley*, St. John's wort, skullcap, valerian**

Other
almond milk, dulse, honey, kelp, nuts (especially almonds), tofu, whole grains (especially oats)

* If you are pregnant, limit your intake of parsley to ½ tsp (2 mL) dried or one sprig fresh per day. Do not take parsley if you are suffering from kidney inflammation.

** Valerian has an adverse effect on some people.

What to Do

Maximize
- Fresh fruits and vegetable fiber to boost general health, which allows you to cope better with stress
- Foods rich in B vitamins (whole grains, leafy greens) to support the nervous system
- Foods that are high in calcium and magnesium (kelp, dulse, soy products, almonds, kale, parsley*), which help ease nervous tension
- Herbs that help you relax and that improve sleep (German chamomile, lavender, skullcap)
- Meditation and relaxation exercises to help release nervous energy, allowing a more balanced emotional state

Eliminate
- Caffeine (found in coffee, black and green tea, chocolate and soft drinks)
- Alcohol
- Refined flour and sugar
- Artificial food additives
- Food allergies and intolerances (see Appendix A: Food Allergies, page 373)

Healing Smoothies

- Almond Banana, page 158
- Apricot and Oatmeal Breakfast Special, page 163
- Banana Frappé, page 305
- Calming Chamomile, page 260
- Cream of Broccoli, page 234
- Lavender Smoothie, page 268
- Popeye's Power, page 272

Arthritis
Rheumatoid Arthritis & Osteoarthritis

Rheumatoid arthritis is the most common chronic inflammatory joint disease. It can usually be diagnosed by the presence of antibodies (called rheumatoid factor) in the blood. Since it is blood-related rather than the result of wear and tear, rheumatoid arthritis is a disease that affects the whole body, often resulting in symptoms such as fever, weight loss, fatigue and a general decline in health. The joints (commonly the wrists, elbows, ankles, knees, hips, and hand and foot joints) become swollen and inflamed and are usually affected symmetrically. Neck pain and stiffness result from spinal inflammation. Joints can eventually become deformed due to a buildup of fluid that impairs the healing process in the joint tissue. Pain and stiffness is usually worst in the morning and may wear off during the day.

Osteoarthritis is a wear-and-tear disorder that usually starts after age 50. It is characterized by cartilage degeneration in weight-bearing joints, such as the hips, knees and spine, as well as joints in the hand. As the cartilage degenerates, new bone, cartilage and connective tissues are formed, which remodel the joint, leading to wasted muscle around the joint and limited movement. Inflammation is secondary to the degeneration of cartilage. Pain is usually provoked by movement and disappears with rest, so it typically gets worse as the day progresses. Because osteoarthritis pain is caused by placing weight on the joints, in overweight people, it improves with weight loss. It is often related to a mineral imbalance in the diet and/or a defect that limits the body's ability to absorb minerals. As a result, it may improve with dietary changes and/or support for the digestive system.

Arthritis sufferers often have poor circulation (signified by constantly cold hands and feet), don't perspire, get constipated easily and are overweight. These factors contribute to the retention of waste products and must be addressed first by using some of the herbs listed below (see also Constipation, page 41, and Overweight, page 76). Visit a medical herbalist or other natural-health practitioner for additional advice for your individual situation.

What to Do

Maximize
- Fresh fruits and vegetables
- Fluid intake (drink at least eight large glasses of water, juice and/or herbal tea daily) to dilute and wash out toxins
- Oily fish (salmon, tuna, herring, sardines, trout, cod, mackerel), which are anti-inflammatory
- Herbs that support the digestive system (lemon balm, peppermint, chamomile) to improve nutrient absorption
- Herbal analgesics (German chamomile, meadowsweet) for pain relief
- Anti-inflammatory herbs (German chamomile, ginger, licorice*, meadowsweet) to reduce pain and joint deterioration
- Herbal diuretics (dandelion leaf) and lymphatics (red clover flower) to encourage the elimination of waste products
- Herbs that support the liver (dandelion root, licorice*) to help eliminate toxins
- Herbal circulatory stimulants (ginger, stinging nettle) to improve blood supply to the affected joints

Minimize

- Refined foods
- Tea, coffee and soft drinks
- Salt and salty foods
- Acidic fruits and vegetables (rhubarb, cranberries, plums, spinach, Swiss chard, beet greens)

Eliminate

- Junk food
- Food allergies and intolerances (see Appendix A: Food Allergies, page 373). Problem foods are often corn, dairy products, wheat, eggs, chocolate, peanuts and varieties of the nightshade family, which includes peppers, tomatoes, potatoes and eggplant
- Meat, especially red meat (beef, pork, lamb) and processed meat products (ham, hamburgers, sausages, cold cuts), which can stimulate inflammation
- Margarine, shortening and heat-processed oils (replace with extra virgin olive oil)
- Shellfish. When protein from shellfish is digested, toxins (urea, uric acid, purines) in it are deposited in the fat and at the ends of the long bones (joints), where they lead to slow, chronic inflammation. Toxins created when shellfish are digested seem to cause more problems than other proteins
- Processed and refined foods
- Sugar and artificial sweeteners (replace with honey, maple syrup or stevia, page 142)
- Citrus fruits, which often cause allergic reactions in people with rheumatoid arthritis
- Vinegar and vinegared foods (pickles), which leach minerals from the body (except apple cider vinegar and brown rice vinegar)
- Alcohol
- Artificial food additives
- Food contaminants from pesticides (eat as much organically produced food as possible)

Healing Smoothies

- Allium Antioxidant, page 258
- Almond Banana, page 158
- Apple Spice Cocktail, page 163
- Asparagus Mango, page 224
- Aspirin in a Glass, page 259
- Breakfast Cocktail, page 173
- Calming Chamomile, page 260
- Cream of Broccoli, page 234
- Detox Delight (use a recommended herb instead of milk thistle), page 179
- Mango Marvel, page 189

ADD & ADHD

Attention Deficit Disorder & Attention Deficit Hyperactivity Disorder

A child may be diagnosed with ADD if he or she is easily distracted, has a short attention span, has difficulty concentrating and impulsively moves from one activity to another. In ADHD, there are also signs of hyperactivity. Studies have shown that increasing a child's intake of whole, nutrient-rich foods increases the supply of nutrients to the brain and improves mental performance. Other studies show that iron deficiency can cause attention deficits.

Introducing fresh juice and smoothies into a child's diet is an easy way to help him or her eat more raw fruits and vegetables. Certain herbs can also help calm a child's nerves while the process of diet detoxification takes place.

What to Do

Maximize
- Whole foods
- Antioxidant-rich fruits and vegetables
- Iron-rich foods (beets; leafy greens; almonds; sea herbs; watercress; and dried fruits, such as figs, raisins and apricots)
- Nuts and seeds to provide zinc, which is necessary for brain function

Minimize
- Foods that limit iron absorption (coffee, tea, chocolate, egg yolks, wheat bran)

Eliminate
- Artificial food additives, colorings, preservatives and sweeteners, which can be toxic to a child
- Sugar and sweet foods and drinks, which deplete the B vitamins necessary for nerve-cell function
- Refined foods, including white flour and white sugar products, which deplete the body's zinc supply
- Food allergies (see Appendix A: Food Allergies, page 373). They are often implicated in ADD, and some of the most common allergens are dairy products (see pages 302–303 for information on milk substitutes), eggs, wheat and oranges

Healing Smoothies

Breastfeeding

A nourishing diet that's rich in minerals is essential for the health of a nursing mother and her baby. Adding fennel, dill or anise to the mother's food or tea helps prevent infant colic. While weaning, drink sage tea to reduce breast milk production.

Healing Foods

Fruits and vegetables
bananas, avocados, carrots, green beans, leafy greens, sweet potatoes, watercress

Herbs
alfalfa, borage leaves and flowers, dandelion leaf and root, fennel seeds, German chamomile, parsley*, red raspberry leaves, stinging nettle

Other
almonds, blackstrap molasses, legumes, pumpkin seeds, sea herbs, sunflower seeds, wheat germ, whole grains, yogurt with active bacterial cultures

* If you are pregnant, limit your intake of parsley to ½ tsp (2 mL) dried or one sprig fresh per day. Do not take parsley if you are suffering from kidney inflammation.

What to Do

Maximize
- Whole foods
- Foods that contain B vitamins (whole grains, leafy greens, sea herbs), which encourage a rich supply of breast milk
- Foods that contain calcium (leafy greens, sea herbs) to support baby's bone development
- Mineral-rich herbal teas (stinging nettle, red raspberry leaf, alfalfa, red clover flower, dandelion)

Minimize
- Garlic, onions and hot peppers, which can create gas in the baby
- Refined foods (white flour, white sugar)

Eliminate
- Artificial food additives, colorings and sweeteners, which can be toxic to a child

Healing Smoothies

- Anise Anise, page 258
- Avocado Pineapple, page 224
- C-Green, page 231
- Green Gold, page 238
- Leafy Luxury, page 240
- Raspberry Raspberry, page 274
- Spinach Salad, page 249

Bronchitis

Bronchitis is an inflammation of the bronchial tubes that is usually characterized by chest congestion and a persistent cough. Typical causes include bacteria, virus, or exposure to smoke or chemicals. Without treatment, the condition can become chronic.

Healing Foods

Fruits and vegetables
apricots, citrus fruits, cranberries, pears, broccoli, cabbage, carrots, leafy greens, onions, red and green bell peppers, turnips, watercress

Herbs
cayenne, cinnamon, elderberries, fenugreek seeds, garlic, ginger, hyssop, licorice*, marshmallow, stinging nettle, parsley**, plantain, thyme

What to Do

Maximize
- Fruits and vegetables, especially those high in vitamin C and beta-carotene
- Raw garlic for its antibiotic effect on the lungs

Minimize
- Meat
- Salt and salty foods

Other
legumes, pumpkin seeds, sesame seeds, soy products, soy yogurt, sunflower seeds

* Avoid licorice if you have high blood pressure. The prolonged use of licorice is not recommended under any circumstances.

** If you are pregnant, limit your intake of parsley to ½ tsp (2 mL) dried or one sprig fresh per day. Do not take parsley if you are suffering from kidney inflammation.

Eliminate
- Dairy products
- Sugar
- Refined flour

Healing Smoothies

- Allium Antioxidant, page 258
- Autumn Refresher, page 165
- C-Blend, page 174
- C-Blitz, page 174
- Citrus Toddy, page 321
- Nectar of the Gods, page 194
- Orange Zinger, page 242
- Spinach Salad, page 249
- Strawberry Sparkle, page 214
- Tart and Tingly, page 216
- Tomato Froth, page 251

- Alcohol
- Food allergies and intolerances (see Appendix A: Food Allergies, page 373)

Cancer Prevention

Risk factors for cancer include the use of tobacco and alcohol, exposure to toxins in food and the environment, and family history of cancer. Factors that protect against cancer include eating a diet that consists primarily of fresh fruits, vegetables and other whole foods; a healthy, active lifestyle; and avoiding foods and toxins that have been linked to cancer (see Eliminate, below).

Healing Foods

Fruits and vegetables
apples, apricots, blueberries, cherries, citrus fruits, cranberries, figs, grapes, kiwis, mangoes, papayas, peaches, raspberries, strawberries, watermelon, asparagus, beets, broccoli, cabbage, carrots, leafy greens, onions, parsnips, squash, sweet potatoes, tomatoes, watercress

Herbs
astragalus, burdock root, calendula, cayenne, echinacea, garlic, green tea, licorice*, parsley**, red clover flower, rosemary, sage***, turmeric

*** Do not take sage if you have high blood pressure or are pregnant or breastfeeding.

What to Do

Maximize
- Organic foods
- Soy products
- Antioxidant-rich fruits and vegetables
- Nuts and seeds

Minimize
- Animal protein in meat and dairy products

Other Recommendations
- Exercise daily, according to your fitness level.

Eliminate
- Margarine, shortening and cooking oils (except extra virgin olive oil)

- Alcohol
- Sugar
- Coffee
- Salt; pickled and salt-cured foods
- Fried foods
- Fried, grilled or barbecued meat, fish and poultry
- Smoked or cured meats (ham, bacon, hot dogs, cold cuts)
- Artificial food additives
- Refined food

Healing Foods

Other
extra virgin olive oil, fish oil, flax seeds, legumes, nuts (except peanuts), pumpkin seeds, shiitake mushrooms, soy products, spirulina, sunflower seeds, yogurt with active bacterial cultures, wheat grass, whole grains

Healing Smoothies

- Açai Berry Combo, page 158
- Allium Antioxidant, page 258
- Brazilian Berry Smoothie, page 172
- Breakfast Cocktail, page 173
- C-Blitz, page 174
- Citrus Cocktail, page 176
- Detox Delight (use a recommended herb instead of milk thistle), page 179
- Eye Opener, page 179
- Fruit of Life, page 180
- Green Gift, page 238
- Green Tea and Blueberries, page 186
- Minestrone, page 241
- Orange Zinger, page 242
- Tomato Juice Cocktail, page 251

Candida

Candida is a yeast infection that typically occurs on the external genitalia. It appears as a discharge in women and a rash in men. It may occur in the mouth, causing a burning sensation, or in the digestive system, causing bloating. General symptoms include fatigue, mood changes, depression, poor memory, headaches, cravings for sweets, bowel irregularities, muscle and joint problems, and skin problems.

Low thyroid function, diabetes, pregnancy, antibiotics, steroids, poor diet and sexual transmission can cause candida. Vaginal deodorants and scented soaps aggravate the condition by irritating the protective mucosa of the vagina. Stress, oral contraceptives, hormones and preservatives in food can encourage chronic candida. Reduce stress by using nerve-nourishing herbs, such as skullcap and oats.

Healing Foods

Fruits and vegetables
cranberries, broccoli, cabbage, carrots, cauliflower, celery, leafy greens, onions, squash, sweet potatoes, red bell peppers

Herbs
calendula, cloves, dandelion leaf and root, echinacea, garlic, ginger, lemon balm, stinging nettle, parsley*, peppermint, rosemary, thyme

Other
caprylic acid, dulse, extra virgin olive oil, kelp, legumes, nuts, seeds, soy products, whole grains, unsweetened yogurt with active bacterial cultures

* If you are pregnant, limit your intake of parsley to ½ tsp (2 mL) dried or one sprig fresh per day. Do not take parsley if you are suffering from kidney inflammation.

What to Do

Maximize
- Antioxidant-rich vegetables
- Vegetable protein (soy products, legumes with rice)
- Raw garlic (several cloves a day) to kill the yeast fungus
- Yogurt with active bacterial cultures to control yeast growth

Minimize
- Fruits and fruit juices to reduce excess fruit sugars that encourage yeast growth
- High-carbohydrate vegetables (potatoes, corn, parsnips)

Eliminate
- Food allergies and intolerances (see Appendix A: Food Allergies, page 373)
- Bananas, citrus fruits, dried fruits and mushrooms
- Alcohol, coffee, chocolate and tea
- Dairy products, which contain sugars that encourage candida growth (except unsweetened yogurt with active bacterial cultures)
- Honey, molasses, soy sauce, sugar and sweeteners

- Meat
- Refined foods
- Vinegared foods (pickles, mustard, ketchup, salad dressings)
- Yeast (including bakery products made with yeast)

Healing Smoothies

- Allium Antioxidant, page 258
- Cream of Broccoli, page 234
- Gingered Greens, page 238
- Green Gift (omit grapes), page 238
- Minestrone, page 241

Chronic Fatigue Syndrome

Chronic fatigue syndrome is not well understood. It is characterized by overwhelming fatigue, lack of energy, sleep disturbances and depression, and often features headaches, sore throats or swollen glands. It often follows a viral infection that has weakened the immune system. Other possible causes are food allergies, poor digestion or nutrient absorption, antibiotic use and long-term stress.

What to Do

Maximize
- Immunity and proper digestion (see Immune Deficiency, page 57, and Indigestion, page 60)
- Antioxidant-rich fruits and vegetables
- Nuts and seeds

Minimize
- Animal protein in meat and dairy products

Other Recommendations
- Get regular daily exercise, according to your fitness level.

Eliminate
- Processed and refined foods
- Caffeine (found in coffee, black and green tea, chocolate and soft drinks)
- Sugar, alcohol, yeast (or foods made with yeast), which can encourage candida infection (see Candida, page 38), which is often a factor in the illness
- Foods allergies and intolerances (see Appendix A: Food Allergies, page 373). Common triggers are dairy products, wheat and corn
- Artificial food additives

Healing Foods

Fruits and vegetables
apples, bananas, citrus fruits, broccoli, carrots, green beans, green and red bell peppers, leafy greens, squash, sweet potatoes, tomatoes, watercress

Herbs
alfalfa, cayenne, dandelion leaf and root, echinacea, evening primrose oil, garlic, ginger, ginseng*, lemon balm, licorice**, milk thistle, parsley***, St. John's wort, stinging nettle

* Do not take ginseng if you have high blood pressure or if you drink coffee. Never take ginseng daily for longer than four weeks.

** Avoid licorice if you have high blood pressure. The prolonged use of licorice is not recommended under any circumstances.

*** If you are pregnant, limit your intake of parsley to ½ tsp (2 mL) dried or one sprig fresh per day. Do not take parsley if you are suffering from kidney inflammation.

Healing Foods

Other
brown rice, cereal grasses, dulse, extra virgin olive oil, fish oils, flax seeds, kelp, legumes, maitake mushrooms, oats, pumpkin seeds, sesame seeds, shiitake mushrooms, sunflower seeds, whole grains, yogurt with active bacterial cultures

Healing Smoothies

- Allium Antioxidant, page 258
- C-Blitz, page 174
- Cream of Broccoli, page 234
- Green Gold, page 238
- Minestrone, page 241
- Peppered Beet, page 244
- Popeye's Power, page 272
- Rustproofer #1, page 248
- Rustproofer #2 (substitute a recommended herb for peppermint), page 248

Common Cold

The common cold is a viral infection of the airways. During cold season, consuming a diet high in fresh fruits, vegetables and garlic is an excellent preventive measure. The severity and duration of any cold can be diminished by promoting elimination through the skin (by sweating) and the bowel (by consuming an abundance of fresh fruit and avoiding slow-digesting meat and dairy products).

Healing Foods

Fruits and vegetables
lemons, citrus fruits, carrots, onions

Herbs
astragalus, cayenne, echinacea, elderflowers and elderberries, garlic, ginger, licorice*, peppermint

Other
honey**

* Avoid licorice if you have high blood pressure. The prolonged use of licorice is not recommended under any circumstances.

** Do not feed honey to children under one year of age.

**** Do not take sage if you have high blood pressure or are pregnant or breastfeeding.

What to Do

Maximize
- Fresh fruits and vegetables and their juices
- Hot herbs (cayenne, ginger) to promote body heat and discourage the virus
- Fluid intake (drink at least eight large glasses of water, juice and/or herbal tea daily)

Eliminate
- Animal protein. The large amount of energy required to digest meat and dairy products is better used as healing energy

---

Help for Common Cold
- Nausea: tea made from peppermint, chamomile, ginger or cinnamon
- Sore throat: gargle or tea made from sage****
- Cough: tea made from thyme, licorice**, hyssop, plantain or marshmallow root

---

- Allium Antioxidant, page 258
- C-Blitz, page 174
- Citrus Toddy, page 321
- Detox Delight (use a recommended herb instead of milk thistle), page 179
- Flaming Antibiotic, page 236
- Fruit of Life, page 180
- Green Gold, page 238
- Orange Pom, page 195
- Popeye's Power, page 272
- Rose Smoothie, page 274
- Rustproofer #1, page 248
- Sage Relief, page 275
- Tomato Juice Cocktail, page 251

Constipation

Constipation may be caused by diseases, such as diverticulitis (see Diverticular Disease, page 45) or anemia (see Anemia, page 31), both of which require treatment. Less-serious causes include stress, lack of exercise, insufficient dietary fiber or the overuse of laxatives, which make the bowel lazy.

Constipation can often be relieved by increasing the amount of fiber in the diet, getting regular exercise and drinking an adequate amount of water (eight or more large glasses a day).

Constipation may be a result of either excessive relaxation or tension of the bowel muscles. Stimulation with cayenne or ginger can benefit a person who is too relaxed. A calming tea of German chamomile, lavender or lemon balm can relax a tense, overstimulated person. Dairy products cause constipation, especially in children. Replacing dairy products with soy- or rice-based dairy substitutes often relieves constipation in a child.

Healing Foods

Fruits and vegetables
apples, pears, prunes, rhubarb, beets, leafy greens, leeks, onions

Herbs
burdock root, German chamomile, cinnamon, dandelion root, fennel seeds, garlic, ginger, lavender, lemon balm, licorice*, peppermint, yellow dock

Other
dried fruit, flax seeds, legumes, molasses, nuts, psyllium seeds, pumpkin seeds, sesame seeds, yogurt with active bacterial cultures

* Avoid licorice if you have high blood pressure. The prolonged use of licorice is not recommended under any circumstances.

What to Do

Maximize
- Whole foods
- Fiber (found in fresh, raw fruits and vegetables; legumes; nuts; seeds; and whole grains)
- Fluid intake (drink at least eight large glasses of water, juice and/or herbal tea daily)
- Bitter herbs (dandelion root; German chamomile; burdock leaf, root or seeds; ginger; fennel; yellow dock) to stimulate the bowel

Eliminate
- Refined foods

Healing Smoothies

- Anise Anise, page 258
- Apple Beet Pear, page 223
- Apple Pear, page 162
- Appled Beet (use a recommended herb instead of thyme), page 223
- Autumn Refresher, page 165
- Beet, page 225
- Blazing Beets, page 225
- Brocco-Carrot, page 226
- Green Gold, page 238
- Loosey-Goosey, page 188
- Prune, page 207
- Pump It Up, page 207
- Rhubarb Apple, page 211
- Rhubarb Pie, page 211
- Spring Celebration, page 150
- Tree Fruit Smoothie, page 217

Depression

Depression, a persistently low mood, is often accompanied by headaches, insomnia or constant drowsiness, inability to concentrate and low immunity. Although a long-term cure may require counseling, good nutrition promotes healing by helping to restore nervous-system function.

Healing Foods

Fruits and vegetables
black beans, broccoli, carrots, mangoes, soybeans, spinach, watercress

Herbs
borage, burdock root, cardamom, cayenne, cinnamon, cloves, dandelion root, garlic, German chamomile, ginger, ginkgo, lemon balm, oat seeds, parsley*, rosemary, skullcap, St. John's wort

Other
cereal grasses, evening primrose oil, flax seeds, kelp, nuts, oats (including bran), pumpkin seeds, sunflower seeds, whole grains

* If you are pregnant, limit your intake of parsley to ½ tsp (2 mL) dried or one sprig fresh per day. Do not take parsley if you are suffering from kidney inflammation.

What to Do

Maximize
- A healthy diet
- Foods rich in B vitamins (whole grains, leafy greens) to improve nerve function
- Herbs that encourage relaxation and sleep and that counter stress and anxiety (borage, skullcap, St. John's wort, German chamomile, lemon balm)
- Herbs that support liver function (dandelion root, burdock root, rosemary)
- Nuts and seeds

Eliminate
- Artificial food additives, which can contribute to depression

Healing Smoothies

- Anti-Depression Tonic, page 259
- Brocco-Carrot, page 226
- C-Green, page 231
- Green Energy, page 265
- Smart Smoothie, page 276

Diabetes

Healing Foods

Fruits and vegetables
apples, avocados, blueberries, grapefruits, lemons, limes, pears, broccoli, Jerusalem artichokes, leafy greens, onions

Herbs
cinnamon, cloves, coriander, dandelion root and leaf, evening primrose oil, fenugreek seeds, garlic, ginger, ginkgo, linden flower, stevia, turmeric, yarrow*

Other
extra virgin olive oil, fish oil, flax seeds, legumes, oats, pumpkin seeds, spirulina, tofu, unsweetened yogurt with active bacterial cultures, whole grains

* Avoid yarrow if you are pregnant.

Diabetes mellitus is an insulin deficiency that results in a high blood-sugar level. This deficiency affects the body's ability to metabolize carbohydrates, protein and fat, which often leads to an increase in the incidence of infections. It is important that a health-care practitioner monitor a patient with diabetes. If diabetes is not controlled, changes in the blood vessels can lead to high blood pressure and deterioration of circulation, causing kidney, nerve and eye problems.

Type I diabetes begins in childhood. The pancreas is unable to produce an adequate supply of insulin, so the disease is controlled with daily insulin injections.

Type II diabetes usually occurs in adulthood, and obesity is a major risk factor. The pancreas often produces sufficient insulin, but the body is unable to use it efficiently. High blood sugar can be reversed by diet and weight loss. In type II diabetes, diet and herbs can help regulate blood sugar, improve digestion and intestinal absorption of nutrients, support blood circulation and improve immunity.

What to Do

Maximize

- A mainly vegetarian diet of fresh organic fruits, vegetables, legumes and unrefined grains, which helps regulate blood sugar and boosts the immune system's ability to resist infection
- Omega-3 fatty acids (found in oily fish and fish oils, hemp oil, flax seeds, pumpkin seeds and soybean products), which are beneficial to blood circulation

Minimize

- Animal fats in meat and dairy products (replace some meat meals with fish and vegetable protein; replace dairy products with soy alternatives)

Eliminate

- Food allergies and intolerances (see Appendix A: Food Allergies, page 373)
- Dairy products
- Potatoes
- Dried fruits, sugar and sweeteners (except stevia and small amounts of raw honey)
- Fats and oils (except extra virgin olive oil)
- Processed foods
- Refined foods
- Caffeine (found in coffee, black and green tea, and soft drinks)

Other Recommendations

- Chronic stress affects sugar levels. Skullcap and oats can help calm nervous stress.
- Daily exercise makes an important contribution to regulating blood sugar levels.

Healing Smoothies

- Allium Antioxidant, page 258
- Apple Beet Pear, page 223
- Beta Blast, page 169
- Blue Cherry, page 171
- Cream of Broccoli, page 234
- Green Energy, page 265
- Gingered Greens, page 238
- Minestrone, page 241
- Spa Special, page 276
- Spinach Salad (use grapefruit instead of orange), page 249

Diarrhea

Diarrhea is an inflammation of the bowel caused by bacterial or viral infection, food allergies or intolerances, or malfunctions of the digestive system. Consult a health-care practitioner if diarrhea lasts longer than one week. Diarrhea causes dehydration, which can be life threatening for small children. In such cases, consult your health-care practitioner immediately.

Healing Foods

Fruits and vegetables
cooked apples, bananas, lemons, limes, carrots, potatoes

Herbs
cardamom, German chamomile, fennel seeds, ginger, lemon balm, meadowsweet, nutmeg, red raspberry leaves, slippery elm bark powder

Other
evening primrose oil, flax seeds, pumpkin seeds, rice, sunflower seeds, whole grains, yogurt with active bacterial cultures

What to Do

Maximize
- Water intake (to be safe, boil all water to eliminate any bacteria, then cool to drinking temperature)
- Herbal teas
- Starchy foods (potatoes, carrots, rice)

Minimize
- Raw fruits (except bananas), which can promote diarrhea
- Raw vegetables, as the fiber may irritate an inflamed bowel
- Dried fruits

Eliminate
- Alcohol, caffeine (found in coffee, black and green tea, chocolate and soft drinks), soft drinks
- Dairy products (except yogurt with active bacterial cultures)
- Sugar and sweeteners
- Food allergies and intolerances (see Appendix A: Food Allergies, page 373)

Healing Smoothies

- Slippery Banana, page 276
- Vichyssoise (use yogurt with active bacterial cultures in place of milk, cream or tofu), page 253

Diverticular Disease
Diverticulitis & Diverticulosis

Healing Foods

Fruits and vegetables
apples, bananas, grapes, mangoes, pears, prunes, broccoli, cabbage, carrots, celery, leafy greens, watercress

Herbs
cinnamon, fenugreek seeds, garlic, German chamomile, ginger, licorice*, marshmallow leaf and root, peppermint, psyllium seeds, slippery elm bark powder, valerian**

Other
flax seeds, legumes, oats, spirulina, wheat bran, whole grains, yogurt with active bacterial cultures

* Avoid licorice if you have high blood pressure. The prolonged use of licorice is not recommended under any circumstances.

** Valerian has an adverse effect on some people.

Diverticulosis is characterized by the presence of multiple small pouches (diverticula) on the large intestine. Diverticulitis occurs when these pouches become inflamed. It is usually associated with constipation and caused by a low-fiber diet. Symptoms typically include continuous pain on the left side of the abdomen, flatulence and, sometimes, diarrhea.

What to Do

Maximize
- Fruits and vegetables
- Whole grains and legumes
- Water intake (drink at least eight large glasses daily)

Minimize
- Animal protein in meat and dairy products

Eliminate
- Caffeine (found in coffee, black and green tea, chocolate and soft drinks)
- Alcohol
- Fried foods
- Pickled foods
- Ham, bacon and fatty meats
- Refined and processed foods
- Spicy foods
- Sugar
- Dairy products (except yogurt with active bacterial cultures)
- Constipation, if present (see Constipation, page 41)

Other Recommendations
- Gradually introduce a high-fiber diet to avoid digestive problems.
- During periods of inflammation, avoid high-fiber foods (raw vegetables, bran), which can irritate the bowel.
- Drink plenty of healing vegetable juices (spinach, cabbage, beet, garlic, carrot) with the addition of soothing slippery elm bark powder

Healing Smoothies

- Gingered Greens, page 238
- Green Gift (use a recommended herb instead of parsley), page 238
- Mango Madness, page 188
- Popeye's Power, page 272
- Prune, page 207
- Slippery Banana, page 276

Endometriosis

Endometriosis is a condition in which tissue that is normally found in the uterus wall, or endometrium, is found in places outside the uterus, such as the bladder, bowel or fallopian tubes. This tissue responds to a woman's monthly hormonal cycle, shedding blood at these sites. Symptoms can include pain, irregular bleeding, depression and bowel problems.

Healing Foods

Fruits and vegetables
apples, apricots, cherries, grapefruits, strawberries, beets, broccoli, cabbage, leafy greens, peas, red and green bell peppers, squash, sweet potatoes

Herbs
calendula, chasteberry, dandelion leaf and root, evening primrose oil, German chamomile, meadowsweet, passionflower, rosemary, turmeric, valerian*

Other
barley, extra virgin olive oil, fish oils, legumes, nuts, oats, seeds, soy yogurt with active bacterial cultures, tofu, whole grains

* Valerian has an adverse effect on some people.

What to Do

Maximize
- Antioxidants (preferably from vegetable sources) to support the immune system in eliminating imperfect or misplaced tissues
- Essential fatty acids (found in nuts, seeds and grains), which have a healing effect

Minimize
- Animal protein in meat and dairy products. Use organic meats, which are sure to be hormone-free, if possible
- Fruits, which may contribute to blood-sugar problems. Candida (see page 38) is often associated with endometriosis

Eliminate
- Sugar and sweeteners
- Yeast and foods made with yeast (bread)
- Coffee
- Alcohol
- Junk food

- Food allergies and intolerances (see Appendix A: Food Allergies, page 373). Dairy and wheat products are common culprits

Other Recommendations
- Balance hormones with chasteberry (*Vitex agnus-castus*).
- Take analgesic herbs (German chamomile, meadowsweet, passionflower, rosemary, valerian) for pain.
- Take nervous-system tonics (passionflower, valerian).
- Use turmeric for its antimicrobial/antiseptic/anti-inflammatory properties.
- Consume herbs that support the liver (calendula, dandelion root, rosemary).
- Evening primrose oil is an antidepressant and helps to support the immune system in eliminating imperfect or misplaced tissues.

Healing Smoothies

- Appled Beet (use a recommended herb instead of thyme), page 223
- Apricot and Oatmeal Breakfast Special (omit the yogurt and dates, and add apple or strawberries), page 163
- Beet, page 225
- Cherry Sunrise, page 175
- Peas Please, page 243

Eye Problems
Cataracts, Glaucoma & Macular Degeneration

Research shows that your risk of cataracts, glaucoma and macular degeneration decreases if you eat a diet rich in antioxidants.

Healing Foods

Fruits and vegetables
apricots, blackberries, blueberries, citrus fruits, cranberries, grapes, mangoes, peaches, raspberries, strawberries, watermelon, asparagus, avocados, broccoli, cabbage, carrots, green and red bell peppers, leafy greens, pumpkin, squash, sweet potatoes, tomatoes, watercress

Herbs
dandelion leaf, garlic, ginger, ginkgo, parsley*, rosemary, turmeric

Other
extra virgin olive oil, nuts, pumpkin seeds, wheat germ, yogurt with active bacterial cultures

* If you are pregnant, limit your intake of parsley to ½ tsp (2 mL) dried or one sprig fresh per day. Do not take parsley if you are suffering from kidney inflammation.

What to Do

Maximize
- Antioxidant-rich fruits and vegetables (see pages 104 and 116) to protect the eyes from free-radical damage. Carrot juice, spinach and blueberries are especially effective
- Fresh garlic, which is a strong antioxidant

Minimize
- Fat in meat and dairy products

Eliminate
- Refined foods
- Fried foods
- Sugar and sweeteners

Healing Smoothies

- Açai Berry Combo, page 158
- Asparagus Mango, page 224
- Berry Yogurt Flip, page 168
- Black Pineapple, page 170
- Blue Water, page 172
- Blueberry, page 171
- Brazilian Berry Smoothie, page 172
- C-Blend, page 174
- C-Blitz, page 174
- Citrus Cocktail, page 176
- Granate Berry, page 183
- Green Tea and Blueberries, page 186
- Liquid Gold, page 187
- Mango Madness, page 188
- Squash Special, page 250
- Sunrise Supreme, page 215
- Tomato Juice Cocktail, page 251

Fatigue

Fatigue is a symptom of many diseases — including anemia, diabetes, hepatitis, hypoglycemia and thyroid disease — and can be determined by blood tests and diagnosed by your doctor. Common nondisease factors often come from a lack of lifestyle balance, which includes diet, exercise, work and social life. A balanced diet provides the digestive enzymes the body requires for processing nutrients and converting food into energy.

Healing Foods

Fruits and vegetables
bananas, grapes, limes, mangoes, oranges, pineapple, strawberries, broccoli, carrots, leafy greens, onions, spinach, watercress

Herbs
alfalfa, burdock root, cardamom, cayenne, cinnamon, cloves, dandelion leaf and root, garlic, ginger, ginseng*, licorice**, parsley***, peppermint, red raspberry leaf, rose hips, stinging nettle, yellow dock

What to Do

Maximize
- Fresh fruits and vegetables
- Whole grains
- Nuts and seeds
- Essential fatty acids

Minimize
- Fat in meat and dairy products
- Fried foods

Healing Foods

Other

almonds, cereal grasses, dates, fish oil, flax seeds, oats, pumpkin seeds, sea herbs, sunflower seeds, tofu, wheat germ, whole grains, yogurt with active bacterial cultures

* Do not take ginseng if you have high blood pressure or if you drink coffee. Never take ginseng daily for longer than four weeks.

** Avoid licorice if you have high blood pressure. The prolonged use of licorice is not recommended under any circumstances.

*** If you are pregnant, limit your intake of parsley to ½ tsp (2 mL) dried or one sprig fresh per day. Do not take parsley if you are suffering from kidney inflammation.

What to Do

Eliminate

- Caffeine and sugar, which can cause fatigue
- Refined flour products, which rob the body of nutrients
- Processed foods, which are often low in nutrients and high in chemical additives
- Margarine, shortening and salad oils (except extra virgin olive oil)
- Alcohol

Other Recommendations

- Exercise daily, according to your fitness level.
- Eat smaller, more-frequent meals to maintain a constant blood-sugar level.
- Practice stress-reduction techniques, such as yoga, tai chi and meditation. Stress depletes vitality.
- Take herbs that support the liver (dandelion root, burdock root) to stimulate metabolism and remove toxins that can cause fatigue.

Healing Smoothies

- Apple Fresh, page 161
- B-Vitamin, page 173
- Brocco-Carrot, page 226
- Carrot Lime, page 227
- Carrot Pineapple, page 228
- Eye Opener, page 179
- Gingered Greens, page 238
- Green Energy, page 265
- Mango Madness, page 188
- Pineapple-C, page 201
- Spiced Carrot, page 249
- Sunrise Supreme, page 215
- Taste of the Tropics, page 216

Fibromyalgia

Fibromyalgia is characterized by tender, aching muscles, joint pain similar to that of rheumatoid arthritis, fatigue and sleep disturbances. The areas typically affected are the neck, shoulders, lower back, chest and thighs. It is considered a form of chronic fatigue syndrome, with pain rather than fatigue as the dominant feature. Depression is often a feature, due to lack of sleep. The cause can be viral or a buildup of toxins. Food, drugs, allergies and nutritional deficiencies can also be involved. Neither the cause nor the cure is well understood, but good nutrition can help recovery.

Healing Foods

Fruits and vegetables

apples, beets, broccoli, cabbage, cauliflower, celery, fennel, green beans, Jerusalem artichokes, onions, squash, sweet potatoes, watercress

Herbs

alfalfa, astragalus, burdock root and seeds, calendula, dandelion leaf and root, echinacea, evening primrose oil, garlic, licorice*, milk thistle, parsley**, passionflower, slippery elm bark powder, St. John's wort, turmeric

What to Do

Maximize

- Antioxidant-rich vegetables
- Vegetable protein
- Nuts and seeds
- Legumes

Healing Foods

Other
barley grass, fish oil, flax seeds, legumes, pumpkin seeds, soy products, sunflower seeds, unsweetened yogurt with active bacterial cultures, whole grains (especially brown rice)

* Avoid licorice if you have high blood pressure. The prolonged use of licorice is not recommended under any circumstances.

** If you are pregnant, limit your intake of parsley to ½ tsp (2 mL) dried or one sprig fresh per day. Do not take parsley if you are suffering from kidney inflammation.

What to Do

Minimize
- Fruits, which may contribute to low blood sugar (see Hypoglycemia, page 57)

Other Recommendations
- Eat oily fish (salmon, mackerel, sardines, tuna) two or three times a week.
- Practice stress-reduction techniques, such as tai chi, yoga and meditation.
- Exercise daily, according to your fitness level.

Eliminate
- Sugar; products that contain sugar; and high-sugar fruits, such as dried fruit, bananas and watermelon
- Refined flour
- Artificial food additives
- Alcohol
- Food allergies and intolerances (see Appendix A: Food Allergies, page 373). Gluten (in wheat products) and members of the nightshade family (potatoes, tomatoes, eggplant and all peppers) often cause problems
- Caffeine (found in coffee, black and green tea, chocolate and soft drinks), which decreases mineral absorption and contributes to the condition
- Dairy products (replace with soy- or rice-based alternatives)
- Salty and pickled foods
- Fried foods
- Pork, shellfish and fatty meats

Healing Smoothies

- Allium Antioxidant, page 258
- Apple Beet Pear, page 223
- Beet, page 225
- Blazing Beets, page 225
- Brocco-Carrot, page 226
- Cream of Broccoli, page 234
- Gingered Beets (use a recommended herb instead of ginger), page 237
- Minestrone, page 241
- Rustproofer #2, page 248

Flatulence

Healing Foods

Fruits and vegetables
apples, kiwis, papayas

Herbs
basil, cardamom, cayenne, German chamomile, cinnamon, cloves, coriander, cumin, dill, fennel seeds, garlic, ginger, mustard seeds, peppermint, thyme

Other
yogurt with active bacterial cultures

Gas is a normal result when food is digested. Foods high in carbohydrates, such as beans, produce more gas because they are not entirely broken down by digestive enzymes. When bacteria ferment the undigested carbohydrates, gas is released. Other foods produce excess gas when the digestive enzyme they require is not available. The most common example is the enzyme needed to digest lactose in dairy products. Artificial sweeteners can also cause gas.

Changing your diet to include more high-fiber foods, such as beans and legumes, may also increase the incidence of gas. Consequently, dietary changes intended to increase the quantity of fiber should be made gradually, over a four- to six-week period.

Tip: To reduce the "gas effect" of legumes, soak them overnight in plenty of water. Discard the soaking water before cooking and rinse the cooked legumes well before adding them to recipes. Cook beans (and other foods) that give you gas with the recommended herbs, which expel gas from the digestive tract.

What to Do

Maximize
- Digestive herbal teas, such as chamomile and fennel, between meals
- Food-combining techniques (see Food Combining, pages 17 and 375), taking care to eat fruits at least half an hour before or two hours after meals

Eliminate
- Artificial sweeteners and all foods that contain them
- Dairy products

Healing Smoothies

- Apple Mint, page 161
- Apple Pie, page 162
- Digestive Drink, page 262
- Gas Guzzler, page 264

Gallstones

Healing Foods

Fruits and vegetables
apples, blackberries, blueberries, cherries, citrus fruits, lemons, pears, raspberries, red grapes, asparagus, beets, broccoli, carrots, celery, leafy greens, radishes, tomatoes, watercress

Herbs
dandelion leaf and root, garlic, ginger, milk thistle, parsley*, turmeric

* If you are pregnant, limit your intake of parsley to ½ tsp (2 mL) dried or one sprig fresh per day. Do not take parsley if you are suffering from kidney inflammation.

Cholesterol from animal fats is a major factor in the formation of gallstones. Symptoms include indigestion, severe pain in the upper right abdomen, constipation, flatulence, nausea and vomiting. If a gallstone remains stuck in the bile duct, causing inflammation, it may need to be surgically removed.

Vegetarians are less likely to develop gallstones than people who eat meat, and dietary changes can reduce the risk of gallstone formation.

What to Do

Maximize
- Vegetable protein
- Fruits, vegetables and whole grains

Minimize
- Fatty meats
- Dairy products

Eliminate
- Sugar
- Refined foods
- Coffee
- Food allergies and intolerances (see Appendix A: Food Allergies, page 373). Often, eggs, pork, onions, coffee, milk, corn, beans and nuts affect gallstone sufferers

Other Recommendations
- Eat oily fish (salmon, mackerel, sardines, tuna) to help lower cholesterol levels.
- Consume bitter foods (dandelion leaf, endive, radicchio, watercress) to increase bile flow, which helps prevent gallstone formation.
- Increase consumption of extra virgin olive oil to discourage gallstone formation.

Healing Foods

Other
extra virgin olive oil,
flax seeds, lecithin, oats,
whole grains

Healing Smoothies

- Apple Beet Pear, page 223
- Apple Mint, page 161
- Autumn Refresher, page 165
- Beet, page 225
- Berry Best, page 166
- Brocco-Carrot, page 226
- C-Blitz, page 174
- C-Green, page 231
- Cherry Berry, page 175
- Digestive Drink, page 262
- Gingered Greens, page 238
- Raspberry, page 209
- Red, Black and Blue, page 210
- Spinach Salad, page 249
- Tomato Froth, page 251
- Tomato Juice Cocktail, page 251
- Zippy Tomato, page 254

Gout

Healing Foods

Fruits and vegetables
bananas, blackberries,
cherries, raspberries,
strawberries, avocados,
carrots, celery

Herbs
burdock root and seeds,
celery seeds, dandelion leaf,
fennel seeds, garlic, ginger,
licorice*, parsley**, stinging
nettle, turmeric, yarrow***,
yellow dock

Other
flax seeds

* Avoid licorice if you have high
blood pressure. The prolonged
use of licorice is not
recommended under any
circumstances.

** If you are pregnant, limit your
intake of parsley to ½ tsp
(2 mL) dried or one sprig fresh
per day. Do not take parsley if
you are suffering from kidney
inflammation.

*** Avoid yarrow if you are
pregnant.

Gout is an inflammatory joint problem characterized by increased production of uric acid, which is deposited in the joints, especially those of the fingers and toes. It may be hereditary or may be caused by the consumption of excess alcohol, meat or starchy food, which increases the production of uric acid. Decreasing the production of uric acid and increasing its excretion in the urine helps control gout.

What to Do

Maximize
- Water intake (drink at least eight large glasses daily) to assist in the elimination of uric acid
- A vegetarian diet
- Herbal teas that dissolve uric acid (celery seed) and help eliminate uric acid (dandelion leaf, stinging nettle)

Minimize
- Protein (chicken, turkey and whitefish are fine in moderation)
- Fat in meat and dairy products
- Salt and salty foods
- Eggs (those from free-range chickens are preferable)
- Wheat, which is acid forming (use brown rice and buckwheat, which produce less acid)

Eliminate
- *Foods and substances that form acid in the body, including:*
- pork and beef;
- preserved meats, such as salami;
- tomatoes and spinach;
- vinegar (except apple cider vinegar);
- refined sugar and flour;
- coffee and tea;
- cheese;
- artificial food additives; and
- alcohol.
- *Foods that are high in purines, including:*
- organ meats (kidney, liver);
- shellfish, herring, sardines, anchovies and mackerel;
- peanuts;
- asparagus;
- mushrooms; and
- legumes (peas, beans, lentils).

Healing Smoothies

- Berry Best, page 166
- Cherry Berry, page 175
- Gout Gone, page 265
- Strawberry Sparkle (use

raspberry juice instead of cranberry juice), page 215
- Sweet and Sour Strawberry (omit the balsamic vinegar), page 214

Hangover

Healing Foods

Fruits and vegetables
apples, bananas, lemons, limes

Herbs
cumin, evening primrose oil, ginger, German chamomile, lavender, meadowsweet, slippery elm bark powder

Other
foods that are rich in B vitamins (whole grains, leafy greens)

Drinking too much alcohol can result in headache, fatigue, nausea, dizziness and depression, which together are called hangover. Hangovers occur because alcohol dehydrates the body, increases acidity in the digestive system, causes the loss of potassium and vitamins, and affects the liver and nervous system. You may get faster relief from hangover symptoms if you follow these recommendations, preferably before retiring.

What to Do

Maximize
- Water to hydrate the body before, during and after drinking
- Juices that are high in vitamin C

- Herbal teas that settle the stomach (chamomile)
- Slippery elm bark powder to protect the stomach from excess acid

Healing Smoothies

- Calming Chamomile, page 260
- Hangover Remedy, page 266

- Morning After, page 270
- Slippery Banana, page 276

Headaches
(Non-Migraine)

Healing Foods

Fruits and vegetables
apples, bananas, broccoli, leafy greens, watercress

Herbs
cayenne, evening primrose oil, German chamomile, lavender, lemon balm, linden flower, passionflower, rosemary, skullcap, thyme, valerian*

Headaches, other than migraines, can be caused by many factors, including muscular and nervous tension, digestive disorders, blood pressure changes, low blood sugar, caffeine, alcohol or drug withdrawal, eye strain, food allergies, a stuffy room, weather changes or poor posture. Avoiding foods that are common headache triggers (see Eliminate, opposite) may help reduce the incidence of headaches.

Other

almonds, legumes, oats, sunflower seeds, tofu, walnuts, wheat germ, whole grains, yogurt with active bacterial cultures

* Valerian has an adverse effect on some people.

What to Do

Maximize

- Foods that are high in magnesium (whole grains, legumes, sea herbs, wheat germ, apples, bananas, nuts, seeds, fish), which relaxes muscles and helps reduce spasms

Minimize

- Salt and salty foods
- Fatty foods

Eliminate

- Artificial food additives, especially monosodium glutamate (MSG)
- Food allergies and intolerances (see Appendix A: Food Allergies, page 373). Dairy products, wheat, corn, oranges and eggs commonly trigger headaches
- Meats preserved with nitrates (bacon, ham, hot dogs)
- Aspartame and foods that are sweetened with aspartame
- Caffeine (found in coffee, black and green tea, chocolate and soft drinks)
- Cheese and red wine

Other Recommendations

- Lemon balm and meadowsweet tea may help relieve headaches caused by digestive disorders.
- Skullcap and valerian * teas can be helpful for stress-related headaches.
- Antispasmodic herbs (cayenne, German chamomile, lemon balm, linden flower, passionflower, skullcap, thyme, valerian *) may help when a headache is caused by muscular tension.

Healing Smoothies

- Brocco-Carrot, page 226
- C Green, page 231
- Cream of Broccoli, page 234
- Green Energy (substitute skullcap for ginkgo), page 265
- Green Gift (use a recommended herb instead of parsley), page 238

Heart Problems
High Cholesterol, High Blood Pressure, Cardiovascular Disease, Heart Failure & Stroke

Family history, cigarette smoking, high alcohol consumption and high "bad" cholesterol are major risk factors for high blood pressure, circulation disorders and cardiovascular disease. In most cardiovascular diseases and circulation disorders, cholesterol deposits narrow the arteries, constricting the flow of blood.

Healing Foods

Fruits and vegetables
apples, apricots, blackberries, blueberries, cranberries, grapefruit*, grapes, kiwis, mangoes, melons, oranges, papayas, pineapple, strawberries, asparagus, avocados, broccoli, carrots, celery, leafy greens, lettuce, onions, parsnips, peas, all peppers, squash, watercress

Herbs
cayenne, dandelion leaf and root, fenugreek seeds, garlic, ginger, linden flowers, parsley**, rosemary, stinging nettle, turmeric

Other
almonds, barley, extra virgin olive oil, fish oil, kelp, lecithin, legumes, oats, seeds (flax, pumpkin, sesame, sunflower), soy products, sprouted seeds and beans, walnuts, whole grains, yogurt with active bacterial cultures

* Avoid grapefruit if you are using calcium channel blocker medication.

** If you are pregnant, limit your intake of parsley to ½ tsp (2 mL) dried or one sprig fresh per day. Do not take parsley if you are suffering from kidney inflammation.

Cholesterol is necessary to sustain life. There are two types in human blood: low-density lipoprotein (LDL, or "bad" cholesterol), which increases the risk of high blood pressure, heart disease and gallstones; and high-density lipoprotein (HDL, or "good" cholesterol), which reduces these risks. To improve health, eat a diet that lowers LDL and raises HDL.

What to Do

Maximize
- Fresh fruits and vegetables, whole grains, nuts and seeds, all of which help regulate blood pressure, reduce LDL and raise HDL
- Garlic and onions to reduce blood pressure and cholesterol
- Antioxidant-rich fruits and vegetables to help prevent cholesterol deposits from forming on artery walls
- Red grape juice to prevent blood clotting

Minimize
- Alcohol
- Coffee
- Eggs
- Salt and salty foods (processed foods)
- Sugar and products that contain sugar

Eliminate
- High-fat meats (such as bacon, pork, beef) and dairy products (except skim milk)

- Margarine and salad oils (except extra virgin olive oil)
- Fried foods
- Pastries
- Milk chocolate
- Alcohol
- Refined sugar and flour
- Coconut

Other Recommendations
- Supportive therapy for heart problems includes daily exercise (such as walking for 30 minutes a day, depending on your level of fitness) and stress-reduction techniques, such as yoga, tai chi and meditation.
- Eat oily fish (salmon, mackerel, sardines, tuna) two to three times a week.
- Substitute vegetable protein for some meat meals.
- Use herbs (see left) to help lower cholesterol and improve circulation.

Healing Smoothies

Heartburn

Heartburn is a burning sensation in the chest that is related to digestive problems. It may be caused by a hiatal hernia, indigestion or inflammation of the stomach. Check with your health-care practitioner to determine the cause. It is especially important to eliminate the possibility of heart disease. Frequent drinks of therapeutic fruit and vegetable juices, antacid herbs (dandelion root, meadowsweet) and soothing herbs (marshmallow root, slippery elm bark powder) can offer relief.

Healing Foods

Fruits and vegetables
bananas, papayas, beets, cabbage, carrots, celery, cucumbers, parsnips

Herbs
calendula, cardamom, dandelion root, dill, fennel, ginger, German chamomile, licorice*, marshmallow root, meadowsweet, parsley**, slippery elm bark powder

Other
flax seeds

* Avoid licorice if you have high blood pressure. The prolonged use of licorice is not recommended under any circumstances.

** If you are pregnant, limit your intake of parsley to ½ tsp (2 mL) dried or one sprig fresh per day. Do not take parsley if you are suffering from kidney inflammation.

What to Do

Maximize
- Fresh fruits and vegetables
- Water intake (drink at least eight large glasses daily, between meals only)
- Slippery elm bark powder (especially at night) to protect the stomach from excess acid

Eliminate
- Coffee, soft drinks, alcohol and chocolate
- Fried, fatty and spicy foods
- Citrus fruits and tomatoes
- Pickled foods
- Refined flour and sugar
- Cigarette smoking
- Large meals
- Antacid and anti-inflammatory drugs, which can irritate the stomach lining

Minimize
- Acid-forming foods (meat, dairy products)

Healing Smoothies

- Apple Carrot Cucumber (use carrot juice instead of apple and lemon juice), page 223
- Beet, page 225
- Slippery Banana, page 276

Herpes Simplex
Cold Sores & Genital Herpes

Herpes simplex virus type 1 can cause cold sores. Genital herpes is caused by herpes simplex virus type 2 and should always be treated by a doctor. Once contracted, the virus remains dormant in the nerve endings and may reactivate when triggered by factors such as lowered immune system function; high stress; alcohol; or certain foods, such as processed foods and foods that are high in arginine (see Eliminate, below). Diet can be used to complement therapy prescribed by a qualified health-care practitioner. The most effective therapy is to avoid outbreaks by keeping immunity high, managing stress and avoiding foods that trigger the virus. Herbs can help by supporting the immune system and nourishing the nerves, where the virus resides.

What to Do

Maximize
- Antioxidant-rich vegetables
- Fish (salmon, sardines, tuna, halibut), legumes and nutritional yeast. These foods are high in the amino acid lysine, which appears to inhibit the virus from replicating
- Antiviral herbs (astragalus, calendula, echinacea, garlic, lemon balm, St. John's wort)
- Immunity-boosting herbs (astragalus, echinacea, burdock (leaf, root or seeds)
- Antistress herbs (ginseng, St. John's wort, lemon balm)

Minimize
- Fruits
- Whole grains, seeds and brown rice. While these foods are high in arginine (see Eliminate, below), they can be balanced with vegetables that are high in lysine

Eliminate
- Foods that are high in arginine (nuts, wheat, caffeine, chocolate, carob, bacon, coffee, sugars, tomatoes, eggplants, all peppers, mushrooms). Arginine is an amino acid that encourages the herpes virus to replicate
- Alcohol, processed foods and refined foods, which depress the immune system

Other Recommendations
- Practice stress-reduction techniques, such as meditation, yoga and breathing exercises.

Healing Smoothies

- Açai Berry Combo, page 158
- Allium Antioxidant, page 258
- Berry Yogurt Flip, page 168
- Brazilian Berry Smoothie, page 173
- Breakfast Cocktail, page 173
- Brocco-Carrot, page 226
- C-Green, page 231
- Fruit of Life, page 180
- Herb-eze, page 267

Hypoglycemia

Healing Foods

Fruits and vegetables
apples, cherries, grapefruits, plums, raw beets, broccoli, cabbage, cauliflower, raw carrots, Jerusalem artichokes, leafy greens, tomatoes

Herbs
dandelion root, German chamomile, ginseng, licorice*

Other
cereal grasses, flax seeds, kelp, legumes, nuts, seeds, spirulina, whole grains, yogurt with active bacterial cultures

* Avoid licorice if you have high blood pressure. The prolonged use of licorice is not recommended under any circumstances.

Hypoglycemia, or low blood sugar, is a disorder characterized by an overproduction of insulin. Symptoms can include aches and pains, constant hunger, dizziness, headache, fatigue, insomnia, digestive disorders, palpitations, tremors, sweating, nausea and nervous tension. You may notice some of these symptoms if you miss a regular meal. Attention to diet can help control blood-sugar levels.

What to Do

Maximize
- Whole grains, vegetables and legumes
- Smaller meals, eaten more frequently
- Cruciferous vegetables (broccoli, cabbage, cauliflower) to help control blood sugar
- Protein with each meal

Minimize
- Sweet foods, including fruits (particularly bananas, watermelon and dried fruits)

Eliminate
- Refined flour and sugar
- Black tea, coffee, soft drinks and alcohol
- Cigarette smoking, which interferes with blood-sugar mechanisms

Healing Smoothies

- Cauliflower Cocktail, page 230
- Cherry Sunrise, page 175
- Green Gift (omit grapes and use a recommended herb instead of parsley), page 238
- Spinach Salad (use grapefruit instead of orange), page 249

Immune Deficiency

Healing Foods

Fruits and vegetables
brightly colored fruits and vegetables, such as apricots, carrots, melons, broccoli, leafy greens

A healthy immune system is the key to resisting infections, allergies and chronic illnesses. The immune system protects and defends the body against viruses, bacteria, parasites and fungi. If it is not in top condition, it won't be able to resist these disease-causing agents. Balance in all areas of life — diet, exercise, mental perspective, social activity and spirituality — helps protect the immune system and keep it functioning well.

Healing Foods

Herbs
astragalus, burdock (leaf, root and seeds), cayenne, cloves, echinacea, elderflower and elderberries, garlic, ginseng, green tea, licorice*, parsley**, red clover, rosemary, sage***, St. John's wort, thyme, turmeric, yarrow****

Other
cereal grasses, legumes, nuts, seeds, shiitake mushrooms, whole grains, yogurt with active bacterial cultures

* Avoid licorice if you have high blood pressure. The prolonged use of licorice is not recommended under any circumstances.

** If you are pregnant, limit your intake of parsley to ½ tsp (2 mL) dried or one sprig fresh per day. Do not take parsley if you are suffering from kidney inflammation.

*** Do not take sage if you have high blood pressure or are pregnant or breastfeeding.

**** Do not take yarrow if you are pregnant.

What to Do

Maximize
- Whole foods
- Fresh, raw, organic fruits and vegetables to provide the vitamins, minerals, digestive enzymes and antioxidants necessary for a healthy immune system
- Whole grains
- Essential fatty acids (found in legumes; nuts; seeds; and oily fish, such as salmon, mackerel, sardines and tuna), which is necessary for growth and maintenance of cells
- Fluid intake (drink at least eight large glasses of water, juice and/or herbal tea daily)

Minimize
- Non-organic meat, which is likely to contain antibiotics and steroid hormones, which depress immunity
- Excess animal fat, which suppresses immunity
- Antibiotics and corticosteroids. While these drugs can be lifesaving, overuse can deplete the immune system, causing more-complex health problems

Eliminate
- Sugar, which depletes vitamins and minerals, impairs the immune system and promotes yeast infections
- Refined, processed or preserved foods and soft drinks, which disrupt mineral levels, leading to poor metabolism of essential fatty acids
- Artificial food additives and pesticides likely found in non-organic food
- Alcohol, which depresses immune function
- Margarine, salad dressings and cooking oils (except extra virgin olive oil and some other cold-pressed oils)
- Nitrates in bacon and sausage, which are converted to toxic substances in the body
- Food allergies and intolerances (see Appendix A: Food Allergies, page 373). Dairy products, gluten, corn products, eggs, oranges, strawberries, pork, tomatoes, coffee, tea, peanuts and chocolate often affect the immune system

Other Recommendations
- Consume sufficient protein, which helps build antibodies and healthy tissue and organs.
- Optimize digestion to improve the absorption of nutrients (see Indigestion, page 60).
- Stress depletes the immune system. Practice stress-reduction techniques, such as yoga, meditation and tai chi.
- Use herbs that are immune-system regulators (astragalus, echinacea, garlic, licorice*, thyme).
- Use antibiotic herbs (burdock leaf, root and seeds; cayenne; cloves; echinacea; garlic; red clover flower; thyme).
- Use antiviral herbs (burdock leaf, root and seeds; elderflower and elderberries; garlic; ginger; lemon balm; licorice*; marjoram; St. John's wort; yarrow****).
- Use antioxidant herbs (astragalus, ginkgo, green tea, hawthorn, milk thistle, rosemary, sage, turmeric).

Healing Smoothies

- Açai Berry Combo, page 158
- Allium Antioxidant, page 258
- Apple Beet Pear, page 223
- Berry Best, page 166
- Berry Yogurt Flip, page 168
- Black Pineapple, page 170
- Blazing Beets, page 225
- Brazilian Berry Smoothie, page 172
- Breakfast Cocktail, page 173
- Brocco-Carrot, page 226
- C-Green, page 231
- Chia Aloha, page 176
- Cranberry Pineapple, page 177
- Fruit of Life, page 180
- Granate Berry, page 183
- Grape Heart, page 185
- Green Tea and Blueberries, page 186
- Ki-Lime, page 187
- Leafy Luxury (use apple juice), page 240
- Minestrone, page 241
- Rustproofer #2, page 248
- Spiced Carrot, page 249

Impotence

Healing Foods

Fruits and vegetables
all

Herbs
cinnamon, cayenne, dandelion leaf, evening primrose oil, garlic, ginger, ginkgo, ginseng, nutmeg, saw palmetto, stinging nettle

Other
fish oil, flax seeds, kelp, legumes, nuts, oats, pumpkin seeds, soy products, sunflower seeds, wheat germ

Impotence, a man's inability to achieve or maintain an erection, may be caused by stress, insufficient blood supply to the penis (from cholesterol deposits in the blood vessels), excess alcohol, drugs, tobacco, diabetes, prostate enlargement or low testosterone.

A whole-food diet helps provide the vitamins and minerals necessary for sexual health. Herbal circulatory stimulants, such as ginger and cayenne, are often helpful for impotence caused by deficient circulation. See Anxiety States, page 32, for suggestions on alleviating emotional stress.

What to Do

Maximize

- Fresh fruits and vegetables, whole grains, nuts and seeds
- Foods that contain vitamin E (whole-grain cereals, brown rice, nuts, seeds, wheat germ, soy products, kelp, dandelion leaf, extra virgin olive oil) to protect the arteries that go to the penis from free-radical damage. Recent studies indicate better antioxidant effects occur when vitamin E comes from food rather than supplements

Minimize

- Animal protein (except for that in fish and chicken)

Eliminate

- Fried foods and junk foods
- Sugar
- Caffeine (found in coffee, black and green tea, chocolate and soft drinks)
- Refined flour
- Alcohol

Healing Smoothies

- Açai Berry Combo, page 158
- Berry Yogurt Flip, page 168
- Blazing Beets, page 225
- Brazilian Berry Smoothie, page 172
- B-Vitamin, page 173
- Cajun Cocktail, page 227
- Chia Aloha, page 176
- Flaming Antibiotic, page 236
- Fruit of Life, page 180
- Granate Berry, page 183
- Green Energy, page 265
- Green Tea and Blueberries, page 186

Indigestion

Healing Foods

Fruits and vegetables
apricots, bananas, lemons, mangoes, melons, papayas, pineapple, Jerusalem artichokes, leafy greens, squash, sweet potatoes

Herbs
cardamom, cayenne, coriander seeds, dandelion root, dill, cinnamon, cumin, fennel, German chamomile, ginger, lemon balm, meadowsweet, peppermint, slippery elm bark powder, turmeric

Other
almonds, apple cider vinegar, barley, flax seeds, rice, yogurt with active bacterial cultures

To avoid indigestion, be sure to wait at least one hour after a meal before drinking fruit smoothies. If fruit is eaten immediately after a meal, digestive problems may result (see Food Combining, pages 17 and 375).

Overeating, irregular eating, excess alcohol or nervous tension may cause occasional indigestion. Symptoms can include abdominal discomfort, nausea or gastric reflux (flowing of stomach and small-intestine contents backward into the esophagus). Chronic indigestion can be caused by irritable bowel syndrome, food intolerances, ulcer or gallbladder disorder. Symptoms of chronic indigestion can include bloating, fatigue, diarrhea and constipation.

What to Do

Maximize
- Relaxed, unhurried meals
- Daily intake of yogurt with active bacterial cultures
- Antioxidant-rich fruits and vegetables
- Digestive herbal teas, such as chamomile, fennel, ginger, lemon balm or peppermint, taken regularly between meals

Minimize
- Alcohol
- Tea
- Eggs and meat

Eliminate
- Food allergies and intolerances (see Appendix A: Food Allergies, page 373)
- Sugar and artificial sweeteners
- Cold drinks, especially during or after meals
- Fruit juices
- High-fat and fried foods
- Dairy products (except yogurt with active bacterial cultures)
- Salty and spicy foods
- Refined foods
- Heavy meals
- Coffee

Healing Smoothies

- Breakfast Cocktail, page 173
- Digestive Drink, page 262
- Peppermint Aperitif (replace ice cubes with 1/4 cup/50 mL water), page 271
- Slippery Banana, page 276

Natural Aids to Digestion

- Acidophilus (see Yogurt and Yogurt Products, page 150). *Lactobacillus acidophilus* is "friendly" bacteria used to ferment milk into yogurt. This bacteria can replace intestinal bacteria necessary for digestion when it has been destroyed by antibiotics.

- Calendula (*Calendula officinalis*), page 120. Because it stimulates bile production, calendula aids digestion. Calendula may be included in smoothies (use 1 tbsp/15 mL fresh petals) and makes an attractive garnish for drinks.

- Cinnamon (*Cinnamomum zeylanicum*), page 122. A warming carminative used to promote digestion, cinnamon adds a pleasant taste to smoothies.

- Dandelion root (*Taraxacum officinale*), page 124. An easily obtained, fairly mild but bitter laxative. Dandelion stimulates the liver and gallbladder and increases the flow of bile to aid digestion. Dandelion leaf acts as a diuretic.

- Fennel (*Foeniculum vulgare*), pages 110 and 126. Add a chopped fresh fennel bulb or an infusion of fennel seeds to smoothies to aid digestion and soothe discomfort from heartburn and indigestion.

- Fiber, page 368. Insoluble fiber in fruits, vegetables and whole grains helps prevent constipation and digestive diseases, such as diverticulosis and colon cancer.

- German chamomile (*Matricaria recutita*), page 127. As Peter Rabbit's mother knew, chamomile soothes upset tummies and inflammations and reduces flatulence and gas pains.

- Ginger (*Zingiber officinale*), page 128. Ginger is used to stimulate blood flow to the digestive system and to increase the absorption of nutrients. It increases the action of the gallbladder while protecting the liver against toxins.

- Kiwifruits (*Actinidia chinensis*), page 97. The enzymes in kiwis help digestion.

- Licorice (*Glycyrrhiza glabra*), page 133. Soothes gastric mucous membranes and eases spasms of the large intestine. Avoid licorice if you have high blood pressure.

- Papayas (*Carica papaya*), page 99. Papaya is a traditional remedy for indigestion. It contains an enzyme called papain, which is similar to pepsin, an enzyme that helps digest protein in the body.

- Peppermint (*Mentha piperita*), page 137. Because it contains flavonoids that stimulate the liver and gallbladder, peppermint increases the flow of bile. It has an antispasmodic effect on the smooth muscles of the digestive tract, making peppermint tea a good choice as an after-dinner drink.

- Pineapples (*Ananas comosus*), page 100. Pineapple is rich in the antibacterial enzyme bromelain. It is also anti-inflammatory and helps in the digestive process. Due to its digestive properties, raw pineapple prevents gelatin from setting and cannot be used in molded salads.

- Turmeric (*Curcuma longa*), page 143. Increases bile production and bile flow, which improves digestion.

Infertility — Female

Healing Foods

Fruits and vegetables
apricots, oranges, peaches, raspberries, asparagus, avocados, beets, broccoli, carrots, leafy greens, sweet potatoes

Herbs
dandelion leaf and root, evening primrose oil, red clover flower, red raspberry leaf, rosemary, stinging nettle

Other
adzuki beans, almonds, Brazil nuts, bulgur, kidney beans, sea herbs, seeds (sunflower, pumpkin, flax, sesame), soy products, wheat germ, yogurt with active bacterial cultures

Factors that affect female fertility include age, vaginal infections, artificial lubricants, surgical scarring, ovarian cysts, endometriosis, uterine fibroids, low thyroid function and diets deficient in the nutrients required for healthy pregnancy, stress relief and hormone balance.

The most important factor in ensuring a healthy pregnancy and birth is the mother's health before and during pregnancy. Whole, fresh, natural foods provide the vitamins and minerals necessary for good health. To help ensure the baby's good health, it is worth taking a few months to improve the mother's health before pregnancy.

An irregular menstrual cycle is a sign of hormonal imbalance. The herb chasteberry, also known as *Vitex agnus-castus* (see page 144), and herbs that support the liver, such as dandelion root (see page 124), may be used to regulate hormone production.

What to Do

Maximize
- Whole foods
- Antioxidant-rich fruits and vegetables
- Nuts and seeds
- Foods that contain folic acid (bulgur, orange juice, spinach, beans, sunflower seeds, wheat germ)

Minimize
- Acid-forming foods (meat, fish, grains, cheese, eggs, tea, coffee, alcohol, cranberries, plums, prunes, lentils, chickpeas, peanuts, walnuts), which can make cervical mucus acidic, which will destroy sperm

Eliminate
- Refined flour
- Cigarette smoking
- Sugar
- Artificial food additives

Other Recommendations
- Drink tea made from nerve-nourishing herbs (German chamomile, skullcap, oat straw) and regularly include relaxing activities, such as walking, meditation, yoga and tai chi, to reduce stress.
- Balance your intake of meat and fish protein (organic if possible) with vegetable protein, such as that in soybean products or beans with rice.

Healing Smoothies

- Açai Berry Combo, page 158
- Apricot and Oatmeal Breakfast Special, page 163
- Apricot Peach, page 164
- Asparagus Mango, page 224
- Beet, page 225
- Berry Yogurt Flip, page 168
- Beta Blast, page 169
- Brocco-Carrot, page 226
- B-Vitamin, page 173
- Fruit of Life, page 180
- Raspberry, page 209
- Rustproofer #2, page 248

Infertility — Male

Male infertility is characterized by low sperm count and low sperm motility (a situation in which the semen is too thick to allow proper sperm mobility). Causes can be related to a deficiency in dietary nutrients, hormone imbalance or stress. There is some evidence that suggests that the estrogens in pesticides and other chemical pollutants may be a cause of declining sperm counts over the past 50 years.

Healing Foods

Fruits and vegetables
berries, cantaloupe, grapefruits, kiwis, oranges, strawberries, asparagus, avocados, broccoli, cabbage, cauliflower, leafy greens (especially spinach), red and green bell peppers

Herbs
astragalus, cayenne, ginger, ginkgo, ginseng, red raspberry leaf

Other
bran, fish oil, legumes, nuts, oats, seeds (especially sunflower and pumpkin), soybean products, whole grains

What to Do

Maximize

- Antioxidant-rich fruits and vegetables, especially those that contain vitamin C. Studies have shown that high sperm motility requires a sufficient intake of vitamin C
- Foods that contain zinc (seafood, legumes, whole grains, sunflower seeds, pumpkin seeds), which is required for sperm motility
- Herbs that improve circulation (cayenne, ginger) of all body fluids, including semen

Minimize

- Iodized salt. Excess iodine lowers sperm count
- Refined foods (white rice, white flour, white sugar)
- Animal fats in meat and dairy products

Eliminate

- Alcohol, coffee, tea and soft drinks, which decrease sperm health

Other Recommendations

- Drink tea made from nerve-nourishing herbs (German chamomile, skullcap, oat straw) and regularly include relaxing activities, such as walking, meditation, yoga and tai chi, to reduce stress.

Healing Smoothies

- Açai Berry Combo, page 158
- Asparagus Mango, page 224
- Berry Fine Cocktail, page 168
- Brazilian Berry Smoothie, page 172
- C-Blitz, page 174
- Citrus Cocktail, page 176
- Spinach Salad, page 249

Inflammatory Bowel Disease

Crohn's disease and ulcerative colitis are serious diseases. Read all reference information on these diseases and consult with an experienced medical practitioner.

Healing Foods

Fruits and vegetables
juice of beets and beet tops, carrot juice and boiled carrots, spinach juice

Herbs
garlic, German chamomile, marshmallow root, slippery elm bark powder, valerian*

Other
ground flax seeds, kelp, psyllium seed, rice

* Valerian has an adverse effect on some people.

What to Do

Maximize
- Rice and cooked root vegetables
- Beet juice, which provides nutrition, cleanses the blood and supports detoxification in the liver
- Raw garlic daily, to cleanse the bowel of toxins
- Food combining (see page 17) to optimize nutrition and absorption of nutrients
- Water and herbal teas between meals

Eliminate
- Red meat, which contributes to inflammation. Substitute with oily fish (salmon, sardines, tuna) and a little white chicken meat
- All foods that commonly cause bowel irritation: coffee, chocolate, mushrooms, alcohol, soft drinks, all junk food, all artificial coloring and flavoring, fried foods, salt

Eliminate
- Foods that trigger allergies and intolerances: commonly dairy products, wheat, rye, oats and corn products, citrus fruits, eggs, cruciferous vegetables (broccoli, cabbage, cauliflower, Brussels sprouts), tomatoes, yeast (see Appendix A: Food Allergies, page 373)
- Sugar and sugar products
- Cigarettes

Healing Smoothies

- Apple Beet Pear, page 223
- Beet Smoothie, page 225
- Calm Beet page, 232
- Green Energy, page 265
- Green Goddess, page 185
- Green Gold, page 238

Influenza

Influenza (flu) is a viral infection of the respiratory tract. Symptoms include chills, fever, cough, headache, aches, fatigue and lack of appetite. Treating the flu early can shorten recovery time and help prevent more-serious disease. Top priorities are getting rest to allow the body's energies to focus on healing and drinking plenty of fluids to encourage the elimination of toxins.

Healing Foods

Fruits and vegetables
lemons, oranges, pineapple, strawberries, broccoli, carrots, Jerusalem artichokes, spinach, watercress

Eating small meals, mainly of vegetable juices, reduces the energy required for digestion, allowing more energy to be focused on healing. "Hot" herbs, such as ginger and cayenne, increase body temperature, which discourages the influenza virus from multiplying.

What to Do

Maximize
- Fresh fruits and vegetables
- Fluid intake (drink at least eight large glasses of water, juice and/or herbal tea daily)

Eliminate
- Alcohol, sugar and sugar products, which decrease immunity

Healing Smoothies

- Brocco-Carrot, page 226
- Detox Delight (use a recommended herb instead of milk thistle), page 179
- Flaming Antibiotic, page 236
- Flu Fighter #1, page 180
- Flu Fighter #2, page 263

- Fruit of Life, page 180
- Gold Star Smoothie, page 182
- Hot Flu Toddy, page 267
- Pineapple Citrus, page 202
- Pineapple Crush, page 202
- Spring Celebration, page 250

Insomnia

Insomnia, or the inability to sleep, may be caused by low blood-sugar levels (see Hypoglycemia, page 57), anxiety, depression, temperature (too hot or too cold) or caffeine ingestion. Foods high in B vitamins, calcium and magnesium supply nutrients that calm the nervous tension that can prevent sleep (see Anxiety States, page 32, and Depression, page 42).

What to Do

Maximize
- Calming, caffeine-free drinks
- Foods that are high in B vitamins (whole grains, leafy greens, broccoli, wheat germ), calcium (yogurt, tofu, broccoli) and magnesium (apples, avocados, dark grapes, nuts, brown rice)

Eliminate
- Alcohol
- Caffeine (found in coffee, black and green tea, chocolate and soft drinks)
- Artificial food additives

Healing Smoothies

- Almond Banana, page 158

- Sleepytime Smoothie, page 275

Irritable Bowel Syndrome

Irritable bowel syndrome is a long-standing bowel dysfunction for which no organic cause can be found. It is characterized by bloating, abdominal pain, and diarrhea or constipation. Healing factors include diet, stress management and elimination of allergens. Herbs can be used to soothe the intestines, reduce inflammation, improve digestion, calm the nerves and promote intestinal healing.

Healing Foods

Fruits and vegetables
apples, apricots, kiwis, lemons, papayas, pineapple, broccoli, cabbage, carrots, spinach, tomatoes

Herbs
cinnamon, dandelion (root, leaves and flowers), fennel, German chamomile, ginger, lemon balm, licorice*, parsley**, peppermint, slippery elm bark powder

Other
flax seeds, nuts, oat bran, tofu, yogurt with active bacterial cultures

* Avoid licorice if you have high blood pressure. The prolonged use of licorice is not recommended under any circumstances.

** If you are pregnant, limit your intake of parsley to ½ tsp (2 mL) dried or one sprig fresh per day. Do not take parsley if you are suffering from kidney inflammation.

What to Do

Maximize
- Fish and vegetable proteins (nuts, seeds, tofu, beans, legumes)
- Raw fruits and vegetables to provide immunity-boosting vitamins C and E, improve bowel function and eliminate toxins
- Flax seeds and flax seed oil, which are soothing and anti-inflammatory and help heal the bowel and improve bowel function

Eliminate
- Alcohol
- Coffee
- Red meat
- Refined sugar and flour
- Artificial sweeteners
- Fats and oils (except extra virgin olive oil)
- Foods allergies and intolerances (see Appendix A: Food Allergies, page 373). Common culprits are dairy products and citrus fruits
- Caffeine, wheat and corn

Healing Smoothies

- Beet, page 225
- Brocco-Carrot, page 226
- Calming Chamomile, page 260
- Cauliflower Cocktail, page 230
- Cream of Broccoli, page 234

- Pineapple Crush, page 202
- Pineapple Tang, page 204
- Rustproofer #1, page 248
- Slippery Banana, page 276
- Spiced Carrot (omit cayenne), page 249

Kidney Stones

Kidney stones are 60% less common in people who follow vegetarian diets. A high-fiber, high-fluid, low-protein diet is the best preventive medicine. Diets high in animal protein encourage stone formation.

Kidney stones are usually made of calcium and oxalic acid. For this type of stone, limit foods that contain oxalic acid and large amounts of salt (sodium can stimulate calcium excretion). Stones

Healing Foods

Fruits and vegetables
apricots, mangoes, melons, peaches, asparagus, broccoli, celery, corn, fennel, leeks, onions

Herbs
goldenrod, marshmallow leaf and root, plantain, stinging nettle

Other
brown rice, seeds (flax, pumpkin, sesame, sunflower), whole grains

that are made of uric acid and other minerals are less common. Eliminating shellfish can help prevent uric acid stones. Consult your health-care practitioner to determine which type of stone you have and what the possible causes are.

What to Do

Maximize
- Water intake (drink at least two large glasses of water four times a day between meals) to flush out stones and prevent bacterial buildup
- Alkaline-forming foods (oranges, lemons, all vegetables) for uric acid stones

Minimize
- Animal protein in meat and dairy products

Eliminate
- Salt and high-sodium foods (bacon, processed foods)
- Sugar

- High-oxalate foods (leafy greens, rhubarb, coffee, tea, chocolate, grapefruits, parsley, peanuts, strawberries, tomatoes) for oxalic acid stones
- Seafood for uric acid stones
- Alcohol
- Refined flour

Other Recommendations
- Replace animal protein with soy and other vegetable proteins.
- Marshmallow leaf tea, which is soothing to the urinary system, may help break up stones.

Healing Smoothies

- Allium Antioxidant, page 258
- Apricot and Oatmeal Breakfast Special, page 163
- Apricot Peach, page 164

- Asparagus Mango, page 224
- Mango Madness, page 188
- Peachy Melon, page 199

Laryngitis

Healing Foods

Fruits and vegetables
all fruits, carrot juice

Herbs
garlic, ginger, sage*, thyme

Other
honey**

* Avoid sage if you have high blood pressure or are pregnant or breastfeeding.

** Do not give honey to children under one year of age.

Laryngitis is an inflammation of the vocal cords that may be associated with a cold or other infection, or caused by excessive use of the voice. It is important to rest the voice for a few days. If laryngitis is accompanied by fever and a cough or lasts longer than two days, consult your health-care practitioner.

What to Do

Maximize
- Fruits and fruit juices

- Herbal teas and gargles (thyme and sage)

Healing Smoothies

- Açai Berry Combo, page 158
- Apricot Peach, page 164
- Berry Yogurt Flip, page 168
- Beta Blast, page 169
- Brazilian Berry Smoothie, page 172
- C-Blend, page 174
- Chia Aloha, page 176

Liver Problems

The liver is responsible for removing toxins from the blood that can interfere with the functions of the heart, nervous system, digestive system and circulatory system. Excess fat, chemicals, intoxicants, and refined and processed foods disrupt liver function. Anger, nervous tension, mood swings, depression, skin problems, gallbladder problems, menstrual and menopausal difficulties and candida infections can result from poor liver function. It can be improved by diet, and the following dietary suggestions can complement traditional treatment of liver diseases, such as hepatitis, which must be treated by a physician.

Healing Foods

Fruits and vegetables
apples, blackberries, dark grapes, plums, raspberries, beets, carrots, celery, leafy greens, onions, tomatoes, watercress

Herbs
alfalfa, astragalus, burdock root, cayenne, dandelion leaf and root, fennel, fenugreek, German chamomile, garlic, ginger, lemon balm, licorice*, milk thistle, parsley**, rosemary, stinging nettle, turmeric, yellow dock

Other
cereal grasses, extra virgin olive oil, flax seeds, lecithin, legumes, sea herbs, spirulina, whole grains

* Avoid licorice if you have high blood pressure. The prolonged use of licorice is not recommended under any circumstances.

** If you are pregnant, limit your intake of parsley to ½ tsp (2 mL) dried or one sprig fresh per day. Do not take parsley if you are suffering from kidney inflammation.

What to Do

Maximize
- Fruits and vegetables
- Legumes and whole grains
- Bitter foods and herbs (asparagus; citrus peel; dandelion leaf, root and flowers; milk thistle seeds; German chamomile flowers) to stimulate liver function
- Water intake (drink at least eight large glasses of water daily)
- Dandelion root tea

Minimize
- Animal protein (replace with small amounts of fish and vegetable protein)

Eliminate
- Foods that interfere with liver function (animal fats, dairy products, eggs, refined foods, margarine, shortening, oils — except extra virgin olive oil — alcohol, processed foods)
- Fried foods
- All tobacco products
- Sugar, sweets and junk foods
- Non-organic foods, which may contain pesticide residues or toxins

Healing Smoothies

- Apple Beet Pear, page 223
- Apple Carrot Cucumber, page 223
- Appled Beet (use a recommended herb instead of thyme), page 223
- Apple Fresh, page 161
- Beet, page 225

- Green Tea and Blueberries, page 186
- Popeye's Power, page 272
- Red Horizon, page 210
- Sunrise Supreme (use blackberries instead of strawberries), page 215

Low Libido

You can remedy low libido, a lack of sexual interest or energy, by nourishing the reproductive organs and boosting your overall energy level. A diet that consists of whole foods, which provide basic vitamins and minerals, as well as valuable phytochemicals, will encourage sexual health. Antioxidant-rich fruits and vegetables improve circulation by preventing cholesterol deposits from forming on blood-vessel walls. The essential fatty acids in nuts and seeds are especially important in regulating sexual response. If stress is a factor, use nerve-nourishing oats, lemon balm or skullcap.

Healing Foods

Fruits and vegetables
apples, lemons, red grapes, beets, leafy greens, leeks, onions, watercress

Herbs
cayenne, cinnamon, cloves, fennel seeds, garlic, ginger, ginseng, mustard, parsley*, peppermint, rose petals, rosemary, stinging nettle

Other
almonds, Brazil nuts, cereal grasses, fish oil, flax seeds, honey, legumes, oats, pumpkin seeds, soy products, sunflower seeds, walnuts, wheat germ, whole grains

* If you are pregnant, limit your intake of parsley to ½ tsp (2 mL) dried or one sprig fresh per day. Do not take parsley if you are suffering from kidney inflammation.

What to Do

Maximize
- Antioxidant-rich fruits and vegetables
- Nuts and seeds
- Whole grains
- Herbs that stimulate circulation and energy (cayenne, cinnamon, cloves, garlic, ginger, rosemary)
- Herbs such as ginseng, fennel, parsley*, nutmeg, lavender, mustard and rose, which have been traditionally used as aphrodisiacs

Minimize
- Meat

Eliminate
- Alcohol
- Coffee
- Dairy products
- Refined and processed foods
- Sugar

Healing Smoothies

- Açai Berry Combo, page 158
- Allium Antioxidant, page 258
- Appled Beet (use a recommended herb instead of thyme), page 223

- Apple Fresh, page 161
- Beet, page 225
- Blazing Beets, page 225
- Green Energy, page 265

Lupus

Fruits and vegetables
apples, apricots, blackberries, black currants, blueberries, cantaloupe, cherries, grapes, pineapple, avocados, broccoli, cabbage, carrots, cauliflower, fennel, leafy greens, onions, squash, watercress

Herbs
burdock root, dandelion root and leaf, echinacea, elderflower, evening primrose oil, fennel, garlic, ginger, lemon balm, licorice*, meadowsweet, parsley**, red clover flower, St. John's wort, stinging nettle, thyme, turmeric

Other
cereal grasses, extra virgin olive oil, fish oil, flax seeds, legumes, seeds, shiitake mushrooms, soy products, soy yogurt, whole grains,

* Avoid licorice if you have high blood pressure. The prolonged use of licorice is not recommended under any circumstances.

** If you are pregnant, limit your intake of parsley to ½ tsp (2 mL) dried or one sprig fresh per day. Do not take parsley if you are suffering from kidney inflammation.

There are two forms of this autoimmune disease: discoid lupus erythematosus (DLE), which affects only the skin, and systemic lupus erythematosus (SLE), which affects the connective tissues throughout the body. In DLE, the skin lesions are red and scaly. Early symptoms of SLE are fatigue, weight loss and fever, which progress to arthritis-like joint pain. In the later stages, SLE may affect the kidneys and heart. Because this disease attacks the body's immune system, it is important to avoid viral infections, stress and fatigue. Nutrition and herbs can help by providing support and nourishment to the immune system and the organs through which detoxification takes place: skin, lungs, kidneys, liver and bowels. Relaxation exercises and plenty of sleep also support the immune system.

What to Do

Maximize
- Antioxidant-rich fruits and vegetables
- Water intake (drink at least eight large glasses of water daily) to eliminate toxins
- Essential fatty acids (found in nuts and seeds, especially freshly ground flax seeds) to strengthen the immune system and improve blood flow

Eliminate
- Animal protein in meat and dairy products, which contributes to the progression of lupus. Substitute vegetable proteins in soy products and legumes with rice
- Food allergies and intolerances (see Appendix A: Food Allergies, page 373). Keep a diet diary to note symptom changes in relation to food eaten
- Salad and cooking oils (except extra virgin olive oil), which promote inflammation
- Sugar and alcohol, which inhibit immune function
- Alfalfa seeds and sprouts, which can cause inflammation

Other Recommendations
- Eat oily fish (salmon, mackerel, sardines and tuna), which provide healing omega-6 oils, three times a week.
- Use anti-inflammatory herbs (German chamomile, elderflower, fennel, ginger, meadowsweet, turmeric).
- Use herbs that help eliminate toxins (burdock leaf, root and seeds; dandelion root and leaf; parsley**).
- Consume herbs and foods that support the immune system (echinacea, garlic, shiitake mushrooms, cereal grasses).
- Exercise daily, according to your fitness level.

- Açai Berry Combo, page 158
- Apricot Peach, page 164
- Black Pineapple, page 170
- Brocco-Carrot, page 226
- C-Green, page 231

- Fruit of Life (use elderberries or black currants), page 180
- Granate Berry, page 183
- Peachy Currant, page 198
- Pine-Berry, page 204

Menopause

Healing Foods

Fruits and vegetables
apples, avocados, bananas, berries, grapes, peaches, pears, asparagus, carrots, celery, fennel, green bell peppers, leafy greens, tomatoes, watercress

Herbs
dandelion root, fennel, garlic, ginseng, lemon balm, licorice*, motherwort, red clover flower, rosemary, sage**

Other
dried fruits, extra virgin olive oil, flax seeds, lentils, pumpkin seeds, sea herbs, soy products, sunflower seeds, wheat germ, whole grains, yogurt with active bacterial cultures

* Avoid licorice if you have high blood pressure. The prolonged use of licorice is not recommended under any circumstances.

** Do not take sage if you have high blood pressure or are pregnant or breastfeeding.

Menopause occurs when menstruation ceases. Hormonal changes around that transitional time can result in irregular menstruation and other symptoms, such as hot flashes, mood swings and vaginal dryness. Stress magnifies these symptoms.

After menopause, a woman's estrogen level decreases. Decreased estrogen is one of the many factors involved in the development of osteoporosis and heart disease. Daily exercise, relaxation and good diet will help you make a smooth transition and decrease your risk of heart disease and osteoporosis. Nutritional and herbal support help balance hormone levels, improve blood circulation, eliminate toxins and reduce nervous tension.

In addition to the transition-smoothing herbs listed on the left, use the following herbs for specific conditions and symptoms:
- chasteberry (also known as *Vitex agnus-castus*) to balance hormones;
- ginseng, skullcap or oats for stress and nervous tension;
- valerian for insomnia;
- black cohosh for joint pain, hot flashes or depression; and
- hawthorn berries for women with a family history of heart disease.

What to Do

Maximize
- Antioxidant-rich fruits and vegetables (see pages 104 and 116)
- Nuts and seeds
- Whole grains

Minimize
- Animal fats in meat and dairy products

Eliminate
- Caffeine (found in coffee, black and green tea, chocolate and soft drinks)
- Sugar
- Cigarette smoking
- Alcohol

Healing Smoothies

- Apple Fresh, page 161
- Asparagus Mango, page 224
- Best Berries, page 168
- Green Energy (use ginseng instead of ginkgo), page 265
- Leafy Pear (use a recommended herb instead of parsley), page 187
- Pear Fennel, page 199
- Peppery Tomato Cocktail, page 245
- Spring Celebration, page 250
- Tree Fruit Smoothie, page 217

Menstrual Disorders

Healing Foods

Fruits and vegetables
apricots, blueberries, blackberries, citrus fruits, grapes, strawberries, beets and beet greens, broccoli, carrots, leafy greens

Herbs
chasteberry, dandelion root and leaf, evening primrose oil, garlic, ginger, parsley*, skullcap, stinging nettle, yarrow**

Other
almonds, dulse, fish oil, flax seeds, kelp, lecithin, legumes, nuts, pumpkin seeds, sesame seeds, soy products, sunflower seeds, whole grains

* If you are pregnant, limit your intake of parsley to ½ tsp (2 mL) dried or one sprig fresh per day. Do not take parsley if you are suffering from kidney inflammation.

** Do not take yarrow if you are pregnant.

Amenorrhea (absence of menstruation), dysmenorrhea (painful menstruation) and premenstrual syndrome (PMS) are often caused by a hormone imbalance, which is sometimes related to excess stress, exercise or animal products in the diet. Other factors can include poor circulation and insufficient blood or lymphatic circulation.

The natural approach is to:
- balance hormones;
- support blood (and lymphatic) circulation to the pelvic organs;
- promote relaxation, regular moderate exercise and good nutrition; and
- improve digestion and elimination to improve nutrient absorption and regulate hormones.

What to Do

Maximize
- Fruits and vegetables, especially those listed left

Minimize
- Salt and salty foods
- Alcohol

Eliminate
- Refined foods, which lack minerals and vitamins and contain potentially harmful additives
- Caffeine, which depletes calcium and other minerals
- Sugar and sweeteners
- Non-organic meat and dairy products, which can contain artificial hormones and toxins

Other Recommendations
- Balance your intake of lean meat or fish protein with vegetable protein.
- Get sufficient dietary calcium by eating foods such as yogurt, broccoli and tofu.
- Exercise daily.

Healing Smoothies

- Appled Beet (use a recommended herb instead of thyme), page 223
- Beet, page 225
- Best Berries, page 168
- Brocco-Carrot, page 226
- C-Green, page 231
- Cramp Crusher, page 261
- Eye Opener (use blueberries, blackberries or strawberries), page 179
- Popeye's Power, page 272
- Pump It Up, page 207
- Sunrise Supreme, page 215
- Woman's Smoothie, page 280

Migraines

A migraine headache starts with the constriction of blood vessels in the brain, which is then followed by an expansion, which causes pain. Warning symptoms (such as vision changes or mood swings) can come with the blood-vessel constriction. The pain usually starts on one side of the head but may spread to both sides, and may be accompanied by nausea or dizziness. Migraine triggers can include strong emotions, hormonal changes, food allergies and some medications, including oral contraceptives.

Healing Foods

Fruits and vegetables
blackberries, cantaloupe, beets, broccoli, carrots, celery, leafy greens, onions

Herbs
cayenne, cinnamon, dandelion leaf and root, feverfew, garlic, German chamomile, ginger, lemon balm, parsley*

Other
brown rice and rice bran, flax seeds, legumes, pumpkin seeds, sunflower seeds, whole grains

* If you are pregnant, limit your intake of parsley to ½ tsp (2 mL) dried or one sprig fresh per day. Do not take parsley if you are suffering from kidney inflammation.

What to Do

Maximize
- Vegetable protein
- Fresh fruits and vegetables

Minimize
- Animal fats in meat and dairy products
- Sugar

Eliminate
- Caffeine (found in coffee, black and green tea, chocolate and soft drinks)
- Foods that precipitate migraine attacks by causing constriction of the blood vessels (red wine, cheese, corn, smoked or pickled fish, sausages, hot dogs and all other preserved meats, pork, shellfish, walnuts)
- Artificial food additives
- Alcohol
- Food allergies and intolerances (see Appendix A: Food Allergies, page 373), which are usually the cause of migraine headaches. Migraine sufferers are commonly intolerant of dairy products, wheat, eggs, oranges and/or monosodium glutamate (MSG). When food allergies and intolerances are alleviated, the incidence of migraines is either eliminated or greatly reduced

Other Recommendations
- Eat oily fish (salmon, mackerel, sardines and tuna) two or three times a week to maintain steady blood flow to the brain.
- Eat a leaf or two of fresh feverfew daily.
- Practice food-combining techniques (see Food Combining, pages 17 and 375).

Healing Smoothies

- Beet, page 225
- Brocco-Carrot, page 226
- C-Green, page 231
- Gingered Beets, page 237

- Gingered Greens, page 238
- Green Gift, page 238
- Migraine Tonic, page 269

Multiple Sclerosis

Multiple sclerosis is the breakdown of the protective myelin sheaths around the brain and spinal cord. Symptoms may include muscular weakness, numbness, blurred vision, light-headedness and urinary incontinence. Although a cure is not known, dietary changes, such as those recommended below, have shown impressive results in slowing the disease's progress by preventing the breakdown of myelin sheaths and returning to health.

Healing Foods

Fruits and vegetables
apples, avocados, bananas, grapes, pineapple, beets, cabbage, cauliflower, leafy greens

Herbs
astragalus, dandelion root, evening primrose oil, ginger, ginseng, skullcap

Other
brown rice, cereal grasses, extra virgin olive oil, fish oil, flax seeds, lecithin, mung beans, sea herbs, soy milk, tofu, wheat germ

What to Do

Maximize

- Foods that are low in saturated fat
- Essential fatty acids (found in evening primrose oil, flax seeds, fish oil)
- Immunity (see Immune Deficiency, page 57)
- Foods that are high in B vitamins (fish, wheat germ, sea herbs) and magnesium (apples, avocados, bananas, leafy greens, fish, nuts, soy products, brown rice, wheat germ) to nourish nerve tissue
- Lifestyle quality. Evaluate and reduce stress in your life by practicing meditation, yoga, tai chi or taking daily long walks in natural surroundings

Minimize

- Animal fats

Eliminate

- Candida infections (see Candida, page 38)
- Food allergies and intolerances (see Appendix A: Food Allergies, page 373)
- Coffee
- Red meat and dark meat of chicken or turkey
- Dairy products and eggs
- Gluten
- Fats and oils (except cold-pressed oils, such as extra virgin olive oil)

Healing Smoothies

- Almond Banana, page 158
- Appled Beet (use a recommended herb instead of thyme), page 223
- Beet, page 225

- B-Vitamin, page 173
- Minestrone, page 241
- Smart Smoothie, page 276

Osteoporosis

Fruits and vegetables
all raw fruits, except those that are acid forming (cranberries, plums, prunes), broccoli, cabbage, leafy greens and watercress are especially good sources of calcium

Herbs
alfalfa, dandelion leaf, German chamomile, oat straw, parsley*, plantain, stinging nettle

Other
blackstrap molasses, dried fruits, feta cheese, fish and fish oil, legumes, nuts, salmon, sardines, seeds, spirulina, tofu, whole grains, yogurt with active bacterial cultures

Sea herbs are especially good sources of calcium

* If you are pregnant, limit your intake of parsley to ½ tsp (2 mL) dried or one sprig fresh per day. Do not take parsley if you are suffering from kidney inflammation.

Osteoporosis is a disease characterized by progressive bone loss and decreased bone density and strength. It is caused when bones lose calcium. Consumption of calcium- and nutrient-rich foods helps keep bones strong. In order for the body to absorb calcium, it requires adequate levels of certain vitamins and minerals, especially vitamin D and magnesium.

Factors in bone loss are:
- age;
- decreased estrogen level (estrogen enhances calcium absorption);
- not doing weight-bearing exercise, which decreases calcium absorption (doing weight-bearing exercise increases it);
- some prescription drugs, such as corticosteroids, anticonvulsants, diuretics and antacids, which contain aluminum, which interferes with calcium absorption;
- chronic stress, which depletes calcium;
- lack of minerals and vitamins in the diet, which inhibits calcium absorption; and
- disease of the thyroid or adrenal glands.

What to Do

Maximize
- *Foods that promote calcium absorption:*
- raw fruits;
- green vegetables;
- nuts and seeds; and
- legumes.

Minimize
- Foods high in oxalic acid (almonds, Swiss chard, rhubarb, spinach), which inhibits calcium uptake
- Foods that use up calcium while being metabolized by the body (citrus fruits, vinegar, wine)
- Sodium fluoride (found in drinking water, soft drinks, canned food, preserved meats, boxed cereals, and residues of insecticides and fertilizers on commercially grown produce).

Although fluoride is needed in bone formation, an excess inhibits the process.
- Sugar, salt and caffeine, which cause calcium to be excreted in the urine;
- Alcohol;
- High-protein (meat and dairy) diets, which lead to bone loss through calcium excretion in the urine. (This is partly because calcium is used in the process of protein breakdown.) Moderate amounts of fish, poultry, eggs and dairy products can be included in the diet. Note that a lack of protein will also cause weakness in the whole system, including all of the bone-making organs and systems

Minimize

- Phosphorus-rich foods, especially soft drinks, which contribute most to bone loss. Although phosphorus is necessary to bone health, an excess inhibits calcium metabolism
- Refined flour, which is nutrient-depleted, leading to a loss of minerals in the diet
- Vegetables in the nightshade family (tomatoes, potatoes, eggplants, all peppers), which contain the calcium inhibitor solanine
- Commercially prepared foods that contain chemicals, which add toxins and deplete minerals
- Food grown with non-organic fertilizers, which cause depletion of their minerals
- Grains and brans, particularly raw bran, which are high in phytic acid, which binds to calcium, making it unavailable to the body. Soak grains overnight to neutralize phytic acid and make vitamins and minerals available to the body

Healing Smoothies

- Açai Berry Combo, page 158
- Apple Beet Pear, page 223
- Avocado Pineapple, page 224
- Beet, page 225
- Berry Yogurt Flip, page 168
- Black Pineapple, page 170
- Brocco-Carrot, page 226
- B-Vitamin, page 173
- C-Green, page 231
- Cherry Berry, page 175
- Cream of Broccoli, page 234
- Eye Opener, page 165
- Leafy Luxury, page 210
- Red, Black and Blue, page 162
- Rustproofer #2, page 214
- Watercress, page 219

Overweight

Excessive weight is most often caused by insufficient exercise relative to the amount eaten. In a few cases, weight gain can be attributed to hormonal imbalances and some drugs (including corticosteroids and birth control pills). Long-term weight loss is most effectively achieved by adopting a whole-food diet and increasing exercise.

Healing Foods

Fruits and vegetables
apples, blackberries, cherries, citrus fruits, grapes, pineapple, strawberries, watermelon, asparagus, broccoli, cabbage, celery, cucumber, fennel, leafy greens, lettuce, Jerusalem artichokes, radishes, watercress

What to Do

Maximize

- Fresh fruits and vegetables, which help speed up the metabolism and eliminate toxins
- Water intake (drink at least eight large glasses daily) to reduce appetite and eliminate toxins

Healing Foods

Herbs
cayenne, chickweed, dandelion leaf and root, evening primrose oil, fennel, garlic, ginger, parsley*, psyllium seeds

Other
cider vinegar, flax seeds, kelp, legumes, soy products, walnuts, whole grains

* If you are pregnant, limit your intake of parsley to ½ tsp (2 mL) dried or one sprig fresh per day. Do not take parsley if you are suffering from kidney inflammation.

What to Do

Minimize

- Refined flour products, fast foods and junk foods
- Fats in meat, dairy products and salad oils (except extra virgin olive oil)
- Starchy foods (breads, corn, parsnips, potatoes, squash, sweet potatoes)

Eliminate

- Sugar and artificial sweeteners
- Fried foods
- Artificial food additives
- Food allergies and intolerances (see Appendix A: Food Allergies, page 373). Milk products, eggs, oranges and gluten may affect digestion

Other Recommendations

- Eat oily fish (salmon, sardines, mackerel, tuna) two or three times a week to help the body burn excess fat.
- Eat fruit between meals for optimum digestion and to discourage snacking on inappropriate foods.
- Exercise daily, according to your fitness level.
- Replace empty-calorie drinks and snacks with nutrient-rich smoothies.

Healing Smoothies

- Black Pineapple, page 170
- B-Vitamin, page 173
- Carrot Pineapple, page 228
- C-Green, page 231
- Popeye's Power, page 272
- Sea-Straw, page 212
- Strawberry Sparkle, page 214
- Sun on the Water, page 215
- Sweet and Sour Strawberry, page 215

Parkinson's Disease

Symptoms of Parkinson's disease include muscle rigidity, loss of reflexes, slowness of movement, trembling and shaking. It is caused by the degeneration of nerve cells within the brain, which leads to a deficiency of the neurotransmitter dopamine. While there is no cure for Parkinson's disease, dietary therapy can help prevent further degeneration of neurons by neurotoxins. Choose foods that are high in antioxidants and avoid pollutants by choosing fresh, organic foods.

Healing Foods

Fruits and vegetables
bananas, blueberries, strawberries, beets, carrots, leafy greens, lettuce, potatoes

Herbs
alfalfa, evening primrose oil, ginger, ginkgo, milk thistle seed, passionflower, St. John's wort

Other
extra virgin olive oil, legumes, nuts, oats, peanuts, seeds (flax, sesame, sunflower, pumpkin), soy lecithin, spelt flour, whole grains (except wheat)

What to Do

Maximize

- Raw antioxidant-rich organic fruits and vegetables to optimize vitamin and mineral intake and provide digestive enzymes (see pages 104 and 116)
- Legumes, nuts and seeds (especially sunflower seeds) to provide vitamin E, which can slow progression of the disease

Minimize

- Animal protein in meat and dairy products, which aggravates symptoms

What to Do

Eliminate
- Refined and processed foods
- Sugar and artificial sweeteners
- Alcohol
- Wheat and liver, which contain manganese, which may aggravate the disease
- Fatty foods, fried foods, margarine and oils (except extra virgin olive oil)

Other Recommendations
- Eat fava beans (broad beans), which contain levodopa, a precursor to dopamine. Eating ½ cup (125 mL) a day can decrease the amount of medication required. Discuss this with your doctor to avoid overdosing.
- Passionflower can help reduce tremors.
- Ginkgo improves blood circulation to the brain, bringing it more nutrients, which helps prevent cell damage.
- Avoid antacids, cookware, deodorants and water that contain aluminum, which may have adverse effects on Parkinson's sufferers.
- Ground flax seeds help cure and prevent constipation and provide essential fatty acids to nourish brain and nerve tissue.
- Oily fish (salmon, sardines, mackerel, tuna) provides essential fatty acids that nourish brain and nerve tissue.

Healing Smoothies
- Açai Berry Combo, page 158
- Beet, page 225
- Brazilian Berry Smoothie, page 172
- C-Green, page 231
- Detox Delight, page 179
- Eye Opener, page 179
- Pump It Up (use flax seeds instead of protein powder), page 207
- Smart Smoothie, page 276
- Spa Special, page 276

Peptic Ulcers
Gastric & Duodenal Ulcers

Healing Foods

Fruits and vegetables
apples, apricots, bananas, blueberries, cantaloupe, cherries, red grapes (with seeds), mangoes, papayas, pears, avocados, cabbage, carrots, cucumbers, broccoli, leafy greens, onions, watercress

Stomach and intestinal ulcers, called peptic ulcers, occur when the protective mucous lining of the stomach or intestine breaks down. Ulcers can be caused by infection from *Helicobacter pylori* bacteria; a breakdown of the protective mucous lining of the intestine caused by steroid medications, such as Aspirin, or nonsteroidal anti-inflammatory medications, which increase acid secretions that break down the lining; stress; and food allergies. Healing involves minimizing the consumption of acids that erode the stomach and intestinal lining, protecting and soothing the intestinal lining, stimulating the immune system and inhibiting the growth of harmful bacteria. Anti-inflammatory, antibacterial, calming and mucous-protective herbs are also helpful in healing ulcers.

Healing Foods

Herbs
calendula, cinnamon, cloves, dandelion root, echinacea, garlic, German chamomile, ginger, green tea, licorice*, marshmallow root, meadowsweet, parsley**, slippery elm bark powder, turmeric

Other
barley, cereal grasses, extra virgin olive oil, honey, legumes, oats, seeds

* Avoid licorice if you have high blood pressure. The prolonged use of licorice is not recommended under any circumstances.

** If you are pregnant, limit your intake of parsley to ½ tsp (2 mL) dried or one sprig fresh per day. Do not take parsley if you are suffering from kidney inflammation.

What to Do

Maximize
- Fruits and vegetables, which provide healing vitamins and protection from infection. Fully ripe, sweet fruits are more soothing than sour fruits
- Slippery elm bark powder (especially at bedtime) to form a coating in the intestinal tract that protects against acid
- Fluid intake (drink at least eight large glasses of water, juice and/or herbal tea daily, between meals only, to ensure that your digestive juices are not diluted)

Minimize
- Salt

Eliminate
- Caffeine (found in black and green tea, coffee, chocolate, soft drinks and decaffeinated coffee), which stimulates secretion of stomach acid
- Dairy products, which lead to increased stomach acidity
- Alcohol, soft drinks and refined grains, which promote ulceration
- Refined flour and sugar
- Ulcer-causing drugs (steroids, such as Aspirin, and nonsteroidal anti-inflammatories)
- Cigarette smoking
- Very hot liquids, which irritate ulcers
- Fried foods and oils (except extra virgin olive oil)

Other Recommendations
- Eat smaller, more-frequent meals and avoid eating late at night.
- Try stress-reducing techniques, such as meditation, yoga and tai chi.
- Drink raw cabbage juice (1 cup/250 mL taken four times a day on an empty stomach immediately after juicing is effective in healing ulcers).
- Practice food-combining techniques (see Food Combining, pages 17 and 375).

Healing Smoothies

- Berry Best, page 166
- Blue Cherry, page 171
- Fruit of Life, page 180
- Leafy Pear, page 187
- Mango Madness (use apple juice instead of orange juice), page 188
- Pear Fennel, page 199
- Peptic Tonic, page 272
- Pump It Up, page 207

Pregnancy

Nutrition is vital to a baby's health, from preconception to birth. Ideally, a mother should get enough nutrients from food rather than supplements. Whole foods provide high-quality, easily digestible nutrients in forms and proportions that your body can use more easily than supplements. Make natural, unprocessed whole grains, beans, fruits, vegetables, nuts and seeds the basis of your diet. Add sufficient protein in the form of lean meat, fish or soy products.

Healing Foods

Fruits and vegetables
bananas, cantaloupe, citrus fruits, strawberries, avocados, carrots, leafy greens, peas, sweet potatoes, watercress

Herbs
alfalfa, dandelion root and leaf, lemon balm, oat straw, red raspberry leaf, rose hips, stinging nettle

Other
blackstrap molasses, dulse, extra virgin olive oil, flax seeds, kelp, legumes, nuts (especially almonds), seeds (especially sunflower), soy products, wheat germ, yogurt with active bacterial cultures

What to Do

Maximize
- Fruits and vegetables
- Nuts and seeds
- Folic acid (found in egg yolks, wheat germ, leafy greens, soybeans, asparagus, oranges), which is necessary for normal fetal development
- Foods that are rich in omega-3 fatty acids (found in flax seeds; walnuts; and oily fish, such as salmon, tuna, mackerel and sardines), which are needed to maintain a mother's hormone balance and for proper fetal development

Minimize
- *Foods that increase calcium loss (common in pregnancy), such as:*
  - sugar and sweeteners;
  - tea, coffee and soft drinks;
  - fats;
  - refined flour; and
  - bran, tomatoes, potatoes, eggplant and all peppers.

Eliminate
- Alcohol
- Artificial food additives
- Non-organic foods, which can contain pesticide residues
- Junk foods

Healing Smoothies

- Asparagus Mango, page 224
- Avocado Pineapple, page 224
- Best Berries, page 168
- Beta Blast, page 169
- C-Green, page 231
- Citrus Cocktail, page 176
- Green Gold, page 238
- Peas Please, page 243
- Pineapple Citrus, page 202
- Pomegranate Plus, page 206
- Raspberry Raspberry, page 274
- Rustproofer #2 (replace peppermint with red raspberry leaf), page 248
- Sea-Straw, page 212
- Spring Celebration, page 250
- Watercress, page 253

Prostate Enlargement, Benign

Prostate enlargement occurs in 50% of men aged 50, 60% of men aged 60 and so on to 100% of men aged 100. The enlarged prostate blocks the urinary tract, obstructing the flow of urine.

Healing Foods

Fruits and vegetables
apples, bananas, berries, citrus fruits, pears, asparagus, beets, broccoli, cabbage, cauliflower, leafy greens, onions, red and green bell peppers, tomatoes, watercress

Herbs
fresh stinging nettle root, garlic, ginger, goldenrod, green tea, parsley*, plantain, saw palmetto berries, turmeric

Other
almonds, Brazil nuts, cashews, flax seeds, kelp, legumes, pecans, pumpkin seeds, sesame seeds, soy products, sunflower seeds

* If you are pregnant, limit your intake of parsley to ½ tsp (2 mL) dried or one sprig fresh per day. Do not take parsley if you are suffering from kidney inflammation.

What to Do

Maximize
- Antioxidant-rich fruits and vegetables (see pages 104 and 116)
- Tomatoes, which reduce the risk of prostate cancer
- Soy products, which protect the prostate from disease
- Foods that are rich in zinc (shellfish, brown rice, legumes, leafy greens, dried fruits, onions, sunflower seeds, pumpkin seeds, egg yolks) to reduce prostate size
- Foods that contain vitamin C (citrus fruits, berries, leafy greens, parsley, all peppers) to aid zinc absorption
- Foods that are rich in vitamin B_6 (bananas, cabbage, egg yolks, leafy greens, legumes, prunes, raisins, soybeans, sunflower seeds) to improve the effectiveness of zinc

Minimize
- Animal fat in meat and dairy products

Eliminate
- Caffeine (found in coffee, black and green tea, chocolate and soft drinks), which limits calcium absorption
- Alcohol, which flushes zinc out of the system
- Foods that contain artificial additives, pesticides or hormones
- Margarine and cooking oils (except extra virgin olive oil)
- Fried foods
- Sugar and sugar products

Other Recommendations
- Eat oily fish (salmon, mackerel, sardines, tuna) two or three times a week.
- Ensure that you get sufficient dietary protein to help absorb zinc.

Healing Smoothies

- Allium Antioxidant, page 258
- Apple Pear, page 162
- Autumn Refresher, page 165
- Beet, page 225
- Berry Best, page 166
- Berry Fine Cocktail, page 168
- B-Vitamin, page 173
- C-Blend, page 174
- C-Blitz, page 174
- C-Green, page 231
- Cabbage Cocktail, page 226
- Cauliflower Cocktail, page 230
- Citrus Cocktail, page 176
- Cream of Broccoli, page 234
- Leafy Luxury, page 240
- Leafy Pear, page 187
- Pear Pineapple, page 200

Healing Smoothies

- Prostate Power, page 273
- Pure Tomato, page 245
- Spring Celebration, page 250
- Tomato Froth, page 251
- Tomato Juice Cocktail, page 251
- Watercress, page 253

Sinusitis

Sinusitis is an inflammation of the sinuses, which is caused by colds, influenza, allergies or dental infections. The most effective prevention and treatment strategies are to avoid mucus-producing foods and to identify, then avoid, food allergies (see Appendix A: Food Allergies, page 373).

Healing Foods

Fruits and vegetables
apricots, cantaloupe, citrus fruits, mangoes, papayas, strawberries, watermelon, asparagus, broccoli, cabbage, carrots, green beans, leafy greens, pumpkin, red and green bell peppers

Herbs
cayenne, dandelion leaf and root, echinacea, elderflowers, ginger, garlic, parsley*

Other
legumes, lentils, pumpkin seeds, sea herbs, sunflower seeds, wheat germ

* If you are pregnant, limit your intake of parsley to ½ tsp (2 mL) dried or one sprig fresh per day. Do not take parsley if you are suffering from kidney inflammation.

What to Do

Maximize
- Foods that are rich in vitamin C (citrus fruits, strawberries, parsley*)
- Foods that are rich in vitamin E (wheat germ, nuts, seeds, cabbage, soy lecithin, spinach, asparagus)
- Foods that are rich in beta-carotene (carrots, mangoes, cantaloupes, apricots, watermelon, red bell peppers, pumpkin, leafy greens, parsley*, papayas)
- Foods that are rich in zinc (pumpkin seeds, fish, sea herbs)
- Liquid intake (drink at least eight large glasses of water a day)
- Raw garlic to reduce and prevent sinus congestion (take daily)

Minimize
- Starchy foods

Eliminate
- Alcohol
- Bananas
- Dairy products (except yogurt with active bacterial cultures)
- Eggs
- Food allergies and intolerances (see Appendix A: Food Allergies, page 373)
- Refined sugar and flour

Healing Smoothies

- Allium Antioxidant, page 258
- Beta Blast, page 169
- Brocco-Carrot, page 226
- C-Blitz, page 174
- Pumpkin Apricot and Date, page 208
- Sun on the Water, page 215

Skin Conditions
Acne, Dry Skin, Psoriasis & Rosacea

Healing Foods

Fruits and vegetables
apples, apricots, berries, cantaloupe, grapes, mangoes, papayas, pears, beets and beet greens, carrots, cucumbers, leafy greens, pumpkin, squash, watercress

Herbs
burdock root, leaf and seeds; calendula; dandelion root and leaf; echinacea; evening primrose oil; fennel seeds; licorice*; red clover flower; stinging nettle; yellow dock

Other
extra virgin olive oil, flax seeds, lentils, oats, pumpkin seeds, sea herbs, sesame seeds, soy products, spirulina, sunflower seeds, whole grains, yogurt with active bacterial cultures

* Avoid licorice if you have high blood pressure. The prolonged use of licorice is not recommended under any circumstances.

Acne: This condition, characterized by raised red pimples, usually responds to the dietary changes and cleansing herbs listed on the left. When acne is related to the menstrual cycle, include the hormone-balancing herb chasteberry (*Vitex agnus-castus*).

Dry Skin: Adding essential fatty acids to your diet helps nourish dry skin. Food sources include extra virgin olive oil, freshly ground flax seeds, fresh walnuts and hazelnuts, and oily fish (mackerel, sardines, salmon, tuna).

Psoriasis: This condition is caused by an increase in the production of skin cells, causing red, scaly plaques. It usually affects the elbows and knees. The cause is unknown, but it is often related to stress and emotional state; herbs such as German chamomile, skullcap and lemon balm can help calm and relax you. Exposing the plaques to sunlight and bathing in the sea are also helpful. Relaxation techniques, such as meditation, yoga and tai chi, can help bring balance to your life. Avoid nuts, citrus fruits and tomatoes, all of which can aggravate psoriasis.

Rosacea: Acne rosacea is a chronic inflammatory skin disease in which too much oil is produced by the glands in the skin. It is often associated with digestive disorders, and the dietary suggestions and cleansing herbs (left) are usually effective in clearing rosacea up.

What to Do

Maximize
- Fresh fruits and vegetables
- Foods that are rich in beta–carotene (carrots, broccoli, leafy greens, apricots, papayas)
- Blood-cleansing herbs (dandelion root, burdock root, yellow dock)
- Herbal nerve relaxants (German chamomile, skullcap, lemon balm, oat seeds)
- Seeds (flax, pumpkin, sunflower)

Minimize
- Salt and salty foods
- Animal protein (replace with vegetable protein)

Eliminate
- Red meat and shellfish
- Sugar
- Fried foods
- Oranges
- Chocolate
- Refined flour
- Coffee and black tea
- Dairy products
- Soft drinks
- Artificial food additives, including sweeteners
- Alcohol

Other Recommendations
- Drink at least eight glasses of water, juice and/or herbal tea daily to flush out toxins.
- Eat oily fish (salmon, sardines, mackerel, tuna) two or three times a week.

Healing Smoothies

- Apple Carrot Cucumber, page 223
- Appled Beet (use a recommended herb instead of thyme), page 223
- Beet, page 225
- Breakfast Cocktail, page 173
- Leafy Pear, page 187
- Pear Fennel, page 199
- Popeye's Power, page 272
- Psoria-Smoothie, page 273
- Teenage Tonic, page 276

Smoking — Quitting

Healing Foods

Fruits and vegetables
cantaloupe, citrus fruits, broccoli, carrots, leafy greens

Herbs
German chamomile, red clover (flowering tops), skullcap

Other
oat bran, oats, pumpkin seeds, sunflower seeds, tofu

In addition to being a major cause of heart and lung disease and cancer, smoking encourages the loss of calcium (leading to osteoporosis) and is a risk factor for high blood pressure and ulcers. Smoking constricts the blood vessels, decreasing circulation to peripheral parts of the body, and increases the risk of stroke for both men and women, as well as impotence in men. It also causes wrinkles.

Reduce Cravings

- Maintain constant blood sugar by eating six meals a day that consist mainly of fresh fruits and vegetables, with a little protein and whole grains.
- Ease withdrawal symptoms with a mainly vegetarian diet, which slows down the removal of nicotine from the body.
- Exercise regularly. Walking and breathing exercises are excellent.
- Snack on sunflower and pumpkin seeds — the zinc content may reduce cravings by blocking taste enzymes.
- Eat plenty of oats. Studies show that oats diminish cravings.
- Drink calming herbal teas to soothe your nerves.

Healing Smoothies

- Appled Beet (use a recommended herb instead of thyme), page 223
- Apricot and Oatmeal Breakfast Special, page 163
- Beta Blast, page 169
- Brocco-Carrot, page 226
- C-Blitz, page 174
- Green Energy, page 265
- Leafy Pear, page 187
- Orange Zinger, page 242

Urinary Tract Infections

Healing Foods

Fruits and vegetables
blueberries, cranberries, lemons, watermelon, carrots, celery, fennel, onions, parsnips, turnips

Herbs
buchu, cinnamon, coriander, cumin, dandelion leaf, echinacea, fennel seeds, garlic, marshmallow root, slippery elm bark powder, stinging nettle, yarrow*

Other
barley, pumpkin seeds, yogurt with active bacterial cultures

* Do not take yarrow if you are pregnant.

Urinary tract infections can be caused by yeast or bacteria. The infection can then pass into the bladder. Cystitis, an inflammation of the bladder, is caused when yeast or bacteria settle into the irritated tissue of the bladder. It is characterized by frequent, painful urination.

What to Do

Maximize
- Liquid intake (drink 8 to 10 cups/2 to 2.5 L water, vegetable juice and/or herbal tea daily) to dilute and wash out bacteria
- Unsweetened cranberry and blueberry juices to prevent bacteria from adhering to the bladder wall
- Onions and garlic, which are antibacterial. Raw garlic is best. Add it to main dishes, sauces, dips and smoothies; add freshly crushed to salads and vegetables; or chop into pieces small enough to swallow
- Antibacterial herbs (buchu, yarrow) to soothe the bladder and herbs that promote urination (marshmallow root, buchu, dandelion leaf)

Minimize
- Meat (replace with vegetable protein, such as that found in tofu, or legumes and rice)
- Alcohol, sugar and artificial food additives, which irritate an inflamed bladder
- Refined sugar and flour
- Dairy products

Eliminate
- Caffeine (found in coffee, black and green tea, chocolate and soft drinks)

Healing Smoothies

- Blue Water, page 172
- Cran-Orange, page 178
- Healthy Bladder Blitz, page 266
- Red Delight (use blueberries instead of raspberries), page 210
- Sun on the Water, page 215
- Tart and Tingly, page 216
- Watermelon, page 219

Uterine Fibroids

Uterine fibroids are benign growths that are stimulated by estrogen. They can cause pain, heavy menstrual bleeding, anemia and bladder problems. With the drop in estrogen that occurs at menopause, fibroids usually shrink. Plenty of exercise to improve pelvic circulation is helpful.

Healing Foods

Fruits and vegetables
apples, beets, carrots, celery, leafy greens, watercress

Herbs
burdock root, chasteberry, cinnamon, dandelion leaf and root, garlic, ginger, red clover, red raspberry leaf, stinging nettle, yarrow*, yellow dock

Other
kelp, tofu, whole grains

* Do not take yarrow if you are pregnant.

What to Do

Maximize
- Sea herbs to reduce fibroid growth
- Fiber from fresh fruits and vegetables and whole grains to improve the elimination of toxins
- Hormone-balancing herbs (chasteberry), liver-supporting herbs (dandelion root, burdock root, milk thistle seed) and vegetables (beets, carrots)
- Organic foods

Eliminate
- Caffeine (found in coffee, black and green tea, chocolate and soft drinks), which increases estrogen levels
- Fried foods, margarine and oils (except extra virgin olive oil)
- Alcohol
- Artificial food additives, preservatives and colorings, which contribute to the accumulation of toxins and hormone imbalance

Other Recommendations
- Correct anemia if present (see Anemia, page 31).
- Correct constipation if present (see Constipation, page 41).

Healing Smoothies

- Apple Carrot Cucumber, page 223
- Appled Beet (use a recommended herb instead of thyme), page 223
- Apple Pie, page 162
- Beet (add one ½-inch/1 cm long piece of peeled ginger), page 225
- Spiced Carrot, page 249

Varicose Veins & Hemorrhoids

Varicose veins develop in the legs when there is a restriction in blood flow to the heart, causing blood to pool and stretch the veins. Age and genetic predisposition are factors. Possible causes include heart-valve damage, which alters the flow of blood; high blood pressure, which causes blockage; blood-flow restriction (from tight clothing); excess weight; and lack of exercise. The risk increases during pregnancy and with age. Keep veins in good shape with a diet full of natural foods.

Hemorrhoids are varicose veins around the anus. They may be caused by constipation, pregnancy, obesity, lack of exercise or standing for long periods of time, all of which put extra pressure on the perineal area.

Healing Foods

Fruits and vegetables
berries (blueberries, strawberries, raspberries, blackberries), cherries, citrus fruits, pears, red grapes, broccoli, cabbage, leafy greens, onions, watercress

Herbs
alfalfa, burdock seed and root, cayenne, dandelion leaf and root, garlic, ginger, horse chestnut, parsley*, witch hazel, yarrow**

Other
buckwheat, dulse, extra virgin olive oil, kelp, legumes, nuts, oats, seeds (flax, pumpkin, sesame, sunflower), soy products, wheat germ, whole grains

* If you are pregnant, limit your intake of parsley to ½ tsp (2 mL) dried or one sprig fresh per day. Do not take parsley if you are suffering from kidney inflammation.

** Do not take yarrow if you are pregnant.

What to Do

Maximize
- Foods that are high in vitamin E (whole grains, wheat germ, legumes, nuts, seeds, leafy greens, sea herbs, soy products) to improve circulation
- Foods that are high in vitamin C (citrus fruits, red and green bell peppers, berries, leafy greens) to strengthen blood vessels

Other Recommendations
- Remedy constipation (see Constipation, page 41), which worsens hemorrhoids.
- Eat oily fish (salmon, sardines, mackerel, tuna) two or three times a week to provide essential fatty acids, which maintain elasticity of veins and help circulation.
- Exercise daily, according to your fitness level.
- Avoid hot baths, which relax the veins, or tone the veins immediately afterward by rinsing your legs with cold water and wiping gently with witch hazel.
- Do not massage varicose veins.
- Avoid standing for long periods of time.
- Raise feet whenever possible.

Healing Smoothies
- Açai Berry Combo, page 158
- Berry Best, page 166
- Berry Fine Cocktail, page 168
- C-Blend, page 174
- C-Blitz, page 174
- C Green, page 231
- Cherry Sunrise, page 175
- Fruit of Life, page 180
- Leafy Pear, page 187
- Orange Zinger, page 242
- Real Raspberry, page 209
- Sea Straw, page 212
- Spa Special (use a recommended herb instead of milk thistle), page 276
- Sunrise Supreme, page 215

Water Retention
Edema

Healing Foods

Fruits and vegetables
blueberries, cantaloupe, grapes, strawberries, watermelon, asparagus, beets, broccoli, cabbage, carrots, celery, corn, cucumbers, leafy greens, squash, watercress

Water retention can be a symptom of a serious condition, such as high blood pressure, heart disease, kidney disease or liver disease. Or it may simply be the result of medications, poor circulation, allergies, anemia or protein deficiency. Consult with your health-care practitioner to determine the cause.

Cases of water retention in the late stages of pregnancy must always be referred to a doctor. Strong diuretics and water-loss diets can reduce water retention in the short term but may result in kidney damage over the long term. Water retention can result from too much (or too little) dietary protein, insufficient water intake or as a side effect of premenstrual syndrome (PMS) or menopause. Consult with your health-care practitioner in all cases of water retention.

Healing Foods

Herbs
burdock leaf, root and seeds; dandelion leaf and root; garlic; parsley*; stinging nettle

Other
adzuki beans and other legumes, fish oil, whole grains

* If you are pregnant, limit your intake of parsley to ½ tsp (2 mL) dried or one sprig fresh per day. Do not take parsley if you are suffering from kidney inflammation.

What to Do

Maximize
- Water intake (drink at least eight large glasses daily)
- Raw fruits and vegetables

Minimize
- Table salt, sea salt, soy sauce and salted snacks, which can cause water retention
- Tea and coffee, which are strong diuretics that can cause kidney strain if used excessively

Eliminate
- Food allergies and intolerances (see Appendix A: Food Allergies, page 373). Dairy products and wheat can cause water retention

- Sugar
- Refined flour

Other Recommendations
- Exercise daily, according to your fitness level, to improve circulation and reduce water retention.
- Use stronger diuretics (parsley*, celery) only occasionally.
- Include tonic diuretics (dandelion root, stinging nettle, asparagus, corn, grapes, cantaloupe, cucumbers, watermelon) regularly in your diet. The herbs can be made into teas, which can be used as liquid bases for smoothies.

Healing Smoothies

- Apple Carrot Cucumber, page 223
- Berry Best, page 166
- Blue Water, page 172
- Brocco-Carrot, page 226
- C-Green, page 231
- Diuretic Tonic, page 263
- Leafy Pear, page 187
- Popeye's Power, page 272
- Red Delight (use blueberries instead of raspberries), page 210

Healthy Foods

Healthy Foods for Blending

Buy Fresh

When choosing fruits and vegetables, make sure they are firm and ripe. Herbs should show no signs of wilting, yellowing or rust. Buy only what you plan to use in the next day or two because longer storage will destroy the live enzymes in the plants. Ideally, you should shop daily for the fresh fruits, vegetables and herbs you need to make the recipes in this book. If this is impractical, store produce in the refrigerator for no more than 2 days.

Buy Organic

Organic agriculture is a holistic method of farming based on ecological principles, with the primary goal of creating a sustainable agricultural system. Organic farmers use the principles of recycling, interdependency and diversity in their farm design and farming practices. Organic agriculture is about much more than growing food without synthetic fertilizers and chemical biocides. Organic agriculture uses practices that benefit the planet as well as our bodies.

Because blending uses fresh fruits, vegetables and herbs almost exclusively, organic produce is clearly the best choice.

The USDA National Organic Program defines sustainable agriculture as "optimizing the health and productivity of interdependent communities of soil life, plants, animals and people. Management practices are carefully selected with an intent to restore and then maintain ecological harmony on the farm, its surrounding environment and, ultimately, the whole planetary ecosystem."

Wash Well

All fruits, vegetables and herbs — even if organic — should be washed, scrubbed or soaked in a sink of cool water to which 2 tbsp (25 mL) of food-grade peroxide or vinegar has been added. This will remove any soil, as well as bacteria that may have developed during transportation and handling. Spinach and leeks should be soaked to remove grit. In most cases, organic produce can be juiced with the skin on. Exceptions are noted below.

If you can't find organically grown produce, you can use the conventional variety, but only if you wash as directed above and remove the peel. However, because pesticide concentrations are particularly high in non-organic apples, Chilean grapes, cucumbers, peaches, strawberries and apricots, you might consider refraining from using them in smoothies.

Fruits

Fruit supplies the body with natural sugar that it uses for fuel. This sugar comes in the form of fructose. We use some fruits, such as apples, grapes and mangoes, in vegetable smoothies to make those smoothies more palatable. The fiber in fresh raw fruit is important in maintaining digestion and, for this reason, it is important to eat both fruits and vegetables whole in addition to juicing them.

Caution
Diabetics and people prone to yeast infections and hypoglycemia need to watch how much fruit they use because they cause a rapid rise in blood sugar.

Açai

Euterpe oleracea

A small, round, dark purple berry from an Amazon palm tree, available in frozen form from whole and natural foods stores in North America. The flavor of the berries is an unusual blend of chocolate and blueberry.

Actions: Antioxidant, anticancer.

Uses: Due to an exceptionally high concentration of phenolic pigments and anthocyanins with antioxidant properties, açai is being researched for its role in the prevention of numerous human disease conditions. The berry is high in omega-6 and omega-9 fatty acids, fiber, calcium, copper, iron, magnesium, phosphorus, potassium and zinc.

Buying and Storing: Açai is available in several forms: dried pulp purée; bottled liquid pulp purée; frozen whole or puréed berries; and freeze-dried capsules. Look for whole pulp pure organic açai berries for juicing or pulping.

For Juicing: Açai adds a creamy texture and deep purple color to juices. Thaw and use ½ to 1 cup (125 to 250 mL) in fruit juice blends.

For Smoothies: Often used in fruit smoothies, açai helps thicken the mixture and adds a fresh fruit flavor. Use ½ cup (125 mL) for every 2 cups (500 mL) of smoothie.

Açai Recipes:
- Açai Berry Combo, page 158
- Berry Yogurt Flip, page 168
- Brazilian Berry Smoothie, page 172

- Cranberry Cooler, page 177
- Frozen Berry Slushie, page 346
- Fruit of Life, page 180
- Orange Slushie, page 196
- Strawberry Cooler, page 214

Apples

Malus pumila

Actions: Tonic, digestive, diuretic, detoxifying, laxative, antiseptic, lower blood cholesterol, antirheumatic, liver stimulant.

Uses: Fresh apples help cleanse the system, lower blood cholesterol levels, keep blood sugar level up and aid digestion. The French use the peels in preparations for rheumatism and gout, as well as in urinary tract remedies. Apples are also very useful components in cleansing fasts because they help eliminate toxins. Apples are good sources of vitamin A. They also contain vitamins B and C and riboflavin, and are high in two important phytochemicals: pectin and boron.

Buying and Storing: Look for blemish-free apples with firm, crisp flesh and smooth, tight skin. Because of the widespread use of pesticides on apples, choose organic whenever possible or peel before using. Apples will keep in a cool, dark, dry place (or the crisper drawer of your refrigerator) for one month or more.

For Juicing: Apples are the most versatile fruit for juicing and can be blended with any vegetable juice to give it a natural sweetness. The greener the apple, the sharper its juice. Use the peel (if organic) and core (but not the seeds) when juicing. One pound (500 g), about 4 medium apples, yields about 1 cup (250 mL) juice.

For Smoothies: One apple, peeled and cored, yields approximately 1 cup (250 mL) roughly chopped. Homemade or commercially packaged applesauce may also be used in smoothies.

Apple Recipes:
- Apple Carrot Cucumber, page 223
- Apple Cooler, page 159
- Apple Crisp, page 160

Apricots

Prunus armeniaca

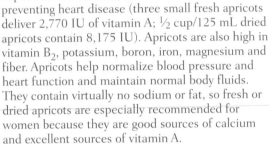

Actions: Antioxidant, anticancer.

Uses: Apricots are very high in beta-carotene, a precursor of vitamin A, which may prevent the formation of cholesterol deposits in the arteries, thus preventing heart disease (three small fresh apricots deliver 2,770 IU of vitamin A; $\frac{1}{2}$ cup/125 mL dried apricots contain 8,175 IU). Apricots are also high in vitamin B_2, potassium, boron, iron, magnesium and fiber. Apricots help normalize blood pressure and heart function and maintain normal body fluids. They contain virtually no sodium or fat, so fresh or dried apricots are especially recommended for women because they are good sources of calcium and excellent sources of vitamin A.

Buying and Storing: Choose firm, fresh apricots that range in color from dark yellow to orange. Keep in a cool, dry place for up to one week.

For Juicing: Choose firm, fresh, dark yellow to orange apricots. Leave peel on if organic but do not use the pit. Apricot juice blends well with berry juice. One pound (500 g), about 4 apricots, yields about $1\frac{1}{2}$ cups (375 mL) juice.

For Smoothies: Dried apricots provide extra sweetness to smoothies. Look for sulfate-free dried apricots, especially if allergies exist.

Apricot Recipes:
- Apricot and Oatmeal Breakfast Special, page 163
- Apricot Apricot, page 164
- Apricot Explosion, page 164
- Apricot Peach, page 164
- Nectar Shake, page 295
- Orange Slushie, page 196

Bananas

Musa cavendishii, syn. *M. chinensis*

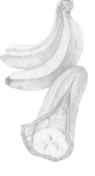

Actions: Antiulcer, antibacterial, boost immunity, lower blood cholesterol levels.

Uses: Due to their ability to strengthen the surface cells of the stomach lining and protect them against acids, bananas are recommended when ulcers or the risk of ulcers is present. High in potassium and vitamin B_6, bananas help prevent heart attacks, strokes and other cardiovascular problems.

Buying and Storing: Look for ripe bananas: they are soft, yellow and slightly speckled with brown. Store in a cool, dark, dry place.

For Smoothies: Often used in fruit smoothies, bananas thicken the mixture and add a fresh fruit flavor. Use one whole banana for every 2 cups (500 mL) of smoothie.

Banana Recipes:
- Almond Banana, page 158
- Banana au Lait, page 289
- Banana Mango, page 165
- Banana Nut, page 166
- Bananarama, page 166
- Brazilian Berry Smoothie, page 172
- Choco-Peanut Parfait, page 345
- CocoNog, page 176
- Frozen Fruit Slurry, page 347
- Grapefruit Greetings, page 184
- Mango Madness, page 188
- Mango Marvel, page 189
- Mexican Mudslide, page 357
- Pumpkin Shake, page 298

Blackberries

Rubus species

Actions: Antioxidant.

Uses: Blackberries are an excellent source of vitamin C and fiber and have high levels of potassium, iron, calcium and manganese.

Buying and Storing: Choose plump, richly colored berries with firm flesh. They're best used immediately (if necessary, store for one day only in the refrigerator). Wash just before using.

For Juicing: Use immediately upon picking or purchasing. If necessary, store for 1 day only in the refrigerator. Wash just before using. One pint (2 cups/500 mL) yields about ¾ cup (175 mL) juice.

For Smoothies: Use fresh, frozen or canned blackberries in smoothies.

Blackberry Recipes:
- Berry Blast, page 167
- Berry Shake, page 290
- Black Belt, page 169
- Blackberry Chiller, page 353
- Blackberry Cream, page 353
- Black Pineapple, page 170
- Green Tea and Blueberries, page 186

Black Currants

Ribes nigrum

Actions: Antioxidant, antibacterial, antidiarrheal, anticancer, boost immunity, promote healing.

Uses: Black currant flesh is extremely high in vitamin C — 200 mg in 3 oz (90 g). Black-currant skins and the outer layers of flesh closest to the skin contain anthocyanins, which have been proven to prevent the growth of bacteria such as *E. coli*. Black currants (especially the seeds) are high in gamma-linolenic acid (GLA), which is important for heart health and a number of bodily functions. For these reasons, whole currants are used in smoothies more often than their juice. Although red currants are not as common, they have similar properties and may be substituted for black.

Buying and Storing: Currants are not widely available but are sometimes found at farmer's markets. While not as fragile as blackberries or raspberries, fresh currants must be stored in the refrigerator, where they will keep for up to one week. Wash just before using.

For Juicing: Use fresh or frozen red or black currants, including the seeds. The flavor is tart, so blend with other, sweeter juices such as apple, apricot and banana. Add the pulp to salsas, quick breads, spreads, dips, slaws and fruit pestos. One pint (2 cups/500 mL) yields about ½ cup (125 mL) juice.

For Smoothies: Use fresh, frozen or dried black or red currants and include the seeds.

Black Currant Recipes:
- Apple Currant, page 160
- Berry Shake, page 290
- Black Currant, page 170
- Flu Fighter #1, page 180
- Peachy Currant, page 198
- Pine-Berry, page 204
- Plum Berry, page 205
- Red, Black and Blue, page 210

Blueberries

Vaccinium species

Actions: Antidiarrheal, antioxidant, antibacterial, antiviral.

Uses: High concentrations of tannins are found in blueberries. They kill bacteria and viruses and help prevent (or relieve) bladder infections. Anthocyanins protect blood vessels against cholesterol buildup. High in pectin, vitamin C, potassium and natural acetylsalicylic acid, blueberries also add extra fiber to smoothies.

Buying and Storing: A silvery "bloom" on blueberries indicates freshness. Choose plump, firm, dark blue berries with smooth skin. Pick over and discard split or soft berries. Blueberries are best used immediately but can be stored in the refrigerator for up to three days. Wash just before using.

For Juicing: Use immediately upon picking or purchasing. If necessary, store for 1 day only in the refrigerator. Wash just before using. Flavor can be tart, especially in wild varieties; treat in the same way as black currants. To prevent or treat bladder infections, juice at least ½ cup (125 mL), add to other ingredients and take daily for a minimum of 3 weeks. One pint (2 cups/500 mL) yields about ½ cup (125 mL) juice.

For Smoothies: Add ¼ to ½ cup (50 to 125 mL) to smoothies for extra healing benefits.

Blueberry Recipes:
- Berry Shake, page 290
- Berry Yogurt Flip, page 168
- Blueberry Smoothie, page 171
- Blue Cherry, page 171
- Blue Water, page 172
- Fruit of Life, page 180

Cantaloupes

See Melons, page 98

Cherries

Prunus species

Actions: Antibacterial, antioxidant, anticancer.

Uses: Cherries are high in ellagic acid (a potent anticancer agent), vitamins A and C, biotin and potassium. Black cherry juice protects against tooth decay.

Buying and Storing: Choose sweet varieties and look for dark red, firm, plump, tight-skinned fruit with the stems attached. Whole ripe cherries are best used immediately but will keep in the refrigerator for up to two days.

For Juicing: Do not use the pits. One pound (500 g), 2 cups (500 mL), yields about ⅔ cup (150 mL) juice.

For Smoothies: When fresh cherries are not available, use pitted frozen, dried or canned cherries in smoothies.

Cherry Recipes:

Citrus Fruits

Citrus species
Oranges, lemons, limes, grapefruits, tangerines

Actions: Antioxidant, anticancer.

Uses: All citrus fruits are high in vitamin C and limonene, which is thought to inhibit breast cancer. Red grapefruit is high in cancer-fighting lycopene. Oranges are a good source of choline, which improves mental function. The combination of carotenoids, flavonoids, terpenes, limonoids and coumarins makes citrus fruits an excellent all-around cancer-fighting package.

Buying and Storing: Purchase plump, juicy fruits that are heavy for their size and yield slightly to pressure. Although citrus fruits will keep for at least a couple of weeks if kept moist in the refrigerator, they are best if used within one week. Organic is preferable — you can be certain the fruits are not injected with gas for transportation.

For Juicing: Remove the peel because it contains bitter elements, but leave as much of the white pith surrounding the sections as possible. The pith contains pectin and bioflavonoids, which help the body absorb vitamin C, act as powerful antioxidants and strengthen the body's capillaries, assisting circulation and enhancing the skin. If you have a centrifugal extractor, use the seeds; they contain limonoids (protect against cancer), calcium, magnesium and potassium.

Citrus juice from a centrifugal extractor is more balanced, thicker, with more of the pith, sweeter tasting and less acidic than juice from a cone juicer. One pound (500 g), about 3 oranges, yields about 1¼ cups (300 mL) juice.

Note: If saving citrus pulp for sauces or breads, remove as much of the bitter white pith as possible before juicing.

For Smoothies: Make fresh citrus juice with a citrus press or juicing machine, or use citrus fruit whole in smoothies. Canned oranges or grapefruits may be used if fresh are not available.

Citrus Recipes:

Cranberries

Vaccinium macrocarpon

Actions: Antibacterial, antiviral, antioxidant, anticancer.

Uses: Cranberries are extremely useful in treating urinary tract and bladder infections. They work like elderberries, preventing the hooks on the bacteria from attaching to the cells of the bladder or urinary tract, rendering them ineffective. Best used as a preventive step against urinary tract and bladder infections, cranberry juice does not take the place of antibiotic drugs, which are more effective in eliminating bacteria once an infection has taken hold. High in vitamins A and C, iodine and calcium, cranberries also prevent kidney stones and deodorize the urine.

Buying and Storing: Choose bright red, plump cranberries that bounce. Keep in the crisper drawer of your refrigerator for two to three weeks. Pure cranberry juice is available (check the label carefully) and is the best to use for its health benefits, but it is very tart. If using pure cranberry juice, taste and add honey, maple syrup or agave nectar to the smoothie as needed.

For Juicing: Fresh cranberry juice is much more effective than the commercial variety, which has a high sugar content. In season during the fall, cranberries freeze very well and can be added frozen to smoothies or juiced without thawing. Wash just before using. Flavor is tart, so blend with sweeter juices such as apple, pineapple, apricot, grape. To prevent or treat bladder infections, juice at least ½ cup (125 mL), blend with other juices as desired, and take every day for a minimum of 3 weeks. One pound (500 g) yields about ¾ cup (175 mL) juice.

For Smoothies: Because their flavor is so tart, you may wish to cook cranberries with sugar, honey or stevia and a small amount of water or juice before combining with other fruit (such as apples or oranges) and blending for smoothies.

Crenshaw Melons

See Melons, page 98

Dates

Phoenix dactylifera

Actions: Boost estrogen levels, laxative.

Uses: Dates are good sources of boron, which prevents calcium loss, so important in the fight against osteoporosis and weakening of bones. Dates contain vitamins A, B_1 (thiamin), B_2 (riboflavin), C and D and valuable mineral salts as well as fiber.

Caution: Dates may trigger headaches in some people.

Buying and Storing: Dried dates are widely available and keep at room temperature for a couple of months. Fresh dates may be found in season in Middle Eastern grocery stores. Buy firm, plump, fresh dates with dark, shiny skins. Fresh dates will keep for several days in the refrigerator.

For Juicing: Dates have a low water content and do not juice well, although date purée may be added to some vegetable juices to make them more palatable.

For Smoothies: Use 3 or 4 dates to sweeten and thicken smoothies.

Date Recipes:
- Apricot and Oatmeal Breakfast Special, page 163
- Date and Nut, page 307
- Date Time, page 178
- Grapefruit Greetings, page 184
- Pumpkin Apricot and Date, page 208
- Pumpkin Shake, page 298
- Special Date, page 213

Elderberries

Sambucus nigra

Actions: Diuretic, laxative, diaphoretic.

Uses: Elderberries support detoxification by promoting bowel movements, urination, sweating and mucus secretion. They are effective in combating viruses, such as those that cause colds and flu.

Caution: If using wild elder that you have gathered yourself, make absolutely certain you are able to identify it correctly. Raw elderberries can make some people sick. If in doubt, cook first before using in smoothies.

Buying and Storing: Elderberries are still mainly harvested in the wild (although some are now grown commercially in the United States and Canada). They are usually available at farmer's markets from mid- to late summer. Look for plump deep purple–black berries with tight, shiny skin and firm flesh. Use immediately or, if necessary, store for one day in the refrigerator. Wash just before using.

For Juicing: Use up to ¼ cup (50 mL) fresh elderberries with sweet fruits such as apples, pineapple, cherries and grapes.

For Smoothies: Elderberries add a dark blue color and a sweet-to-slightly-tart taste to smoothies. Use fresh or frozen elderberries, about ½ cup (125 mL) per smoothie recipe or 1 to 2 tbsp (15 to 25 mL) elderberry syrup or jam per smoothie.

Elderberry Recipes:
- Berry Yogurt Flip, page 168
- Fruit of Life, page 180
- Red Delight, page 210
- Tart and Tingly, page 216

Figs

Ficus carica

Actions: Antibacterial, anticancer, antiulcer, digestive, demulcent, laxative.

Uses: Figs contain benzaldehyde, a cancer-fighting agent. They are also high in potassium, B vitamins, calcium and magnesium.

Caution: Dried figs can trigger headaches in some people.

Buying and Storing: Dried figs are readily available in supermarkets throughout the year. In summer and early fall, some supermarkets and most Middle Eastern grocery stores carry fresh figs. When purchasing fresh figs, choose soft, plump, dark brown fruit with thin skins.

For Juicing: Figs have a low water content and do not juice well.

For Smoothies: Fresh figs can be found in some supermarkets and most Middle Eastern food markets in summer and early fall. Choose soft, plump figs, remove skin and blend the flesh and seeds.

Use dried or fresh figs or Fig Milk (see page 313) to sweeten and thicken smoothies.

Fig Recipes:
- Figgy Duff, page 179
- Fruity Fig, page 181
- Maple Ginger Fig, page 190
- Tutti-Figgy, page 218

Gooseberries

Ribes grossularia

Actions: Protect skin and gums, laxative.

Uses: High in vitamin C, potassium and pectin, a natural fiber.

For Juicing: The tartness of gooseberries requires that they be sweetened by combining them with apples, grapes or date purée.

For Smoothies: Add ½ cup (125 mL) to smoothies for extra healing benefits.

Gooseberry Recipes:
- Gooseberry Berry, page 182
- Gooseberry Fool, page 183
- Loosey-Goosey, page 188

Grapefruits

See Citrus Fruits, page 94

Grapes

Vitis vinifera

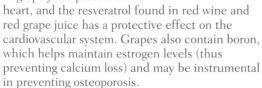

Actions: Antioxidant, antiviral, anticancer.

Uses: Grapes contain large amounts of ellagic and caffeic acids, which deactivate carcinogens, and are a good source of potassium. The flavonoids in grape juice protect the heart, and the resveratrol found in red wine and red grape juice has a protective effect on the cardiovascular system. Grapes also contain boron, which helps maintain estrogen levels (thus preventing calcium loss) and may be instrumental in preventing osteoporosis.

Buying and Storing: Organic grapes are preferable due to the large amounts of pesticides used on non-organic crops. When purchasing grapes, always look for bright color, firm flesh and unwrinkled skin. Wash in food-grade hydrogen peroxide (or other produce cleaner) and store in the crisper drawer of your refrigerator for three or four days.

For Juicing: Common varieties for juicing include Thompson seedless, Concord, red and green seedless grapes. Wash thoroughly and juice whole with skins and seeds intact. Two cups (500 mL) yields about ¾ cup (175 mL) juice.

For Smoothies: Use fresh seedless grapes or raisins in smoothies and blended drinks.

Grape Recipes:
- Apple Fresh, page 161
- Apple Pear, page 162
- Apricot Peach, page 164
- Berry Best, page 166
- Blueberry Smoothie, page 171
- Blue Cherry, page 171
- Grape Glacé, page 184
- Grape Heart, page 185
- Mango Madness, page 188
- Mango Mango, page 189
- Pear Pineapple, page 200
- Raisin Pie, page 208
- Sher-Lime, page 212
- Sunrise Supreme, page 215
- Tangerine, page 216

Honeydew Melons

See Melons, page 98

Kiwifruits

Actinidia chinensis

Actions: Antioxidant, anticancer, aid digestion.

Uses: Kiwis are often used as part of cleansing regimens or to aid digestion. They are high in vitamins C and E (they are one of the few fruits that contain vitamin E), which act as antioxidants and protect cells from free-radical damage. Kiwis are also high in potassium and contain some calcium.

Buying and Storing: Choose ripe fruits that yield to gentle pressure. Kiwis will ripen in a brown paper bag at room temperature after two or three days. They will keep for at least one week in the crisper drawer of the refrigerator.

For Juicing: Choose ripe fruit that yields to gentle pressure. Peel and feed flesh and seeds through juicer. One pound (500 g), about 4 kiwifruits, yields about ⅓ cup (75 mL) juice.

For Smoothies: Use fresh, peel and cut in half or quarters before blending.

Kiwi Recipes:
- Apple Mint, page 161
- C-Blitz, page 174
- Gooseberry Berry, page 182
- Green Cosmo, page 365
- Green Goddess, page 185
- Iced Green Goddess, page 347
- Ki-Lime, page 187
- Mango Marvel, page 189
- Pineapple Kiwi, page 203
- Sher-Lime, page 212
- Tart and Tingly, page 216
- Tropics, page 218

Lemons

See Citrus Fruits, page 94

Limes

See Citrus Fruits, page 94

Mangos

Mangifera indica

Actions: Antioxidant, anticancer.

Uses: High in vitamin A (there are 8,000 IU of beta-carotene in one mango), vitamin C, potassium, niacin and fiber, mangoes help protect against cancer and arteriosclerosis. They also help the body fight infection and maintain bowel regularity.

Buying and Storing: Choose large, firm, unblemished yellow to yellow-red fruit with flesh that gives slightly when gently squeezed. Store in the crisper drawer of your refrigerator for three or four days.

For Juicing: Choose large, firm unblemished fruit, yellow to yellow-red in color. Remove peel and pit before using. Handle carefully since its sap can irritate the skin. Mangos add a creamy texture to juices.

For Smoothies: Add one whole mango to smoothie recipes for added vitamin A.

Mango Recipes:
- Banana Mango, page 165
- Brazilian Berry Smoothie, page 172
- Breakfast Cocktail, page 173
- Detox Delight, page 179
- Fruity Twist, page 182
- Liquid Gold, page 187
- Mango Madness, page 188
- Mango Mango, page 189
- Mango Marvel, page 189
- Mango Tango, page 190
- Pineapple Kiwi, page 203
- Tropical Storm, page 352
- Tropi-Cocktail, page 218

Melons

Cucumis melo
Cantaloupe, honeydew, Crenshaw, Spanish, musk

Actions: Antioxidant, anticancer, anticoagulant (cantaloupe and honeydew).

Uses: Adenosine is an anticoagulant chemical found in melons that lessens the risks of heart attack and stroke. Melons are a good source of vitamin A and contain vitamin C and calcium.

Buying and Storing: Ripe melons are heavy for their size and give off a full, sweet perfume. Avoid soft, blemished fruit.

For Juicing: Choose ripe melons. Peel, cut into wedges and juice with the seeds. Two cups (500 mL) melon chunks yield about ⅔ cup (150 mL) juice.

For Smoothies: Use 1 or 2 peeled wedges per smoothie recipe and coarsely chop the flesh before adding to the blender.

Melon Recipes:
- Berry Best, page 166
- Beta Blast, page 169
- Fruit Explosion, page 180
- Fruit Splash, page 181
- Green Goddess, page 185
- Mega Melon Supreme, page 191

- Mellow Mandarin, page 191
- Melon Morning Cocktail, page 192
- Minted Melon, page 192
- Minty Peach, page 193
- Orange Aid, page 194
- Peachy Melon, page 199
- Plums Up, page 205

Musk Melons

See Melons, page 98

Nectarines

Prunus persica var. *nectarina*

Actions: Antioxidant, anticancer.

Uses: A good source of vitamins A and C and potassium, nectarines are an ancient fruit and not, as many people think, a cross between a peach and a plum.

Buying and Storing: Choose fruit with some bright red areas that are smooth and tight, with no soft patches. Nectarines should be heavy for their size (which means they are full of juice) and firm when pressed. They should not be hard.

For Juicing: Cut in half, remove pit, and juice with skin on. Nectarines are sweeter than peaches and can replace them in juicing recipes. One pound (500 g), about 3 nectarines, yields about 1 cup (250 mL) juice.

For Smoothies: Cut in quarters, remove pit, and add to the blender with other ingredients.

Nectarine Recipes:
- Nectarine on Ice, page 193
- Nectarlicious, page 193
- Nectar of the Gods, page 194
- Nectar Shake, page 295
- Orange Aid, page 194
- Watermelon Wave, page 220

Oranges

See Citrus Fruits, page 94

Papayas

Carica papaya

Actions: Antioxidant, anticancer, aid digestion.

Uses: High in vitamins A and C and potassium.

Buying and Storing: Choose large, firm, unblemished yellow fruit with flesh that gives slightly when gently squeezed. Store in the crisper drawer of your refrigerator for three or four days.

For Juicing: Choose yellow fruit that yields to gentle pressure. Peel, avoiding too much contact with the skin. It is not necessary to remove the seeds before juicing.

For Smoothies: Papayas blend well with other fruits in drinks and serve as a sweet addition that gives a creamy texture to smoothies. Use the seeds, since they contain protein.

Papaya Recipes:
- Fruity Twist, page 182
- Hawaiian Silk, page 186
- Mango Mango, page 189
- Mango Marvel, page 189
- Papaya Passion, page 196
- Taste of the Tropics, page 216
- Tropi-Cocktail, page 218

Peaches

Prunus persica

Actions: Antioxidant, anticancer.

Uses: Rich in vitamin A and potassium, peaches contain boron, niacin, some iron and vitamin C. They help protect against cancer, osteoporosis and heart disease, and their sugar content is low (about 9%).

Buying and Storing: Fruit that is full and heavy for its size, with fuzzy down and lightly firm flesh, is preferable. Store in the crisper drawer of your refrigerator for up to four days. Freestone varieties (such as Loring and Redhaven) are easier to pit than clingstone varieties.

For Juicing: Choose firm, fully-colored fruit with no green that yields to gentle pressure. Cut in half, remove and discard pit, and juice with the skin intact. One pound (500 g), about 4 peaches, yields about ⅔ cup (150 mL) juice.

For Smoothies: Canned peaches add extra nutrients to winter smoothies. Drain and add sliced peaches to winter smoothies.

Peach Recipes:
- Apricot Peach, page 164
- Fruity Fig, page 181
- Liquid Gold, page 187
- Minty Peach, page 193
- Nectar of the Gods, page 194
- Peach Bliss, page 196
- Peach Cobbler, page 197
- Peaches and Cream, page 198
- Peach Paradise, page 197
- Peachy Currant, page 198
- Peachy Melon, page 199
- Rhubarb Pineapple, page 211

Pears

Pyrus communis

Actions: Protect the colon.

Uses: Perhaps one of the oldest cultivated fruits, pears are a good source of vitamin C, boron and potassium. Pears are also a sweet source of fiber.

Buying and Storing: Pears should be lightly firm, unblemished and sweetly pear-scented. They are often available before they are fully ripe, in which case they can be ripened in a brown paper bag at room temperature for one to three days. Ripe pears can be stored in the crisper drawer of your refrigerator for three or four days.

For Juicing: Use varieties such as Bartlett, Comice, Seckel and Bosc. Choose firm unblemished pears and juice the whole fruit. One pound (500 g), about 3 pears, yields about ½ cup (125 mL) juice.

For Smoothies: Use fresh, frozen, dried or canned pears for smoothies. Juicy varieties, such as Bartlett, Comice, Seckel and Bosc are best. Wash, peel (if not organic) and core. Cut into quarters before putting in the blender.

Pear Recipes:
- Apple Pear, page 162
- Autumn Refresher, page 165
- Bananarama, page 166
- Leafy Pear, page 187
- Pear Fennel, page 199
- Pear Raspberry, page 200
- Pink Pear, page 204
- Tree Fruit Smoothie, page 217

Pineapples

Ananas comosus

Actions: Aid digestion.

Uses: Pineapples are a good source of potassium and contain some vitamin C and iron.

Buying and Storing: Choose large, firm fruits (heaviness indicates juiciness) that are yellow all over. Cut off leaves and outer rind of the fruit.

For Juicing: Cut in half and then in wedges without trimming away the woody core. One pound (500 g), about one-third medium pineapple, yields about ½ cup (125 mL) juice.

For Smoothies: One fresh wedge of pineapple equals approximately 1 cup (250 mL) chopped. Frozen, canned or dried pineapple may be substituted for fresh in smoothies.

Pineapple Recipes:
- Apricot Explosion, page 164
- Banana Split, page 343
- B-Vitamin, page 173
- Carrot Pineapple, page 228
- Cherries Jubilee, page 175
- Coconut Cream, page 345
- Cranberry Pineapple, page 177
- Fruity Twist, page 182
- Hawaiian Silk, page 186
- Liquid Gold, page 187
- Mellow Yellow, page 191
- Melon Morning Cocktail, page 192
- Papaya Passion, page 196
- Pineapple-C, page 201
- Pineapple Citrus, page 202
- Pineapple Crush, page 202
- Pineapple Kiwi, page 203
- Pineapple Soy, page 203
- Pineapple Tang, page 204
- Pine-Berry, page 204
- Rhubarb Pineapple, page 211
- Tropics, page 218

Plums

Prunus species

Actions: Antibacterial, antioxidant.

Uses: A good source of vitamin A, plums contain calcium and a small amount of vitamin C.

Buying and Storing:
Ripe plums are firm, with no soft spots or splits. Look for brightly colored (yellow, black or red) plums with tight skins that are heavy for their size and smell sweet. Keep in the crisper drawer of your refrigerator for up to four days.

For Juicing: Use yellow, black or red sweet plums. Pit and juice plums with skin intact. One pound (500 g), about 4 large plums, yields about ¾ cup (175 mL) juice.

For Smoothies: Use whole fresh plums or prunes in smoothies and blended drinks. If using for constipation, use 4 to 6 prunes for every 1 cup (250 mL) of smoothie.

    Prunes are dried plums and are high in pectin and other insoluble fiber, and low in sugar. They act as a natural laxative, and the pectin in them fights colon cancer. Use plump, pitted stewed prunes in juicing or two or three pitted dried prunes per smoothie recipe.

Plum Recipes:
- Fruity Fig, page 181
- Grape Glacé, page 184
- Green Tea and Blueberries, page 186
- Peachy Currant, page 198
- Plum Berry, page 205
- Plum Bliss, page 298
- Plum Lico, page 205
- Plums Up, page 205
- Pomegranate Plus, page 206
- Pom Pom, page 206
- Purple Cosmo, page 360
- Red Horizon, page 210
- Tree Fruit Smoothie, page 217
- Tutti-Figgy, page 218
- Watermelon, page 219

Prune Recipes:
- Loosey-Goosey, page 188
- Prune, page 207

Pomegranates

Punica granatum

Actions: Antidiarrheal, antifever, astringent.

Uses: High levels of antioxidant-rich tannins and flavonoids in the juice and peel make pomegranates beneficial in helping to prevent some forms of cancer. Traditionally used to reduce fevers.

Buying and Storing: Select firm, bright red fruits that are free of bruising and feel heavy. Whole, unpeeled pomegranates keep for up to 2 months in the crisper of the refrigerator. Whole seeds may be frozen and stored for up to 3 months (thaw slightly before juicing).

For Juicing: Peel and remove as much of the white membrane as possible before juicing the seeds. Use the seeds from 1 or 2 whole pomegranates in combination with other fruits.

For Smoothies: Use the juice for pulping. The seeds may be blended in smoothies. Each white pomegranate seed is surrounded by a bright red, sweetly flavored, juicy aril. It is the aril that is pressed and strained to make pure juice. Because the white seed is edible, both the aril and the seed are used in smoothies.

Pomegranate Recipes:
- Granate Berry, page 183
- Orange Pepper, page 242
- Pink Pear, page 204
- Pomegranate Perfect, page 206
- Pomegranate Plus, page 206
- Pom Pom, page 206
- Red Delight, page 210
- Strawberry Sparkle, page 214
- Tutti-Fruity, page 219

Raspberries

Rubus idaeus

Actions: Enhance immunity.

Uses: Raspberries are rich in potassium and niacin and also contain iron and some vitamin C (see also Red Raspberry, page 138).

Buying and Storing:
Buy or pick in peak
season and choose whole,
plump, brightly colored
berries. Sort and discard
soft or broken berries.
Store in the crisper
drawer of your
refrigerator for one day.
Wash just before using.

For Juicing: Do not store
long. Wash just before
juicing. Raspberries blend well with other berries
in juices and the taste is enhanced by a small
amount of citrus juice. One pint (2 cups/500 mL)
yields about ½ cup (125 mL) juice.

For Smoothies: Raspberries blend well with other
berries in smoothies, and their flavor is enhanced by
a small amount of citrus juice. Substitute frozen,
dried or canned raspberries for fresh in blended
drinks. You can also add up to ¼ cup (50 mL)
raspberry jam to smoothies.

Raspberry Recipes:
- Açai Berry Combo, page 158
- Apple Cooler, page 159
- Apricot Ice, page 326
- Berry Blast, page 167
- Berry Bonanza, page 167
- Berry Fine Cocktail, page 168
- Berry Shake, page 290
- Black Pineapple, page 170
- Bloody Orange Vodka, page 355
- Cherry Berry, page 175
- Granate Berry, page 183
- Nectarlicious, page 193
- Peach Bliss, page 196
- Pear Raspberry, page 200
- Perfect in Pink, page 201
- Pink Cosmo, page 359
- Plum Berry, page 205
- Plum Bliss, page 298
- Raspberry, page 209
- Raspberry Cheesecake, page 351
- Razzy Orange, page 209
- Real Raspberry, page 209
- Red Berry Chiller, page 360
- Red, Black and Blue, page 210
- Sour Cherry, page 213
- Summer Strawberry Shake, page 299
- Sweet and Sour Strawberry, page 215
- Tutti-Fruity, page 219

Rhubarb

Rheum species

Actions: Laxative.

Uses: Rhubarb is
actually a vegetable
that is almost always
used as a fruit.
It is high in potassium
and contains a fair
amount of iron.
The calcium in 1 cup (250 mL) of cooked rhubarb
is twice that of the same amount of milk.

Caution: Never use rhubarb leaves, which are toxic
and inedible due to their high concentration of
oxalic acid.

Buying and Storing: If you do not have a rhubarb
patch in your garden, look for rhubarb in farmer's
markets in the spring.
   Choose thin, firm stalks that are at least 90%
red. Rhubarb should snap when bent. Store in a
cool, dry place or the crisper drawer of your
refrigerator for no longer than two days.

For Juicing: Use stalks and roots, but not the
leaves, which contain toxic concentrations of oxalic
acid. Rhubarb can be juiced fresh or frozen. To
soften its tartness, combine rhubarb with sweeter
fruits or juices.

For Smoothies: Use only one raw ripe stalk per
smoothie. Cooking mellows the tart taste and
softens the laxative effect. In a medium saucepan,
combine 1 cup (250 mL) chopped fresh rhubarb,
1 cup (250 mL) chopped apple and 1/4 cup
(50 mL) sugar or liquid honey (or 2 tsp/10 mL
stevia). Cover with water or apple juice and simmer
until soft. Use up to 1/2 cup (125 mL) of this
mixture per smoothie recipe. Cooked frozen or
canned rhubarb may also be used in smoothies.

Rhubarb Recipes:
- Rhubarb Apple, page 211
- Rhubarb Pie, page 211
- Rhubarb Pineapple, page 211
- Rhubarb Smoothie, page 212
- Strawberry Rhubarb Freeze, page 362

Spanish Melons

See Melons, page 98

Starfruits

Averrhoa carambola

A tropical fruit that grows in the shape of a star.

Actions: Antioxidant

Uses: High in vitamin C, potassium, proanthocyanidins, epicatechins and carotene, starfruit is traditionally used to treat arthritis, coughs, diarrhea, hangovers, hemorrhoids, bladder stones, kidney stones and toothache.

Caution: People who suffer from gout or with kidney or other renal problems and/or diabetes should avoid starfruit due to its oxalic acid.

Buying and Storing: Starfruit is delicate, with 5 pointed ribs and should be handled with care. The skin is thin, smooth and waxy. Ripe fruit is golden in color with little or no green. Keep in the crisper section of the refrigerator for up to 4 days.

For Juicing and Smoothies: Starfruit juice is refreshingly thirst quenching, with a tart and slightly citrusy flavor. Use 1 or 2 whole, even-colored and yellow fruits in combination with other fruits in juices and smoothies.

Starfruit Recipes:
- Gold Star Smoothie, page 182
- Grapefruit Greetings, page 184
- Tropical Shake, page 300

Strawberries

Fragaria species

Actions: Antioxidant, antiviral, anticancer.

Uses: Effective against kidney stones, gout, rheumatism and arthritis, strawberries are also used in cleansing juices and as a mild tonic for the liver. Strawberries are high in cancer-fighting ellagic acid and vitamin C. They are also a good source of vitamin A and potassium, and contain some iron. Both the leaves and the fruit are used medicinally. Strawberry leaf tea can be used to treat diarrhea and dysentery.

Buying and Storing: Pick your own or choose brightly colored firm berries with the hulls attached. They are best used immediately but may be stored for no more than two days in the refrigerator. Wash just before using.

For Juicing: Wash just before juicing. Strawberries add a sweet and powerful flavor to juices. They are best blended with only one or two other fruits, although they blend well with other berries in juices. The taste is enhanced by a small amount of citrus juice. One pint (2 cups/500 mL) yields about $\frac{1}{2}$ cup (125 mL) juice.

For Smoothies: Strawberries blend well with bananas and other fruits in blended drinks. The traditional smoothie combination includes strawberry, banana and orange juice. You can substitute frozen strawberries for fresh in any of the smoothie recipes.

Strawberry Recipes:
- Apricot Ice, page 326
- Banana Split, page 343
- Best Berries, page 168
- Blackberry Chiller, page 353
- Frozen Berry Slushie, page 346
- Frozen Fruit Slurry, page 347
- Orange Slushie, page 196
- Peach Blush, page 296
- Peach Mimosas, page 358
- Pineapple-C, page 201
- Pineapple Crush, page 202
- Pomegranate Plus, page 206
- Red Berry Chiller, page 360
- Rhubarb Pie, page 211
- Rose Mimosas, page 361
- Sea-Straw, page 212
- Strawberry Blush, page 213
- Strawberry Cooler, page 214
- Strawberry Margarita, page 362
- Strawberry Rhubarb Freeze, page 362
- Strawberry Sparkle, page 214
- Strawberry Swirl, page 214
- Sweet and Sour Strawberry, page 215
- Tutti-Fruity, page 219
- Wake Up and Shine, page 219
- Whisky Sour, page 364

Tangerines

See Citrus Fruits, page 94

Watermelons

Citrullus vulgaris

Actions: Antibacterial, anticancer.

Uses: Watermelons contain vitamins A and C, iron and potassium. Their high water content makes them good summer refreshments.

Buying and Storing: A watermelon should have a bright green rind and firm flesh (no blemishes or soft spots) and feel heavy for its size. Store in a cool, dark place or in the refrigerator for two or three days.

For Juicing: Remove the rind. Use flesh and seeds, which contain protein, zinc, vitamin E and essential fatty acids. Watermelon is a refreshing summer juice on its own or blended with other fruits as a thirst quencher. Two cups (500 mL) chunked watermelon yields about 1 cup (250 mL) juice.

For Smoothies: One 1½-inch (4 cm) slice watermelon yields approximately 1 cup (250 mL) chopped fruit. Use 1 cup (250 mL) chopped watermelon for each blended drink.

Watermelon Recipes:
- Hot Watermelon Cooler, page 186
- Mega Melon Supreme, page 191
- Melon Morning Cocktail, page 192
- Perfect in Pink, page 201
- Red Delight, page 210
- Sun on the Water, page 215
- Watermelon, page 219
- Watermelon Julep, page 363
- Watermelon-Strawberry Splash, page 220
- Watermelon Wave, page 220

Top Common Antioxidant Fruits

Oxygen Radical Absorbance Capacity (ORAC) is a testing system that measures antioxidant capability of fruits and vegetables. A total of 1,670 ORAC units would be the average equivalent of eating five mixed servings of fruits and vegetables a day; however, juicing or pulping with fruits and vegetables known to be high in antioxidants, or with a high ORAC value, will add much more protection from damaging free radicals.

Fruits	Amount	ORAC Value*
Açai	½ cup (125 mL)	16,140
Pomegranates	2 whole	10,500
Blueberries	1 cup (250 mL) whole cultivated	9,019
Cranberries	1 cup (250 mL) whole	8,983
Blackberries	1 cup (250 mL) whole cultivated	7,701
Prunes	½ cup (125 mL)	7,291
Raspberries	1 cup (250 mL)	6,058
Strawberries	1 cup (250 mL)	5,938
Red Delicious Apple	1	5,900
Sweet Cherries	1 cup (250 mL)	4,873
Black Plum	1	4,844

*Source: USDA data on foods with high levels of antioxidants

Vegetables

Asparagus

Asparagus officinalis

Actions: Antioxidant, anticancer, anti-cataracts, diuretic, promotes healing.

Uses: Asparagus is one of only four vegetables that are high in vitamin E. It is also a source of vitamins A and C, as well as potassium, niacin and some iron.

Buying and Storing: Look for tight buds at the tips and smooth green stalks with some white at the very bottoms. Fresh asparagus will snap at the point where the tender stalk meets the tougher end. Store stalks upright in ½ inch (1 cm) of water in the refrigerator for up to two days.

For Juicing: Wash spears (no need to trim them) and feed through tube stalk-end first. One pound (500 g) of asparagus yields about ¾ cup (175 mL) juice.

For Smoothies: Trim off tough stem bottoms and cook in boiling water for 3 minutes. Drain, cool to room temperature and coarsely chop before adding to smoothies. Frozen or canned asparagus with juices may be substituted when fresh is not available.

Asparagus Recipes:
- Asparagus Mango, page 224
- Gingered Greens, page 238
- Spring Celebration, page 250

Avocados

Persea americana

Actions: Antioxidant.

Uses: Avocados (which are technically fruits) contain more potassium than many other fruits and vegetables (bananas are just slightly higher). High in essential fatty acids, avocados also contain 17 vitamins and minerals, including vitamins A, C and E; all the B vitamins, except B_{12}, and including riboflavin; iron; calcium; copper; phosphorus; zinc; niacin; and magnesium.

They also have the largest amount of protein of any fruit. One avocado blended into a smoothie adds creamy texture and exceptional nutritional value.

Buying and Storing: Look for ripe, heavy avocados that have dull dark green skin with no dents. Ripe avocados give slightly when gently squeezed. Avocados are often sold unripe, but you can ripen them in a paper bag at room temperature and store them in the refrigerator for just over one week once ripe.

For Juicing: Avocados contain little water and do not juice well.

For Smoothies: Peel and cut in half. Remove pit and cut flesh into pieces. Blend with other fruits or vegetables. Brush with lemon juice to keep flesh from turning brown. Because of their relatively low water content, avocados thicken smoothies in much the same way that bananas do. Up to 30% of an avocado's weight may be oil; and for that reason, they should be used sparingly.

Avocado Recipes:
- Asparagus Mango, page 224
- Avocado Orange, page 224
- Avocado Pineapple, page 224
- C-Green, page 231
- Gingered Beets, page 237

Beans and Peas

Phaseolus vulgaris
Pisum sativum
Green, yellow wax, Italian, snap and string beans; also green peas, snow peas

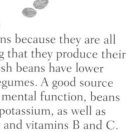

Actions: Improve memory, antioxidant.

Uses: Green beans are the same botanically as dry beans because they are all leguminous plants, meaning that they produce their seeds in pods. However, fresh beans have lower nutrient levels than dried legumes. A good source of choline, which improves mental function, beans also contain vitamin A and potassium, as well as some protein, iron, calcium and vitamins B and C. The amino acids in beans and peas make them a valuable food for vegetarians.

Buying and Storing: Buy fresh peas and beans with firm pods that show no signs of wilting. The bigger the pea or bean inside the pod, the older the vegetable. Fresh yellow or green beans should be pliant but still snap when bent. Store unwashed fresh peas (in their pods) and beans in a plastic bag in the refrigerator for two or three days. Parboiled fresh beans and peas freeze well.

For Juicing: Fresh green or yellow beans may be juiced but because of their low water content, peas work best in smoothies.

For Smoothies: Raw or blanched green peas thicken blended drinks. Wash, shell and add to other fruits or vegetables in the blender in ¼-cup (50 mL) amounts. Soaked dried beans such as red beans, chickpeas and lentils are an excellent addition to smoothies because they add protein and thicken the drink.

Bean Recipes:
- Creamy Chickpea, page 235
- Lima Curry, page 240
- Minestrone, page 241
- Pease Porridge, page 243
- Peas Please, page 243

Beets

Beta vulgaris

Actions: Antibacterial, antioxidant, tonic, cleansing, laxative.

Uses: Beets (the root of the beet plant) are high in vitamin A and the enzyme betaine, which nourishes and strengthens the liver and gallbladder. Beets are also an excellent source of potassium and are cleansing for the liver, kidneys and gallbladder.

Buying and Storing: Bright, glossy, crisp beet greens indicate fresh beets (see Leafy Greens, page 111, for how to use beet greens in smoothies). Buy firm unblemished small beets with greens intact, if possible. To store, cut off tops and treat as leafy greens. Store unwashed beets in a plastic bag in the refrigerator. Beets will keep for up to 1½ weeks. Wash just before cooking.

For Juicing: Scrub roots and leave skin on. Feed tops through juicer first and follow with roots,

tapping them through the tube. One pound (500 g), 2 medium beets with greens, yields about 1 cup (250 mL) juice.

For Smoothies: Use cooked fresh, frozen or canned beets with juices.

Beet Recipes:
- Apple Beet Pear, page 223
- Appled Beet, page 223
- Beet, page 225
- Blazing Beets, page 225
- Clam Beet, page 232
- Gingered Beets, page 237
- Peppered Beet, page 244
- Red Rocket, page 246

Broccoli

Brassica oleracea

Actions: Antioxidant, anticancer, promotes healing, anti-cataracts.

Uses: Broccoli is one of only four vegetables that are high in vitamin E. It is also high in cancer-fighting indoles and glucosinolates and has fair amounts of vitamins A, B and C.

Buying and Storing: Broccoli yellows as it ages, so deep green color and firm tight buds are signs of freshness. Thin stalks are more tender than thick or hollow ones. Store in a vented plastic bag in the crisper drawer of the refrigerator for up to three days.

For Juicing: Use thick stalks and leaves as well as tops. Wash and cut into spears.

For Smoothies: Use cooked fresh, frozen or canned broccoli with juices.

Broccoli Recipes:
- Brocco-Carrot, page 226
- Cheesy Broccoli, page 231
- Gingered Greens, page 238
- Green Gift, page 238

Brussels Sprouts

See Cabbage, opposite

Cabbage

Brassica oleracea var. *capitata*
Green, red, Savoy, bok choy and Chinese cabbage; kohlrabi; and Brussels sprouts

Actions: Antibacterial, anticancer, helps memory, antioxidant, detoxifying, diuretic, anti-inflammatory, tonic, antiseptic, restorative, antiulcer, boosts immunity, anti-cataracts, promotes healing.

Uses: High in cancer-fighting indoles and a good source of choline, which improves mental function, cabbage is one of only four vegetables that are high in vitamin E. An excellent remedy for anemia, cabbage has also been used as a nutritive tonic to restore strength in cases of debility and during convalescence. Beneficial to the liver, cabbage is also effective in preventing colon cancer and may be of help to people with diabetes by reducing blood sugar levels. Cabbage juice is especially effective in preventing and healing ulcers.

Buying and Storing: Fresh cabbage has loose outer leaves around a firm center head. Stored cabbage does not have the outer wrapper leaves and tends to be paler in color. Cabbage will keep for up to two weeks in a plastic bag in the refrigerator. Wash and cut or slice just before using.

For Juicing: Wash and cut into wedges, leaving dark green outer leaves and core intact. Juice Brussels sprouts whole. One pound (500 g) cabbage (about one-third head) yields about 1 cup (250 mL) juice.

For Smoothies: Shred or cut fresh or frozen cabbage into chunks for blending into smoothies.

Cabbage Recipes:
- Cabbage Cocktail, page 226
- Minestrone, page 241
- Red Rocket, page 246

Carrots

Daucus carota subsp. *sativus*

Actions: Antioxidant, anticancer, protect arteries, expectorant, antiseptic, diuretic, boost immunity, antibacterial, lower blood cholesterol levels, prevent constipation.

Uses: Carrots are extremely nutritious and rich in vitamins A, B and C; iron; calcium; potassium; and sodium. They have a cleansing effect on the liver and digestive system, help prevent the formation of kidney stones and relieve arthritis and gout. Their antioxidant properties come from carotenoids (including beta-carotene), which have been shown to cut cancer risk, protect against arterial and cardiac disease, and lower blood cholesterol. Carrots enhance mental function and decrease the risk of cataracts and macular degeneration.

Buying and Storing: The green tops continue to draw nutrients out of the carrot, so choose fresh carrots that are sold loose without the tops, or remove the tops immediately after purchase. Choose firm well-shaped carrots with no cracks. If stored unwashed in a cold, moist place, carrots should not shrivel. Keep for up to two weeks in a vented plastic bag in the crisper drawer of your refrigerator.

For Juicing: Carrots are the sweetest, most versatile vegetable and can be used in almost any juicing recipe. The deeper the color, the higher the concentration of beta-carotene. Do not use carrot greens for juicing. One pound (500 g), about 6 medium, yields approximately 1 cup (250 mL) or more juice.

For Smoothies: Cooking frees up carotenes (precursors to vitamin A), the anticancer agents in carrots. Steam or simmer carrots just until tender, then add to the blender with other fruits or vegetables.

Carrot Recipes:
- Apple Carrot Cucumber, page 223
- Beet, page 225
- Brocco-Carrot, page 226
- Carrot Raisin Cooler, page 228
- Cauliflower Cocktail, page 230
- Flaming Antibiotic, page 236
- Garden Goodness, page 236
- Minestrone, page 241
- Orange Zinger, page 242
- Parsnip, page 242
- Pease Please, page 243
- Peas Porridge, page 243
- Rustproofer #1, page 248
- Spiced Carrot, page 249
- Turnip Parsnip Carrot, page 252

Cauliflower

Brassica oleracea var. *botrytis*

Actions: Antioxidant, anticancer.

Uses: Like all cruciferous vegetables (cabbage, Brussels sprouts, broccoli, collard greens, kohlrabi), cauliflower is rich in cancer-fighting indoles. Cauliflower contains vitamin C and potassium, as well as some protein and iron.

Buying and Storing: Fresh cauliflower has dense, tightly packed florets, and the head is surrounded by crisp green leaves. Keep loosely covered in a perforated plastic bag in the refrigerator for no longer than one week.

For Juicing: Wash and cut into pieces, leaving core and leaves intact. One pound (500 g) flowerets yields approximately 1 cup (250 mL) juice.

For Smoothies: Cut into pieces and cook before blending. Use some of the core if it is not too woody.

Cauliflower Recipes:
• Cauliflower Cocktail, page 230
• Cream of Broccoli, page 234
• Herbed Cauliflower, page 239

Celery

Apium graveolens var. *dulce*
Celeriac *Apium graveolens* var. *rapaceum*

Actions: Mild diuretic, anticancer.

Uses: Sometimes used as a treatment for high blood pressure (two to four stalks per day), celery also helps detoxify carcinogens (see also Celery Seeds, page 122, for their healing properties).

Buying and Storing: Fresh celery has crisp green leaves and firm, crisp ribs. (The leaves are removed from older stalks.) Store for up to two weeks in a vented plastic bag in the refrigerator.

For Juicing: Use stalks and leaves. One stalk yields about ¼ cup (50 mL) juice. Cut celeriac to fit the diameter of the feed tube.

For Smoothies: Use celery stalks and leaves in vegetable cocktails to add natural saltiness. Cut into chunks before adding to the blender. Celeriac, the root of a different variety of celery than common table celery, adds a stronger celery flavor to smoothies. Peel off the tough outer skin, then slice and chop before adding to the blender.

Celery Recipes:
• Blazing Beets, page 225
• Cabbage Cocktail, page 226
• Clam Beet, page 232
• Celery Cream, page 230
• Minestrone, page 241
• Red Rocket, page 246

Celeriac

See Celery, left

Chile Peppers

Capsicum annuum

See also Cayenne, page 121

Actions: Stimulant, tonic, diaphoretic, rubefacient, carminative, antiseptic, antibacterial, expectorant, anti-bronchitis, anti-emphysema, decongestant, blood thinner.

Uses: Chiles are hot peppers that contain the active element capsaicin. They are high in vitamin A and contain some vitamin C, calcium, iron, magnesium, phosphorus and potassium. Chile peppers help people with bronchitis and related problems by irritating the bronchial tubes and sinuses, causing the secretion of fluid that thins the constricting mucus and helps move it out of the body. Capsaicin also blocks pain messages from the brain, making it an effective pain reliever. In addition, it also helps prevent heart attacks (if taken on a consistent basis), as it has clot-dissolving properties. Cayenne (see page 121) is a variety of chile. It appears in the

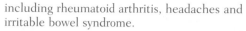

Herb Profiles section because it is used medicinally, as well as in cooking.

Buying and Storing: Look for firm, crisp chile peppers with smooth skin and no blemishes. Store in a paper bag in the crisper drawer of your refrigerator for up to four days. Peppers freeze well and may be added frozen to smoothies. When purchasing dried chile peppers, make sure they are clean and fully dried. Store them in a cool, dry place.

For Juicing: Wash peppers and remove stems. Wash hands thoroughly after handling, since capsaicin will irritate skin and is very painful if it contacts the eyes, lips or nasal passages. When first using chile peppers for juicing, juice after all other ingredients have been put through the machine and keep the juice separate. Add it to vegetable juice blends 1 tsp (5 mL) at a time until you reach the level of heat with which you are comfortable. Alternatively, whisk in a drop of hot or jerk sauce (or ¼ tsp/1 mL powdered cayenne) to juices and blended drinks.

For Smoothies: Use fresh, reconstituted or dried or canned chiles in smoothies. Adding yogurt to chile drinks helps extinguish the fire.

Chile Pepper Recipes:
- Blazing Beets, page 225
- Cajun Cocktail, page 227
- Flaming Antibiotic, page 236
- Peppered Potato, page 244
- Peppery Tomato Cocktail, page 245
- Zippy Tomato, page 254

Collard Greens

See Leafy Greens, page 111

Corn

Zea mays

Actions: Anticancer, antiviral, raises estrogen level, neutralizes stomach acid, high fiber helps with kidney stones and water retention.

Uses: Used in moderation, corn adds fiber to the diet.

Caution: Corn and corn products (cereals, corn chips or foods made with cornstarch) may trigger food intolerances that lead to chronic conditions, including rheumatoid arthritis, headaches and irritable bowel syndrome.

Buying and Storing: Fresh corn is best if cooked within minutes of picking. When that is not possible, buy corn that has been kept cold and use as soon as possible.

For Juicing: Corn is not generally juiced, but if you want to add it to a smoothie, cut the kernels off the cob and juice along with other vegetables.

For smoothies: Use leftover cooked fresh corn by slicing kernels off the cob with a sharp knife. Frozen or canned whole-kernel corn packed in water can be used when fresh is not available.

Corn Smoothies
- Corn Chowder, page 233

Cucumbers

Cucumis sativus

Actions: Diuretic.

Uses: Moderate sources of vitamin A, iron and potassium, cucumbers are high in water, making them good vegetables for smoothies. Cucumbers contain sterols, which may help the heart by reducing cholesterol.

Buying and Storing: Choose shiny, bright green, firm cucumbers. Avoid those with yellow spots (although this is a sign of ripeness, the seeds will be bitter and the flesh too soft) and wax on the skin (which is not good to eat and usually a sign of age). Store in the crisper drawer of the refrigerator for four or five days.

For Juicing: Peel if skin has been waxed. Use whole or cut in half lengthwise and leave seeds intact. One pound (500 g), about 1 large, yields approximately 1¼ cups (300 mL) juice.

For Smoothies: Cut into cubes but leave the seeds intact for blending into smoothies.

Cucumber Recipes:
- Apple Carrot Cucumber, page 223
- Flaming Antibiotic, page 236
- Gazpacho, page 237
- Green Gold, page 238
- Tomato Froth, page 251
- Turnip-Tomato Tango, page 252
- Watercress, page 253
- Zuke and Cuke, page 254

Eggplants

Solanum melongena

Actions: Antibacterial, diuretic, may lower blood cholesterol levels, may prevent cancer.

Uses: Now used topically to treat skin cancer, the terpenes in eggplants may also work internally to deactivate steroidal hormones that promote certain cancers. Eggplants contain a fair amount of potassium, which normalizes blood pressure. They are also low in fat and calories.

Buying and Storing: Choose small deep-purple eggplants with firm, smooth skin that has no scrapes, cuts or bruises. Use immediately or keep for one or two days in the crisper drawer of the refrigerator.

For Smoothies: Wash before using, peel (if not organic) and cut into cubes, leaving the seeds intact. One slice of fresh eggplant can be used in any vegetable smoothie. It adds fiber, which thickens drinks without changing the taste of the main ingredients.

Eggplant Smoothies
- Roasted Eggplant, page 247

Fennel

Foeniculum vulgare

Actions: Antioxidant, seeds are digestive.

Uses: A bulb-like vegetable similar to celery but with a distinctly sweet anise taste, fennel is a good source of vitamin A.

Buying and Storing: Avoid wilted or browning stalks on fennel. The bulb should be firm and white with a light green tinge. Remove leaves if not using immediately and keep for up to one week in the refrigerator.

For Juicing: Use the leaves if attached to the stalks. Use only one-quarter of the bulb (or less) per serving of juice. Larger amounts will make the flavor overpowering.

For Smoothies: Use one-quarter chopped raw, cooked or frozen fennel bulb in smoothies.

Fennel Recipes:
- Anise Anise, page 258
- Celery Cream, page 230
- Creamed Onions, page 234
- Creamy Fennel, page 235
- Gingered Beets, page 237
- Peas Please, page 243
- Peppery Tomato Cocktail, page 245

Garlic

See page 127

Garlic Recipes:
- Allium Antioxidant, page 258
- Blazing Beets, page 225
- Cajun Cocktail, page 227
- Cheesy Broccoli, page 231
- Flaming Antibiotic, page 236
- Gazpacho, page 237
- Minestrone, page 241
- Peppery Tomato Cocktail, page 245

Jerusalem Artichoke

Helianthus tuberosus

Actions: Antibacterial.

Uses: Jerusalem artichokes are the tuberous roots of a plant related to the sunflower (which is why they are often sold as "sunchokes.") Their sweet, nutty flavor blends well in juices. People with diabetes easily digest the inulin, a type of carbohydrate, found in Jerusalem artichokes. They are also a source of calcium, iron and magnesium.

For Juicing: Scrub well and cut larger tubers in half. One cup (250 mL) Jerusalem artichokes yields about ½ cup (125 mL) juice.

For Smoothies: Blanch in boiling water for 3 minutes, cool and chop coarsely before adding to blended drinks.

Kale

See Leafy Greens, below

Kohlrabi

See Cabbage, page 107

Leafy Greens

Kale, Swiss chard, collard greens, mustard greens, turnip greens, lettuce

Actions: Antioxidant, anticancer.

Uses: Excellent sources of vitamin A and chlorophyll, leafy greens are also good sources of vitamin C, with some calcium, iron, folic acid and potassium, as well.

Buying and Storing: Buy bright green, crisp (not wilted) greens and store unwashed in a vented plastic bag in the crisper drawer of your refrigerator. Leafy greens are very tender and will sag and yellow (or brown) when not stored or handled properly. Store away from fruits.

For Juicing: Wash, roll along stem into a long cylinder and feed through tube by tapping.

For Smoothies: Remove tough ribs and stems, shred or chop coarsely before adding to the blender.

Greens Recipes:
• Garden Goodness, page236
• Green Gift, page 238
• Leafy Luxury, page 240

Leeks

Allium ampeloprasum var. *porrum*

Actions: Expectorant, diuretic, relaxant, laxative, antiseptic, digestive, hypotensive.

Uses: Easily digested, leeks are used in tonics, especially during convalescence from illness. They can be blended into toddies for relief from sore

throats, thanks to their warming, expectorant and stimulating qualities.

Buying and Storing: Bright green ends showing no signs of slime or wilt, with crisp white roots intact, means that leeks are fresh. Unwashed and kept in a vented plastic bag in the refrigerator, leeks should last for one to two weeks.

For Juicing: Leave roots and dark green leaves intact, split and wash inner layers well. Use one-half to one leek per serving.

For Smoothies: Leeks can be gritty, so it is important to clean them thoroughly before using. Trim the white roots and outer green leaves off, then split leeks lengthwise and wash the inner layers well. Cut into chunks. Leeks may be used raw but mellow and soften when cooked.

Leek Recipes:
• Vichyssoise, page 253

Lettuce

See Leafy Greens, left

Mustard Greens

See Leafy Greens, left

Onions

Allium species

Actions: Antibacterial, anticancer, antioxidant, circulatory and digestive stimulant, antiseptic, detoxifying, lower blood cholesterol levels, hypotensive, lower blood sugar level, diuretic, cardioprotective.

Uses: Onions help prevent thrombosis, reduce high blood pressure, lower blood sugar, prevent inflammatory responses and prohibit the growth of cancer cells. Shallots and yellow or red onions are the richest dietary sources of quercetin, a potent antioxidant and cancer-inhibiting phytochemical.

Buying and Storing: Examine each onion to make sure it has dry, tight skin and is firm. Avoid onions with woody centers in the neck and black powdery patches. If stored in a cool, dry place with good air circulation, onions will keep for up to two weeks (one month or more in the refrigerator).

For Juicing: Leave skin on and cut in half if necessary to fit feed tube. Blend with other juices. One medium onion yields approximately 3 tbsp (45 mL) juice.

For Smoothies: Vidalia or red onions are preferable for smoothies because they are milder in flavor. Peel and quarter before adding to the blender.

Onion Recipes:
- Allium Antioxidant, page 258
- Clam Beet, page 232
- Corn Chowder, page 233
- Creamed Onions, page 234
- Creamy Chickpea, page 235
- Gazpacho, page 237
- Herbed Cauliflower, page 239
- Minestrone, page 241
- Peppered Potato, page 244
- Quick Vichyssoise, page 246
- Roasted Eggplant, page 247
- Vichyssoise, page 253

Parsnips

Pastinaca sativa

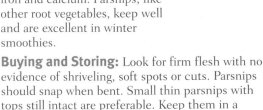

Actions: Anti-inflammatory, anticancer.

Uses: Parsnips are best fresh after frost has concentrated their carbohydrates into sugar, making them sweeter. Good sources of vitamins C and E and potassium, they also contain some protein, iron and calcium. Parsnips, like other root vegetables, keep well and are excellent in winter smoothies.

Buying and Storing: Look for firm flesh with no evidence of shriveling, soft spots or cuts. Parsnips should snap when bent. Small thin parsnips with tops still intact are preferable. Keep them in a plastic bag in the refrigerator for up to 1½ weeks.

For Juicing: Choose firm, small parsnips. Juice with both ends intact. One pound (500 g) yields approximately 1 cup (250 mL) juice.

For Smoothies: Pair with apples and/or carrots in smoothies. Steam or blanch before adding to ingredients in smoothies.

Parsnip Recipes:
- Creamed Onions, page 234
- Parsnip, page 242

Peas

See Beans and Peas, page 105

Peppers

Capsicum annuum
Bell or sweet pepper: green, red, yellow and orange

Actions: Antioxidant, anticancer, cardioprotective.

Uses: Use green, yellow, orange, purple and red peppers in vegetable cocktails and blended drinks — they are all high in vitamins A and C and contain some potassium.

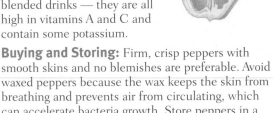

Buying and Storing: Firm, crisp peppers with smooth skins and no blemishes are preferable. Avoid waxed peppers because the wax keeps the skin from breathing and prevents air from circulating, which can accelerate bacteria growth. Store peppers in a paper bag in the crisper drawer of the refrigerator for up to four days. Peppers freeze well and may be added to smoothies without thawing.

For Juicing: Choose thick, fleshy, smooth-skinned peppers. Wash before using. Discard stem, but use seeds. One pound (500 g) yields about 1½ cups (375 mL) juice.

For Smoothies: Frozen, canned, or reconstituted dried peppers may be used in place of fresh in smoothies.

Pepper Recipes:
- Garden Goodness, page 236
- Orange Pepper, page 242
- Peppered Beet, page 244
- Peppered Potato, page 244
- Peppery Tomato Cocktail, page 245

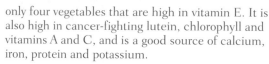

Potatoes

Solanum tuberosum

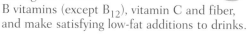

Actions: Anticancer, cardioprotective.

Uses: Potatoes are high in potassium, which may help prevent high blood pressure and strokes. They are a good source of B vitamins (except B_{12}), vitamin C and fiber, and make satisfying low-fat additions to drinks.

Buying and Storing: Select clean, smooth, well-shaped potatoes. Avoid those with wrinkled skin, soft spots or bruises. One medium potato weighs about 8 oz (250 g) and makes about 1 cup (250 mL) diced. If kept in a cool, dry place (for example, a cellar or porch), potatoes will last for up to one month. Keep covered with brown paper or burlap, as light causes potatoes to turn green.

For Juicing: Potatoes are not generally juiced due to their starch content.

For Smoothies: Cook potatoes before adding to smoothies. You can also use canned or leftover cooked potatoes.

Potato Recipes:
- Cheesy Broccoli, page 231
- Corn Chowder, page 233
- Creamy Chickpea, page 235
- Pease Porridge, page 243
- Peppered Potato, page 244
- Quick Vichyssoise, page 246
- Vichyssoise, page 253

Pumpkin

See Squash, right

Spinach

Spinacia oleracea

Actions: Anticancer, improves memory, antioxidant, promotes healing, anti-cataracts, anti-anemia.

Uses: A good source of choline, which improves mental function, and folic acid, a heart protector, spinach is one of only four vegetables that are high in vitamin E. It is also high in cancer-fighting lutein, chlorophyll and vitamins A and C, and is a good source of calcium, iron, protein and potassium.

Buying and Storing: Choose loose spinach, which is fresher than prepackaged, when available. However, be sure to wash it thoroughly, as it tends to be gritty. Look for broad, crisp, deep green leaves with no signs of yellowing, wilting or softness. Spinach keeps for up to three days in a perforated plastic bag in the crisper drawer of the refrigerator. Pick over and remove yellow or wilted leaves of prepackaged spinach before using.

For Juicing: Wash well. Roll into a long cylinder along stem and feed through tube by tapping.

For Smoothies: Use fresh, frozen or canned spinach in blended drinks. Remove tough ribs and stems, and coarsely chop the leaves before adding to the blender.

Spinach Recipes:
- Appled Beet, page 223
- Brocco-Carrot, page 226
- C-Green, page 231
- Cream of Broccoli, page 234
- Green Gold, page 238
- Pease Porridge, page 243
- Spinach Salad, page 249
- Spring Celebration, page 250

Squash

Cucurbita species
Acorn, butternut, Hubbard, pumpkin, turban

Actions: Antioxidant, anticancer.

Uses: Squash is a good winter vegetable that is high in vitamin A.

Buying and Storing: Summer squash are small and tender, with pliable skins and seeds. Winter squash have been allowed to mature on the vine, and their rinds and seeds are tough and woody. Keep whole squash in a cold, moist place or in a perforated plastic bag in the refrigerator. Winter squash may keep for up to one month if stored properly. Cooked squash freezes well for use in smoothies.

For Juicing: Scrub and remove stem. Use skin (if not too thick or waxed) and juice with seeds (high in cancer-fighting chemicals). One pound (500 g), about half a medium squash, yields about ½ cup (125 mL) juice.

For Smoothies: Frozen, canned or leftover cooked squash is the easiest to use in smoothies.

Squash Recipes:
- Carrot Squash, page 229
- Rustproofer #2, page 248
- Squash Special, page 250

Swiss Chard

See Leafy Greens, page 111

Tomatoes

Lycopersicon esculentum

Actions: Antioxidant, anticancer.

Uses: High in lycopene and glutathione, two powerful antioxidants, tomatoes are thought to reduce the risk of many cancers. Lycopene is also thought to help maintain mental and physical functions and is absorbed by the body more efficiently when tomatoes are juiced (or cooked). Tomatoes also contain glutamic acid, which is converted in the body to gamma-aminobutyric acid (GABA), a calming agent known to be effective in reducing kidney hypertension. Drink tomato juice or smoothies made with tomatoes to relax after a stressful day.

Buying and Storing: Vine-ripened heritage varieties are the most flavorful. Tomatoes are best bought fresh only when in season (use canned or reconstituted dried at other times). Local tomatoes are not treated with ethylene gas to force reddening. Plump, heavy, firm-skinned, bright red tomatoes keep for two or three days at room temperature. When almost overripe, store tomatoes in the refrigerator for only one or two more days.

For Juicing: Wash. Discard stem and leaves. Use skin and seeds. Twelve ounces (375 g), about 3 small tomatoes, yields 1 cup (250 mL) or more juice.

For Smoothies: Skin and seeds are blended finely in smoothies and do not need to be removed.

Tomato Recipes:
- Cajun Cocktail, page 227
- Cauliflower Cocktail, page 230
- Celery Cream, page 230
- Clam Tomato, page 232

- Flaming Antibiotic, page 236
- Gazpacho, page 237
- Icy Carrot Cooler, page 239
- Minestrone, page 241
- Orange Pepper, page 242
- Peppery Tomato Cocktail, page 245
- Pure Tomato, page 245
- Roasted Eggplant, page 247
- Rustproofer #1, page 248
- Tomato Froth, page 251
- Tomato Juice Cocktail, page 251
- Turnip-Tomato Tango, page 252
- Zippy Tomato, page 254

Turnips

Brassica rapa

Actions: Tonic, decongestant, antibacterial, anticancer, diuretic.

Uses: Turnips have a beneficial effect on the urinary system, purify the blood and aid in the elimination of toxins. For this reason, they make a good addition to cleansing smoothies. Both the root and the green tops (see Leafy Greens, page 111) are high in glucosinolates, which are thought to block the development of cancer. Good sources of calcium, iron and protein, small tender turnips are available in the spring and sometimes in the fall.

Buying and Storing: Small firm white turnips with dark green leaves that show no signs of wilting or yellowing are best. Turnips will keep for up to one week in a plastic bag in the refrigerator.

For Juicing: Choose fresh turnips with tops intact. Remove tops and wash. Scrub bulbs and juice alternately with tops.

For Smoothies: Cooked fresh spring turnip is a pleasant addition to smoothies. Treat young turnips the same way as parsnips.

Turnip Recipes:
- Turnip Parsnip Carrot, page 252
- Turnip-Tomato Tango, page 252

Watercress

Nasturtium officinale

Actions: Antioxidant, diuretic, anticancer, tonic, antibiotic, cleansing.

Uses: High in fiber and vitamin C and a good source of vitamin A, watercress grows wild around streams and wet areas. Be careful not to harvest it in areas where fields drain directly into streams, because watercress takes in chemical runoff and the by-products of animal feces through its roots.

Buying and Storing: Pick watercress just before using. If purchasing, choose crisp bright green sprigs with intact leaves. Sort through and remove any yellow or wilted stems. Watercress is fragile and should be used immediately. Wrapped in a towel in the crisper drawer of the refrigerator, it will keep for one or two days.

For Juicing: Wash well and feed through tube alternately with other vegetables. Watercress adds a slightly hot bite to juice drinks.

For Smoothies: Use sparingly. Add up to 3 sprigs watercress (leaves and stems) to blended drinks.

Watercress Recipes:
- Watercress, page 253

Wild Greens

Dandelion, mustard, sorrel, turnip, wild garlic and wild leek (ramp)

See Leafy Greens, page 111

Zucchinis

Cucurbita pepo
Italian, yellow straightneck, yellow crookneck

Actions: Antioxidant.

Uses: A good source of vitamins A and C, potassium and niacin, zucchinis are mild tasting and blend well with stronger vegetables.

Buying and Storing: Although zucchinis grow quite large, the smaller they are, the more tender. Look for soft thin skin with no cuts or bruises, and intact stem ends.

For Juicing: Choose small, firm zucchini. Scrub well, leaving skin and blossom end on. Ten ounces (300 g), about 1 medium zucchini, yields about 1 cup (250 mL) of juice.

For Smoothies: Coarsely chop before adding to the blender.

Zucchini Recipes:
- Zuke and Cuke, page 254

Top Common Antioxidant Vegetables

Oxygen Radical Absorbance Capacity (ORAC) is a testing system that measures the antioxidant capability of fruits and vegetables. A total of 1,670 ORAC units would be the average equivalent of eating five mixed servings of fruits and vegetables a day; however, juicing or pulping with fruits and vegetables known to be high in antioxidants, or with a high ORAC value, will add much more protection from damaging free radicals.

Vegetables	Amount	ORAC Value*
Red Beans	½ cup (125 mL)	13,727
Red Kidney Beans	½ cup (125 mL)	13,259
Pinto Beans	½ cup (125 mL)	11,864
Artichoke Hearts	1 cup (250 mL) cooked	7,904
Russet Potato	1, cooked	4,649
Black Beans	½ cup (125 mL)	4,181
Kale	1 cup (250 mL)	2,540

*Source: USDA data on foods with high levels of antioxidants

Herbs

Some herbal practitioners recommend using whole fresh herbs for juicing. This is because only the whole fresh juice, taken immediately, captures the entire synergistic complex of healing ingredients locked within the cellular structure of the living plant. (Sigfried Gursche, *Healing with Herbal Juices,* Alive Books, 1993.)

Most herbalists work with the dried form of herbs for medicinal teas because dried herbs are the most widely available and the easiest to store, transport and work with. For the same reasons, with some exceptions, dried herbs are recommended for use in the tea recipes and some of the juice recipes in this book. However, if fresh herbs are available, be sure to use them.

For each measure of dried herbs called for in a recipe, use 3 times the quantity of fresh.

Most of the herbs profiled in the following section are available dried from whole or natural food stores. Many can be grown in pots or in your garden and some can be wildcrafted (gathered from the wild). See the Sources section (page 372) for information on how to obtain herbs, tinctures and flower essences by mail.

For the greatest medicinal value, dried herbs should be as fresh as possible. Purchase organic dried herbs from a farm or health/alternativestore in small quantities and store for up to 8 to 10 months. If you store your herbs and spices for longer periods, you may not experience the desired effect from them.

Tinctures

A popular and widely available method of herbal medication is the herbal tincture. Tinctures are highly concentrated liquid extracts of the healing herbal properties of medicinal herbs. Tinctures are easy to make and high-quality organic preparations are available from whole or natural food stores.

Water or vinegar may be used but alcohol is the most popular method of extracting the active components in herbs. Alcohol tinctures will last for many years. For each herb listed in this section, we have given the medicinal dose for using the of that herb.

Caution

Herbs contain active medicinal components and should be taken in small amounts or under the advisement of a medical herbalist. There are many herbs that should not be taken in medicinal amounts during pregnancy. It is wise to avoid all herbs during pregnancy unless following the advice of a midwife.

Alfalfa

Medicago sativa

A hardy perennial easily grown in most parts of North America.

Parts Used

Leaves, flowers and sprouted seeds.

Healing Properties

Actions: Tonic, nutritive, lowers blood cholesterol, antianemia.
Uses: Alfalfa is a cell nutritive and overall tonic for the body. It promotes strong teeth, bones and connective tissues. Alfalfa is one of the best sources of chlorophyll, which stimulates new skin growth; heals wounds and burns; diminishes the symptoms of arthritis, gout and rheumatism; lowers blood cholesterol level; reduces inflammation; and improves the body's resistance to cancer.

Caution

Alfalfa seeds and sprouts are rich in the amino acid canavanine, which can contribute to inflammation in rheumatoid arthritis, systemic lupus erythematosus and other rheumatoid and inflammatory conditions. Alfalfa leaves are not a source of canavanine and can be used for inflammatory and rheumatic conditions.

Availability

Whole or cut dried leaves are available in alternative/health stores. Sprouted seeds are readily available in supermarkets.

How to Use in Smoothies

Fresh sprigs: Wash, pat dry and remove leaves and flowers from stem. Use leaves and flower petals; discard stem and green flower center. Use 1 tbsp (15 mL) for each smoothie recipe.
Dried leaves and flowers: Crush dried leaves and flowers to a fine powder. Use up to 1 tbsp (15 mL) per smoothie.
Infusion: In a teapot, pour 1/4 cup (50 mL) boiling water over 2 tbsp (25 mL) chopped fresh leaves (or 2 tsp/10 mL powdered dried leaves). Cover and steep for 10 minutes. Cool (no need to strain) and use to replace 1/4 cup (50 mL) liquid in smoothie recipes.
Tincture: Add 1 tsp (5 mL) tincture to each smoothie recipe.

Astragalus

Astragalus membranaceus

A hardy shrub-like perennial native to eastern Asia but grown in temperate regions.

Parts Used
Root.

Healing Properties
Actions: Immunostimulant, antimicrobial, cardiotonic, diuretic, promotes tissue regeneration.
Uses: Used throughout Asia as a tonic, astragalus is a powerful stimulator for virtually every kind of immune-system activity. It has also been shown to alleviate the adverse effects of steroids and chemotherapy on the immune system, and can be used during traditional cancer treatment.

Availability
While more and more North American herb farms are growing this exceptional medicinal herb, the most-reliable sources for the dried root are Asian herb stores in large urban areas. However, alternative/health stores carry cut or ground dried astragalus, as well as the tincture form.

How to Use in Smoothies
Ground dried root: Add 1 tsp (5 mL) to each 1 cup (250 mL) of smoothie.
Decoction: In a small saucepan, combine ¼ cup (50 mL) boiling water with one 1-inch (2.5 cm) slice dried root (or 1 tsp/5 mL chopped dried root). Cover and simmer for 10 minutes. Remove from heat; steep for 10 minutes. Strain, discard root and let cool. Use to replace ¼ cup (50 mL) liquid in smoothie recipes.
Tincture: Add 10 to 20 drops tincture to each 1 cup (250 mL) of smoothie.

Basil

Ocimum basilicum

A bushy annual with large, waxy, deep green leaves and small tubular flowers on long spikes.

Parts Used
Leaves and flowering tops.

Healing Properties
Actions: Antispasmodic, soothing digestive, antibacterial, antidepressant, adrenal gland stimulant.
Uses: Indigestion, nervous tension, stress, tension headaches.

Availability
Fresh sprigs are sold in season at farmer's markets and supermarkets. Sifted chopped dried leaves are available at alternative/health stores.

How to Use in Smoothies
Fresh leaves: Use 1 to 3 leaves for each 1 cup (250 mL) of smoothie. Wash, pat dry and strip leaves off stem. Discard stem and roughly chop leaves before adding to the blender.

Black Cohosh

Cimicifuga racemosa

A tall, wild woodland perennial native to North America with broad leaves and spikes of fragrant white flowers.

Parts Used
Root and rhizome.

Healing Properties
Actions: Antirheumatic, antispasmodic, mild pain reliever, estrogenic, sedative, anti-inflammatory, uterine stimulant.
Uses: A bitter, tonic herb that soothes aches and pains, black cohosh is used to treat rheumatoid arthritis, sciatica, bronchial spasms, menstrual cramps, menopausal problems, and labor and postpartum pains.

Caution
Do not take if you are pregnant or breastfeeding unless otherwise advised by your health-care practitioner. Excessive doses can cause headaches.

Availability
Seeds, rootlets and plants are available for growing. Dried roots and tinctures are available at alternative/health stores.

How to Use in Smoothies
Decoction: In a small saucepan, combine ¼ cup (50 mL) boiling water with ½ tsp (2 mL) chopped or ground dried root. Cover and simmer for 10 minutes. Remove from heat; steep for 10 minutes. Strain, discard root and let cool. Use to replace ¼ cup (50 mL) liquid in smoothie recipes.
Tincture: Add 8 drops tincture to each 1 cup (250 mL) of smoothie.
Note: Do not add to smoothies more than once a day.

Borage

Borago officinalis

A self-seeding annual with a branching, hollow stem that supports alternating long oval leaves. Small blue star-shaped flowers hang in wide, drooping clusters. The whole plant is covered with prickly silver hairs.

Parts Used
Leaves and flowering tops.

Healing Properties
Actions: Adrenal gland restorative, expectorant, increases milk in breastfeeding.
Uses: Coughs, depression, stress, to strengthen adrenal glands after treatment with corticosteroid drugs.

Caution
Borage leaves contain very small amounts of pyrrolizidine alkaloids, which can be toxic to the liver but are considered safe for occasional use under the supervision of a qualified health-care practitioner.

Availability
Easy to grow in containers or gardens, fresh borage is not readily available for purchase. Dried leaves are sometimes available in alternative/health stores. Use fresh whenever possible, as dried leaves have lost most of their medicinal effectiveness.

How to Use in Smoothies
Fresh sprigs: Use half to 1 whole leaf and up to 4 fresh flowers. Wash, pat dry and strip leaves and flowers off stem. Discard stem and chop leaf and flowers before adding to the blender.
Infusion: In a teapot, pour ¼ cup (50 mL) boiling water over 1 tbsp (15 mL) chopped fresh leaves. Cover and steep for 10 minutes. Cool (no need to strain) and use to replace ¼ cup (50 mL) liquid in smoothie recipes.

Buchu

Agathosma betulina

A small green shrub native to South Africa. Plants in this genus have attractive flowers and aromatic bright green ovate leaves that make them popular as ornamentals.

Parts Used
Leaves.

Healing Properties
Actions: Diuretic, urinary antiseptic.
Uses: Used to treat urinary disorders, such as painful urination, cystisis, prostatitis and urethritis. Research indicates that buchu contains properties that block ultraviolet light, which could be helpful in skin preparations.

Availability
Dried leaves and tinctures are available in alternative/health stores.

How to Use in Smoothies
Ground dried leaves: Use 1 tsp (5 mL) ground dried leaves for each smoothie recipe. Add to other ingredients before blending.
Infusion: In a teapot, pour ¼ cup (50 mL) boiling water over 1 tsp (5 mL) chopped or ground dried leaves. Cover and steep for 10 minutes. Cool (no need to strain) and use to replace ¼ cup (50 mL) liquid in smoothie recipes.
Tincture: Add 20 to 40 drops tincture to each 1 cup (250 mL) of smoothie.

Burdock

Arctium lappa

A hardy biennial that produces fruiting heads covered with hooked burrs that catch on clothing and animal fur. Grows wild extensively in North America. Due to its wide availability in rural and urban waste areas, burdock can be easily foraged. Avoid collecting it from roadsides, ditches, streams close to field runoff, or other areas likely to be polluted by car exhaust or chemical runoff.

Parts Used
Root, stalk, leaves and seeds.

Burdock Leaf

Healing Properties
Actions: Mild laxative, diuretic.
Uses: Leaves may be used in the same way that the root is (see Burdock Root, page 120), though they are less effective.

Availability
Dried leaves and tinctures are available in alternative/health stores.

How to Use in Smoothies
Fresh leaves: Use 1 tbsp (15 mL) chopped fresh leaves in any smoothie recipe. Add to other ingredients before blending.

Dried leaves: Crush to a fine powder. Use 1 to 2 tsp (5 to 10 mL) for each 1 cup (250 mL) of smoothie. Add to other ingredients before blending.

Infusion: In a teapot, pour $\frac{1}{4}$ cup (50 mL) boiling water over 1 tbsp (15 mL) chopped fresh leaves (or 1 tsp/5 mL chopped or ground dried leaves). Cover and steep for 10 minutes. Cool (no need to strain) and use to replace $\frac{1}{4}$ cup (50 mL) liquid in smoothie recipes.

Tincture: Add 10 to 40 drops tincture to each 1 cup (250 mL) of smoothie.

Burdock Root

Healing Properties
Actions: Mild laxative, antirheumatic, antibiotic, diaphoretic, diuretic, skin and blood cleanser, soothing demulcent, tonic, soothes kidneys, lymphatic cleanser.

Uses: Burdock root is used as a cleansing, eliminative remedy. It helps remove toxins that cause skin problems (including eczema, acne, rashes and boils), digestive sluggishness and arthritis pain. It supports the liver, lymphatic glands and digestive system.

Availability
Dig roots in the wild in the fall. Scrub and chop, then dry for storage. Chopped dried root and tinctures are available in alternative/health stores.

How to Use in Smoothies
Fresh root: Scrub, coarsely chop and add to other ingredients before blending. Use 1 tbsp (15 mL) chopped fresh root for each 1 cup (250 mL) of smoothie.

Dried root: Crush to a fine powder. Use 1 tsp (5 mL) for each 1 cup (250 mL) of smoothie. Add to other ingredients before blending.

Decoction: In a small saucepan, gently simmer 1 tsp (5 mL) dried root in $\frac{1}{4}$ cup (50 mL) water for 15 minutes. Strain, discard root and let cool. Use to replace $\frac{1}{4}$ cup (50 mL) liquid in smoothie recipes.

Tincture: Add 10 to 20 drops tincture to each 1 cup (250 mL) of smoothie.

Burdock Seeds

Healing Properties
Actions: Antipyretic, anti-inflammatory, antibacterial, reduce blood sugar level.

Uses: Lymphatic cleanser, soothing demulcent, tonic, soothe kidneys.

Availability
Seeds can be gathered easily in the wild in late summer and early fall (see Burdock, page 119). They are not always available in alternative/health stores, but burdock tinctures are.

How to Use in Smoothies
Infusion: In a teapot, pour $\frac{1}{4}$ cup (50 mL) boiling water over 1 tsp (5 mL) bruised fresh or dried seeds. Cover and steep for 10 minutes. Strain, discard seeds and let cool. Use to replace $\frac{1}{4}$ cup (50 mL) liquid in smoothie recipes.

Tincture: Add 10 to 40 drops tincture to each 1 cup (250 mL) of smoothie.

Calendula

Calendula officinalis

A prolific annual easily grown from seed, with bright yellow to orange marigold-like flowers.

Parts Used
Petals.

Healing Properties
Actions: Astringent, antiseptic, antifungal, anti-inflammatory, heals wounds, menstrual regulator, stimulates bile production.

Uses: Calendula acts as a digestive aid and general tonic. It improves menopausal problems, menstrual pain, gastritis, peptic ulcers, gallbladder problems, indigestion and fungal infections.

Availability
Whole dried flower heads are available in alternative/health stores.

How to Use in Smoothies
Infusion: In a teapot, pour $\frac{1}{4}$ cup (50 mL) boiling water over 1 tbsp (15 mL) fresh petals (or 1 tsp/ 5 mL dried petals). Cover and steep for 10 minutes if using dried petals, or 15 minutes if using fresh. Cool (no need to strain) and use to replace $\frac{1}{4}$ cup (50 mL) liquid in smoothie recipes.

Tincture: Add 5 to 20 drops tincture to each 1 cup (250 mL) of smoothie.

Cardamom

Elettaria cardamomum

A rhizomatous perennial with large lanceolate leaves originally from the Indian rain forests. For centuries it has been exported to Europe, mainly for its fragrance. When coaxed into bloom, the flowers are white with dark pink–striped lips.

Parts Used
Seeds.

Healing Properties
Actions: Antispasmodic, carminative, digestive stimulant, expectorant.
Uses: A pungent herb with stimulating, tonic effects that work best on the digestive system, cardamom relaxes spasms, stimulates appetite and relieves flatulence.

Availability
Whole or ground dried seeds are widely available in supermarkets and alternative/health stores.

How to Use in Smoothies
Ground dried seeds: Add 1 tsp (5 mL) ground dried seeds to other ingredients before blending.
Infusion: In a teapot, pour ¼ cup (50 mL) boiling water over 1 tsp (5 mL) lightly crushed dried seeds. Cover and steep for 10 minutes. Strain, discard seeds and let cool. Use to replace ¼ cup (50 mL) liquid in smoothie recipes.

Catnip

Nepeta cataria

A hardy perennial — and a favorite of cats — with erect branched stems that bear gray-green toothed ovate leaves and whorls of white tubular flowers.

Parts Used
Leaves, stems and flowers.

Healing Properties
Actions: Antispasmodic, astringent, carminative, diaphoretic, cooling, sedative.
Uses: Catnip lowers fever, relaxes spasms, increases perspiration and is often taken at night to ensure sleep. It is also used for diarrhea, stomach upsets, colic, colds, flu, inflammation, pain and convulsions. It is especially useful for lowering children's fevers.

Availability
Catnip is easily grown in North America, but dried leaves, stems and flowers are available in alternative/health stores.

How to Use in Smoothies
Fresh sprigs: Use 2 or 3 leaves for each 1 cup (250 mL) of smoothie. Wash, pat dry and strip leaves and flowers from stem. Discard stem and coarsely chop leaves and flowers.
Dried leaves and flowers: Crush to a fine powder. Use 1 tsp (5 mL) for each 1 cup (250 mL) of smoothie. Add to other ingredients before blending.
Infusion: In a teapot, pour ¼ cup (50 mL) boiling water over 1 tbsp (15 mL) chopped fresh catnip (or 1 tsp/5 mL chopped or ground dried). Cover and steep for 10 minutes. Cool (no need to strain) and use to replace ¼ cup (50 mL) liquid in smoothie recipes.

Cayenne

Capsicum annuum and *Capsicum frutescens*

A tropical perennial grown as an annual in temperate zones (see also Chile Peppers, page 108). Although many varieties of chile peppers are used in cooking to add flavor and heat, the cayenne pepper is also used frequently as an herb because of its healing powers.

Parts Used
Red pepper fruit.

Healing Properties
Actions: Stimulant, tonic, carminative, diaphoretic, rubefacient, antiseptic, antibacterial.
Uses: Cayenne stimulates blood circulation, purifies the blood, promotes fluid elimination and sweating, and is most often used as a stimulating nerve tonic. Applied externally, over-the-counter creams and ointments that contain active capsaicin extract are often effective in relieving the pain of osteoarthritis, rheumatoid arthritis and shingles, as well as the burning pain in the toes, feet and legs caused by diabetic neuropathy and fibromyalgia.

Caution
Cayenne contains an irritating compound that, when applied externally, heals inflammations on unbroken skin by bringing blood to the surface. If used on broken skin, cayenne will irritate the wound and not be as effective. Natural-medicine practitioners often advise that capsaicin not be taken internally in cases of chronic inflammation of

the intestinal tract, such as in irritable bowel syndrome, ulcerative colitis and Crohn's disease. It should be used sparingly during pregnancy.

Availability
Fresh whole cayenne peppers are available in Latin American markets, supermarkets and alternative/ health stores. Dried whole cayenne peppers and ground cayenne pepper are widely available.

How to Use in Smoothies
Use fresh or reconstituted dried cayenne peppers, ground dried cayenne pepper or canned cayenne peppers in smoothies. If unavailable, whisk in a drop of hot pepper or jerk sauce. Taste and add more if desired.

Fresh pepper: Wash and handle carefully and wash hands thoroughly after handling, as capsaicin will irritate the skin and is very painful if it gets into the eyes or nasal passages or onto lips. Remove and discard stem, ribs and seeds. When first using cayenne peppers, add half of the recommended amount to the blender after all other ingredients have been pureed. Taste and add more if desired.

Ground dried pepper: Add $\frac{1}{8}$ to $\frac{1}{4}$ tsp (0.5 to 1 mL) ground dried cayenne pepper to other ingredients before blending. Gradually add more (up to 1 tsp/5 mL) if taste allows.

Celery Seeds

Apium graveolens

A biennial with a bulbous, fleshy root and thick, grooved stems. Although the stalk, leaves and, sometimes, the seeds are used in cooking (see Celery, page 108), it is the seeds collected from wild celery that are used for medicinal purposes.

Parts Used
Seeds.

Healing Properties
Actions: Anti-inflammatory, antioxidant, carminative, sedative, urinary antiseptic.
Uses: Celery seeds are an aromatic, tonic herb that relieve muscle spasms and are used to treat gout, inflammation of the urinary tract, cystitis, osteoarthritis and rheumatoid arthritis.

Caution
Do not use celery seeds if you are pregnant.

Availability
Purchase celery seeds from herbalists or alternative/ health stores only.

How to Use in Smoothies
Dried seeds: Crush to a fine powder. Use $\frac{1}{4}$ tsp (1 mL) for each 1 cup (250 mL) of smoothie. Add to other ingredients before blending.
Infusion: In a teapot, pour $\frac{1}{4}$ cup (50 mL) boiling water over $\frac{1}{4}$ tsp (1 mL) lightly crushed dried seeds. Cover and steep for 10 minutes. Strain, discard seeds and let cool. Use to replace $\frac{1}{4}$ cup (50 mL) liquid in smoothie recipes.

Chamomile

See German Chamomile, page 127

Chickweed

Stellaria media

A low, spreading annual with diffusely branched stems, ovate leaves and white star-shaped flowers found in most parts of North America.

Parts Used
Roots, leaves, flowers and stems.

Healing Properties
Actions: Anticancer, anti-inflammatory, antirheumatic, astringent, heals wounds, demulcent.
Uses: Chickweed is used internally to treat rheumatism, constipation, mucus in the lungs, coughs, colds, tumors and blood disorders. It is used externally to treat eczema, psoriasis and other skin conditions.

Availability
A common weed, chickweed may be wildcrafted from summer through fall. Dried aerial parts (stem, leaves and flowers) and roots are available in alternative/health stores.

How to Use in Smoothies
Fresh sprigs: Use 1 or 2 leaves and/or flowers in each smoothie recipe. Wash, pat dry and strip leaves and flowers off stem. Discard stem and coarsely chop leaves and flowers before blending.
Dried leaves and flowers: Crush to a fine powder. Use 2 tsp (10 mL) for each 1 cup (250 mL) of smoothie. Add to other ingredients before blending.
Infusion: In a teapot, pour $\frac{1}{4}$ cup (50 mL) boiling water over 2 tbsp (25 mL) chopped fresh leaves, flowers or stems (or 2 tsp/10 mL chopped or ground dried). Cover and steep for 10 minutes. Cool (no need to strain) and use to replace $\frac{1}{4}$ cup (50 mL) liquid in smoothie recipes.

Cinnamon

Cinnamomum zeylanicum
and *C. cassia*

The dried smooth inner bark of a cultivated laurel-like tree that grows in the hot, wet tropical regions of India, Brazil, the East and West Indies, and islands in the Indian Ocean.

Parts Used
Bark.

Healing Properties
Actions: Carminative, diaphoretic, astringent, stimulant, antimicrobial.
Uses: Cinnamon is a warming carminative used to promote digestion and relieve nausea, vomiting and diarrhea. It is used for upset stomach and to treat irritable bowel syndrome (see page 66). Recent research has shown that cinnamon helps the body use insulin more efficiently, which may be helpful in the management of diabetes.

Availability
Dried rolled sticks are sold in 2- to 18-inch (5 to 45 cm) lengths. Powdered cinnamon and ground cinnamon, which is coarser, are widely available.

How to Use in Smoothies
Ground: Add up to ½ tsp (2 mL) ground cinnamon to other ingredients before blending.
Infusion: In a teapot, pour ¼ cup (50 mL) boiling water over 1 tsp (5 mL) ground cinnamon (or one 1-inch/2.5 cm long stick cinnamon, broken into pieces). Cover and steep for 10 minutes. Strain, discard stick (if using) and let cool. Use to replace ¼ cup (50 mL) liquid in smoothie recipes.

Clove

Syzygium aromaticum

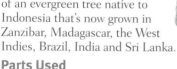

The pink unopened flower buds of an evergreen tree native to Indonesia that's now grown in Zanzibar, Madagascar, the West Indies, Brazil, India and Sri Lanka.

Parts Used
Dried buds.

Healing Properties
Actions: Antioxidant, anesthetic, antiseptic, anti-inflammatory, anodyne, antispasmodic, carminative, stimulant, antiemetic, antihistamine, warming.

Uses: Cloves are used to treat asthma, bronchitis, nausea, vomiting, flatulence, diarrhea and hypothermia. Some studies indicate that cloves may have anticoagulant properties and may stimulate the production of enzymes that fight cancer. Clove oil is the active ingredient in some mouthwashes, toothpastes, soaps, insect repellents, perfumes, foods and veterinary medications, as well as many over-the-counter toothache remedies.

Availability
Whole and ground dried cloves are widely available.

How to Use in Smoothies
Ground: Use ¼ tsp (1 mL) for each smoothie recipe. Add to other ingredients before blending.
Infusion: In a teapot, pour ¼ cup (50 mL) boiling water over ¼ tsp (1 mL) lightly crushed whole cloves. Cover and steep for 10 minutes. Strain, discard cloves and let cool. Use to replace ¼ cup (50 mL) liquid in smoothie recipes.

Coriander Seeds

Coriandrum sativum

A hardy annual with slender, erect branched stems that bear aromatic pinnate parsley-like leaves. Small flat umbels of tiny white to pale mauve flowers yield round green berries (seeds) that ripen to a brownish yellow.

Parts Used
Seeds.

Healing Properties
Actions: Soothing digestive, appetite stimulant, improve digestion and nutrient absorption.
Uses: Digestive problems, flatulence.

Availability
Dried seeds are readily available in alternative/health stores and Indian markets.

How to Use in Smoothies
Dried seeds: Crush to a powder. Add ½ tsp (2 mL) to other ingredients before blending.
Infusion: In a teapot, pour ¼ cup (50 mL) boiling water over 1 tsp (5 mL) lightly crushed dried seeds. Cover and steep for 10 minutes. Strain, discard seeds and let cool. Use to replace ¼ cup (50 mL) liquid in smoothie recipes.

Cumin

Cuminum cyminum

A slender annual with dark
green leaves found wild from the
Mediterranean to Sudan in Africa
and in central Asia. Umbels of tiny
white or pink flowers are followed
by bristly oval seeds.

Parts Used
Seeds.

Healing Properties
Actions: Stimulant, soothing digestive, antispasmodic,
diuretic, increases milk in breastfeeding.
Uses: Indigestion, flatulence.

Availability
Dried seeds are readily available in
alternative/health stores and Indian markets.

How to Use in Smoothies
Dried seeds: Crush to a powder. Add ½ tsp
(2 mL) to other ingredients before blending.
Infusion: In a teapot, pour ¼ cup (50 mL)
boiling water over ½ tsp (2 mL) lightly crushed
dried seeds. Cover and steep for 10 minutes.
Strain, discard seeds and let cool. Use to replace
¼ cup (50 mL) liquid in smoothie recipes.

Dandelion

Taraxacum officinale

A hardy herbaceous perennial
commonly found in most parts
of North America.

Parts Used
Roots, stems, leaves and flowers.

Dandelion Leaf

Healing Properties
Actions: Diuretic, liver and digestive tonic.
Uses: Dandelion is used for liver, gallbladder, kidney
and bladder ailments, including hepatitis and
jaundice. It is also used as a diuretic. The leaves are
used specifically to support the kidneys.

Availability
Whole plants are easily foraged from spring through
fall. Look for fresh leaves in some supermarkets,
farmer's markets and alternative/health stores;
chopped dried leaves are available in alternative/
health stores.

How to Use in Smoothies
Fresh leaves: Wash, pat dry and roughly chop
before adding to the blender. Use 1 to 2 tbsp (15 to
25 mL) in each smoothie recipe.
Dried leaves: Crush to a powder. Use 1 tsp (5 mL)
for each smoothie recipe. Add to other ingredients
before blending.
Infusion: In a teapot, pour 1/4 cup (50 mL) boiling
water over 1 tbsp (15 mL) chopped fresh dandelion
leaves (or 1 tsp/5 mL dried). Cover and steep for
10 minutes. Cool (no need to strain) and use to
replace 1/4 cup (50 mL) liquid in smoothie recipes.

Dandelion Root

Healing Properties
Actions: Liver tonic, promotes bile flow, diuretic,
mild laxative, antirheumatic.
Uses: Dandelion is used for liver, gallbladder, kidney
and bladder ailments, including hepatitis and
jaundice. It is also used as a diuretic. The root is
used specifically to support the liver.

Availability
Dig fresh roots in the fall. Chopped dried roots and
tinctures are available in alternative/health stores.

How to Use in Smoothies
Fresh root: Scrub, chop and add 1 tsp (15 mL) to
other ingredients before blending.
Dried root: Crush to a fine powder. Use 1 tsp
(5 mL) for each 1 cup (250 mL) of smoothie. Add
to other ingredients before blending.

Decoction: In a small saucepan, gently simmer
1 tsp (5 mL) chopped dried root in ¼ cup
(50 mL) water for 10 minutes. Strain, discard root
and let cool. Use to replace ¼ cup (50 mL) liquid
in smoothie recipes.
Tincture: Add 1 tsp (5 mL) tincture to each 1 cup
(250 mL) of smoothie.

Dill

Anethum graveolens

A tall top-heavy annual
with a long hollow stem
growing out of a spindly
taproot. Terminal flower
heads, which grow out of
the top of the stem, appear
in a wide, flat umbel of numerous yellow flowers.
Branches along the stem support feathery blue-
green leaflets.

Parts Used
Seeds.

Healing Properties
Actions: Soothing digestive, antispasmodic, increases milk in breastfeeding.
Uses: Flatulence, infant colic, bad breath.

Availability
Easy to grow, dill seeds can be harvested from late summer through early fall. Dried seeds are readily available in alternative/health stores and supermarkets.

How to Use in Smoothies
Dried seeds: Crush to a powder. Add ½ tsp (2 mL) to other ingredients before blending.
Infusion: In a teapot, pour ¼ cup (50 mL) boiling water over 1 tsp (5 mL) lightly crushed dried seeds. Cover and steep for 10 minutes. Strain, discard seeds and let cool. Use to replace ¼ cup (50 mL) liquid in smoothie recipes.

Echinacea

Echinacea angustifolia or *E. purpurea*

A hardy perennial also known as coneflower that is native to North America, with bright purple petals surrounding a brown cone.

Parts Used
Leaves, seeds, flowers, roots, stems.

Healing Properties
Actions: Immune modulating, anti-inflammatory, antibiotic, antimicrobial, antiseptic, analgesic, antiallergenic, lymphatic tonic.
Uses: Echinacea is used clinically to prevent and treat infections in the respiratory, urinary and digestive systems. It is useful in chronic candida and sinus infections and to support the health of patients undergoing chemotherapy. Externally, echinacea speeds healing of skin infections and wounds. Evidence shows that echinacea is effective because it increases the activity of phagocytes, which play an important role in preventing and overcoming bacterial, viral and fungal infections. Test-tube studies of its antiviral properties indicate that the aboveground parts of *E. purpurea* may be effective in inhibiting the viruses that cause herpes, influenza and polio. The roots of *E. angustifolia*, *E. pallida* and *E. purpurea* may be effective in defending the body against the herpes simplex and influenza viruses.

Availability
Whole or chopped dried root, stems and leaves are available in alternative/health stores. Echinacea is also available in tincture and tablet form.

How to Use in Smoothies
Decoction: In a small saucepan, gently simmer 1 tsp (5 mL) chopped dried root in ¼ cup (50 mL) water for 10 minutes. Strain, discard root and let cool. Use to replace ¼ cup (50 mL) liquid in smoothie recipes.
Tincture: Add ½ tsp (2 mL) tincture to each 1 cup (250 mL) of smoothie.

Elder

Sambucus nigra

A fast-growing hardy perennial shrub common in many parts of North America.

Parts Used
Bark, flowers and berries.

Healing Properties
Actions: (Flowers) Expectorant, reduce phlegm, circulatory stimulant, diaphoretic, diuretic, topically anti-inflammatory. (Berries) Diaphoretic, diuretic, laxative. (Bark) Purgative, large doses are emetic, diuretic.
Uses: (Flowers) Elderflowers can be taken early in allergy season to strengthen the upper respiratory tract and help prevent hay fever.
(Berries) Elderberries support detoxification by promoting bowel movements, urination, sweating and mucus secretion. Elderberries are effective in combating viruses, including those that cause colds and flu.

Caution
If using wild elder that you have gathered yourself, make absolutely certain you are able to identify it correctly. Raw elderberries can make some people sick. If in doubt, cook first before using in smoothies.

Availability
Fresh elderberries are found in season at farmer's markets. Dried flowers, fresh or dried berries and elder tinctures are available in alternative/health stores.

How to Use in Smoothies
Fresh flowers: Wash, pat dry and chop. Add 1 tbsp (15 mL) to other ingredients before blending.
Dried flowers: Add 1 tsp (5 mL) to other ingredients before blending.
Infusion, flowers: In a teapot, pour ¼ cup (50 mL) boiling water over 1 tbsp (15 mL) fresh elderflowers (or 1 tsp/5 mL dried). Cover and steep for 10 minutes if using dried flowers, or for 15 minutes if using fresh flowers. Cool (no need to strain) and use to replace ¼ cup (50 mL) liquid in smoothie recipes.

Fresh berries: Add up to ¼ cup (50 mL) fresh elderberries to other ingredients before blending.
Infusion, berries: Pour ¼ cup (50 mL) boiling water over 1 tbsp (15 mL) fresh elderberries (or 1 tsp/5 mL lightly crushed dried elderberries). Cover and steep for 10 minutes. Cool (no need to strain) and use to replace ¼ cup (50 mL) liquid in smoothie recipes.
Tincture: Add 1 tsp (5 mL) tincture to each 1 cup (250 mL) of smoothie.

Evening Primrose

Oenothera biennis

An erect biennial with a rosette of basal leaves. In summer, yellow flowers open at night. Downy pods that contain tiny black seeds follow blooms.

Parts Used
Seed oil.

Healing Properties
Actions: Anticoagulant, anti-inflammatory, improves blood circulation, nutritive, the essential fatty acids in the seed oil help repair tissues.
Uses: Acne, anxiety, arthritis, asthma, breast tenderness, diabetes, dry skin, eczema, hangover, inflammation, high blood pressure, hyperactivity in children, migraines, multiple sclerosis, premenstrual syndrome.

Availability
Evening primrose oil is widely available in gel capsule form and sometimes in bulk in alternative/health stores.

How to Use in Smoothies
Oil: If using capsules, slit open and collect oil in a measuring spoon. Add 1 tsp (5 mL) oil to other ingredients before blending.

Fennel Seeds

Foeniculum vulgare

The fennel plant looks like a larger version of dill. Stout, solid stems support bright yellow, large umbel clusters of flowers. Thread-like, feathery green leaves alternately branch out from joints on the stem. Flowers appear in summer, followed by gray-brown seeds, which are used for medicinal purposes.

Parts Used
Seeds.

Healing Properties
Actions: Soothing diuretic, anti-inflammatory, antispasmodic, soothing digestive, increases milk in breastfeeding, mild expectorant.
Uses: Indigestion, flatulence, increases milk in breastfeeding, relieves colic in babies when taken by nursing mother. Fennel seed infusion is safe to treat colic and coughs in babies and children.

Caution
Avoid large doses if you are pregnant, as fennel seeds are a uterine stimulant.

Availability
Fennel grows wild in Mediterranean Europe and Asia and has become naturalized in many other parts of the world, where the fleshy bulb is harvested and used as a vegetable (see page 110). Harvest seeds in late summer and early fall. Dried seeds are readily available in alternative/health stores and supermarkets.

How to Use in Smoothies
Dried seeds: Crush to a powder. Add ¼ tsp (1 mL) to other ingredients before blending.
Infusion: In a teapot, pour ¼ cup (50 mL) boiling water over ¼ to ½ tsp (1 to 2 mL) lightly crushed dried seeds. Cover and steep for 15 minutes. Strain, discard seeds and let cool. Use to replace ¼ cup (50 mL) liquid in smoothie recipes.

Fenugreek

Trigonella foenum-graecum

Grown as a fodder crop in southern and central Europe, fenugreek is widely naturalized from the Mediterranean to southern Africa to Australia. This annual has aromatic trifoliate leaves and solitary or paired yellow-white flowers, followed by beaked pods with yellow-brown seeds.

Parts Used
Aerial parts (stem, leaves and flowers) and seeds.

Healing Properties
Actions: Expectorant, soothing digestive, protects intestinal surfaces, reduces blood sugar level, increases milk in breastfeeding.
Uses: Bronchitis, coughs, diabetes, diverticular disease, ulcerative colitis, Crohn's disease, menstrual pain, peptic ulcers, stomach upsets.

Availability
Dried seeds are available in alternative/health stores.

How to Use in Smoothies
Decoction: In a small saucepan, gently simmer 1 to 2 tsp (5 to 10 mL) lightly crushed dried seeds or aerial parts (stem, leaves and flowers) in 1 cup (250 mL) water for 10 minutes. Strain, discard solids and let cool. Use to replace up to 1 cup (250 mL) liquid in smoothie recipes.

Feverfew

Tanacetum parthenium

A perennial that appears throughout northern temperate regions. Bright green oblong leaves contain pungent volatile oils that may cause unpleasant reactions if handled or consumed in excess. Flowers are small and daisy-like.

Parts Used
Leaves.

Healing Properties
Actions: Anti-inflammatory, vasodilator, digestive.
Uses: Prevention of migraine headaches, rheumatoid arthritis, menstrual pain.

Caution
Do not take feverfew if you are pregnant, since it stimulates the uterus. Fresh leaves may cause mouth ulcers in sensitive people.

Availability
Easily grown, fresh leaves may be harvested from June through late fall. Chopped dried leaves are available in alternative/health stores.

How to Use in Smoothies
Fresh leaves: Use 1 leaf in each smoothie recipe. Wash, pat dry and add to other ingredients before blending.
Dried leaves: Crush to a fine powder. Use 1 tsp (5 mL) for each 1 cup (250 mL) of smoothie. Add to other ingredients before blending.
Tincture: Add 5 to 20 drops tincture to 1 cup (250 mL) of smoothie.

Garlic

Allium sativum

A hardy perennial with an onion-like bulb that's easily grown in North America.

Parts Used
Bulb or "bud" at the root of the plant.

Healing Properties
Actions: Antimicrobial, antibiotic, cardioprotective, hypotensive, anticancer, diaphoretic, anticoagulant, lowers blood cholesterol level, lowers blood sugar level, expectorant, digestive stimulant, diuretic, antihistamine, antiparasitic.
Uses: Research has shown that garlic inhibits cancer-cell formation and proliferation. It lowers total and low-density lipoprotein (LDL) cholesterol in humans and reduces blood clotting, thereby reducing the risks of blocked arteries and heart disease. Garlic is also an antioxidant and stimulates the immune system. It has strong antibiotic and anti-inflammatory properties, making it a good topical medicine. Garlic protects organs from damage inflicted by synthetic drugs, chemical pollutants and radiation.

Availability
Buy fresh whole organic bulbs at farmer's markets and supermarkets.

How to Use In Smoothies
Fresh cloves: Only fresh cloves of garlic have medicinal value. Add half to 1 whole fresh clove to other ingredients before blending.

German Chamomile

Matricaria recutita

A low-growing hardy annual easily grown in North America. Flowers have daisy-like petals that surround rounded yellow centers.

Parts Used
Flower heads and petals.

Healing Properties
Actions: Gentle sedative, anti-inflammatory, mild antiseptic, antiemetic, antispasmodic, carminative, nervine, emmenagogue, mild pain reliever.
Uses: Anxiety, insomnia, indigestion, peptic ulcer, motion sickness, inflammation (such as gastritis) and menstrual cramps. Chamomile also reduces flatulence and gas pains.

Availability
Whole dried flower heads and tinctures are available in alternative/health stores.

How to Use in Smoothies
Fresh petals and flower heads: Add 1 tbsp (15 mL) to other ingredients before blending.

Infusion: In a teapot, pour $\frac{1}{4}$ cup (50 mL) boiling water over 1 tbsp (15 L) fresh flower heads (or 1 tsp/5 mL dried). Cover and steep for 10 minutes. Cool (no need to strain) and use to replace $\frac{1}{4}$ cup (50 mL) liquid in smoothie recipes.

Tincture: Add 1 tsp (5 mL) tincture to 1 cup (250 mL) of smoothie.

Ginger

Zingiber officinale

A tender perennial edible rhizome native to Southeast Asia.

Parts Used
Root.

Healing Properties
Actions: Antinausea, relieves headaches and arthritis, anti-inflammatory, circulatory stimulant, expectorant, antispasmodic, antiseptic, diaphoretic, anticoagulant, peripheral vasodilator, anti-emetic, carminative, antioxidant.

Uses: Gingerroot calms nausea and morning sickness and prevents vomiting. It is a cleansing, warming herb. Ginger stimulates blood flow to the digestive system and increases nutrient absorption. It increases the action of the gallbladder while protecting the liver against toxins and preventing the formation of ulcers. Studies show that ginger gives some relief from the pain and swelling of arthritis without side-effects. Ginger is also used to control flatulence, circulation problems and impotence, and to prevent nausea after chemotherapy.

Caution
Ginger can be irritating to the intestinal mucosa and should be taken with or after meals. Ginger is contraindicated for people who are suffering from kidney disease.

Availability
Fresh gingerroot and ground dried ginger are widely available in supermarkets, Asian and Indian markets, and alternative/health stores.

How to Use in Smoothies
Fresh root: Fresh and clean-tasting with a hot bite, ginger blends well with most fruits in smoothies. Cut one $\frac{1}{2}$-inch (1 cm) slice of fresh gingerroot and peel (if not organic). Cut into 4 pieces and add to other ingredients before blending.

Infusion: In a teapot, pour $\frac{1}{4}$ cup (50 mL) boiling water over 1 tsp (5 mL) grated peeled fresh gingerroot. Cover and steep for 10 minutes. Cool (no need to strain) and use the infusion to replace $\frac{1}{4}$ cup (50 mL) liquid in smoothie recipes.

Ground dried root: Add 1 tsp (5 mL) ground dried ginger to other ingredients before blending.

Ginkgo

Ginkgo biloba

A deciduous tree and one of the oldest trees to survive to the present day, ginkgo originated in central China but is grown as an ornamental in central North America. Light green fan-shaped leaves with two lobes turn yellow in autumn.

Parts Used
Leaves.

Healing Properties
Actions: Antioxidant, circulatory stimulant, increases blood flow to the brain, relieves bronchial spasms.

Uses: Asthma, tinnitus, cold hands and feet, varicose veins, hemorrhoids, headache, hangover, age-related memory loss, hearing loss, eyesight changes, Alzheimer's disease, Raynaud's disease, retinopathy, impotence.

Availability
Leaves can be gathered when yellow in the fall. Dried ginkgo leaves are available in alternative/ health stores.

How to Use in Smoothies
Dried leaves: Crush to a fine powder. Use 1 tsp (5 mL) for each 1 cup (250 mL) of smoothie. Add to other ingredients before blending.

Infusion: In a teapot, pour $\frac{1}{4}$ cup (50 mL) boiling water over 1 tbsp (15 mL) chopped fresh leaves (or 1 tsp/5 mL dried). Cover and steep for 10 minutes. Cool (no need to strain) and use to replace $\frac{1}{4}$ cup (50 mL) liquid in smoothie recipes.

Liquid extract: Add 40 drops liquid extract to each 1 cup (250 mL) of smoothie.

Ginseng

Siberian: *Eleutherococcus senticosis,* North American: *Panax quinquefolius,* Asian: *Panax ginseng*

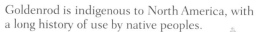

A hardy perennial native to cool wooded areas of eastern and central North America.

Parts Used
Root (from plants more than four years old) and leaves (if organic).

Healing Properties
Actions: Antioxidant, adaptogen, tonic, stimulant, regulates blood sugar and cholesterol levels, stimulates the immune system.
Uses: Ginseng helps the body resist and adapt to stress. It is a mild stimulant and, as a tonic, promotes long-term overall health. Along with increasing resistance to diabetes, cancer, heart disease and various infections, ginseng is also credited with improving memory, increasing fertility, protecting the liver against toxins and protecting the body against radiation. It is also used to treat impotence and depression.

Caution
Avoid ginseng if you have a fever, asthma, bronchitis, emphysema, high blood pressure or cardiac arrhythmia. Do not take ginseng if you are pregnant or if you drink coffee, and never give ginseng to a hyperactive child. Do not take continuously for a period of more than four weeks.

Availability
Whole or chopped dried root, tea, powdered and tinctures are all available in alternative/health stores and Asian grocery stores. In its native North American woodlands, ginseng has been harvested to near extinction. Please do not collect it in the wild or purchase wildcrafted North American ginseng.

How to Use in Smoothies
Fresh root: Wash and chop one 1-inch (2.5 cm) long piece. Add to other ingredients before blending. Only use organic ginseng and leave the peel on.
Dried root: Grate finely. Add $\frac{1}{4}$ tsp (1 mL) to each 1 cup (250 mL) of smoothie.
Decoction: In a small saucepan, gently simmer 1 tsp (5 mL) chopped dried root in $\frac{1}{4}$ cup (50 mL) water for 10 minutes. Strain, discard root and let cool. Use to replace $\frac{1}{4}$ cup (50 mL) liquid in smoothie recipes.
Tincture: Add 10 to 20 drops tincture to each 1 cup (250 mL) of smoothie.

Goldenrod

Solidago virgaurea

A perennial with upright stems, oval leaves and yellow flowers that appear in late summer.

Goldenrod is indigenous to North America, with a long history of use by native peoples.

Parts Used
Aerial parts (stem, leaves and flowers).

Healing Properties
Actions: Anticatarrhal, anti-inflammatory, antiseptic to mucous membranes, urinary antiseptic, diuretic, diaphoretic.
Uses: Bronchitis, coughs, respiratory congestion, urethritis, tonsillitis, prostatitis, kidney and bladder problems.

Availability
Goldenrod is widely available in the wild and in wastelands. Harvest from July through fall. Chopped dried leaves, stems and flowers are available in alternative/health stores.

How to Use in Smoothies
Fresh sprigs: Use 1 sprig for each 1 cup (250 mL) of smoothie. Wash, pat dry and strip leaves and flowering tops off stem. Discard stem and coarsely chop leaves and flowering tops before adding to blender.
Dried leaves and flowers: Crush to a fine powder. Use $\frac{1}{4}$ to $\frac{1}{2}$ tsp (1 to 2 mL) for each 1 cup (250 mL) of smoothie. Add to other ingredients before blending.
Infusion: In a teapot, pour $\frac{1}{4}$ cup (50 mL) boiling water over 1 tbsp (15 mL) fresh goldenrod (or 1 tsp/5 mL dried). Cover and steep for 10 minutes. Cool (no need to strain) and use to replace $\frac{1}{4}$ cup (50 mL) liquid in smoothie recipes.

Gotu Kola

Centella asiatica

A small, creeping tropical perennial, this plant has been used for centuries in India for its rejuvenating properties.

Parts Used
Aerial parts.

Healing Properties
Actions: Blood tonic, digestive, central nervous system relaxant, laxative, strengthens adrenal glands
Uses: Exhaustion, age-related memory loss, nervous disorders, Parkinson's disease, stress

Caution

Gotu Kola should not be used in pregnancy or by people with epilepsy. Do not use for longer than 6 weeks without a break. May aggravate itching. In large doses, may cause headache.

Availability

Dried aerial parts may be available at health/alternative stores. Tincture is available where tablets are sold.

How to Use in Smoothies

Dried leaf and flowers: Crush to a fine powder and whisk into fresh juice or add to ingredients in blended drinks, use ½ tsp (2 mL) for each 1 cup (250 mL) of juice or smoothie.

Infusion: In a teapot, pour ¼ cup (50 mL) of boiling water over ½ tsp (2 mL) gotu kola. Steep for 10 minutes. Strain, discard herb, and add liquid to 1 cup (250 mL) of juice or smoothie.

Tincture: Add ½ to 1 tsp (2 to 5 mL) to 1 cup (250 mL) of juice or smoothie.

Green Tea

Camellia sinensis

Green and black tea leaves come from a shrub or small tree indigenous to the wet forests of Asia. It is now cultivated commercially in Asia, Africa, South America and North America.

Parts Used

Leaves.

Healing Properties

Actions: Antioxidant, diuretic, recently found to have anticancer properties.

Uses: Cancer prevention, protection against radiation if taken daily at least a week before exposure.

Caution

Green tea contains caffeine, so minimize your intake of it if you have a health condition that is aggravated by caffeine.

Availability

Available dried in bulk in Asian grocery stores and alternative/health stores, or individually wrapped in supermarkets.

How to Use in Smoothies

Dried leaves: Crush to a fine powder. Use 1 tsp (5 mL) for each 1 cup (250 mL) of smoothie. Add to other ingredients before blending.

Infusion: In a teapot, pour ¼ cup (50 mL) boiling water over 1 tsp (5 mL) dried green tea leaves. Cover and steep for 10 minutes. Cool (no need to strain) and use to replace ¼ cup (50 mL) liquid in smoothie recipes.

Hawthorn

Crataegus laevigata

A thorny shrub found throughout northern temperate regions, hawthorn grows wild in hedgerows in Europe and the northeastern United States and Canada. Scented white flowers bear dark red oval fruit with stony pits.

Parts Used

Flowering tops and fruit.

Healing Properties

Actions: Heart tonic, improves coronary circulation.

Uses: Angina, hypertension, poor circulation.

Caution

Consult your health-care practitioner before taking hawthorn if you are taking other heart medications.

Availability

Harvest flowering tops in the spring and fresh fruit in late summer and dry for medicinal use. Dried hawthorn "berries" are available in alternative/health stores.

How to Use in Smoothies

Fresh berries: The pits in hawthorn berries make it difficult to remove the flesh for smoothies. If enough flesh can be separated (up to ½ cup/125 mL), add to any fruit or berry smoothie for an excellent heart tonic.

Infusion: In a teapot, pour ¼ cup (50 mL) boiling water over 1 to 2 tsp (5 to 10 mL) bruised fresh or dried hawthorn blossoms or lightly crushed fresh or dried berries. Cover and steep for 10 minutes. Cool, strain and discard berries with pits (no need to strain blossoms). Use to replace ¼ cup (50 mL) liquid in smoothie recipes.

Tincture: Add 10 to 20 drops tincture to each 1 cup (250 mL) of smoothie.

Horse Chestnut

Aesculus hippocastanum

A large tree common in North America and southeastern Europe with palmate leaves and long spikes of white flowers that appear in the spring.

Globular green-brown spiny fruits replace flowers in summer.

Parts Used
Bark and seeds.

Healing Properties
Actions: Astringent, anti-inflammatory, circulatory tonic, strengthens and tones veins.
Uses: Varicose veins, hemorrhoids, phlebitis. Horse chestnut tea can be used externally to treat bruises and leg ulcers.

Availability
Dried bark and seeds are available in alternative/health stores.

How to Use in Smoothies
Infusion: In a teapot, pour $\frac{1}{4}$ cup (50 mL) boiling water over $\frac{1}{2}$ tsp (2 mL) lightly crushed bark and seeds. Cover and steep for 15 minutes. Cool, strain and discard bark and seeds. Use to replace $\frac{1}{4}$ cup (50 mL) liquid in smoothie recipes.
Tincture: Add 30 drops tincture to each 1 cup (250 mL) of smoothie.

Hyssop

Hyssopus officinalis

A bushy evergreen woody perennial native to central and southern Europe, western Asia and northern Africa. The square, upright stems have linear opposite leaves and dense spikes at the tops that bear whorls of purple flowers.

Parts Used
Leaves and flowering tops.

Healing Properties
Actions: Antispasmodic, expectorant, diaphoretic, mild pain reliever, diuretic, antiviral against herpes simplex, reduces phlegm, soothing digestive.
Uses: Asthma, bronchitis, colds, coughs, influenza, fevers, flatulence.

Availability
Hyssop is easy to grow and can be harvested from May through fall in central and northern North America. Dried leaves are available in alternative/health stores.

How to Use in Smoothies
Fresh sprigs: Use 1 to 3 leaves per smoothie recipe. Wash, pat dry, strip leaves and flowering tops off stems (discard stems if woody) and chop before adding to the blender.

Dried leaves and flowers: Crush to a fine powder. Use 1 tsp (5 mL) for each 1 cup (250 mL) of smoothie. Add to other ingredients before blending.
Infusion: In a teapot, pour $\frac{1}{4}$ cup (50 mL) boiling water over 1 tbsp (15 mL) chopped fresh hyssop (or 1 tsp/5 mL dried). Cover and steep for 10 minutes. Cool (no need to strain) and use to replace $\frac{1}{4}$ cup (50 mL) liquid in smoothie recipes.

Kava

Piper methysticum

An evergreen shrub grown and used in Polynesia that belongs to the pepper (*Piper*) genus of plants.

Parts Used
Root and rhizome.

Healing Properties
Actions: Antimicrobial, especially to the genitourinary system; antispasmodic; nerve and muscle relaxant; diuretic; stimulant.
Uses: Stress; anxiety; chronic fatigue syndrome; fibromyalgia; insomnia; infections of the kidneys, bladder, vagina, prostate or urethra.

Caution
Do not use kava if you are pregnant or breastfeeding. Consult with your health-care practitioner before taking kava with other drugs that act on the nervous system. Do not take for a period of more than three months unless advised to do so by your health-care practitioner. Do not drive or operate heavy machinery while taking kava and do not use if you drink alcohol or take drugs that affect the liver.

Availability
Dried root and liquid extracts are available in alternative/health stores.

How to Use in Smoothies
Decoction: In a small saucepan, combine $\frac{1}{2}$ cup (125 mL) boiling water with 1 tsp (5 mL) dried root. Cover and simmer for 10 minutes or until light brown. Cool, strain and discard root. Use part to replace $\frac{1}{4}$ cup (50 mL) liquid in smoothie recipes.
Liquid extract: Add $\frac{1}{2}$ to 1 tsp (2 to 5 mL) to each 1 cup (250 mL) of smoothie.

Lavender

Lavandula spp

A shrub-like plant with dense, woody stems from which linear pine-like gray-green leaves grow. Whorls of tiny flowers grow on spikes that branch off the long stems.

Parts Used
Leaves, stems and flowering tops.

Healing Properties
Actions: Relaxant, antispasmodic, antidepressant, nervous system tonic, circulatory stimulant, antibacterial, antiseptic, carminative, promotes bile flow.
Uses: Colic, depression, exhaustion, indigestion, insomnia, stress, tension headaches.

Caution
Avoid large doses if you are pregnant because it is a uterine stimulant.

Availability
Easily grown in temperate climates, lavender can be harvested from June through fall. Dried flower buds are available at alternative/health stores.

How to Use in Smoothies
Fresh sprigs: Use up to 1 tsp (5 mL) chopped fresh leaves and flowers per smoothie recipe. Start with a small amount because lavender has a distinctive taste. Wash, pat dry and strip leaves and flowers off stems. Discard stems and chop leaves and flowers before adding to the blender.
Dried flowers: Crush to a fine powder. Use ¼ to ½ tsp (1 to 2 mL) per smoothie recipe. Add to other ingredients before blending.
Infusion: In a teapot, pour ¼ cup (50 mL) boiling water over 1 tsp (5 mL) chopped fresh lavender flowers (or ½ tsp/2 mL dried). Cover and steep for 15 minutes. Cool (no need to strain) and use to replace ¼ cup (50 mL) liquid in smoothie recipes.

Lemon Balm

Melissa officinalis

A bushy perennial with strongly lemon-scented opposite oval leaves that grow on thin, square stems. White or yellow tubular flowers grow in clusters at the base of the leaves.

Parts Used
Leaves and flowering tops.

Healing Properties
Actions: Antioxidant, antihistamine, carminative, antispasmodic, antiviral, antibacterial, nerve relaxant, antidepressant, stimulates bile flow, hypotensive.
Uses: Anxiety, depression, stress, flatulence, indigestion, insomnia.

Availability
An easily grown perennial, lemon balm leaves and flowers can be harvested from June through autumn. Dried leaves are available in alternative/health stores.

How to Use in Smoothies
Fresh sprigs: Use up to 3 leaves and/or flowers in each smoothie recipe. Wash, pat dry and strip leaves and flowers off stem. Discard stem and chop leaves and flowers. Add to other ingredients before blending.
Dried leaves and flowers: Crush to a fine powder. Use 1 tsp (5 mL) per smoothie recipe. Add to other ingredients before blending.
Infusion: In a teapot, pour ¼ cup (50 mL) boiling water over 1 tbsp (15 mL) chopped fresh leaves and flowers (or 1 tsp/5 mL dried). Cover and steep for 10 minutes. Cool (no need to strain) and use to replace ¼ cup (50 mL) liquid in smoothie recipes.

Lemon Verbena

Aloysia triphylla

A fast-growing deciduous shrub native to South America that grows to a height of over six feet (180 cm) in zones 8 to 10. Long, pointed green leaves grow on erect stems that grow out of green-to-brown bark and turn woody when mature. Tiny lavender-colored flowers grow in spikes.

Parts Used
Leaves.

Healing Properties
Actions: Antispasmodic, digestive.
Uses: Indigestion, flatulence.

Availability
Dried leaves may be available in alternative/health stores.

How to Use in Smoothies

Fresh sprigs: Use up to 3 leaves in each smoothie recipe. Wash, pat dry and strip leaves off stem. Discard stem and chop leaves before adding to the blender.

Dried leaves: Crush to a fine powder. Use 1 tsp (5 mL) per smoothie recipe. Add to other ingredients before blending.

Infusion: In a teapot, pour $\frac{1}{4}$ cup (50 mL) boiling water over 1 tbsp (15 mL) bruised fresh leaves (or 1 tsp/5 mL dried). Cover and steep for 10 minutes. Cool (no need to strain) and use to replace $\frac{1}{4}$ cup (50 mL) liquid in smoothie recipes.

Licorice

Glycyrrhiza glabra

A tender perennial native to the Mediterranean region and southwest Asia.

Parts Used
Root.

Healing Properties

Actions: Gentle laxative, tonic, anti-inflammatory, antibacterial, anti-arthritic, soothes gastric and intestinal mucous membranes, expectorant.

Uses: Licorice root is considered one of the best tonic herbs because it provides nutrients to almost all body systems. It detoxifies, regulates blood sugar level and recharges depleted adrenal glands. It has also been shown to heal peptic ulcers, soothe irritated membranes and loosen and expel phlegm in the upper respiratory tract. It is also used to treat sore throats, urinary tract infections, coughs, bronchitis, gastritis and constipation.

Caution

Large amounts taken over long periods of time may cause fluid retention and lower blood potassium levels. Avoid if you have high blood pressure.

Availability
Whole or ground dried root is available in alternative/health stores.
Note: Extracts lack the tonic action.

How to Use in Smoothies

Decoction: Gently simmer 1 tsp (5 mL) chopped dried root in $\frac{1}{4}$ cup (50 mL) water for 10 minutes. Cool, strain and discard root. Use to replace $\frac{1}{4}$ cup (50 mL) liquid in smoothie recipes.

Linden Flower

(Lime Flowers) *Tilia cordata* or *T.* x *eurpaea*

A deciduous tree with shiny dark green heart-shaped leaves and yellow-white flowers that appear in midsummer. Found throughout northern temperate regions, linden is often grown as an ornamental in North American cities.

Parts Used
Leaves and flowering tops.

Healing Properties

Actions: Antispasmodic, diaphoretic (hot tea), diuretic (warm tea), hypotensive, relaxant, mild astringent.

Uses: Linden flower tea is a pleasant-tasting, relaxing remedy for stress, anxiety, tension headache and insomnia. It relaxes and nourishes blood vessels, making it a useful treatment for high blood pressure and heart disease. Because it promotes sweating, it is helpful in treating colds, flu and fevers. The tea can be given to children as a calming remedy or to reduce fever.

Availability

Harvest flowers in mid-June and leaves from early summer through fall. Dried leaves and flowers are available in alternative/health stores. Linden tea bags are often available in supermarkets.

How to Use in Smoothies

Fresh or dried leaves and flowers: Part of linden's actions are due to its essential oils, which are only released when exposed to heat. For this reason, fresh or dried linden is not added to smoothies except as a cooled tea (see Infusion, below).

Infusion: In a teapot, pour $\frac{1}{4}$ cup (50 mL) boiling water over 1 tbsp (15 mL) chopped fresh or dried leaves and flowers. Cover and steep for 10 minutes. Cool (no need to strain) and use to replace $\frac{1}{4}$ cup (50 mL) liquid in smoothie recipes.

Marshmallow

Althaea officinalis

A robust perennial with a fleshy taproot and upright stems that bear toothed oval leaves and pale pink flowers. Marshmallow is partial to wet ground and is often found in the wild in the United States, southern Canada, western Europe, central

Asia and northern Africa. Hollyhock (*A. rosea*) is in the same genus.

Parts Used
Flowers, leaves and root.

Healing Properties
Actions: (Root and leaves) Soothes mucous membranes; diuretic; expectorant; soothes, cleanses and heals external wounds. (Flower) Expectorant.
Uses: The high mucilage content of marshmallow root makes it useful for soothing inflammation in the digestive tract, kidneys and bladder; peptic ulcers; ulcerative colitis; Crohn's disease; urethritis; hiatal hernia; cystitis; diarrhea; and gastritis. Marshmallow leaves are used to treat bronchial inflammations, such as bronchitis, and in teas for internal ulcerative conditions. Marshmallow flower is used in expectorant cough syrups.

Availability
Gather leaves and flowers from mid-June through fall and harvest roots in the fall. Dried root is available in alternative/health stores.

How to Use in Smoothies
Fresh sprigs: Use 1 or 2 leaves and/or flowers per smoothie recipe. Wash, pat dry and strip leaves and flowers off stem. Discard stem and chop leaves and flowers before adding to the blender.
Dried leaves and flowers: Crush to a fine powder. Use 1 tsp (5 mL) for each 1 cup (250 mL) of smoothie. Add to other ingredients before blending.
Infusion: In a teapot, pour ¼ cup (50 mL) boiling water over 1 tbsp (15 mL) chopped fresh leaves and flowers (or 1 tsp/5 mL dried). Cover and steep for 10 minutes. Cool (no need to strain) and use to replace ¼ cup (50 mL) liquid in smoothie recipes.
Fresh root: Scrub and chop. Use a ½-inch (1 cm) piece for each 1 cup (250 mL) of smoothie. Add to other ingredients before blending.
Decoction: In a small saucepan, pour ¼ cup (50 mL) boiling water over 1 tsp (5 mL) chopped dried root. Cover and simmer for 10 minutes. Remove from heat; steep for 10 minutes. Cool, strain and discard root. Use to replace ¼ cup (50 mL) liquid in smoothie recipes.

Meadowsweet

Filipendula ulmaria

A hardy herbaceous perennial found in moist or boggy soils throughout Europe, North America and temperate Asia. Toothed pinnate leaves grow on upright stems. Creamy white almond-scented flowers appear from midsummer to early autumn.

Parts Used
Aerial parts (stem, leaves and flowers).

Healing Properties
Actions: Antacid, anti-inflammatory, anticoagulant, astringent, antirheumatic, diuretic, liver supportive, diaphoretic.
Uses: The anti-inflammatory and antacid actions of meadowsweet are useful in treating rheumatoid arthritis, cystitis, peptic ulcer, hyperacidity and gastric reflux. As an astringent, it is used to treat some types of diarrhea. Meadowsweet contains salicylic acid and can be used instead of Aspirin as an anti-inflammatory. Because it protects the mucous membranes of the digestive tract, unlike Aspirin, long-term use does not cause stomach bleeding.

Availability
Harvest leaves and flowers from mid-July through fall. Dried leaves and flowers are available in alternative/health stores.

How to Use in Smoothies
Dried leaves and flowers: Crush to a fine powder. Use 1 tsp (5 mL) for each 1 cup (250 mL) of smoothie. Add to other ingredients before blending.
Infusion: In a teapot, pour ¼ cup (50 mL) boiling water over 1 tbsp (15 mL) chopped fresh stem, leaves and flowers (or 1 tsp /5 mL dried). Cover and steep for 10 minutes. Cool (no need to strain) and use to replace ¼ cup (50 mL) liquid in smoothie recipes.
Tincture: Add 40 drops tincture to each 1 cup (250 mL) of smoothie.

Milk Thistle

Silybum marianum

Milk thistle is a stout annual or biennial with large oblong leaves and purple flowers. Black seeds, each bearing a tuft of white hairs, appear in mid- to late summer.

Parts Used
Seeds.

Healing Properties
Actions: Antioxidant, promotes bile production and flow, protects the liver by promoting development of new liver cells and repairing existing liver cells, detoxifies, increases milk in breastfeeding.
Uses: Milk thistle's strong liver-protective action is important in treating diseases such as alcoholism, cirrhosis and hepatitis, as well as in chronic

conditions that cause liver congestion, such as constipation, bloating and premenstrual syndrome.

Availability
Seeds may be collected in the wild in midsummer but are widely available in alternative/health stores.

How to Use in Smoothies
Dried seeds: Crush to a fine powder. Use 1 tbsp (15 mL) for each 1 cup (250 mL) of smoothie. Add to other ingredients before blending.
Infusion: In a teapot, pour ¼ cup (50 mL) boiling water over 1 tsp (5 mL) ground dried seeds. Cover and steep for 15 minutes. Cool, strain and discard seeds. Use to replace ¼ cup (50 mL) liquid in smoothie recipes.
Tincture: Add 10 to 20 drops tincture to each 1 cup (250 mL) of smoothie.

Motherwort

Leonurus cardiaca

A strong-smelling perennial found throughout temperate Europe, Asia and North America. Deeply lobed palmate leaves grow out of purple stems. Mauve-pink to white flowers grow in whorls from single stems from midsummer to mid-autumn.

Parts Used
Aerial parts (stem, leaves and flowers).

Healing Properties
Actions: Antispasmodic, nerve and heart sedative, hypotensive, uterine stimulant.
Uses: Motherwort has long been used to ease menstrual pain. It eases hot flashes and other menopausal symptoms, as well as the anxiety associated with premenstrual syndrome. As a heart tonic, motherwort is especially useful for palpitations and other heart conditions in which anxiety and tension play a part. Its relaxing action makes it helpful in reducing withdrawal symptoms from antidepressant drugs.

Caution
Do not take if you are pregnant or during heavy menstrual bleeding.

Availability
Gather aerial parts (stem, leaves and flowers) from midsummer to mid-fall. Dried leaves and flowers are available in alternative/health stores.

How to Use in Smoothies
Fresh leaves: Use up to 3 leaves in each smoothie recipe. Wash, pat dry and strip leaves off stem.

Discard stem and chop leaves before adding to the blender.
Dried leaves and flowers: Crush to a fine powder. Use 1 tsp (5 mL) for each 1 cup (250 mL) of smoothie. Add to other ingredients before blending.
Infusion: In a teapot, pour ¼ cup (50 mL) boiling water over 1 tbsp (15 mL) chopped fresh stem, leaves and flowers (or 1 tsp/5 mL dried). Cover and steep for 15 minutes. Cool (no need to strain) and use to replace ¼ cup (50 mL) liquid in smoothie recipes.
Tincture: Add 1 tsp (5 mL) tincture to each 1 cup (250 mL) of smoothie.

Nutmeg

Myristica fragrans

A bushy evergreen tree native to the tropical rain forests in the Moluccas and the Banda Islands that is now grown commercially in Asia, Australia, Indonesia and Sri Lanka. Pale yellow flowers produced in axillary clusters are followed by fleshy yellow globe- to pear-shaped fruits (generally called seeds).

Parts Used
Dried kernel of the nutmeg fruit.

Healing Properties
Actions: Anti-inflammatory, antispasmodic, carminative, digestive stimulant, sedative.
Uses: Colic, diarrhea, flatulence, nausea, vomiting, muscle tension.

Caution
Do not use in medicinal doses if you are pregnant, as nutmeg has strong volatile oil components.

Availability
Whole dried nutmeg seeds are available in alternative/health stores, specialty stores and many supermarkets. Ground nutmeg is widely available.

How to Use in Smoothies
Dried seeds: Grate to a fine powder. Use ¼ tsp (1 mL) per smoothie recipe. Add to other ingredients before blending.

Oats

Avena sativa

A grain commonly grown throughout North America.

Parts Used

All, including seeds.

Healing Properties

Actions: Antioxidant, nerve restorative, antidepressant, nourishes brain and nerves, improves stamina, can increase libido if taken regularly.

Uses: Anxiety, depression, stress, withdrawal from alcohol and antidepressant drugs.

Availability

Oat seeds, oat straw and oatmeal are available at alternative/health stores. Oatmeal is available in supermarkets.

How to Use in Smoothies

Dried seeds, leaves and straw: Crush to a fine powder. Use 1 tsp (5 mL) per smoothie recipe. Add to other ingredients before blending.

Infusion: In a teapot, pour ¼ cup (50 mL) boiling water over 1 tsp (5 mL) dried oat straw or seeds. Cover and steep for 10 minutes. Cool, strain and discard straw or seeds. Use to replace ¼ cup (50 mL) liquid in smoothie recipes.

Oregon Grape

Mahonia aquifolium

Also called mountain grape, Oregon grape is the state flower of Oregon. It bears holly-like leaves and bright yellow flowers that mature into grape-like berry clusters. It grows in the mountainous regions of the West Coast of the United States and southern British Columbia.

Parts Used

Root and rhizome.

Healing Properties

Actions: Laxative; blood tonic; increases bile flow; liver stimulant; digestive; antimicrobial in the digestive tract; stimulates salivary and stomach secretions, including hydrochloric acid.

Uses: Eczema, psoriasis, constipation, indigestion, liver and gallbladder problems, gum and tooth problems.

Availability

Dried root and powdered dried root are available in alternative/health stores or by mail order.

How to Use in Smoothies

Powdered dried root: Add ¼ to ½ tsp (1 to 2 mL) ground dried root to other ingredients before blending.

Decoction: In a small saucepan, combine ¼ cup (50 mL) boiling water and 1 tsp (5 mL) chopped dried root. Cover and steep for 10 minutes. Cool, strain and discard root. Use to replace ¼ cup (50 mL) liquid in smoothie recipes.

Parsley

Petroselinum crispum

A hardy biennial native to the Mediterranean and grown as an annual in colder climates.

Parts Used

Leaves, stems and root.

Healing Properties

Actions: Antioxidant, tonic, digestive, diuretic.

Uses: As a diuretic, parsley helps the body expel excess water and flush the kidneys. Always look for and treat underlying causes of water retention. Parsley is one of the richest food sources of vitamin C.

Caution

Do not take large doses of parsley if you are pregnant because it is a uterine stimulant. Parsley is also contraindicated if you are suffering from kidney inflammation.

Availability

Fresh sprigs are available in most supermarkets year-round.

How to Use in Smoothies

Fresh sprigs: Use 1 or 2 sprigs for each 1 cup (250 mL) of smoothie. Wash, pat dry and chop before adding to the blender.

Dried leaves: Add 1 tsp (5 mL) ground leaves to other ingredients before blending.

Infusion: In a teapot, pour ¼ cup (50 mL) boiling water over 1 tbsp (15 mL) chopped fresh parsley (or 1 tsp/5 mL dried). Cover and steep for 10 minutes. Cool (no need to strain) and use to replace ¼ cup (50 mL) liquid in smoothie recipes.

Passionflower

Passiflora incarnata

A perennial climbing vine with deeply lobed leaves and showy, fragrant, white-to-purple flowers. Some 350 species of passionflower are native to the southeastern United States and Mexico. Other species grow in tropical Asia and Australia.

Parts Used
Leaves and flowers.

Healing Properties
Actions: Antispasmodic, mild sedative, mild pain reliever, central nervous system relaxant.
Uses: Anxiety, asthma, insomnia, restlessness, headache, Parkinson's disease, withdrawal from antidepressant drugs and alcohol.

Availability
Passionflower can be harvested from May through July in the wild or in cultivated gardens. Dried passionflower is available in alternative/health stores.

How to Use in Smoothies
Dried leaves and flowers: Crush to a fine powder. Use ¼ tsp (1 mL) for each 1 cup (250 mL) of smoothie. Add to other ingredients before blending.
Infusion: In a teapot, pour ¼ cup (50 mL) boiling water over 1 tbsp (15 mL) chopped fresh passionflower (or ½ tsp/2 mL dried). Cover and steep for 15 minutes. Cool (no need to strain) and use to replace ¼ cup (50 mL) liquid in smoothie recipes.
Tincture: Add 40 drops tincture to each 1 cup (250 mL) of smoothie.

Peppermint

Mentha x *piperita*

An invasive hardy perennial native to Europe and Asia but easily grown in North America. It has aromatic bright green oval leaves on purple stems and small pink, white or purple flowers in elongated conical spikes at the tops of the stems.

Parts Used
Leaves and flowers.

Healing Properties
Actions: Antispasmodic, digestive tonic, anti-emetic, carminative, peripheral vasodilator, diaphoretic, promotes bile flow, analgesic.
Uses: Taking peppermint before eating helps stimulate the liver and gallbladder by increasing bile flow to the liver and intestines. It is well known for its ability to quell nausea and vomiting. Peppermint is used to treat ulcerative colitis, Crohn's disease, diverticular disease, motion sickness, fevers, colds and flu, and to improve appetite.

Caution
Do not use if you are pregnant or give to a child.

Availability
Fresh sprigs appear in some farmer's markets and supermarkets year-round. Dried leaves are available in alternative/health stores. Peppermint tea in bulk and bags is widely available.

How to Use in Smoothies
Fresh leaves: Use 3 to 4 leaves for each 1 cup (250 mL) of smoothie. Wash, pat dry and strip leaves and flowers off stem. Discard stem and chop leaves and flowers. Add to other ingredients before blending.
Dried leaves: Add 1 tsp (5 mL) ground dried leaves to each smoothie recipe.
Infusion: In a teapot, pour ¼ cup (50 mL) boiling water over 1 tbsp (15 mL) chopped fresh peppermint (or 1 tsp/5 mL dried). Cover and steep for 10 minutes. Cool (no need to strain) and use to replace ¼ cup (50 mL) liquid in smoothie recipes.

Plantain

Plantago major and *P. lanceolata*

Broad-leaved plantain and narrow-leaved plantain are common weeds found in waste areas throughout North America. Leaves grow in a basal rosette, and flowers top long cylindrical spikes that grow up to six inches (15 cm) above leaves.

Parts Used
Leaves.

Healing Properties
Actions: Antibacterial, soothing expectorant, provides mucilage-rich protection to digestive tract, nutritive, antihistamine, astringent.
Uses: Coughs, bronchitis, allergies, irritable bowel syndrome, gastric ulcers.

Availability
The leaves can be collected throughout the summer. Dried leaves are available in alternative/health stores.

How to Use in Smoothies
Fresh leaves: Use 1 leaf per smoothie recipe. Wash, pat dry and chop before adding to the blender.
Infusion: In a teapot, pour $\frac{1}{4}$ cup (50 mL) boiling water over 1 tbsp (15 mL) chopped fresh plantain leaves (or 1 tsp/5 mL dried). Cover and steep for 10 minutes. Cool (no need to strain) and use to replace $\frac{1}{4}$ cup (50 mL) liquid in smoothie recipes.

Psyllium

Plantago psyllium

The mucilage-rich seeds of *Plantago psyllium* (native to the Mediterranean) are similar to those of broad-leaved plantain (Plantago major), and are common in Europe and naturalized in North America.

Parts Used
Seeds.

Healing Properties
Actions: Soothing, digestive, safe and gentle laxative, lowers cholesterol.
Uses: Constipation, irritable bowel syndrome, diverticular disease, detoxification, and obesity. The seeds act as a laxative by bulking up the stool and lubricating the bowel. It is necessary to drink at least one large glass of water when taking 1 to 2 tsp (5 to 10 mL) of the seeds. Drink another 8 glasses of water throughout the day.

Caution
Psyllium can cause an allergic reaction in sensitive individuals; discontinue immediately if a reaction develops. It should be avoided by people with asthma. Psyllium must not be taken in cases of bowel obstruction.

Availability
Psyllium seeds are widely available in pharmacies and health/alternative stores.

How to Use in Smoothies
Whole seeds: Whisk 1 to 2 tsp (5 to 10 mL) seeds into 1 cup (250 mL) fresh juice or blended drink and drink immediately before they can absorb the moisture. Drink one large glass of water and eight more glasses over the course of the day.

Red Clover

Trifolium pratense

A perennial with tubular pink-to-red flowers throughout the summer, red clover grows in fields throughout North America. Its three long oval leaflets distinguish it as a clover.

Parts Used
Flowering tops.

Healing Properties
Actions: Antispasmodic, expectorant, balances hormones, nutritive, anticoagulant, lymphatic cleanser.
Uses: Coughs, bronchitis, whooping cough, menstrual problems.

Caution
Because it helps thin the blood, don't use red clover during heavy menstrual flow.

Availability
The flowering tops can be harvested from May through September in the wild or in cultivated gardens. Dried flowers are available in alternative/health stores. Dried clover that has turned brown is of little use; be sure that the flowers are still pink.

How to Use in Smoothies
Fresh sprigs: Use 1 or 2 sprigs per smoothie recipe. Wash, pat dry and strip leaves and flowers off stems. Discard stems and green centers of flowers and chop leaves and petals before adding to blender.
Dried leaves and flowers: Crush to a fine powder. Use 1 tsp (5 mL) for each 1 cup (250 mL) of smoothie. Add to other ingredients before blending.
Infusion: In a teapot, pour $\frac{1}{4}$ cup (50 mL) boiling water over 1 tbsp (15 mL) chopped fresh red clover (or 1 tsp/5 mL dried). Cover and steep for 15 minutes. Cool (no need to strain) and use to replace $\frac{1}{4}$ cup (50 mL) liquid in smoothie recipes.

Red Raspberry

Rubus idaeus

A deciduous shrub with prickly stems and pinnately divided leaves that is widespread in Europe, Asia and North America. Small white flowers appear in clusters, and aromatic, juicy red fruit follow in early summer.

Parts Used

Leaves.

Healing Properties

Actions: Antispasmodic, astringent, increases milk in breastfeeding.

Uses: Red raspberry leaves have long been used to tone the uterus during pregnancy and labor, resulting in less risk of miscarriage, relief of morning sickness and safer, easier birth. As an astringent, raspberry leaves ease sore throat and diarrhea.

Availability

Harvest leaves from early summer through fall. Dried leaves are available in alternative/health stores.

How to Use in Smoothies

Fresh leaves: Use 1 or 2 leaves per smoothie recipe. Wash, pat dry and chop before adding to the blender.

Dried leaves: Crush to a fine powder. Use 1 tsp (5 mL) for each 1 cup (250 mL) of smoothie. Add to other ingredients before blending.

Infusion: In a teapot, pour $1/4$ cup (50 mL) boiling water over 1 tbsp (15 mL) chopped fresh leaves (or 2 tsp/10 mL dried). Cover and steep for 15 minutes. Cool (no need to strain) and use to replace $1/4$ cup (50 mL) liquid in smoothie recipes.

Rose

Rosa species

Cultivation of roses dates back thousands of years, with *R. rugosa*, *R. gallica*, *R. rubra* and *R. x damascena* being among the oldest varieties. *R. rugosa* is a deciduous shrub with thorny stems and dark green oval leaves; dark pink or white flowers appear in summer and are followed by large globular bright red rose hips (fruit). Wild roses (including *R. canina* of North America) grow in northern temperate regions throughout the world.

Parts Used

Petals and hips.

Healing Properties

Actions: (Rose hips from *R. canina*) Contain vitamin C, diuretic, astringent, mild laxative. (Rose petals from *R. gallica*, *R. x damascena*, *R. centifolia*, *R. rugosa*) Antidepressant, anti-inflammatory, astringent, blood tonic.

Uses: (Rose hips) The nutrient value of rose hips makes them useful in preventing the common cold. A tasty addition to herbal teas, rose hips improve immune function. As an astringent, they are used to treat diarrhea. (Rose petals) Add them to teas for their relaxing and uplifting fragrance. Used in baths, they ease the pain of rheumatoid arthritis.

Availability

Harvest petals from midsummer through fall and hips in the fall from pesticide-free bushes.

How to Use in Smoothies

Dried flowers or hips: Crush to a fine powder. Use $1/2$ tsp (2 mL) for each 1 cup (250 mL) of smoothie. Add to other ingredients before blending.

Infusion: In a teapot, pour $1/4$ cup (50 mL) boiling water over 1 tbsp (15 mL) fresh rose petals or chopped fresh rose hips (or 1 tsp/5 mL dried petals or crushed dried hips). Cover and steep for 10 minutes. Cool (no need to strain) and use to replace $1/4$ cup (50 mL) liquid in smoothie recipes.

Rosemary

Rosmarinus officinalis

An evergreen shrub native to the Mediterranean that grows to a height of six feet (180 cm) in warm climates.

Parts Used

Leaves and flowers.

Healing Properties

Actions: Antioxidant, anti-inflammatory, astringent, nervine, carminative, antiseptic, diuretic, diaphoretic, promotes bile flow, antidepressant, circulatory stimulant, antispasmodic, nervous system and cardiac tonic.

Uses: An effective food preservative, rosemary may help prevent breast cancer and fight the deterioration of brain function. It is also useful in treating migraine and tension headaches, nervous tension, flatulence, depression, chronic fatigue syndrome and joint pain.

Caution

Do not take large amounts if you are pregnant, as rosemary contains strong volatile oil components.

Availability

Look for fresh sprigs in farmer's markets and supermarkets year-round. Dried whole and ground leaves are widely found in supermarkets and alternative/health stores.

How to Use in Smoothies

Fresh sprigs: Use ½ tsp (2 mL) chopped fresh rosemary leaves and flowers per smoothie recipe. Wash, pat dry and strip leaves and flowers off stem. Discard stem and chop leaves and flowers before adding to the blender.

Infusion: In a teapot, pour ¼ cup (50 mL) boiling water over 1 tbsp (15 mL) chopped fresh rosemary (or 1 tsp/5 mL dried). Cover and steep for 10 minutes. Cool (no need to strain) and use to replace ¼ cup (50 mL) liquid in smoothie recipes.

Sage

Salvia officinalis

A hardy evergreen woody perennial shrub native to the western United States and Mexico, with wrinkled gray-green oval leaves and purple, pink or white flowers.

Parts Used

Leaves and flowers.

Healing Properties

Actions: Antioxidant, antimicrobial, antibiotic, antiseptic, carminative, antispasmodic, anti-inflammatory, circulatory stimulant, estrogenic, peripheral vasodilator, reduces perspiration, uterine stimulant.

Uses: Sage's volatile oil kills bacteria and fungi — even those that are resistant to penicillin. It makes a very good gargle for sore throats, laryngitis and mouth ulcers. It is also used to reduce breast milk production and to relieve night sweats and hot flashes during menopause.

Caution

Sage can cause convulsions in very large doses. Do not use if you have high blood pressure or epilepsy or if you are pregnant.

Availability

Fresh sprigs can be found at some supermarkets and farmer's markets. Whole, rubbed or ground dried sage is available at most supermarkets.

How to Use in Smoothies

Fresh leaves: Use 1 leaf per smoothie recipe. Wash, pat dry and strip leaves off stem (discard stem if woody). Chop before adding to the blender.

Dried leaves and flowers: Crush to a fine powder. Use ½ tsp (2 mL) for each 1 cup (250 mL) of smoothie. Add to other ingredients before blending.

Infusion: In a teapot, pour ¼ cup (50 mL) boiling water over 1 tbsp (15 mL) chopped fresh sage (or 1 tsp/5 mL dried). Cover and steep for 10 minutes. Cool (no need to strain) and use to replace ¼ cup (50 mL) liquid in smoothie recipes.

Saw Palmetto

Serenoa repens

A clump-forming evergreen palm with long blue-green leaves and blue-black berries. It grows mainly along coastal areas of southeastern North America and forms dense thickets along the Atlantic coasts of Georgia and Florida.

Parts Used

Berries.

Healing Properties

Actions: Diuretic, urinary antiseptic, stimulates the hormone-secreting glands.

Uses: Benign prostate enlargement, low libido.

Availability

The berries can be harvested from September though January. Dried berries are available ground and in tablet form in alternative/health stores.

How to Use in Smoothies

Ground dried berries: Use ¼ tsp (1 mL) per smoothie recipe. Add to other ingredients before blending.

Infusion: In a teapot, pour ¼ cup (50 mL) boiling water over 1 tsp (5 mL) crushed fresh berries (or ½ tsp/2 mL crushed dried). Cover and steep for 10 minutes. Cool, strain and discard berries. Use to replace ¼ cup (50 mL) liquid in smoothie recipes.

Liquid extract: Add 10 to 25 drops liquid extract to each 1 cup (250 mL) of smoothie.

Skullcap

Scutellaria laterifolia

A perennial member of the mint family that features hooded violet-blue flowers. It grows in wooded areas in most of the United States and southern Canada, except along the West Coast.

Parts Used
Aerial parts (stem, leaves and flowers).

Healing Properties
Actions: Antispasmodic, nourishes central nervous system, relaxant, sedative.

Uses: Drug addiction withdrawal, premenstrual tension, headaches, migraines, mental exhaustion, insomnia, stress.

Availability
Aerial parts (stem, leaves and flowers) can be collected while the plant is in flower. Dried skullcap is available in alternative/health stores.

How to Use in Smoothies
Fresh sprigs: Use 1 leaf and/or flower per smoothie recipe. Wash, pat dry and strip leaves and flowers off stem. Discard stem and chop leaves and flowers before adding to the blender.
Dried leaves and flowers: Crush to a fine powder. Use 1 tsp (5 mL) for each 1 cup (250 mL) of smoothie. Add to other ingredients before blending.
Infusion: In a teapot, pour $^1/_4$ cup (50 mL) boiling water over 1 tbsp (15 mL) chopped fresh skullcap (or 1 tsp/5 mL dried). Cover and steep for 10 minutes. Cool (no need to strain) and use to replace $^1/_4$ cup (50 mL) liquid in smoothie recipes.
Tincture: Add 40 drops tincture to each 1 cup (250 mL) of smoothie.

Slippery Elm

Ulmus rubra

A deciduous tree found in moist woods in the eastern and midwestern United States and southeastern Canada.

Parts Used
Dried inner bark.

Healing Properties
Actions: Soothing digestive, antacid, nutritive, provides mucilage-rich protection to the digestive tract.
Uses: Peptic ulcers, indigestion, heartburn, hiatal hernia, Crohn's disease, ulcerative colitis, irritable bowel syndrome, diarrhea. A paste of slippery elm bark powder can be used to soothe and heal wounds and burns. It is one of the most useful herbs in herbal medicine.

Availability
Ground dried inner bark and lozenges are available in alternative/health stores.

How to Use in Smoothies
Smoothies are a great medium in which to take slippery elm, which is so soothing for the bowel but so difficult to consume because the powder doesn't dissolve in or mix with liquids.
Ground dried bark: Add 1 tsp (5 mL) to each 1 cup (250 mL) of smoothie.

Spearmint

Mentha spicata

A hardy invasive perennial found in wet soil in most of North America. Like all mints, it has a square stem with bright green lanceolate leaves and lilac, pink or white flowers that form in a terminal, cylindrical spike.

Parts Used
Leaves and flowering tops.

Healing Properties
Actions: Antispasmodic, digestive, diaphoretic.
Uses: Common cold, influenza, indigestion, flatulence, lack of appetite. Spearmint is milder than peppermint, so it is often used to treat children's colds and flus.

Availability
The leaves are best harvested just before the flowers open. Dried leaves are available in alternative/health stores.

How to Use in Smoothies
Fresh sprigs: Use 2 to 3 leaves per smoothie recipe. Wash, pat dry and strip leaves and flowers off stems. Discard stems and chop leaves and flowers before adding to the blender.
Dried leaves and flowers: Crush to a fine powder. Use $^1/_2$ tsp (2 mL) for each 1 cup (250 mL) of smoothie. Add to other ingredients before blending.
Infusion: In a teapot, pour $^1/_4$ cup (50 mL) boiling water over 1 tbsp (15 mL) chopped fresh spearmint (or 1 tsp/5 mL dried). Cover and steep for 10 minutes. Cool (no need to strain) and use to replace $^1/_4$ cup (50 mL) liquid in smoothie recipes.

St. John's Wort

Hypericum perforatum

A perennial native of woodlands in Europe and temperate Asia that has also naturalized in temperate areas of the United States and Canada. It is an upright plant with straight stems that are woody at the base and has five-petaled yellow flowers growing from the tips of the branched stems. When rubbed, the yellow petals stain the fingers red.

Parts Used
Flowering tops.

Healing Properties
Actions: Astringent, antiviral, anti-inflammatory, antidepressant, nervous system tonic, sedative.
Uses: St. John's wort is widely used as an antidepressant. It has become popular because of its effectiveness and lack of side-effects. As a sedative and nervous-system tonic, it is useful in treating neuralgia, shingles, sciatica, tension, anxiety, and emotional instability in premenstrual syndrome and menopause.

Caution
Recent studies suggest that St. John's wort increases the metabolism of certain drugs, reducing their effectiveness. If you are taking prescription drugs, consult with your herbalist, doctor or pharmacist about possible drug interactions before taking St. John's wort. Of particular concern are oral contraceptives, anticonvulsants, antidepressants (especially selective serotonin reuptake inhibitors), HIV drugs, anticoagulants (warfarin), cyclosporine (an immunosuppressant drug given after transplants) and digoxin.

Availability
Harvest flowering tops for two to three weeks in midsummer. Dried aerial parts (stem, leaves and flowers) and tinctures are available in alternative/health stores.

How to Use in Smoothies
Dried leaves and flowers: Crush to a fine powder. Use 1 tsp (5 mL) for each 1 cup (250 mL) of smoothie. Add to other ingredients before blending.
Infusion: In a teapot, pour ¼ cup (50 mL) boiling water over 1 tbsp (15 mL) chopped fresh flowers (or 1 tsp/5 mL dried). Cover and steep for 15 minutes. Cool (no need to strain) and use to replace ¼ cup (50 mL) liquid in smoothie recipes.

Tincture: Add 20 to 40 drops tincture to each 1 cup (250 mL) of smoothie.

Stevia

Stevia rebaudiana

A small tender shrub native to northeastern Paraguay and adjacent areas of Brazil.

Parts Used
Leaves.

Healing Properties
Actions: Energy booster, natural sweetener (without calories), tonic, digestive, diuretic.
Uses: Stevia's main benefit is that it is a safe sweetener and sugar alternative. With its powerful sweet licorice flavor (stevia is 200 to 300 times sweeter than sugar), it prevents cavities and does not trigger a rise in blood sugar. It increases energy and improves digestion by stimulating the pancreas without feeding yeast or fungi.

Availability
Cut and dried ground leaves and liquid extracts are available in alternative/health stores.

How to Use in Smoothies
Fresh leaves: Use 1 leaf per smoothie. Wash, pat dry and strip leaves off stem. Discard stem and chop leaves before adding to the blender.
Dried leaves: Crush to a fine powder. Use ⅛ tsp (0.5 mL) for each 1 cup (250 mL) of smoothie. Add to other ingredients before blending.
Infusion: In a teapot, pour ¼ cup (50 mL) boiling water over 1 tsp (5 mL) chopped fresh leaves (or ¼ tsp/1 mL dried). Cover and steep for 10 minutes. Cool (no need to strain) and use to replace ¼ cup (50 mL) liquid in smoothie recipes.
Liquid extract: Add 1 or 2 drops liquid extract to each 1 cup (250 mL) of smoothie.

Stinging Nettle

Urtica dioica

A perennial widespread in temperate regions of Europe, North America and Eurasia with bristly stinging hairs on the stems and toothed ovate leaves that cause minor skin irritation when touched. Minute green flowers appear in clusters during the summer.

Parts Used
Leaves, root and seeds.

Healing Properties

Actions: (Leaves and flowers) Astringent, blood tonic, circulatory stimulant, diuretic, eliminates uric acid from the body, nutritive (high in iron, chlorophyll and vitamin C), increases milk in breastfeeding. (Fresh root) Astringent, diuretic.

Uses: (Leaves and flowers) A valuable herb, stinging nettle is useful as a general, everyday nourishing tonic, as well as for treatment of iron-deficiency anemia, gout, arthritis and kidney stones. It is also a good blood tonic to take during pregnancy or if you have diabetes, poor circulation or a chronic skin disease, such as eczema. (Fresh root) Fresh stinging nettle root has a strong effect on the urinary system. It is useful in treating water retention, kidney stones, urinary tract infections, cystitis, prostatitis and prostate enlargement.

Availability

Gather leaves and flowers while flowering in summer and root in fall. Use gloves to protect your hands from its uric acid, which dissipates with drying or cooking. Dried leaves and flowers are available in alternative/health stores.

How to Use in Smoothies

Infusion: In a teapot, pour ¼ cup (50 mL) boiling water over 1 tbsp (15 mL) chopped fresh leaves (or 1 tsp/5 mL dried). Cover and steep for 15 minutes. Cool (no need to strain) and use to replace ¼ cup (50 mL) liquid in smoothie recipes.

Tincture: Add 1 tsp (5 mL) tincture to each 1 cup (250 mL) of smoothie.

Thyme

Thymus species

A bushy low-growing shrub easily grown in North America.

Parts Used

Leaves and flowers.

Healing Properties

Actions: Antioxidant, expectorant, antiseptic, antispasmodic, astringent, tonic, antimicrobial, antibiotic, heals wounds, carminative, calms coughs, nervine.

Uses: Thyme is ideal for deep-seated chest infections, such as chronic coughs and bronchitis. It is also used to treat sinusitis, laryngitis, asthma and irritable bowel syndrome.

Caution

Do not take if you are pregnant. Children under two years of age and people with thyroid problems should not take thyme.

Availability

Fresh sprigs are available in season at farmer's markets and most supermarkets year-round. Dried whole leaves can be found in alternative/health stores.

How to Use in Smoothies

Fresh sprigs: Use 1 sprig per smoothie recipe. Wash, pat dry and strip leaves and flowers off stem (discard stem if woody). Chop before adding to the blender.

Dried leaves and flowers: Add 1 tsp (5 mL) dried leaves and crushed flowers to each 1 cup (250 mL) of smoothie.

Infusion: In a teapot, pour ¼ cup (50 mL) boiling water over 1 tbsp (15 mL) chopped fresh thyme (or 1 tsp/5 mL dried). Cover and steep for 15 minutes. Cool (no need to strain) and use to replace ¼ cup (50 mL) liquid in smoothie recipes.

Turmeric

Curcuma longa

A deciduous tender perennial in the ginger family native to southeast Asia that is hardy to zone 10. The long rhizome resembles ginger but is thinner and rounder, with brilliant orange flesh.

Parts Used

Root.

Healing Properties

Actions: Antioxidant, anti-inflammatory, antimicrobial, antibacterial, antifungal, antiviral, anticoagulant, analgesic, lowers blood cholesterol, reduces postexercise pain, heals wounds, antispasmodic, protects liver cells, increases bile production and flow.

Uses: Turmeric appears to inhibit colon and breast cancer and is used to treat hepatitis, nausea and digestive disturbances. It also helps people whose gallbladders have been removed. It boosts insulin activity and reduces the risk of stroke. Turmeric is also used to treat rheumatoid arthritis, cancer, candida, AIDS, Crohn's disease and eczema.

Availability

Asian stores stock fresh, frozen or dried whole rhizomes. Alternative/health stores offer dried whole rhizomes, and supermarkets sell ground turmeric.

How to Use in Smoothies

Fresh root: Use one $\frac{1}{2}$- to 1-inch (1 to 2.5 cm) long piece per smoothie recipe. Scrub, peel (if not organic) and cut into quarters before adding to the blender.

Ground dried root: Use 1 tsp (5 mL) ground dried root for each 1 cup (250 mL) of smoothie. Add to other ingredients before blending.

Infusion: In a teapot, pour $\frac{1}{4}$ cup (50 mL) boiling water over 1 tbsp (15 mL) freshly grated turmeric (or 1 tsp/5 mL chopped or ground dried root). Cover and steep for 10 minutes. Cool, strain and discard root. Use to replace $\frac{1}{4}$ cup (50 mL) liquid in smoothie recipes.

Valerian

Valeriana officinalis

A tall hardy perennial with strong-smelling white clustered flowers that grows wild in eastern Canada and the northeastern United States.

Parts Used

Root.

Healing Properties

Actions: Sedative, relaxant, antispasmodic.

Uses: High blood pressure, insomnia, anxiety, tension headaches, muscle cramps, migraines.

Caution

Some people experience adverse reactions to valerian.

Availability

Roots can be harvested in late fall in the wild or in cultivated gardens. Dried roots and tinctures are available in alternative/health stores.

How to Use in Smoothies

Fresh root: Valerian roots are a mass of thin rootlets. After digging up, immerse in water to remove loose soil, then scrub and chop. Wrap

fresh root in a towel and store in the refrigerator for one to two weeks. Dry chopped root to store longer. Use 2 tsp (10 mL) chopped fresh root per smoothie recipe.

Decoction: In a small saucepan, pour $\frac{1}{4}$ cup (50 mL) boiling water over 1 tbsp (15 mL) chopped fresh root (or 1 tsp/5 mL chopped dried). Cover and simmer for 10 minutes. Cool, strain and discard root. Use to replace $\frac{1}{4}$ cup (50 mL) liquid in smoothie recipes.

Tincture: Add 20 to 40 drops tincture to each 1 cup (250 mL) of smoothie.

Vitex

(Chaste Tree) *Vitex agnus-castus*

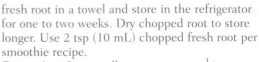

A deciduous aromatic shrub or small tree native to southern Europe. Grown in temperate climates (zones 7 to 10), chaste tree bears palmate leaves and small tubular lilac scented flowers and fleshy red-black fruits.

Parts Used

Berries.

Healing Properties

Actions: Balances female sex hormones by acting on the anterior pituitary gland.

Uses: Premenstrual symptoms, painful menstruation, menopausal symptoms.

Caution

Do not take with progesterone drugs.

Availability

Dried berries are available in health/alternative stores. Vitex is also available as a tincture.

How to Use in Smoothies

Infusion: In a teapot, pour $\frac{1}{4}$ cup (50 mL) boiling water over 1 tbsp (15 mL) lightly crushed fresh chasteberries (or 1 tsp/5 mL lightly crushed dried). Cover and steep for 10 minutes. Strain, discard berries and let cool. Use to replace $\frac{1}{4}$ cup (50 mL) liquid in smoothie recipes.

Tincture: Add 10 to 20 drops tincture to each 1 cup (250 mL) of smoothie.

Wild Lettuce

Lactuca virosa

A tall biennial with lanceolate leaves and dandelion-like flowers that grows easily from seed.

Parts Used
Leaves and flowers.

Healing Properties
Actions: Nerve relaxant, mild sedative, mild pain reliever.
Uses: Anxiety, insomnia, hyperactivity in children.

Availability
Gather leaves in June and July, otherwise not widely available.

How to Use in Smoothies
Dried leaves and flowers: Crush to a fine powder. Use 1 tsp (5 mL) for each 1 cup (250 mL) of smoothie. Add to other ingredients before blending.
Infusion: In a teapot, pour $\frac{1}{4}$ cup (50 mL) boiling water over 1 tbsp (15 mL) chopped fresh leaves (or 1 tsp/5 mL ground dried leaves). Cover and steep for 10 minutes. Cool (no need to strain) and use to replace $\frac{1}{4}$ cup (50 mL) liquid in smoothie recipes.

Yarrow

Achillea millefolium

A one- to three-foot (30 to 90 cm) tall hardy perennial with feathery leaves and white (occasionally pink) flowers that grows wild in fields throughout North America and is easily grown in the garden.

Parts Used
Stem, leaves and flowers.

Healing Properties
Actions: Anti-inflammatory, bitter, promotes bile flow, diaphoretic, digestive, relaxant, promotes blood circulation, heals wounds.
Uses: High blood pressure, colds, fevers, influenza, varicose veins.

Caution
Large doses of yarrow are toxic if taken over a long period of time.

Availability
Harvest aboveground parts while flowering in the wild from June through September. Dried stems, leaves and flowers and tinctures are available in alternative/health stores.

How to Use in Smoothies
Dried stems, leaves and flowers: Crush to a fine powder. Use 1 tsp (5 mL) for each 1 cup (250 mL) of smoothie. Add to other ingredients before blending.
Infusion: In a teapot, pour $\frac{1}{4}$ cup (50 mL) boiling water over 1 tbsp (15 mL) chopped fresh flowers (or 1 tsp/5 mL dried). Cover and steep for 10 minutes. Cool (no need to strain) and use to replace $\frac{1}{4}$ cup (50 mL) liquid in smoothie recipes.
Tincture: Add 40 drops tincture to each 1 cup (250 mL) of smoothie.

Yellow Dock

Rumex crispus

A large one- to five-foot (30 to 150 cm) tall perennial with small green-to-red flowers that grows in waste areas throughout North America.

Parts Used
Root.

Healing Properties
Actions: Bitter, laxative, lymphatic, increases bile flow.
Uses: Fresh roots are rich in iron and can be used to treat iron-deficiency anemia. Yellow dock also helps cleanse the body by supporting liver function and eliminating toxins through the bile. It is an especially helpful cleanser for skin diseases, rheumatoid arthritis, swollen lymph glands and constipation.

Availability
The root can be harvested in the wild from September through November. Dried root is available in alternative/health stores.

How to Use in Smoothies
Fresh root: Immerse root in water to remove loose soil, then scrub and chop (leave skin on if it has been wildcrafted and you are certain is has not been contaminated by pesticides or waste). Wrap fresh root in a towel and store in the refrigerator for one to two weeks. Dry chopped root to store longer. Use 2 tsp (10 mL) fresh chopped root per smoothie recipe.
Ground dried root: Add 1 tsp (5 mL) ground dried root to each 1 cup (250 mL) of smoothie.
Decoction: In a small saucepan, pour $\frac{1}{4}$ cup (50 mL) boiling water over 1 tbsp (15 mL) chopped fresh root (or 1 tsp/5 mL chopped dried). Cover and simmer for 10 minutes. Cool, strain and discard root. Use to replace $\frac{1}{4}$ cup (50 mL) liquid in smoothie recipes.

Other Ingredients

Blackstrap Molasses

Molasses is a thick syrup by-product of sugar refining, in which the sucrose (sugar) is separated from the liquid and nutrients from the raw cane plant. Several grades of molasses are available, but blackstrap contains the least sugar and the most nutrients: iron, six of the B vitamins, calcium, phosphorus and potassium.

For Juicing and Smoothies: Molasses has a strong flavor, so use sparingly, about 1 to 2 tsp (5 to 10 mL) per 1 cup (250 mL) in juice or tea that requires additional sweetening.

Carob

Ceratonia siliqua

Carob, which is powdered carob beans, is used as a substitute for cocoa and chocolate. Carob is healthier than chocolate because, unlike cocoa (from which chocolate is made), it has no caffeine, does not need extra sugar, is lower in fat and provides some calcium and phosphorus. It is available in baking chips, which can be used in hot drinks, as well as in powdered form, which can be blended into smoothies (see also Coconut Carob Milk, page 328).

For Juicing: To add sweetness to juices, whisk up to 1 tbsp (15 mL) carob into 1 cup (250 mL) of juice.

For Smoothies: Add up to 2 tbsp (25 mL) carob to ingredients before blending.

Cheese

Cheese contains almost all of the nutrients in milk in concentrated form. People with milk intolerances cannot eat cheese made from cow's milk. While hard cheeses usually cannot be blended into drinks, soft and semisoft cheeses — such as feta, blue, cream and cottage cheeses, among many others — can be added to smoothies. Because softer cheeses are usually higher in fat, they should be used sparingly.

For Smoothies: When using semisoft cheese, bring it to room temperature, remove the rind if there is one and chop before adding to the blender.

The amount varies with the cheese, but a good rule of thumb is to add no more than 1/4 cup (50 mL) per smoothie recipe.

Cider Vinegar

Distilled white vinegar is a mixture of acetic acid and water. It is useful as a disinfectant and cleaning agent but is not valuable as a food. Naturally fermented vinegar made from wine or fruit juice, such as the cider vinegar widely available in grocery stores, contains some nutrients. However, the most nutritious cider vinegar is available at alternative/ health stores. It is made from juice extracted from certified organic apples that is naturally fermented (without heat or the addition of clarifiers, enzymes or preservatives). This process yields a natural cider vinegar that contains some pectin and trace minerals, as well as beneficial bacteria and enzymes.

For Juicing and Smoothies: For overall health, add 1 tsp (5 mL) natural apple cider vinegar to juice and smoothie drinks.

Flax Seeds

Linum usitatissimum

Flax seed oil is the best vegetable source of essential omega-3 fatty acids, which help lubricate the joints and prevent absorption of toxins by stimulating digestion.

For Juicing: Whisk in 1 tbsp (15 mL) flax seed oil for up to 2 cups (500 mL) juice.

For Smoothies: Add 1 tbsp (15 mL) whole flax seeds to other ingredients before blending.

Grains

Oats, wheat, rye, buckwheat, spelt, amaranth, quinoa

Whole grains are unrefined and therefore retain all the nutritional value of the bran and germ. They also add fiber and complex carbohydrates to the diet. In all, whole grains offer protein, carbohydrates, phytate, vitamin E, fiber (including lignins), and some B vitamins (thiamin, riboflavin, niacin, folacin), iron, zinc and magnesium.

Actions: Anti-cancer, antioxidant, fight heart disease, anti-obesity, lower blood sugar level.

For Smoothies: Add 2 to 3 tbsp (25 to 45 mL) whole grain flakes to 1 cup (250 mL) blended drinks and milk shakes. Add to roots and nuts for roasted coffee-substitute blends.

Grasses

Wheat, barley

Wheat and barley grass are grown from the seeds (or "berries") of the wheat or barley plant. Harvested when 5 to 6 inches (12.5 to 15 cm) high, the grass is then eaten or juiced fresh, dried and used in powdered form, or pressed into pills. High in chlorophyll (a powerful healing agent and infection fighter), beta-carotene and vitamins C and E, these green foods are easily added to juices and blended drinks. They are also one of the best plant sources of protein — even better than soy and legumes.

Actions: Antioxidant, anti-inflammatory, anticancer, antibiotic, blood cleanser, protects against radiation

For Juicing and Smoothies: Fresh wheat and barley grasses require a special juicer or attachment to extract their liquid. They have a strong flavor, so mix with water or vegetable juice, not fruit juices. Whisk 1 tbsp (15 mL) powdered wheat or barley grass with 1 to 2 cups (250 to 500 mL) vegetable juice or blended drinks.

Caution: Start with small amounts (no more than 2 tbsp/25 mL) wheat grass juice daily. Large amounts may cause diarrhea and nausea.

Green Algae

Chlorella, spirulina

Rich in carotenoids and chlorophyll, these microscopic single-celled green algae have been shown to be effective in reducing the effects of radiation and may be helpful in treating HIV infections. Available in capsules or bulk loose powder.

Actions: Antioxidant, anticancer, boost immunity, reduce heavy-metal toxicity, hypotensive.

For Juicing and Smoothies: Add 2 tsp (10 mL) to juice and blended drinks.

Hemp

Cannabis sativa

Hemp seeds are high in protein and contain about 30% oil, which is high in essential fatty acids — omega-3 and omega-6, as well as gamma-linolenic acid (GLA). Hemp nuts, the hulled seeds of the hemp plant, can be used in nut butters, baked products, dips and spreads, and incorporated into blended drinks.

For Smoothies: Add 2 to 3 tbsp (25 to 45 mL) hemp nuts to blended drinks.

Honey

Honey is almost as sweet as granulated white sugar. The difference is that honey has small amounts of B vitamins, calcium, iron, zinc, potassium and phosphorus. It also acts as a potent bacteria killer. One tbsp (15 mL) contains just under 2% of the recommended daily intake of vitamins A and C, iron and calcium. Generally, the darker the honey, the higher its antioxidant value.

Actions: Antioxidant, antibacterial, antimicrobial, calms nerves, antidiarrheal.

For Juicing and Smoothies: Use honey as a sweetener for bitter vegetable juices or add to hot toddies and cold remedies to soothe sore throats.

Caution: The National Honey Board, along with other health organizations, recommends that honey not be fed to infants under one year of age.

Honey-Related Products

Bee pollen is the male seeds of flower blossoms, which collect on the legs of the bees as they work. The bees clean it off, mix it with nectar and their own enzymes. It contains proteins, vitamins A, B, C and E, calcium, magnesium, selenium, nucleic acids and lecithin and may be added to blended drinks. Use 1 tbsp (15 mL) bee pollen for up to 2 cups (500 mL) smoothie.

Propolis is a sticky resinous substance collected from coniferous trees. It is supportive of the immune system and is used as a tonic. Propolis can be added to blended drinks, 1 tsp (5 mL) for each 1 cup (250 mL) of juice or smoothie.

Royal jelly is the milky product fed exclusively to the queen bee. It is known to be rich in B vitamins, as well as vitamins A, C, D and E. Refrigerate fresh royal jelly or purchase it freeze-dried for use in juices and blended drinks. Add

1 tbsp (15 mL) royal jelly for up to 2 cups (500 mL) juice or smoothie.

Lecithin

Lecithin is one of the best sources of choline, which is known to improve memory by strengthening neurons in the brain's memory centers. Lecithin is available in alternative/health stores in capsule or granular form. Add two capsules or 1 tbsp (15 mL) lecithin granules to 1 to 2 cups (250 to 500 mL) of smoothie.

Maple Syrup

The sap from sugar maples (*Acer saccharum*), red maples (*A. rubrum*) and silver maples (*A. saccharinum*) is collected in the spring when it is flowing from the roots back into the aerial parts of the tree to provide energy for growth. The sap is 95 to 97% water, but when it is boiled down, a thick, sweet syrup composed of 65% sucrose is left behind. The syrup also contains organic acids, minerals (mainly potassium and calcium) and traces of amino acids and vitamins. One-quarter cup (50 mL) maple syrup provides 6% of the recommended daily intake of calcium and thiamin, and 2% of magnesium and riboflavin.

For Juicing and Smoothies: Stir 1 to 2 tbsp (15 to 25 mL) pure maple syrup (avoid "maple-flavored" syrup, which is primarily corn syrup with artificial flavor) into 1 to 2 cups (250 to 500 mL) juice or smoothie if a sweetener is required.

Nuts

All nuts — including peanuts, which are technically legumes — contain large amounts of protein, vitamin E, fiber and protease inhibitors, which are known to prevent cancer in laboratory animals. Although nuts are extremely high in fat, their oils are polyunsaturated and, as such, reduce blood cholesterol levels. Nuts also contain essential fatty acids, which are necessary for healthy skin, hair, glands, mucous membranes, nerves and arteries, as well as being helpful in preventing cardiovascular disease. Nuts allow a slow, steady rise in blood sugar and insulin, making them good foods for people with diabetes (see also Nut Milks, page 314).

Actions: Anticancer, lower blood cholesterol levels, regulate blood sugar level.

For Juicing: Use ground nuts as a garnish for juices.

For Smoothies: Add up to ¼ cup (50 mL) whole nuts or Nut Milk (see pages 314–316) for blending with other ingredients in smoothies and blended drinks.

Caution: Nuts can cause extreme allergic reactions in some people. Also, peanuts and peanut butter may be contaminated by aflatoxin mold, a carcinogen.

Protein Powder

Soy protein (the protein extracted from soybeans) is believed to help reduce the risk of cancers of the breast, endometrium and prostate if it contains isoflavones. Isoflavones mimic the action of estrogen and thus reduce the symptoms of menopause and help prevent the loss of calcium, which is linked to osteoporosis. Research has shown that soy protein reduces both the overall cholesterol level and the low-density lipoprotein (LDL), or "bad," cholesterol level. Choose raw soy protein powder made from soybeans that are water-washed (not washed in alcohol), organically grown and specifically tested for high isoflavone levels.

For Smoothies: Add up to 3 tbsp (45 mL) to ingredients before blending.

Caution: There is growing concern over the prolonged use of soy (see Soy Products, opposite).

Psyllium Seeds

See page 138

Pumpkin Seeds

Pumpkin seeds are important to men because they contain high concentrations of amino acids that can reduce the symptoms of prostate enlargement.

For Smoothies: Add 2 tbsp (25 mL) fresh hulled pumpkin seeds to ingredients for blending.

Ready-to-Use Juices

Juice from fresh raw fruits, vegetables and herbs is the best source of nutrients and live energy. Canned or bottled juices have been processed at high heat and may contain added ingredients such as sugar, artificial flavorings, stabilizers, thickeners/thinners, and chemical preservatives. Should you wish to blend ready-to-use juices with fresh juice, choose pure juice with no sugar or additives.

Sea Herbs

Arame, dulse, nori, wakame, kelp

Their high concentrations of vitamin A, protein, calcium, iron and other minerals make sea herbs important to overall health.

Actions: Anticancer, diuretic, antibacterial, boost immune function.

For Juicing: Add the soaking water from sea herbs to fresh juices; the salty taste blends well in vegetable juices. Sprinkle powdered or finely cut sea herbs over juice as a garnish.

For Smoothies: Add ¼ to ½ cup (50 to 125 mL) soaked, simmered sea herbs to other ingredients for smoothies or blended drinks.

Sesame Seeds

Sesamum indicum

High in calcium and a good source of incomplete protein, sesame seeds lend a light, nutty taste to juices and blended drinks. Sesame seed oil is exceptionally stable and is a source of vitamin E and coenzyme Q10, an essential coenzyme for metabolism, or the rate at which the body produces energy (or burns calories).

Actions: Emollient, laxative, antioxidant.

For Juicing: Sprinkle seeds over juices as a garnish or whisk 1 tsp (5 mL) sesame oil into juices.

For Smoothies: Add 1 tbsp (15 mL) to other ingredients for blending.

Soy Products

Soybeans are the only known plant source of complete protein, meaning that they contain all of the essential amino acids in the appropriate proportions that are essential for the growth and maintenance of cells. Because soy products are often rich in isoflavones, diets high in soy were once thought to prevent cancers of the prostate, breast, uterus, lungs, colon, stomach, liver, pancreas, bladder and skin. However, recent studies have shown conflicting conclusions.

Actions: May be anticancer, lower blood cholesterol level, boost immunity.

Caution: Due to new research and the effects of genetic modification and heavy chemical use on soybeans, buy only organic fresh or dried soybeans and soy products.

Availability: Available raw, dried or canned whole, or in paste (miso), soy milk, tofu and tempeh.

For Juicing and Smoothies: Whisk ¼ cup (50 mL) soy milk into fresh juice or smoothies.

Caution: A large percentage of soybeans grown today are genetically modified and are produced using high amounts of pesticides. Fresh soybeans contain enzyme inhibitors that block protein digestion and may cause serious gastric distress and organ damage. The inhibitors are not present in such high amounts in the fermented bean products of tofu, tempeh or soy sauce. The high amounts of phytic acid in soybeans and soy foods may block the uptake of essential minerals and cause deficiencies. Isoflavones — once thought to minimize cell damage from free radicals, block the damaging effects of hormonal or synthetic estrogens, and inhibit tumor cell growth — may, in fact, be toxic.

Soybeans and soy foods contain goitrogens, naturally occurring substances in certain foods that can interfere with the functioning of the thyroid gland. Individuals with already existing and untreated thyroid problems may want to avoid soy foods.

Textured vegetable protein (TVP) is made from soybeans and is produced using chemicals and harmful techniques. It is not considered a whole food.

Excessive soy intake should be avoided during pregnancy, and soy-based baby formulas should not be used.

Tofu is a curd made from soybeans that is high in B vitamins, potassium and iron, as well as calcium, so long as that mineral has been used as the curdling agent (check the label). Tofu thickens and "smoothes" the taste of blended drinks. Silken tofu works best in smoothies. Add ¼ to ½ cup (50 to 125 mL) to any smoothie recipe.

Tempeh, a mild, firm cake made from fermented cooked soybeans, may also be used in smoothies. It is usually sold frozen. Add ¼ cup (50 mL) crumbled tempeh to any smoothie recipe.

Canned soybeans or cooked reconstituted dried soybeans are also good in smoothies and produce a thicker result. Add ½ cup (125 mL) canned or cooked soybeans per smoothie recipe.

Sprouts

A good source of B vitamins (except B_{12}), sprouts also contain vitamins A and C, as well as bioflavonoids and enzymes. They add a green, living nutritional boost to juices and blended drinks. Alfalfa (and other grains), bean, pea and herb seeds are easy to sprout in a warm, moist environment and offer a concentrated blast of the nutrients found in the mature plants. Grow sprouts in the winter months, when fresh leafy greens are not at their best.

Caution: The safety of seed sprouts depends upon the quality of the water in which they are grown. Some sprouts have been linked with harmful bacteria, and water is the culprit in generating that bacteria. The best source for sprouts is to grow them from clean, organic seeds in water that has been boiled or that is known to be free of contaminants.

Buying and Storing: For reasons stated above, grow your own or purchase sprouts from reliable growers. Look for moist, crisp sprouts with no evidence of slime or wilting. Store in the refrigerator for up to one week.

For Juicing: Feed through tube interspersed with firm fruit or vegetables.

For Smoothies: Add up to 1 cup (250 mL) to blended drinks.

Sunflower Seeds

Helianthus annuus

A good source of vitamin E and zinc, sunflower seeds can be added to other ingredients before blending into smoothies.

For Smoothies: Use 2 tbsp (25 mL) for up to 2 cups (500 mL) smoothie.

Tofu

See Soy Products, page 149

Wheat Germ

A good source of vitamin E and thiamin, wheat germ may be added to other ingredients before blending.

For Juicing and Smoothies: Use 2 tbsp (25 mL) for up to 2 cups (500 mL) juice or smoothie.

Wheat Grass

See Grasses, page 147

Yogurt and Yogurt Products

Yogurt is produced from fermented milk. A beneficial type of bacteria (called lactobacilli) in yogurt restores and maintains a normal microbial balance in the intestinal tract. The acidophilus culture in yogurt also helps protect against colon cancer. When buying, check the label to ensure that it "contains active cultures." Yogurt is usually safe for people with milk allergies and is essential to a vegetarian diet.

Actions: Antibacterial, anticancer, anti-ulcer, immune building, lowers blood cholesterol.

For Juicing and Smoothies: Add up to 1 cup (250 mL) yogurt to blended drinks and stir up to ¼ cup (50 mL) into fruit or vegetable juices.

The Recipes

Smoothie Guidelines

Bursting with flavor and nutrition, smoothies are filled with healthful antioxidants, important vitamins, minerals, enzymes, fiber, water and other vital phytochemicals. Unlike juices, which lack insoluble fiber, smoothies deliver all the natural fiber that's present in whole raw fruits and vegetables. They are a great way to start the day, to snack between meals and, occasionally, to replace a midday meal. If you make them with milk, yogurt, tofu or fortified soy milk, they also add bone-building calcium to your diet.

Buy Organic

Buy organic produce whenever possible to reduce your intake of potentially harmful chemicals. When you purchase organic fruits and vegetables, you support a sustainable system of soil regeneration that is important to our future food supply while reducing your exposure to toxins. To keep nutrient levels from diminishing, store fresh vegetables properly: they will stay fresh in the crisper drawer of your refrigerator for a few days to just over one week. Large quantities of fresh vegetables may be stored for longer in a root cellar.

Look for smooth, blemish-free skins and choose produce at the peak of ripeness. Underripe fruit and vegetables produce smoothies that are chalky, lumpy and somewhat bitter — and they may cause diarrhea or stomach cramps. Overripe fruit may start to ferment and can cause the same symptoms.

To ripen soft-fleshed fruits and vegetables (peaches, apricots, pears, plums and avocados), place in a brown paper bag and keep at room temperature for two or three days or until ripe.

Tips for Blending Fruits and Vegetables

- Measure the ingredients into the blender jug in the order listed in the recipe, pouring liquid into the jug first. This is essential for the blender to work properly.
- Blend on the low or mix setting for 10 to 30 seconds, then increase the speed to the high, purée or liquefy setting for another 10 to 30 seconds. This allows the blades to chop the bigger chunks finely before they spin faster and lift the mixture up and out of range. This method actually shortens the time needed to liquefy the ingredients for drinking.
- Always chop ice with some liquid in the jug.

- Smoothie too thin? Add a couple of ice cubes, a banana or frozen fruit.
- Smoothie too thick? Add more liquid — juice, soy milk, milk or water.
- Smoothie too sweet? Add lemon juice, 1 tbsp (15 mL) at a time, until taste is corrected.
- Smoothie too sour? Add chopped sweet fruit (banana, apple, grapes, pineapple or dried apricots or dates), in 1/4-cup (50 mL) increments, until desired sweetness is achieved.
- Blend, drink and enjoy — every day!

Fruit and Vegetable Juices

Fruit and vegetable juices are often used as liquids in smoothies. The best possible juice is made from fresh organic produce and should be consumed immediately. When it is not possible to make your own juice, commercially prepared unsweetened organic juice is the next best choice. For convenience, keep a variety of frozen concentrated fruit juices, bottled vegetable juices and meat broths on hand. Look for unsweetened concentrates made from organic fruit and avoid monosodium glutamate (MSG), sugar and other unwanted additives in commercially prepared vegetable juices and cocktails.

Canned Fruit and Vegetables

When fresh produce is not in season, keeping a variety of canned fruits and vegetables on hand is a convenient way to make a variety of flavorful smoothies. Studies show that canned fruits are very nutritious. When Ken Sammonds, an associate professor of human nutrition at the University of Massachusetts, compared two versions of the same fruit smoothie recipe — one made with canned fruit, the other made with fresh fruit — he found that many vitamin levels were comparable. "The ingredients you choose, not the form of the ingredients, are what really determine a recipe's nutrient content," he concluded. However, commercially processed foods may contain additives, pesticide residues or large amounts of sugar. Organic produce packed in its own juice or water with no sugar added (available at natural food stores) is preferable.

To substitute canned for fresh, use one 14-oz (398 mL) can for each 1 cup (250 mL) sliced or chopped fresh fruit or vegetable. Use the liquid in the can (if it is not a heavy sugar syrup) but reduce the amount of other liquids in the recipe by 1/4 cup (50 mL).

Using Frozen Fruits and Vegetables

Smoothies are colder, thicker and smoother when they're made with frozen produce. In fact, combining fresh and frozen fruit or vegetables in the same drink is ideal. To make the most-economical use of your blender, purchase large quantities of fresh seasonal produce and freeze it in individual servings. A more expensive but more convenient option is to use commercially frozen fruit or vegetables, especially in winter, when fresh local produce is out of season. Look for frozen produce that has no added sugar and avoid packages that are stained or show evidence of leakage, which are both indications that the contents have thawed and refrozen.

Freezing fresh fruit and vegetables: Peel, seed or pit, and cut into slices or chunks. (If using berries, pick them over, discarding any wrinkled, split or soft berries, then wash and pat dry.) Arrange the pieces in a single layer on a baking sheet and freeze in the coldest part of the freezer. Transfer to a resealable plastic freezer bag, then seal and label. Use three or four frozen pieces of fruit or vegetable or $\frac{1}{2}$ cup (125 mL) frozen berries, peas or beans (no need to thaw) in smoothies. Frozen produce will keep for up to six months in the freezer.

Fruit Smoothies

continued on next page

Sugar Alert

Fruits are high in natural sugar, which the body uses for fuel. However, people with diabetes and those who are prone to yeast infections and hypoglycemia must limit their consumption of fruits and fruit juices because overconsumption can cause a rapid rise in blood sugar.

Most juices, particularly those made from concentrated fruit, contain a lot of natural sugar — 1 cup (250 mL) unsweetened apple juice contains, on average, 25 g sugar — and sugar is often added to commercially prepared juices. Since many smoothies rely on fruit juice for the liquid, this is a concern to people for whom sugar is an issue. This book provides many vegetable smoothies for people who wish to limit their fruit consumption and yet still enjoy the benefits of smoothies.

Using Dried Fruit

Dried fruit may also be used in smoothies, either as is or in fruit milks (see pages 312 to 313). Drying concentrates the sugars (glucose, fructose and sucrose) and fiber in fruits. This means that smoothies made with dried fruit are sweeter than those made with fresh and have more cleansing power because they are higher in fiber. (That's why prunes are a more effective laxative than fresh plums.) Fresh apricots, for example, are approximately 2% fiber, but dried apricots are about 20% fiber.

Substituting dried fruit: When substituting dried fruit for fresh, frozen or canned, add ¼ cup (50 mL) extra liquid to the recipe, or reconstitute the dried fruit before using.

Reconstituting dried fruit: Measure whole, sliced or halved dried fruit into a small bowl and pour boiling water over it to cover. Steep for 30 minutes to 1 hour or until fruit is plump and soft. Drain (reserve liquid to add to other liquid in recipe) and chop fruit before adding to the blender.

Caution: Commercially dried fruits (except dates and figs) are usually fumigated with sulfur dioxide, a gas that is poisonous and destroys B vitamins. Buy unsulfured fruits whenever possible, especially if you are feeding them to children, and wash thoroughly before using. To make your own dried fruit, buy organic fruit in season and dry in the oven or using a food dehydrator.

Açai Berry Combo

Serves 2

¼ cup	raspberry or grape juice	50 mL
1 tbsp	freshly squeezed lemon juice	15 mL
1 cup	frozen whole açai berries or açai berry pulp, partially thawed	250 mL
½ cup	blueberries	125 mL
½ cup	raspberries or pitted cherries	125 mL

1. In a blender, combine raspberry juice, lemon juice, açai berries, blueberries and raspberries. Secure lid and blend (from low to high if using a variable speed blender) until smooth.

Almond Banana

Serves 1 or 2

Tip
Although many of the recipes call for unflavored soy milk, some flavored soy milks work equally well in fruit smoothies. Feel free to substitute your favorite flavor.

1 cup	soy milk or Almond Milk (page 314)	250 mL
3 tbsp	chopped almonds	45 mL
2	bananas, cut into chunks	2
Pinch	ground nutmeg	Pinch

1. In a blender, combine soy milk, almonds, bananas and nutmeg. Secure lid and blend (from low to high if using a variable speed blender) until smooth.

Serves 2 or 3

Almond Date

Tip

Although many of the recipes call for unflavored soy milk, some flavored soy milks work equally well in fruit smoothies. Feel free to substitute your favorite flavor.

¾ cup	soy milk or Almond Milk (page 314)	175 mL
¼ cup	pitted dates	50 mL
2 tbsp	chopped almonds or pecans	25 mL
3 tbsp	cream cheese	45 mL
1	banana, cut into chunks	1
⅛ tsp	ground cinnamon	0.5 mL
Pinch	ground nutmeg	Pinch

1. In a blender, combine soy milk, dates, almonds, cream cheese, banana, cinnamon and nutmeg. Secure lid and blend (from low to high if using a variable speed blender) until smooth.

Serves 2

Apple Cooler

½ cup	freshly squeezed orange juice	125 mL
2	apples, quartered	2
1	orange, seeded and sectioned	1
½ cup	frozen raspberries	125 mL

1. In a blender, combine orange juice, apples, orange and raspberries. Secure lid and blend (from low to high if using a variable speed blender) until smooth.

Apple Crisp

Serves 4

¾ cup	apple juice	175 mL
2	apples, quartered	2
½ cup	frozen raspberries	125 mL
¼ cup	cranberry sauce	50 mL
½	banana, cut in chunks	½
1 tbsp	steel-cut or rolled oats	15 mL
¼ tsp	ground cinnamon	1 mL
Pinch	ground nutmeg	Pinch

1. In a blender, combine apple juice, apples, raspberries, cranberry sauce, banana, oats, cinnamon and nutmeg. Secure lid and blend (from low to high if using a variable speed blender) until smooth.

Apple Currant

Serves 1 or 2

Tip
You can use fresh and frozen fruit interchangeably in most smoothies, although the results will differ. Frozen fruit not only chills a smoothie, it thickens it as well.

⅔ cup	apple juice	150 mL
½ cup	black currants	125 mL
1	apple, quartered	1
½ cup	applesauce	125 mL

1. In a blender, combine apple juice, black currants, apple quarters and applesauce. Secure lid and blend (from low to high if using a variable speed blender) until smooth.

| Serves 3 | | |

Apple Fresh

¾ cup	apple juice	175 mL
2	apples, quartered	2
1 cup	seedless red grapes	250 mL
½	lemon, peeled and seeded	½
½ tsp	powdered ginseng, optional	2 mL

1. In a blender, combine apple juice, apples, grapes, lemon, and ginseng, if using. Secure lid and blend (from low to high if using a variable speed blender) until smooth.

| Serves 3 or 4 | | |

Apple Mint

Tip
The sweetness of this smoothie will increase significantly if you use sweetened frozen yogurt rather than plain yogurt.

½ cup	cooled peppermint infusion (page 137)	125 mL
¼ cup	plain or frozen yogurt	50 mL
1	apple, quartered	1
1	kiwifruit, quartered	1
1 tbsp	chopped fresh peppermint leaves	15 mL
¼ tsp	fennel seeds	1 mL
¼ cup	applesauce	50 mL

1. In a blender, combine infusion, yogurt, apple, kiwi, peppermint, fennel seeds and applesauce. Secure lid and blend (from low to high if using a variable speed blender) until smooth.

Apple Pear

Serves 3 or 4

1	can (14 or 15 oz/398 or 425 mL) pears in juice	1
1 tbsp	freshly squeezed lemon juice	15 mL
¼ cup	applesauce	50 mL
1	apple, quartered	1
½ cup	seedless red or green grapes	125 mL

1. In a blender, combine pears with juice, lemon juice, applesauce, apple and grapes. Secure lid and blend (from low to high if using a variable speed blender) until smooth.

Apple Pie

Serves 2

¼ cup	apple cider	50 mL
½ cup	silken tofu	125 mL
2	apples, quartered	2
2 tbsp	spelt flakes, optional	25 mL
¼ tsp	ground cinnamon	1 mL
⅛ tsp	ground cloves	0.5 mL
⅛ tsp	ground nutmeg	0.5 mL
Pinch	ground ginger, optional	Pinch
½ cup	applesauce	125 mL

1. In a blender, combine cider, tofu, apples, spelt flakes, if using, cinnamon, cloves, nutmeg, ginger, if using, and applesauce. Secure lid and blend (from low to high if using a variable speed blender) until smooth.

Apple Spice Cocktail

Serves 2

¾ cup	apple juice	175 mL
3	apples, quartered	3
1	piece (½ inch/1 cm) gingerroot, peeled	1
⅛ tsp	ground cardamom, optional	0.5 mL
⅛ tsp	ground nutmeg	0.5 mL
¼ cup	cranberry sauce	50 mL

1. In a blender, combine apple juice, apples, ginger, cardamom, if using, nutmeg and cranberry sauce. Secure lid and blend (from low to high if using a variable speed blender) until smooth.

Apricot and Oatmeal Breakfast Special

Serves 2

Tips

Start the prep for this in the evening for a nutritious breakfast drink.

This is a substantial and very thick mixture that may be thinned with more juice.

½ cup	chopped dried apricots	125 mL
1	package (1 oz/30 g) instant oatmeal (about ½ cup/125 mL)	1
1 cup	boiling water	250 mL
1½ cups	orange juice, preferably freshly squeezed	375 mL
2 tbsp	plain yogurt	25 mL
2	pitted dates	2

1. In a small bowl, combine apricots, instant oatmeal and boiling water. Cover and let soak for at least 20 minutes or overnight.

2. In a blender or food processor, combine orange juice, apricot-oatmeal mixture and any soaking liquid, yogurt and dates. Secure lid and blend (from low to high if using a variable speed blender) until smooth.

Apricot Apricot

¼ cup	orange or carrot juice	50 mL
1	can (14 oz/398 mL) apricots with juice	1
½ cup	chopped dried apricots	125 mL
1	banana, cut into chunks	1

1. In a blender, combine orange juice, canned apricots with juice, dried apricots and banana. Secure lid and blend (from low to high if using a variable speed blender) until smooth.

Apricot Explosion

½ cup	pineapple juice	125 mL
2	apricots, halved	2
1	pineapple wedge, cut into chunks	1
¼ cup	apricot- or peach-flavored frozen yogurt	50 mL

1. In a blender, combine pineapple juice, apricots, chopped pineapple and frozen yogurt. Secure lid and blend (from low to high if using a variable speed blender) until smooth.

Apricot Peach

½ cup	freshly squeezed orange juice	125 mL
2	apricots, halved	2
2	peaches, halved	2
½ cup	green grapes	125 mL

1. In a blender, combine orange juice, apricots, peaches and grapes. Secure lid and blend (from low to high if using a variable speed blender) until smooth.

Autumn Refresher

Serves 3

¼ cup	freshly squeezed orange juice	50 mL
3 tbsp	freshly squeezed lime juice	45 mL
2	pears, quartered	2
1	peach, chopped	1
1	apple, quartered	1

1. In a blender, combine orange juice, lime juice, pears, peach and apple. Secure lid and blend (from low to high if using a variable speed blender) until smooth.

Banana Mango

Serves 2 or 3

½ cup	mango, apricot or peach nectar	125 mL
⅓ cup	silken tofu	75 mL
1	banana, cut into chunks	1
1	mango, halved	1
½ cup	apricot halves	125 mL

1. In a blender, combine mango nectar, tofu, banana, mango and apricots. Secure lid and blend (from low to high if using a variable speed blender) until smooth.

Banana Nut

Serves 3

Tip
Use unflavored or vanilla soy milk in place of the pineapple juice to reduce the sweetness of this smoothie.

½ cup	pineapple juice	125 mL
3 tbsp	chopped almonds	45 mL
2	pineapple wedges, cut into chunks	2
1	banana, cut into chunks	1
¼ cup	banana-flavored frozen yogurt	50 mL
⅛ tsp	ground cinnamon	0.5 mL
Pinch	ground nutmeg	Pinch

1. In a blender, combine pineapple juice, almonds, pineapple wedges, chopped banana, frozen yogurt, cinnamon and nutmeg. Secure lid and blend (from low to high if using a variable speed blender) until smooth.

Serves 1

Bananarama

⅔ cup	pear nectar	150 mL
2 tbsp	freshly squeezed lemon juice	25 mL
4	frozen banana chunks	4
1	pear, quartered	1

1. In a blender, combine pear nectar, lemon juice, banana and pear. Secure lid and blend (from low to high if using a variable speed blender) until smooth.

Serves 2

Berry Best

½ cup	raspberry juice	125 mL
½ cup	blueberries	125 mL
½ cup	pitted cherries	125 mL
½ cup	seedless grapes	125 mL
¼	cantaloupe, cubed	¼

1. In a blender, combine raspberry juice, blueberries, cherries, grapes and cantaloupe. Secure lid and blend (from low to high if using a variable speed blender) until smooth.

Berry Blast

Serves 2 or 3

¾ cup	raspberry juice	175 mL
2 tbsp	freshly squeezed lemon juice	25 mL
6	frozen strawberries	6
6	frozen raspberries	6
½ cup	blackberries	125 mL
½ cup	blueberries	125 mL

1. In a blender, combine raspberry juice, lemon juice, strawberries, raspberries, blackberries and blueberries. Secure lid and blend (from low to high if using a variable speed blender) until smooth.

Berry Bonanza

Serves 2

* Raw elderberries can make some people sick. If in doubt, cook in a small amount of water, cool and drain.

½ cup	raspberry or cranberry-raspberry juice	125 mL
2 tbsp	freshly squeezed lemon juice	25 mL
½ cup	elderberries* or blueberries	125 mL
6	frozen strawberries	6
½ cup	frozen raspberries	125 mL

1. In a blender, combine raspberry juice, lemon juice, elderberries, strawberries and raspberries. Secure lid and blend (from low to high if using a variable speed blender) until smooth.

Berry Fine Cocktail

⅔ cup	pineapple juice	150 mL
1 cup	raspberries	250 mL
12	strawberries	12
¼ cup	cranberries	50 mL
4	ice cubes	4

1. In a blender, combine pineapple juice, raspberries, strawberries, cranberries and ice cubes. Secure lid and process using the chop or pulse function until smooth.

Berry Yogurt Flip

* Raw elderberries can make some people sick. If in doubt, cook in a small amount of water, cool and drain.

½ cup	cranberry-raspberry juice	125 mL
1 cup	blueberries or elderberries*	250 mL
½ cup	frozen whole açai berries or açai berry pulp, partially thawed	125 mL
6	almonds	6
½ cup	plain yogurt	125 mL

1. In a blender, combine cranberry-raspberry juice, blueberries, açai berries and almonds. Secure lid and blend on low for 30 seconds. Add yogurt and blend on high until smooth.

Best Berries

¾ cup	pineapple juice	175 mL
2 tbsp	freshly squeezed lemon juice	25 mL
3 tbsp	plain or frozen yogurt	45 mL
12	strawberries	12
1	banana, cut into chunks	1

1. In a blender, combine pineapple juice, lemon juice, yogurt, strawberries and banana. Secure lid and blend (from low to high if using a variable speed blender) until smooth.

Serves 1 or 2

Beta Blast

½ cup	freshly squeezed orange juice	125 mL
¼ cup	carrot juice	50 mL
½	cantaloupe, cubed	½
¼ cup	chopped apricots	50 mL
¼ cup	silken tofu, optional	50 mL

1. In a blender, combine orange juice, carrot juice, cantaloupe, apricots, and tofu, if using. Secure lid and blend (from low to high if using a variable speed blender) until smooth.

Serves 2

Black Belt

¾ cup	freshly squeezed orange juice	175 mL
½ cup	frozen blackberries	125 mL
¼ cup	frozen blueberries	50 mL
4	frozen banana chunks	4

1. In a blender, combine orange juice, blackberries, blueberries and banana. Secure lid and blend (from low to high if using a variable speed blender) until smooth.

Black Currant

Serves 2

²⁄₃ cup	apple juice	150 mL
½ cup	black currants	125 mL
1	banana, cut into chunks	1
⅓ cup	plain yogurt	75 mL
2 tbsp	liquid honey, or to taste	25 mL

1. In a blender, combine apple juice, currants, banana, yogurt and honey. Secure lid and blend (from low to high if using a variable speed blender) until smooth.

Black Pineapple

Serves 3

Tip

Replacing fresh berries with frozen (or frozen with fresh) is fine in smoothie recipes. Keep in mind that if you use all frozen berries, the smoothie will be colder and thicker.

* If you are pregnant, limit your intake of parsley to ½ tsp (2 mL) dried or one sprig fresh per day. Do not take parsley if you are suffering from kidney inflammation.

1 cup	pineapple juice	250 mL
2 tbsp	freshly squeezed lemon juice	25 mL
½ cup	blackberries	125 mL
½ cup	blueberries	125 mL
½ cup	raspberries	125 mL
1 tbsp	chopped fresh parsley*	15 mL

1. In a blender, combine pineapple juice, lemon juice, blackberries, blueberries, raspberries and parsley. Secure lid and blend (from low to high if using a variable speed blender) until smooth.

Serves 2		

Blueberry Smoothie

²⁄₃ cup	cranberry-raspberry juice	150 mL
1 cup	blueberries	250 mL
½ cup	seedless red grapes	125 mL
¼ cup	silken tofu or plain yogurt	50 mL

1. In a blender, combine cranberry-raspberry juice, blueberries, grapes and tofu. Secure lid and blend (from low to high if using a variable speed blender) until smooth.

Serves 3 or 4		

Blue Cherry

½ cup	soy or rice milk	125 mL
1 tbsp	freshly squeezed lemon juice	15 mL
1 cup	blueberries	250 mL
1 cup	pitted cherries	250 mL
½ cup	seedless red grapes	125 mL
¼ cup	silken tofu or fruit-flavored frozen yogurt	50 mL

1. In a blender, combine soy milk, lemon juice, blueberries, cherries, grapes and tofu. Secure lid and blend (from low to high if using a variable speed blender) until smooth.

Blue Water

Serves 3 or 4

¾ cup	cranberry juice	175 mL
¼ cup	crushed ice	50 mL
1 cup	chopped watermelon	250 mL
½ cup	blueberries	125 mL
¼ cup	cranberry sauce	50 mL

1. In a blender, combine cranberry juice, ice, watermelon, blueberries and cranberry sauce. Secure lid and blend (from low to high if using a variable speed blender) until smooth.

Brazilian Berry Smoothie

Serves 2

½ cup	freshly squeezed orange juice	125 mL
1	banana, cut into chunks	1
1	mango, quartered	1
2 cups	frozen whole açai berries or açai berry pulp, partially thawed	500 mL

1. In a blender, combine orange juice, banana, mango and açai berries. Secure lid and blend (from low to high if using a variable speed blender) until smooth.

Serves 3	# Breakfast Cocktail	

½ cup	carrot juice	125 mL
1	mango, halved	1
1	papaya, quartered	1
1	apple, quartered	1
1	piece (½ inch/1 cm) gingerroot, peeled	1
¼ cup	plain yogurt	50 mL

1. In a blender, combine carrot juice, mango, papaya, apple, ginger and yogurt. Secure lid and blend (from low to high if using a variable speed blender) until smooth.

Serves 4	# B-Vitamin	

½ cup	pineapple juice	125 mL
¼ cup	soy or rice milk	50 mL
1 cup	chopped pineapple	250 mL
¼ cup	apricot halves	50 mL
1	banana, cut into chunks	1
1 tbsp	wheat germ	15 mL
2 tsp	flax seeds	10 mL
1 tsp	cod liver or hemp oil, optional	5 mL

1. In a blender, combine pineapple juice, soy milk, pineapple, apricots, banana, wheat germ, flax seeds, and oil, if using. Secure lid and blend (from low to high if using a variable speed blender) until smooth.

C-Blend

Serves 2 or 3

¼ cup	freshly squeezed orange juice	50 mL
¼ cup	cranberry sauce	50 mL
	Juice of 1 lime	
2	oranges, sectioned and seeded	2
½	grapefruit, sectioned and seeded	½
1 tbsp	chopped fresh parsley*	15 mL
1 tbsp	liquid honey, optional	15 mL

1. In a blender, combine orange juice, cranberry sauce, lime juice, oranges, grapefruit, parsley, and honey, if using. Secure lid and blend (from low to high if using a variable speed blender) until smooth.

C-Blitz

Serves 2 or 3

¼ cup	freshly squeezed orange juice	50 mL
	Juice of 1 lemon	
2	kiwifruits, quartered	2
1	orange, sectioned and seeded	1
½	grapefruit, sectioned and seeded	½
1 tbsp	chopped fresh parsley* (see above)	15 mL

1. In a blender, combine orange juice, lemon juice, kiwis, orange, grapefruit and parsley. Secure lid and blend (from low to high if using a variable speed blender) until smooth.

Serves 3

Cherries Jubilee

1 cup	soy or rice milk	250 mL
1 cup	pitted cherries	250 mL
2	pineapple wedges, cut into chunks	2
2	frozen banana chunks	2
1 tbsp	flax seeds	15 mL
⅛ tsp	almond extract	0.5 mL

1. In a blender, combine soy milk, cherries, pineapple, banana, flax seeds and almond extract. Secure lid and blend (from low to high if using a variable speed blender) until smooth.

Serves 3

Cherry Berry

Tip
To substitute fresh cherries for canned in this recipe, use 1 cup (250 mL) chopped pitted cherries. Add ¼ cup (50 mL) raspberry or orange juice.

1	can (14 oz/398 mL) sweet cherries with juice	1
½ cup	raspberries or blueberries	125 mL
6	strawberries	6

1. In a blender, combine cherries with juice, raspberries and strawberries. Secure lid and blend (from low to high if using a variable speed blender) until smooth.

Serves 3 or 4

Cherry Sunrise

1 cup	grapefruit juice	250 mL
1 cup	pitted cherries	250 mL
6	strawberries	6
1	apple, quartered	1
1 tbsp	fresh chamomile flowers, optional	15 mL

1. In a blender, combine grapefruit juice, cherries, strawberries, apple, and chamomile flowers, if using. Secure lid and blend (from low to high if using a variable speed blender) until smooth.

Chia Aloha

Serves 1 or 2

1 tbsp	chia seeds or flax seeds	15 mL
3 tbsp	freshly squeezed orange juice	45 mL
½ cup	milk	125 mL
1	can (14 oz/398 mL) guavas, drained	1

1. In a blender, combine chia seeds, orange juice, milk and guavas. Secure lid and blend (from low to high if using a variable speed blender) until smooth.

Citrus Cocktail

Serves 2 or 3

Tip
The sweetness of this smoothie will increase significantly if you use sweetened frozen yogurt rather than plain yogurt. Try using Fruit Yogurt Slush (page 341) for the frozen yogurt in this recipe.

½ cup	freshly squeezed orange juice	125 mL
¼ cup	grapefruit juice	50 mL
12	strawberries	12
1	piece (½ inch/1 cm) gingerroot, peeled	1
1 tbsp	wheat germ or chopped almonds	15 mL
¼ cup	plain or frozen yogurt	50 mL

1. In a blender, combine orange juice, grapefruit juice, strawberries, ginger, wheat germ and yogurt. Secure lid and blend (from low to high if using a variable speed blender) until smooth.

CocoNog

Serves 1

Tip
Use canned coconut milk or homemade Coconut Milk (page 315) in this smoothie.

½ cup	coconut cream or coconut milk (see Tip, left)	125 mL
4	frozen banana chunks	4
½ cup	plain yogurt, drained	125 mL
Pinch	ground nutmeg	Pinch
3	ice cubes	3

1. In a blender, combine coconut cream, banana, yogurt, nutmeg and ice. Secure lid and blend (from low to high if using a variable speed blender) until smooth.

Serves 2	# Cran-Apple	
¾ cup	apple juice	175 mL
¼ cup	cranberry sauce	50 mL
1	apple, quartered	1
1	orange, sectioned and seeded	1
1 tbsp	flax seeds	15 mL

1. In a blender, combine apple juice, cranberry sauce, apple, orange and flax seeds. Secure lid and blend (from low to high if using a variable speed blender) until smooth.

Serves 2	# Cranberry Cooler	
½ cup	cranberry juice	125 mL
½ cup	cranberry sauce	125 mL
1 cup	frozen whole açai berries or açai berry pulp, partially thawed	250 mL
½ cup	plain yogurt	125 mL
	Honey, to taste	

1. In a blender, combine cranberry juice, cranberry sauce, açai berries and yogurt. Secure lid and blend (from low to high if using a variable speed blender) until smooth. Taste and add honey, if desired.

Serves 2	# Cranberry Pineapple	
¾ cup	pineapple juice	175 mL
¼ cup	cranberries	50 mL
2	pineapple wedges, cut into chunks	2
1	apple, quartered	1

1. In a blender, combine pineapple juice, cranberries, pineapple and apple. Secure lid and blend (from low to high if using a variable speed blender) until smooth.

Cran-Cherry

Serves 2 or 3

¾ cup	apple juice	175 mL
⅓ cup	dried cherries or cranberries	75 mL
¼ cup	frozen cherries	50 mL
¼ cup	cranberry sauce	50 mL

1. In a blender, combine apple juice, dried cherries, frozen cherries and cranberry sauce. Secure lid and blend (from low to high if using a variable speed blender) until smooth.

Cran-Orange

Serves 1 or 2

¾ cup	freshly squeezed orange juice	175 mL
¼ cup	silken tofu	50 mL
2 tbsp	dried cranberries	25 mL
1	orange, sectioned and seeded	1
2 tsp	grated gingerroot	10 mL

1. In a blender, combine orange juice, tofu, cranberries, orange and ginger. Secure lid and blend (from low to high if using a variable speed blender) until smooth.

Date Time

Serves 2

¾ cup	freshly squeezed orange juice	175 mL
¼ cup	pitted dates	50 mL
¼ cup	cranberries or cranberry sauce	50 mL
1	apple, quartered	1

1. In a blender, combine orange juice, dates, cranberries and apple. Secure lid and blend (from low to high if using a variable speed blender) until smooth.

Detox Delight

1 cup	cranberry juice	250 mL
1	grapefruit, sectioned and seeded	1
1	mango, halved	1
1	beet, grated	1
15 to 20	drops milk thistle tincture	15 to 20

1. In a blender, combine cranberry juice, grapefruit, mango, beet and milk thistle. Secure lid and blend (from low to high if using a variable speed blender) until smooth.

Eye Opener

1/3 cup	freshly squeezed orange juice	75 mL
1 cup	pitted cherries	250 mL
12	strawberries	12
1	orange, sectioned and seeded	1

1. In a blender, combine orange juice, cherries, strawberries and orange sections. Secure lid and blend (from low to high if using a variable speed blender) until smooth.

Figgy Duff

1/2 cup	pineapple juice	125 mL
5	fresh or dried figs	5
1 tbsp	flax seeds	15 mL
2 tsp	steel-cut or rolled oats	10 mL
1 tsp	extra virgin olive oil or hemp oil	5 mL

1. In a blender, combine pineapple juice, figs, flax seeds, oats and oil. Secure lid and blend (from low to high if using a variable speed blender) until smooth.

Flu Fighter #1

Serves 2

½ cup	freshly squeezed orange juice	125 mL
⅓ cup	freshly squeezed lemon juice	75 mL
½ cup	elderberries	125 mL
¼ cup	cranberry sauce	50 mL
2 tbsp	black currant jelly or liquid honey	25 mL

1. In a blender, combine orange juice, lemon juice, elderberries, cranberry sauce and black currant jelly. Secure lid and blend (from low to high if using a variable speed blender) until smooth.

Fruit Explosion

Serves 2

¾ cup	apple juice	175 mL
¼ cup	dried cranberries	50 mL
¼	cantaloupe, cubed	¼
5	frozen strawberries	5

1. In a blender, combine apple juice, cranberries, cantaloupe and strawberries. Secure lid and blend (from low to high if using a variable speed blender) until smooth.

Fruit of Life

Serves 2

* Raw elderberries can make some people sick. If in doubt, cook in a small amount of water, cool and drain.

½ cup	cranberry juice	125 mL
½ cup	frozen whole açai berries or açai berry pulp, partially thawed	125 mL
	Seeds of 1 pomegranate	
1 cup	blueberries or elderberries*	250 mL

1. In a blender, combine cranberry juice, açai berries, pomegranate seeds and blueberries. Secure lid and blend (from low to high if using a variable speed blender) until smooth.

Serves 2		

Fruit Splash

¾ cup	grapefruit juice	175 mL
¼ cup	cranberry sauce	50 mL
¼	cantaloupe, cubed	¼
¼ cup	frozen raspberries	50 mL

1. In a blender, combine grapefruit juice, cranberry sauce, cantaloupe and raspberries. Secure lid and blend (from low to high if using a variable speed blender) until smooth.

Serves 2		

Fruity Fig

½ cup	peach or apple juice	125 mL
	Juice of ½ lemon	
2	fresh or dried figs	2
2	apricots, halved	2
1	peach, halved	1
1	plum, halved	1

1. In a blender, combine peach juice, lemon juice, figs, apricots, peach and plum. Secure lid and blend (from low to high if using a variable speed blender) until smooth.

Fruity Twist

Serves 4

¾ cup	freshly squeezed orange juice	175 mL
1	pineapple wedge, cut into chunks	1
1	slice watermelon, cubed	1
1	mango, halved	1
½	papaya	½
1	banana, cut into chunks	1

1. In a blender, combine orange juice, pineapple, watermelon, mango, papaya and banana. Secure lid and blend (from low to high if using a variable speed blender) until smooth.

Gold Star Smoothie

Serves 1

¼ cup	pineapple juice	50 mL
2	starfruit, halved	2
2	golden plums, halved	2
2	pineapple wedges, cut into chunks	2

1. In a blender, combine pineapple juice, starfruit, plums and pineapple. Secure lid and blend (from low to high if using a variable speed blender) until smooth.

Gooseberry Berry

Serves 2

½ cup	raspberry or cranberry juice	125 mL
½ cup	green or red gooseberries	125 mL
3	kiwifruits, quartered	3
2	ice cubes	2
	Honey, to taste	

1. In a blender, combine raspberry juice, gooseberries, kiwis and ice cubes. Secure lid and process using the chop or pulse function until smooth. Taste and add honey, if desired.

Serves 1	# Gooseberry Fool	
¼ cup	pineapple juice	50 mL
¼ cup	raspberry-flavored frozen yogurt	50 mL
1 cup	gooseberries	250 mL
1 tbsp	liquid honey, or to taste	15 mL

1. In a blender, combine pineapple juice, yogurt, gooseberries and honey. Secure lid and blend (from low to high if using a variable speed blender) until smooth.

Serves 1	# Granate Berry	
½ cup	pomegranate juice	125 mL
½ cup	pomegranate seeds	125 mL
½ cup	raspberries	125 mL
2 tbsp	plain yogurt	25 mL

1. In a blender, combine pomegranate juice, pomegranate seeds and raspberries. Secure lid and blend (from low to high if using a variable speed blender) until smooth. Pour into glass and stir in yogurt.

Grapefruit Greetings

Serves 2

1	can (10 oz/284 mL) mandarin orange sections with juice	1
2 tbsp	freshly squeezed lemon juice	25 mL
1	grapefruit, sectioned and seeded	1
1	banana, cut into chunks	1
1	starfruit, halved	1
2	pitted dates	2
½ cup	plain yogurt	125 mL

1. In a blender, combine oranges with juice, lemon juice, grapefruit, banana, starfruit, dates and yogurt. Secure lid and blend (from low to high if using a variable speed blender) until smooth.

Grape Glacé

Serves 1

½ cup	grape juice	125 mL
½ cup	ice cubes	125 mL
2 cups	seedless red grapes	500 mL
1	plum, halved	1

1. In a blender, combine grape juice, ice cubes, grapes and plum. Secure lid and process using the chop or pulse function until smooth.

Serves 2

Grape Heart

½ cup	grape or grapefruit juice	125 mL
1 tbsp	chopped almonds	15 mL
2 cups	seedless red grapes	500 mL
½ cup	blueberries	125 mL
½	grapefruit, sectioned and seeded	½

1. In a blender, combine grape juice, almonds, grapes, blueberries and grapefruit. Secure lid and blend (from low to high if using a variable speed blender) until smooth.

Serves 4

Green Goddess

Tip
You can substitute cantaloupe for the musk melon in this recipe and the result will be a Goddess, just not a green one.

⅓ cup	kiwi or grapefruit juice	75 mL
	Juice of 1 lime	
¼	musk melon, cubed	¼
2	kiwifruits, quartered	2
2	banana chunks	2
1 tbsp	chopped fresh peppermint leaves	15 mL

1. In a blender, combine kiwi juice, lime juice, melon, kiwis, banana and peppermint. Secure lid and blend (from low to high if using a variable speed blender) until smooth.

Serves 2

Green Tea and Blueberries

½ cup	steeped green tea, chilled	125 mL
1 cup	blueberries	250 mL
1 cup	blackberries	250 mL
2	black plums, halved	2

1. In a blender, combine green tea, blueberries, blackberries and plums. Secure lid and blend (from low to high if using a variable speed blender) until smooth.

Serves 2

Hawaiian Silk

Tip
Use canned coconut milk or homemade Coconut Milk (page 315) in this smoothie.

½ cup	coconut milk (see Tip, left)	125 mL
¼ cup	pineapple juice	50 mL
1	papaya, halved	1
1	pineapple wedge, cut into cubes	1

1. In a blender, combine coconut milk, pineapple juice, papaya and pineapple. Secure lid and blend (from low to high if using a variable speed blender) until smooth.

Serves 2

Hot Watermelon Cooler

½ cup	cranberry juice	125 mL
2 tbsp	freshly squeezed lime juice	25 mL
1	slice watermelon, cut into chunks	1
2 tbsp	chopped hot green chiles	25 mL
2	ice cubes	2

1. In a blender, combine cranberry juice, lime juice, watermelon, chiles and ice. Secure lid and process using the chop or pulse function until smooth.

Ki-Lime

Serves 1

½ cup	white grape juice	125 mL
2 tbsp	freshly squeezed lime juice	25 mL
2	kiwifruits, quartered	2
½	papaya	½

1. In a blender, combine grape juice, lime juice, kiwis and papaya. Secure lid and blend (from low to high if using a variable speed blender) until smooth.

Leafy Pear

Serves 1

½ cup	apple juice	125 mL
2	pears, quartered	2
2	kale leaves, chopped	2
1 tbsp	chopped fresh parsley	15 mL
2	ice cubes	2

1. In a blender, combine apple juice, pears, kale, parsley and ice. Secure lid and process using the chop or pulse function until smooth.

Liquid Gold

Serves 4

½ cup	freshly squeezed orange juice	125 mL
3 tbsp	freshly squeezed lemon juice	45 mL
2	apricots, halved	2
2	peaches, halved	2
1	pineapple wedge, cut into chunks	1
½	mango	½
½	banana, cut into chunks	½

1. In a blender, combine orange juice, lemon juice, apricots, peaches, pineapple, mango and banana. Secure lid and blend (from low to high if using a variable speed blender) until smooth.

Loosey-Goosey

Tip

Be careful with this drink — it works as a laxative.

* Avoid licorice if you have high blood pressure. The prolonged use of licorice is not recommended under any circumstances.

¼ cup	apple juice	50 mL
¼ cup	gooseberries	50 mL
1	apple, quartered	1
3 tbsp	chopped pitted dates	45 mL
3 tbsp	chopped pitted prunes	45 mL
¼ tsp	ground licorice*, ginger or cinnamon	1 mL

1. In a blender, combine apple juice, gooseberries, apple, dates, prunes and licorice. Secure lid and blend (from low to high if using a variable speed blender) until smooth.

Mango Madness

½ cup	freshly squeezed orange juice	125 mL
1	mango, halved	1
1	banana, cut into chunks	1
1 cup	seedless green grapes	250 mL
1	piece (¼ inch/0.5 cm) gingerroot, peeled	1

1. In a blender, combine orange juice, mango, banana, grapes and ginger. Secure lid and blend (from low to high if using a variable speed blender) until smooth.

Serves 2	# Mango Mango	
½ cup	mango or papaya nectar	125 mL
1	mango, halved	1
1	slice watermelon, cubed	1
½ cup	seedless red grapes	125 mL

1. In a blender, combine mango nectar, mango, watermelon and grapes. Secure lid and blend (from low to high if using a variable speed blender) until smooth.

Serves 2	# Mango Marvel	
½ cup	freshly squeezed orange juice	125 mL
1	mango, quartered	1
1	kiwifruit, quartered	1
½	papaya	½
4	frozen banana chunks	4
1	scoop vanilla-flavored frozen yogurt	1

1. In a blender, combine orange juice, mango, kiwi, papaya, banana and frozen yogurt. Secure lid and blend (from low to high if using a variable speed blender) until smooth.

Mango Tango

Serves 3 or 4

1 cup	freshly squeezed orange juice	250 mL
½	mango	½
1	pineapple wedge, cut into chunks	1
1	slice watermelon, cubed	1
½	papaya	½
5	frozen strawberries	5

1. In a blender, combine orange juice, mango, pineapple, watermelon, papaya and strawberries. Secure lid and blend (from low to high if using a variable speed blender) until smooth.

Maple Ginger Fig

Serves 1

¼ cup	freshly squeezed orange juice	50 mL
4	fresh or dried figs	4
⅓ cup	plain or fruit-flavored yogurt	75 mL
3 tbsp	pure maple syrup	45 mL
1 tsp	grated gingerroot	5 mL

1. In a blender, combine orange juice, figs, yogurt, maple syrup and ginger. Secure lid and blend (from low to high if using a variable speed blender) until smooth.

Serves 4	# Mega Melon Supreme	
½ cup	freshly squeezed orange juice or Apricot Milk (page 312)	125 mL
½ cup	chopped watermelon	125 mL
½ cup	chopped cantaloupe	125 mL
½ cup	chopped honeydew melon	125 mL
½ cup	vanilla-flavored frozen yogurt	125 mL

1. In a blender, combine orange juice, watermelon, cantaloupe, honeydew and frozen yogurt. Secure lid and blend (from low to high if using a variable speed blender) until smooth.

Serves 2	# Mellow Mandarin	
1	can (10 oz/284 mL) mandarin orange sections with juice	1
¼	honeydew melon, cubed	¼
6	frozen strawberries	6
1	piece (½ inch/1 cm) gingerroot, peeled	1

1. In a blender, combine mandarins with juice, melon, strawberries and ginger. Secure lid and blend (from low to high if using a variable speed blender) until smooth.

Serves 2	# Mellow Yellow	
½ cup	white grape juice	125 mL
1	grapefruit, sectioned and seeded	1
1	pineapple wedge, cut into chunks	1
1	banana, cut into chunks	1

1. In a blender, combine grape juice, grapefruit, pineapple and banana. Secure lid and blend (from low to high if using a variable speed blender) until smooth.

Melon Morning Cocktail

Serves 4

½ cup	freshly squeezed orange juice	125 mL
1 cup	chopped watermelon	250 mL
¼	cantaloupe, cubed	¼
1	orange, sectioned and seeded	1
1	pineapple wedge, cut into chunks	1

1. In a blender, combine orange juice, watermelon, cantaloupe, orange and pineapple. Secure lid and blend (from low to high if using a variable speed blender) until smooth.

Minted Melon

Serves 2

½ cup	pineapple juice	125 mL
1 tbsp	freshly squeezed lime juice	15 mL
2	kiwifruits, quartered	2
½	honeydew melon, cut into chunks	½
1 tbsp	chopped fresh peppermint	15 mL
2	ice cubes	2

1. In a blender, combine pineapple juice, lime juice, kiwis, melon, peppermint and ice. Secure lid and process using the chop or pulse function until smooth.

Apple Fresh (page 161)

Apple Pear (page 162)

Berry Bonanza (page 167)

Leafy Pear (page 187)

Apricot Explosion (page 164)

Banana Mango (page 165)

Blueberry Smoothie (page 171)

Fruit of Life (page 180)

Hot Watermelon Cooler (page 186)

Tropics (page 218)

Orange Pom (page 195), Mango Marvel (page 189)
and Blueberry Banana (page 285)

Minted Melon (page 192)

Apple Carrot Cucumber (page 223)

Carrot Lime (page 227)

Beet (page 225)

C-Green (page 231)

Minty Peach

Serves 2 or 3

½ cup	peach or apricot nectar	125 mL
¼ cup	plain yogurt	50 mL
2 tbsp	freshly squeezed lemon juice	25 mL
1 cup	frozen peach slices	250 mL
1	honeydew melon wedge, cubed	1
1 tbsp	chopped fresh peppermint	15 mL

1. In a blender, combine peach nectar, yogurt, lemon juice, peaches, melon and peppermint. Secure lid and blend (from low to high if using a variable speed blender) until smooth.

Nectarine on Ice

Serves 3

Tip
Use fresh apricots when in season, dried at other times.

¼ cup	frozen orange juice concentrate	50 mL
½ cup	water	125 mL
4	ice cubes	4
2	nectarines, halved	2
2	apricots, halved (see Tip, left)	2

1. In a blender, combine orange juice concentrate, water, ice, nectarines and apricots. Secure lid and process using the chop or pulse function until smooth.

Nectarlicious

Serves 3

1 cup	freshly squeezed orange juice	250 mL
2	nectarines, halved	2
¼ cup	blackberries	50 mL
¼ cup	raspberries	50 mL

1. In a blender, combine orange juice, nectarines, blackberries and raspberries. Secure lid and blend (from low to high if using a variable speed blender) until smooth.

Serves 2 or 3		

Nectar of the Gods

½ cup	peach or apricot nectar or pineapple juice	125 mL
1 tbsp	freshly squeezed lemon juice	15 mL
2	nectarines, halved	2
2	peaches, halved	2
½ cup	sparkling mineral water or soda water	125 mL

1. In a blender, combine peach nectar, lemon juice, nectarines and peaches. Secure lid and blend (from low to high if using a variable speed blender) until smooth. Pour into glasses and top up with mineral water.

Serves 3		

Orange Aid

¾ cup	freshly squeezed orange juice	175 mL
2 tsp	freshly squeezed lemon juice	10 mL
2	nectarines, halved	2
1	orange, sectioned and seeded	1
1	cantaloupe wedge, cubed	1

1. In a blender, combine orange juice, lemon juice, nectarines, orange and cantaloupe. Secure lid and blend (from low to high if using a variable speed blender) until smooth.

Orange Silk

Serves 1

1 tsp	grated orange zest	5 mL
¼ cup	freshly squeezed orange juice	50 mL
3 tbsp	soy or rice milk	45 mL
1 tbsp	orange flax seed oil	15 mL
1	orange, sectioned and seeded	1
½ cup	silken tofu	125 mL

1. In a blender, combine orange zest and juice, soy milk, flax seed oil, orange and tofu. Secure lid and blend (from low to high if using a variable speed blender) until smooth.

Orange Pom

Serves 2

½ cup	freshly squeezed orange juice	125 mL
½ cup	pomegranate seeds	125 mL
1	orange, sectioned and seeded	1
1	carrot, cut into chunks	1
1	apple, quartered	1

1. In a blender, combine orange juice, pomegranate seeds, orange, carrot and apple. Secure lid and blend (from low to high if using a variable speed blender) until smooth.

Orange Slushie

Serves 2

¼ cup	plain yogurt	50 mL
3	apricots, halved	3
1	orange, sectioned and seeded	1
¼ cup	frozen strawberries	50 mL
¼ cup	frozen whole açai berries or açai berry pulp, partially thawed	50 mL

1. In a blender, combine yogurt, apricots, orange, strawberries and açai berries. Secure lid and blend (from low to high if using a variable speed blender) until smooth. Serve with a spoon.

Papaya Passion

Serves 2

½ cup	freshly squeezed orange juice	125 mL
¼ cup	carrot juice	50 mL
1	pineapple wedge, cut into chunks	1
½ cup	chopped papaya	125 mL

1. In a blender, combine orange juice, carrot juice, pineapple and papaya. Secure lid and blend (from low to high if using a variable speed blender) until smooth.

Peach Bliss

Serves 2

½ cup	grapefruit juice	125 mL
1 cup	frozen peach slices	250 mL
¼ cup	frozen raspberries	50 mL
¼ cup	chopped dried peaches or chopped mixed dried fruit	50 mL

1. In a blender, combine grapefruit juice, peach slices, raspberries and dried peaches. Secure lid and blend (from low to high if using a variable speed blender) until smooth.

Peach Cobbler

Serves 4

Tip

You can use fresh and frozen fruit interchangeably in most smoothies, although the results will differ. Frozen fruit not only chills a smoothie, it thickens it as well.

1	can (14 oz/398 mL) peach halves or slices with juice	1
4	ice cubes	4
½ cup	evaporated milk or Almond Milk (page 314)	125 mL
¼ cup	peach-flavored yogurt	50 mL
2	apricots, halved	2
⅓ cup	peach sherbet	75 mL
Pinch	ground nutmeg	Pinch

1. In a blender, combine peaches with juice, ice, evaporated milk, yogurt, apricots, sherbet and nutmeg. Secure lid and process using the chop or pulse function until smooth.

Peach Paradise

Serves 3 or 4

Tip

Use soy or rice milk or regular milk if you prefer. Evaporated milk makes a thicker smoothie.

½ cup	evaporated milk (see Tip, left)	125 mL
¼ cup	blueberries	50 mL
2	peaches, halved	2
3 tbsp	plain or peach-flavored yogurt	45 mL
2 tbsp	chopped almonds	25 mL
¼ tsp	ground cinnamon	1 mL

1. In a blender, combine evaporated milk, blueberries, peaches, yogurt, almonds and cinnamon. Secure lid and process using the chop or pulse function until smooth.

Peaches and Cream

Serves 3 or 4

Tip

Use soy or rice milk or regular milk if you prefer. Evaporated milk makes a thicker smoothie.

1	can (14 oz/398 mL) peach halves or slices, drained	1
½ cup	evaporated milk (see Tip, left)	125 mL
½ cup	frozen peach slices	125 mL
¼ cup	silken tofu	50 mL
¼ tsp	almond extract	1 mL

1. In a blender, combine drained canned peaches, evaporated milk, frozen peaches, tofu and almond extract. Secure lid and blend (from low to high if using a variable speed blender) until smooth.

Peachy Currant

Serves 2

½ cup	freshly squeezed orange juice	125 mL
2	peaches, halved	2
1	red plum, halved	1
½ cup	black or red currants or raspberries	125 mL
2	ice cubes	2

1. In a blender, combine orange juice, peaches, plum, currants and ice. Secure lid and process using the chop or pulse function until smooth.

Serves 3 or 4	# Peachy Melon	
	½ cup	peach nectar	125 mL

Peachy Melon

½ cup	peach nectar	125 mL
¼ cup	freshly squeezed orange juice or mango nectar	50 mL
2	peaches, halved	2
2	apricots, halved	2
½ cup	chopped mango	125 mL
¼	cantaloupe, cubed	¼

Serves 3 or 4

1. In a blender, combine peach nectar, orange juice, peaches, apricots, mango and cantaloupe. Secure lid and blend (from low to high if using a variable speed blender) until smooth.

Pear Fennel

Serves 3

* Avoid licorice if you have high blood pressure. The prolonged use of licorice is not recommended under any circumstances.

½ cup	pear nectar or apple juice	125 mL
¼ cup	applesauce	50 mL
2	pears, quartered	2
1	banana, cut into chunks	1
½ cup	chopped fennel bulb	125 mL
¼ tsp	ground licorice*, optional	1 mL

1. In a blender, combine pear nectar, applesauce, pears, banana, fennel, and licorice, if using. Secure lid and blend (from low to high if using a variable speed blender) until smooth.

Pear Pineapple

¼ cup	grapefruit juice	50 mL
	Juice of 1 lemon	
1	pineapple wedge, cut into chunks	1
1	pear, quartered	1
½ cup	seedless red or green grapes	125 mL

1. In a blender, combine grapefruit juice, lemon juice, pineapple, pear and grapes. Secure lid and blend (from low to high if using a variable speed blender) until smooth.

Pear Raspberry

¼ cup	raspberry juice	50 mL
2 tbsp	freshly squeezed lemon juice	25 mL
2	pears, quartered	2
1 cup	raspberries	250 mL
¼ cup	vanilla-flavored frozen yogurt	50 mL

1. In a blender, combine raspberry juice, lemon juice, pears, raspberries and frozen yogurt. Secure lid and blend (from low to high if using a variable speed blender) until smooth.

Serves 3

Perfect in Pink

Tip
You can use fresh and frozen fruit interchangeably in most smoothies, although the results will differ. Frozen fruit not only chills a smoothie, it thickens it as well.

¼ cup	cranberry juice	50 mL
1 tbsp	freshly squeezed lemon juice	15 mL
1 cup	chopped watermelon	250 mL
½ cup	pitted cherries	125 mL
¼ cup	frozen raspberries	50 mL

1. In a blender, combine cranberry juice, lemon juice, watermelon, cherries and raspberries. Secure lid and blend (from low to high if using a variable speed blender) until smooth.

Serves 3

Pineapple-C

½ cup	freshly squeezed orange or pineapple juice	125 mL
	Juice of 1 lime	
2 tbsp	freshly squeezed lemon juice	25 mL
12	strawberries	12
1	pineapple wedge, cut into chunks	1

1. In a blender, combine orange juice, lime juice, lemon juice, strawberries and pineapple. Secure lid and blend (from low to high if using a variable speed blender) until smooth.

Pineapple Citrus

Serves 3

¼ cup	pineapple juice	50 mL
¼ cup	freshly squeezed orange juice	50 mL
	Juice of 1 lemon	
1	orange, sectioned and seeded	1
1	pineapple wedge, cut into chunks	1
1 tbsp	chopped fresh peppermint	15 mL

1. In a blender, combine pineapple juice, orange juice, lemon juice, orange, pineapple and peppermint. Secure lid and blend (from low to high if using a variable speed blender) until smooth.

Pineapple Crush

Serves 2

½ cup	pineapple juice	125 mL
1	red grapefruit, sectioned and seeded	1
1	pineapple wedge, cut into chunks	1
½ cup	halved strawberries	125 mL
2	ice cubes	2

1. In a blender, combine pineapple juice, grapefruit, pineapple, strawberries and ice. Secure lid and process using the chop or pulse function until smooth.

Pineapple Kiwi

½ cup	pineapple juice	125 mL
2	kiwifruits, quartered	2
2	apricots, halved	2
1	mango, halved	1
½ cup	plain yogurt	125 mL
¼ tsp	ground ginger	1 mL

1. In a blender, combine pineapple juice, kiwis, apricots, mango, yogurt and ginger. Secure lid and blend (from low to high if using a variable speed blender) until smooth.

Pineapple Soy

Tip

The sweetness of this smoothie will increase significantly if you use sweetened frozen yogurt rather than plain yogurt.

¼ cup	pineapple juice	50 mL
¼ cup	soy or rice milk	50 mL
1	banana, cut into chunks	1
2	pineapple wedges, cut into chunks	2
½ cup	plain yogurt or fruit-flavored frozen yogurt	125 mL

1. In a blender, combine pineapple juice, soy milk, banana, pineapple and yogurt. Secure lid and blend (from low to high if using a variable speed blender) until smooth.

Serves 1 or 2

Pineapple Tang

½ cup	pineapple juice	125 mL
2 tbsp	freshly squeezed lime juice	25 mL
1	pineapple wedge, cut into chunks	1
¼ cup	plain yogurt	50 mL

1. In a blender, combine pineapple juice, lime juice, pineapple and yogurt. Secure lid and blend (from low to high if using a variable speed blender) until smooth.

Serves 4

Pine-Berry

Tip

Try using homemade frozen yogurt (see recipes, pages 339 and 341) in this smoothie.

1	can (14 oz/398 mL) cherries with juice	1
¼ cup	plain or frozen yogurt	50 mL
2	pineapple wedges, cut into chunks	2
1 cup	blueberries	250 mL
½ cup	black currants	125 mL

1. In a blender, combine cherries with juice, yogurt, pineapple, blueberries and black currants. Secure lid and blend (from low to high if using a variable speed blender) until smooth.

Serves 1

Pink Pear

¼ cup	raspberry juice	50 mL
1	pear, quartered	1
1	orange, sectioned and seeded	1
½ cup	pomegranate seeds	125 mL
Pinch	ground nutmeg	Pinch

1. In a blender, combine raspberry juice, pear, orange sections and pomegranate seeds. Secure lid and blend (from low to high if using a variable speed blender) until smooth. Pour into glass and garnish with nutmeg.

Plum Berry

¾ cup	raspberry juice	175 mL
¼ cup	black currant or raspberry jam	50 mL
2	plums, quartered	2
1 cup	raspberries	250 mL

1. In a blender, combine raspberry juice, jam, plums and raspberries. Secure lid and blend (from low to high if using a variable speed blender) until smooth.

Plum Lico

* Avoid licorice if you have high blood pressure. The prolonged use of licorice is not recommended under any circumstances.

¼ cup	pineapple juice	50 mL
¼ cup	plain yogurt	50 mL
2	plums, quartered	2
1 cup	pitted cherries	250 mL
½	grapefruit, sectioned and seeded	½
¼ tsp	ground licorice*, optional	1 mL

1. In a blender, combine pineapple juice, yogurt, plums, cherries, grapefruit, and licorice, if using. Secure lid and blend (from low to high if using a variable speed blender) until smooth.

Plums Up

¾ cup	freshly squeezed orange juice	175 mL
2 tbsp	freshly squeezed lemon juice	25 mL
2	plums, quartered	2
1	pineapple wedge, cut into chunks	1
¼	cantaloupe, cubed	¼

1. In a blender, combine orange juice, lemon juice, plums, pineapple and cantaloupe. Secure lid and blend (from low to high if using a variable speed blender) until smooth.

Pomegranate Perfect

Serves 1

Tip
Use canned coconut milk or homemade Coconut Milk (page 315) in this smoothie.

½ cup	coconut milk (see Tip, left)	125 mL
1	slice watermelon, cut into chunks	1
½ cup	raspberries	125 mL
¼ cup	pomegranate seeds	50 mL

1. In a blender, combine coconut milk, watermelon, raspberries and pomegranate seeds. Secure lid and blend (from low to high if using a variable speed blender) until smooth.

Pomegranate Plus

Serves 2

½ cup	freshly squeezed orange juice	125 mL
½ cup	pomegranate seeds	125 mL
½ cup	pitted black cherries	125 mL
½ cup	halved strawberries	125 mL
1	red or black plum, halved	1

1. In a blender, combine orange juice, pomegranate seeds, cherries, strawberries and plum. Secure lid and blend (from low to high if using a variable speed blender) until smooth.

Pom Pom

Serves 2

¼ cup	pomegranate juice	50 mL
1	apple, quartered	1
1	red or black plum, halved	1
½ cup	pomegranate seeds	125 mL
½ cup	pitted cherries	125 mL

1. In a blender, combine pomegranate juice, apple, plum, pomegranate seeds and cherries. Secure lid and blend (from low to high if using a variable speed blender) until smooth.

Prune

1 cup	soy or rice milk	250 mL
¼ cup	chopped prunes	50 mL
1	banana, cut into chunks	1

1. In a blender, combine soy milk, prunes and banana. Secure lid and blend (from low to high if using a variable speed blender) until smooth.

Pump It Up

¾ cup	soy or rice milk	175 mL
½ cup	pitted cherries	125 mL
1	banana, cut into chunks	1
¼ cup	blueberries	50 mL
1 tbsp	protein powder	15 mL
2 tbsp	chopped almonds	25 mL

1. In a blender, combine soy milk, cherries, banana, blueberries, protein powder and almonds. Secure lid and blend (from low to high if using a variable speed blender) until smooth.

Serves 1

Pumpkin Apricot and Date

½ cup	soy or rice milk	125 mL
½ cup	pumpkin purée	125 mL
¼ cup	chopped dried apricots	50 mL
3	pitted dates	3
1	slice or cube candied ginger, chopped	1
1 tsp	brown sugar	5 mL
Pinch	ground nutmeg	Pinch
3	ice cubes	3

1. In a blender, combine soy milk, pumpkin, apricots, dates, ginger, brown sugar, nutmeg and ice. Secure lid and process using the chop or pulse function until smooth.

Serves 1

Raisin Pie

½ cup	soy or rice milk	125 mL
1 tbsp	freshly squeezed lemon juice	15 mL
1 cup	seedless red grapes	250 mL
¼ cup	raisins	50 mL
1 tbsp	steel-cut or rolled oats	15 mL
¼ tsp	ground cinnamon	1 mL

1. In a blender, combine soy milk, lemon juice, grapes, raisins, oats and cinnamon. Secure lid and blend (from low to high if using a variable speed blender) until smooth.

Serves 4		

Raspberry

½ cup	freshly squeezed orange juice	125 mL
1 cup	raspberries	250 mL
2	apricots, halved	2
1	peach, halved	1
¼ cup	plain yogurt	50 mL

1. In a blender, combine orange juice, raspberries, apricots, peach and yogurt. Secure lid and blend (from low to high if using a variable speed blender) until smooth.

Serves 2 or 3		

Razzy Orange

½ cup	freshly squeezed orange juice	125 mL
½ cup	frozen raspberries	125 mL
1	orange, sectioned and seeded	1
¼ cup	raspberry- or orange-flavored yogurt	50 mL

1. In a blender, combine orange juice, raspberries, orange and yogurt. Secure lid and blend (from low to high if using a variable speed blender) until smooth.

Serves 2		

Real Raspberry

Tips

The sweetness of this smoothie will increase significantly if you use sweetened frozen yogurt rather than plain yogurt.

You can use any berry — raspberry, strawberry, blueberry or blackberry — in this sweet summer drink.

½ cup	cranberry-raspberry juice	125 mL
1 cup	raspberries	250 mL
½ cup	pitted cherries	125 mL
½ cup	blueberries	125 mL
¼ cup	raspberry-flavored frozen yogurt	50 mL

1. In a blender, combine cranberry-raspberry juice, raspberries, cherries, blueberries and frozen yogurt. Secure lid and blend (from low to high if using a variable speed blender) until smooth.

Red, Black and Blue

Serves 2

Tip

Raspberries vary in sweetness, depending upon the variety and/or growing conditions. Pineapple juice is a natural sweetener, but after blending, taste for yourself and add honey, in 1-tsp (5 mL) increments, until this drink is sweet enough for you.

½ cup	pineapple juice	125 mL
½ cup	black currants or blackberries	125 mL
½ cup	raspberries	125 mL
½ cup	blueberries	125 mL
1	banana, cut into chunks	1
2 tbsp	liquid honey, or to taste	25 mL

1. In a blender, combine pineapple juice, black currants, raspberries, blueberries, banana and honey. Secure lid and blend (from low to high if using a variable speed blender) until smooth.

Red Delight

Serves 2

* Raw elderberries can make some people sick. If in doubt, cook in a small amount of water, cool and drain.

½ cup	cranberry juice	125 mL
1	slice watermelon, cut into cubes	1
½ cup	pomegranate seeds or elderberries*	125 mL
¼ cup	raspberries	50 mL

1. In a blender, combine cranberry juice, watermelon, pomegranate seeds and raspberries. Secure lid and blend (from low to high if using a variable speed blender) until smooth.

Red Horizon

Serves 2

½ cup	freshly squeezed orange juice	125 mL
2	red or black plums, halved	2
1	orange, sectioned and seeded	1
½ cup	pomegranate seeds	125 mL
¼ cup	raspberries	50 mL

1. In a blender, combine orange juice, plums, orange, pomegranate seeds and raspberries. Secure lid and blend (from low to high if using a variable speed blender) until smooth.

Rhubarb Apple

¼ cup	apple juice	50 mL
½ cup	applesauce	125 mL
½ cup	sweetened cooked rhubarb	125 mL
1	apple, quartered	1

Tip

To cook rhubarb: In a saucepan, cover chopped fresh or frozen rhubarb with water. Add ¼ cup (50 mL) granulated sugar (or to taste) for every cup (250 mL) of chopped rhubarb. Bring to a boil over medium heat. Boil, stirring occasionally, for 8 minutes or until soft and water has almost evaporated.

1. In a blender, combine apple juice, applesauce, rhubarb and chopped apple. Secure lid and blend (from low to high if using a variable speed blender) until smooth.

Rhubarb Pie

⅓ cup	raspberry juice	75 mL
1 cup	sweetened cooked rhubarb (see Tip, above)	250 mL
½ cup	halved strawberries	125 mL
2 tbsp	plain yogurt	25 mL

1. In a blender, combine raspberry juice, rhubarb, strawberries and yogurt. Secure lid and blend (from low to high if using a variable speed blender) until smooth.

Rhubarb Pineapple

½ cup	pineapple juice	125 mL
¼ cup	chopped fresh rhubarb (see Tip, left)	50 mL
1	pineapple wedge, cut into chunks	1
1	peach, halved	1

Tip

Use this as a laxative smoothie or use cooked rhubarb.

1. In a blender, combine pineapple juice, rhubarb, pineapple and peach. Secure lid and blend (from low to high if using a variable speed blender) until smooth.

Rhubarb Smoothie

½ cup	cranberry-apple juice	125 mL
¼ cup	sweetened cooked rhubarb (see Tip, page 211)	50 mL
1	banana, cut into chunks	1

1. In a blender, combine cranberry-apple juice, rhubarb and banana. Secure lid and blend (from low to high if using a variable speed blender) until smooth.

Tip
Substitute any dried sea herb (page 149) for the dulse in this recipe.

Sea-Straw

½ cup	grapefruit juice	125 mL
6	strawberries	6
3 tbsp	chopped pitted dates	45 mL
1 tsp	crushed dulse	5 mL

1. In a blender, combine grapefruit juice, strawberries, dates and dulse. Secure lid and blend (from low to high if using a variable speed blender) until smooth.

Sher-Lime

½ cup	freshly squeezed orange juice	125 mL
3 tbsp	freshly squeezed lime juice	45 mL
2	kiwifruits, quartered	2
¼ cup	seedless green grapes	50 mL
¼ cup	lime sherbet	50 mL

1. In a blender, combine orange juice, lime juice, kiwis, grapes and sherbet. Secure lid and blend (from low to high if using a variable speed blender) until smooth.

Sour Cherry

¼ cup	cranberry juice	50 mL
1 cup	pitted black cherries	250 mL
½ cup	raspberries	125 mL
⅓ cup	plain yogurt	75 mL

1. In a blender, combine cranberry juice, cherries, raspberries and yogurt. Secure lid and blend (from low to high if using a variable speed blender) until smooth.

Special Date

Tip

You can use fresh and frozen fruit interchangeably in most smoothies, although the results will differ. Frozen fruit not only chills a smoothie, it also makes it thicker.

¾ cup	freshly squeezed orange juice	175 mL
2 tbsp	freshly squeezed lemon juice	25 mL
¼ cup	pitted dates	50 mL
1	orange, sectioned and seeded	1

1. In a blender, combine orange juice, lemon juice, dates and orange. Secure lid and blend (from low to high if using a variable speed blender) until smooth.

Strawberry Blush

1	can (14 oz/398 mL) diced beets in water	1
¼ cup	cranberry sauce	50 mL
½ cup	strawberries	125 mL
1 tbsp	chopped pitted dates	15 mL
6	ice cubes	6

1. In a blender, combine beets with liquid, cranberry sauce, strawberries, dates and ice cubes. Secure lid and process using the chop or pulse function until smooth.

Strawberry Cooler

Tip
Use canned coconut milk or homemade Coconut Milk (page 315) in this smoothie.

½ cup	coconut milk (see Tip, left)	125 mL
¼ cup	pineapple juice	50 mL
1 cup	halved strawberries	250 mL
½ cup	frozen whole açai berries or açai berry pulp, partially thawed	125 mL

1. In a blender, combine coconut milk, pineapple juice, strawberries and açai berries. Secure lid and blend (from low to high if using a variable speed blender) until smooth.

Strawberry Sparkle

½ cup	cranberry juice	125 mL
½ cup	pomegranate seeds	125 mL
½ cup	frozen raspberries	125 mL
½ cup	halved strawberries	125 mL

1. In a blender, combine cranberry juice, pomegranate seeds, raspberries and strawberries. Secure lid and blend (from low to high if using a variable speed blender) until smooth.

Strawberry Swirl

½ cup	cranberry-raspberry juice	125 mL
2 tbsp	freshly squeezed lemon juice	25 mL
10	frozen strawberries	10
¼ cup	frozen raspberries	50 mL
2 tbsp	plain yogurt	25 mL

1. In a blender, combine cranberry-raspberry juice, lemon juice, strawberries, raspberries and yogurt. Secure lid and blend (from low to high if using a variable speed blender) until smooth.

Sun on the Water

½ cup	freshly squeezed orange juice	125 mL
1 tbsp	freshly squeezed lemon juice	15 mL
1	slice watermelon, cut into chunks	1
1	red grapefruit, sectioned and seeded	1

1. In a blender, combine orange juice, lemon juice, watermelon and grapefruit. Secure lid and blend (from low to high if using a variable speed blender) until smooth.

Sunrise Supreme

½ cup	white grape juice	125 mL
1 cup	seedless red grapes	250 mL
12	strawberries	12
½ cup	raspberries	125 mL
1	orange, sectioned and seeded	1

1. In a blender, combine grape juice, grapes, strawberries, raspberries and orange. Secure lid and blend (from low to high if using a variable speed blender) until smooth.

Sweet and Sour Strawberry

½ cup	raspberry juice	125 mL
1 tsp	balsamic vinegar	5 mL
½ cup	halved strawberries	125 mL
¼ cup	frozen raspberries	50 mL

1. In a blender, combine raspberry juice, balsamic vinegar, strawberries and raspberries. Secure lid and blend (from low to high if using a variable speed blender) until smooth.

Tangerine

Serves 1 or 2

½ cup	freshly squeezed tangerine or orange juice	125 mL
2 tbsp	freshly squeezed lemon juice	25 mL
2	tangerines, sectioned and seeded	2
1 cup	seedless red grapes	250 mL

1. In a blender, combine tangerine juice, lemon juice, tangerines and grapes. Secure lid and blend (from low to high if using a variable speed blender) until smooth.

Tart and Tingly

Serves 1

Tip

You can use fresh and frozen fruit interchangeably in most smoothies, although the results will differ. Frozen fruit not only chills a smoothie, it thickens it as well.

*Some people have an adverse reaction to raw elderberries. If in doubt, cook, cool and drain before using.

¼ cup	cranberry juice	50 mL
2	kiwifruits, quartered	2
½ cup	frozen blueberries or elderberries*	125 mL
	Honey, to taste	

1. In a blender, combine cranberry juice, kiwis and blueberries. Secure lid and blend (from low to high if using a variable speed blender) until smooth. Pour into a glass and add honey, if desired.

Taste of the Tropics

Serves 4

½ cup	freshly squeezed orange juice	125 mL
	Juice of 1 lime	
½	papaya	½
1	pineapple wedge, cut into chunks	1
1 tbsp	chopped fresh peppermint	15 mL

1. In a blender, combine orange juice, lime juice, papaya, pineapple and peppermint. Secure lid and blend (from low to high if using a variable speed blender) until smooth.

Serves 2		

Tree Fruit Smoothie

⅔ cup	apple juice	150 mL
1	pear, quartered	1
1	apple, quartered	1
1	red plum, halved	1
1	black plum, halved	1

1. In a blender, combine apple juice, pear, apple and red and black plums. Secure lid and blend (from low to high if using a variable speed blender) until smooth.

Serves 1 or 2		

Triple A

½ cup	apricot or peach nectar or Apricot Milk (page 312)	125 mL
2	apricots, halved	2
1	apple, quartered	1
2 tbsp	chopped almonds	25 mL
¼ tsp	almond extract, optional	1 mL

1. In a blender, combine apricot nectar, apricots, apple, almonds, and almond extract, if using. Secure lid and blend (from low to high if using a variable speed blender) until smooth.

Tropi-Cocktail

Serves 2

¼ cup	apricot nectar or freshly squeezed orange juice	50 mL
½ cup	plain yogurt	125 mL
¼	cantaloupe or honeydew melon, cubed	¼
½	mango	½
1	slice papaya	1
1	banana, cut into chunks	1

1. In a blender, combine apricot nectar, yogurt, cantaloupe, mango, papaya and banana. Secure lid and blend (from low to high if using a variable speed blender) until smooth.

Tropics

Serves 2

Tip
Use canned coconut milk or homemade Coconut Milk (page 315) in this smoothie.

½ cup	coconut milk (see Tip, left)	125 mL
2	kiwifruits, quartered	2
½	papaya	½
1	banana, cut into chunks	1
½ cup	chopped pineapple	125 mL

1. In a blender, combine coconut milk, kiwis, papaya, banana and pineapple. Secure lid and blend (from low to high if using a variable speed blender) until smooth.

Tutti-Figgy

Serves 1

½ cup	apple juice	125 mL
4	fresh figs	4
4	red or black plums, halved	4
¼ cup	fresh or frozen blueberries	50 mL
1	scoop vanilla-flavored frozen yogurt	1

1. In a blender, combine apple juice, figs, plums, blueberries and frozen yogurt. Secure lid and blend (from low to high if using a variable speed blender) until smooth.

Serves 1

Tutti-Fruity

½ cup	pomegranate-blueberry juice	125 mL
¼ cup	frozen raspberries	50 mL
¼ cup	frozen strawberries	50 mL
¼ cup	frozen blueberries	50 mL
1	scoop vanilla-flavored frozen yogurt	1

1. In a blender, combine pomegranate-blueberry juice, raspberries, strawberries, blueberries and frozen yogurt. Secure lid and blend (from low to high if using a variable speed blender) until smooth.

Tips

Pure pomegranate juice and pomegranate juice mixed with other fruit juice is now widely available, but you may substitute apple or raspberry juice for the pomegranate-blueberry juice, if necessary.

The frozen berries make this a very thick drink. You can use fresh, if desired.

Serves 1

Wake Up and Shine

⅓ cup	freshly squeezed orange juice	75 mL
½ cup	halved strawberries	125 mL
½	grapefruit, sectioned and seeded	½
2 tbsp	plain yogurt	25 mL
1 tsp	blue-green algae, optional	5 mL

1. In a blender, combine orange juice, strawberries, grapefruit, yogurt, and algae, if using. Secure lid and blend (from low to high if using a variable speed blender) until smooth.

Serves 2 or 3

Watermelon

¼ cup	freshly squeezed orange juice	50 mL
1 tbsp	freshly squeezed lemon juice	15 mL
1 cup	chopped watermelon	250 mL
2	plums, quartered	2
⅓ cup	plain yogurt	75 mL

1. In a blender, combine orange juice, lemon juice, watermelon, plums and yogurt. Secure lid and blend (from low to high if using a variable speed blender) until smooth.

Watermelon-Strawberry Splash

Serves 2 or 3

½ cup	raspberry or cranberry juice	125 mL
2 tbsp	freshly squeezed lemon juice	25 mL
1 cup	chopped watermelon	250 mL
6	frozen strawberries	6

1. In a blender, combine raspberry juice, lemon juice, watermelon and strawberries. Secure lid and blend (from low to high if using a variable speed blender) until smooth.

Watermelon Wave

Serves 1 or 2

¼ cup	freshly squeezed orange juice	50 mL
1 tbsp	freshly squeezed lime juice	15 mL
1 cup	chopped watermelon	250 mL
2	nectarines, halved	2

1. In a blender, combine orange juice, lime juice, watermelon and nectarines. Secure lid and blend (from low to high if using a variable speed blender) until smooth.

Vegetable Smoothies

Using Vegetables in Smoothies

Because cooking destroys some nutrients, try smoothies made with milder-tasting raw vegetables, such as celery, carrots, cucumbers, eggplants or zucchini first. Then try stronger-tasting raw vegetables, such as cauliflower, peas or broccoli. If you find their flavor too strong, you will know that you want to cook these vegetables before or after blending. Cooking softens both the taste and the texture of vegetables. Some vegetables, especially hard root vegetables — such as beets, potatoes and parsnips — must be cooked before you can use them in smoothies, because they cannot be liquefied in their raw state by ordinary blenders.

Cooking fresh vegetables: Broccoli, carrots, cauliflower, peas and beans may be parboiled (cooked for one to three minutes in boiling water) before adding to smoothies. Denser vegetables, such as beets, potatoes or parsnips, require a longer cooking time, five to seven minutes or until soft. Roasting vegetables before using them in smoothies adds a rich, sweet taste (see Roasted Eggplant, page 247). Alternatively, after blending, raw vegetable smoothies can be simmered on top of the stove for seven to 12 minutes or until the vegetables are tender. For convenience, save leftover cooked vegetables for use in smoothies.

Frozen vegetables are convenient for smoothies because, in addition to being consistently available, they save cooking time and are easy to measure. Add up to 1 cup (250 mL) cooked frozen vegetables to smoothie recipes.

To freeze fresh vegetables: Peel (if not organic), trim off stems and woody parts and cut into pieces or chunks. Drop vegetable pieces into a large pot of boiling water and return to a simmer (just under a full boil). Simmer for 3 minutes, then drain and immerse in cold water for 3 minutes. Drain, pat dry and seal in a freezer container.

Liquids for Vegetable Smoothies

In addition to vegetable juices, homemade vegetable, meat or poultry stocks and miso soup work well in smoothies, because no unwanted ingredients are added. Canned spaghetti sauce, clams, consommé or liquid soup bases or ready-to-use broth may replace vegetable juices in vegetable smoothie recipes, but look for low-sodium products that contain no additives. Herbal teas (parsley, dandelion, burdock and others) may also be used in vegetable smoothies (see page 256 for how to use medicinal herbal teas in smoothies). Fruit and nut milks (see pages 312 to 316) give extra texture, flavor and/or sweetness to vegetable smoothies.

Apple Beet Pear

Tip

Substitute 1 cup (250 mL) cooked chopped beets for the canned. Increase apple juice by ¼ cup (50 mL).

1	can (14 or 15 oz/398 or 425 mL) diced beets in water	1
1 tbsp	freshly squeezed lemon juice	15 mL
¼ cup	apple juice	50 mL
1	pear, quartered	1
1	apple, quartered	1
1 tsp	chopped fresh savory	5 mL

1. In a blender, combine beets with liquid, lemon juice, apple juice, pear, apple and savory. Secure lid and blend (from low to high if using a variable speed blender) until smooth.

Apple Carrot Cucumber

Serves 1

Tip

Blanching the carrot will make it softer, but try it raw for a change in this smoothie.

¼ cup	apple juice	50 mL
1 tbsp	freshly squeezed lemon juice	15 mL
1	carrot, cut into chunks	1
½	cucumber, cut into chunks	½

1. In a blender, combine apple juice, lemon juice, carrot and cucumber. Secure lid and blend (from low to high if using a variable speed blender) until smooth.

Appled Beet

Serves 1

½ cup	apple juice	125 mL
1 cup	cooked sliced beets	250 mL
1	apple, quartered	1
½ cup	packed spinach	125 mL
1 tsp	fresh thyme	5 mL

1. In a blender, combine apple juice, beets, apple, spinach and thyme. Secure lid and blend (from low to high if using a variable speed blender) until smooth.

Asparagus Mango

Serves 1

½ cup	carrot juice	125 mL
1	mango, quartered	1
1 cup	cooked chopped asparagus	250 mL
½	avocado	½
2	ice cubes	2

1. In a blender, combine carrot juice, mango, asparagus, avocado and ice. Secure lid and process using the chop or pulse function until smooth.

Avocado Orange

Serves 2 or 3

½ cup	freshly squeezed orange juice	125 mL
2 tbsp	freshly squeezed lemon juice	25 mL
1	orange, sectioned and seeded	1
4	fresh or dried figs, quartered	4
½	avocado	½
2	frozen banana chunks	2

1. In a blender, combine orange juice, lemon juice, orange, figs, avocado and banana. Secure lid and blend (from low to high if using a variable speed blender) until smooth.

Avocado Pineapple

Serves 1

¾ cup	raspberry juice	175 mL
1 cup	chopped pineapple	250 mL
1	avocado, halved	1

1. In a blender, combine raspberry juice, pineapple and avocado. Secure lid and blend (from low to high if using a variable speed blender) until smooth.

Beet

Serves 2 or 3

½ cup	beet or carrot juice	125 mL
¾ cup	cooked chopped beets	175 mL
½ cup	cooked chopped carrots	125 mL
½ cup	vegetable or chicken broth	125 mL
¼ tsp	salt, or to taste	1 mL

1. In a blender, combine beet juice, beets, carrots and broth. Secure lid and blend (from low to high if using a variable speed blender) until smooth. Season with salt.

Blazing Beets

Serves 3 or 4

1	can (14 or 15 oz/398 or 425 mL) beets	1
½ cup	apple juice	125 mL
2	apples, quartered	2
2	stalks celery, chopped	2
1	piece (½ inch/1 cm) gingerroot, peeled	1
½	fresh chile pepper, chopped	½
1	clove garlic	1

1. In a blender, combine beets with liquid, apple juice, apples, celery, ginger, chile pepper and garlic. Secure lid and blend (from low to high if using a variable speed blender) until smooth.

Brocco-Carrot

Serves 1

½ cup	carrot juice	125 mL
¼ cup	apple or orange juice	50 mL
1 cup	cooked fresh or thawed frozen spinach	250 mL
½ cup	chopped cooked or thawed frozen broccoli	125 mL
1	apple, quartered	1
¼ tsp	salt, or to taste	1 mL

1. In a blender, combine carrot juice, apple juice, spinach, broccoli and apple. Secure lid and blend (from low to high if using a variable speed blender) until smooth. Season with salt. Serve hot or cold with a spoon.

Cabbage Cocktail

Serves 1 or 2

* If you are pregnant, limit your intake of parsley to ½ tsp (2 mL) dried or one sprig fresh per day. Do not take parsley if you are suffering from kidney inflammation.

½ cup	apple juice	125 mL
¼ cup	carrot juice	50 mL
1 cup	chopped bok choy	250 mL
1	stalk celery, cut into chunks	1
1	sprig parsley*	1
1 tsp	chopped fresh dill	5 mL
¼ tsp	salt, or to taste	1 mL

1. In a blender, combine apple juice, carrot juice, bok choy, celery, parsley and dill. Secure lid and blend (from low to high if using a variable speed blender) until smooth. Season with salt.

Cajun Cocktail

* If you are pregnant, limit your intake of parsley to ½ tsp (2 mL) dried or one sprig fresh per day. Do not take parsley if you are suffering from kidney inflammation.

½ cup	tomato juice	125 mL
	Juice of 1 lime	
2	tomatoes, quartered	2
1	small zucchini, cut into chunks	1
1	clove garlic	1
1	sprig parsley*	1
1	chile pepper, chopped	1
½ tsp	prepared horseradish	2 mL
¼ tsp	dill seeds	1 mL

1. In a blender, combine tomato juice, lime juice, tomatoes, zucchini, garlic, parsley, chile pepper, horseradish and dill seeds. Secure lid and blend (from low to high if using a variable speed blender) until smooth.

Carrot Lime

½ cup	freshly squeezed orange juice	125 mL
1 cup	cooked sliced carrots	250 mL
½	lime, sectioned and seeded	½
¼ cup	plain yogurt	50 mL
2	ice cubes	2

1. In a blender, combine orange juice, carrots, lime, yogurt and ice. Secure lid and process using the chop or pulse function until smooth.

Carrot Pineapple

Serves 1

¼ cup	freshly squeezed orange juice	50 mL
2 tbsp	freshly squeezed lemon juice	25 mL
½ cup	cooked chopped carrots	125 mL
1	pineapple wedge, cut into chunks	1
3	ice cubes	3

1. In a blender, combine orange juice, lemon juice, carrots, pineapple and ice. Secure lid and process using the chop or pulse function until smooth.

Carrot Raisin Cooler

Serves 1 or 2

¼ cup	freshly squeezed orange juice	50 mL
½ cup	chopped carrots	125 mL
½ cup	plain yogurt	125 mL
¼ cup	raisins	50 mL
¼ tsp	ground nutmeg	1 mL
6	ice cubes (page 319)	6

1. In a blender, combine orange juice, carrots, yogurt, raisins, nutmeg and ice cubes. Secure lid and blend (from low to high if using a variable speed blender) until smooth.

Carrot Squash

Serves 4

Variation

Use low-fat yogurt in place of the cream, if desired.

1 cup	vegetable or chicken broth	250 mL
1 cup	cooked squash	250 mL
½ cup	cooked chopped carrots	125 mL
1	apple, quartered	1
¼	onion	¼
½ tsp	garam masala	2 mL
¼ tsp	dry mustard	1 mL
Pinch	ground nutmeg	Pinch
½ cup	table (18%) cream or milk	125 mL
¼ tsp	salt, or to taste	1 mL

Garnish, optional

¼ cup	sour cream	50 mL
½ tsp	ground nutmeg	2 mL

1. In a blender, combine broth, squash, carrots, apple, onion, garam masala, mustard and nutmeg. Secure lid and blend on low for 30 seconds.

2. With blender still running, add cream through opening in center of lid. Blend just until smooth. Season with salt. Serve hot or cold with a spoon.

3. *Garnish:* Top with sour cream and nutmeg, if using.

Cauliflower Cocktail

1 cup	carrot juice	250 mL
¼ cup	cooked chopped cauliflower	50 mL
1	tomato, quartered	1
½ cup	cooked chopped carrot	125 mL
1	stalk celery, cut into chunks	1
1 tsp	flaked kelp	5 mL
¼ tsp	ground turmeric	1 mL

1. In a blender, combine carrot juice, cauliflower, tomato, carrot, celery, kelp and turmeric. Secure lid and blend (from low to high if using a variable speed blender) until smooth.

Celery Cream

½ cup	soy or rice milk	125 mL
¼ cup	chopped celery	50 mL
¼ cup	chopped fennel bulb or celeriac, optional	50 mL
1	tomato, quartered	1
½ tsp	curry powder	2 mL
¼ tsp	ground turmeric	1 mL
Pinch	ground cumin	Pinch

1. In a blender, combine soy milk, celery, fennel, tomato, curry powder, turmeric and cumin. Secure lid and blend (from low to high if using a variable speed blender) until smooth.

C-Green

* If you are pregnant, limit your intake of parsley to ½ tsp (2 mL) dried or one sprig fresh per day. Do not take parsley if you are suffering from kidney inflammation.

¾ cup	apple juice	175 mL
1 cup	chopped spinach	250 mL
½	avocado	½
1 tbsp	chopped fresh parsley*	15 mL
1 tbsp	chopped watercress	15 mL

1. In a blender, combine apple juice, spinach, avocado, parsley and watercress. Secure lid and blend (from low to high if using a variable speed blender) until smooth.

Cheesy Broccoli

Tip

Taste and add up to double the amounts of curry and turmeric, if desired.

1 cup	milk or soy milk	250 mL
½	clove garlic	½
1 cup	cooked potato or rice	250 mL
1 cup	cooked chopped broccoli	250 mL
⅓ cup	shredded Cheddar cheese	75 mL
¼ tsp	curry powder, optional	1 mL
¼ tsp	ground turmeric	1 mL
¼ tsp	salt, or to taste	1 mL

1. In a small saucepan over medium heat, bring milk just to a boil; pour half into blender. Keep remaining milk warm. Add garlic, potato, broccoli, cheese, curry powder (if using), and turmeric to blender. Secure lid and blend on low for 30 seconds.

2. With blender still running, add remaining hot milk through opening in center of lid. Blend just until smooth. Season with salt. Serve hot or cold with a spoon.

Clam Beet

Serves 3 or 4

Tip
Substitute 1 cup (250 mL) cooked chopped beets for the canned. Add ¼ cup (50 mL) vegetable or tomato juice.

1	can (10 oz/284 mL) clams (minced or whole)	1
1	can (14 or 15 oz/398 or 425 mL) diced beets in water	1
1	stalk celery, cut into chunks	1
1 tbsp	chopped onion	15 mL
2 to 4	dashes hot pepper sauce, optional	2 to 4

1. In a blender, combine clams with juice, beets with liquid, celery and onion. Secure lid and blend (from low to high if using a variable speed blender) until smooth. Season with hot pepper sauce if using.

Clam Tomato

Serves 3 or 4

Tip
This is a delicious nonalcoholic substitute for a Bloody Caesar, which is made with vodka.

1	can (10 oz/284 mL) clams (minced or whole)	1
4	tomatoes, quartered	4
¼ cup	spaghetti sauce	50 mL
	Juice of ½ lemon	
1	stalk celery, cut into chunks	1
1 tsp	chopped fresh thyme	5 mL
1 or 2	dashes hot pepper sauce, optional	1 or 2

1. In a blender, combine clams with liquid, tomatoes, spaghetti sauce, lemon juice, celery, thyme, and hot pepper sauce if using. Secure lid and blend (from low to high if using a variable speed blender) until smooth.

Serves 1 or 2

Corn Chowder

1 cup	chicken or vegetable broth	250 mL
1 cup	corn kernels	250 mL
1	small potato, peeled and chopped	1
2 tbsp	chopped onion	25 mL
1	fresh sage leaf	1
1 tsp	fresh thyme	5 mL
¼ cup	milk or table (18%) cream	50 mL
¼ tsp	salt, or to taste	1 mL

1. In a medium saucepan over medium heat, bring broth, corn, potato, onion, sage and thyme just to a boil. Cover, reduce heat to low and simmer for 7 to 10 minutes or until vegetables are tender. Pour into blender and blend on low for 30 seconds.

2. With blender still running, add milk through opening in center of lid. Blend just until smooth. Season with salt. Serve hot or cold with a spoon.

Creamed Onions

¾ cup	milk	175 mL
2	onions, quartered	2
1	stalk celery, cut into chunks	1
1	parsnip, cut into chunks	1
¼ cup	chopped fennel bulb	50 mL
¼ tsp	ground star anise	1 mL
Pinch	ground nutmeg	Pinch

1. In a medium saucepan over medium heat, bring milk just to a boil. Add onions, celery, parsnip and fennel. Reduce heat to low and simmer for 12 minutes or until vegetables are soft.

2. Pour milk mixture into blender. Add star anise and nutmeg. Secure lid and blend (from low to high if using a variable speed blender) until smooth. Thin with more milk, if desired. Serve hot or cold with a spoon.

Cream of Broccoli

Tip
Blanching vegetables makes them easier to blend for drinks. To blanch vegetables, immerse in boiling water for 1 to 2 minutes. Remove and plunge into cold water. Drain well.

¼ cup	soy milk or coconut milk	50 mL
2	spears broccoli, blanched	2
1 cup	cauliflower florets, blanched	250 mL
1 cup	packed spinach	250 mL
3 tbsp	crumbled feta cheese	45 mL
1 tbsp	drained plain yogurt	15 mL

1. In a blender, combine soy milk, broccoli, cauliflower, spinach and feta cheese. Secure lid and blend (from low to high if using a variable speed blender) until smooth. Pour into a glass and garnish with yogurt.

Creamy Chickpea

* If you are pregnant, limit your intake of parsley to ½ tsp (2 mL) dried or one sprig fresh per day. Do not take parsley if you are suffering from kidney inflammation.

1 cup	chicken or vegetable broth	250 mL
½ cup	chopped cooked potato	125 mL
⅓ cup	cooked chickpeas	75 mL
1 tbsp	chopped onion	15 mL
¼	clove garlic	¼
1	sprig parsley*	1
¼ cup	half-and-half (10%) cream or milk	50 mL
¼ tsp	salt, or to taste	1 mL

1. In a small saucepan over high heat, bring broth to a boil; pour half into blender. Reduce heat to low; keep remaining stock warm. Add potato, chickpeas, onion, garlic and parsley to blender. Secure lid and blend on low for 30 seconds or just until smooth.

2. With blender running, add cream through opening in center of lid. Blend just until combined. Season with salt. Serve hot or cold.

Creamy Fennel

Tip

Use canned coconut milk or homemade Coconut Milk (page 315) in this smoothie.

½ cup	coconut milk (see Tip, left)	125 mL
1 cup	chopped fennel bulb	250 mL
1	apple, quartered	1
1 tsp	fennel seeds	5 mL

1. In a blender, combine coconut milk, chopped fennel, apple and fennel seeds. Secure lid and blend (from low to high if using a variable speed blender) until smooth.

Flaming Antibiotic

Serves 2 or 3

½ cup	tomato juice	125 mL
2	tomatoes, quartered	2
1	apple, quartered	1
½ cup	cooked chopped carrots	125 mL
½	cucumber, cut into chunks	½
½	clove garlic	½
1	chile pepper, chopped	1
2 tsp	fresh thyme	10 mL

1. In a blender, combine tomato juice, tomatoes, apple, carrots, cucumber, garlic, chile pepper and thyme. Secure lid and blend (from low to high if using a variable speed blender) until smooth.

Garden Goodness

Serves 2

* If you are pregnant, limit your intake of parsley to ½ tsp (2 mL) dried or one sprig fresh per day. Do not take parsley if you are suffering from kidney inflammation.

¾ cup	quartered fresh or canned tomatoes	175 mL
1 tbsp	freshly squeezed lemon juice	15 mL
½ cup	chopped leafy greens (page 111)	125 mL
¼ cup	chopped carrots	50 mL
2 tbsp	chopped red or green bell pepper	25 mL
1	sprig parsley*	1
1 tbsp	raisins	15 mL
1 tsp	chopped onion	5 mL
¼ tsp	celery seeds	1 mL
1 cup	ice cubes	250 mL

1. In a blender, combine tomatoes, lemon juice, greens, carrots, pepper, parsley, raisins, onion, celery seeds and ice cubes. Secure lid and process using the chop or pulse function until smooth.

Gazpacho

Serves 2 or 3

½ cup	tomato juice or spaghetti sauce	125 mL
2	tomatoes, quartered	2
1	apple, quartered	1
½	cucumber, cut into chunks	½
1 tbsp	chopped onion	15 mL
¼	clove garlic	¼
2 tsp	chopped fresh cilantro	10 mL

1. In a blender, combine tomato juice, tomatoes, apple, cucumber, onion, garlic and cilantro. Secure lid and blend (from low to high if using a variable speed blender) until smooth.

Gingered Beets

Serves 1

¼ cup	vegetable or chicken broth	50 mL
1	beet, chopped and cooked	1
¼	fennel bulb, sliced	¼
½	avocado	½
1 tsp	grated gingerroot	5 mL

1. In a blender, combine broth, beet, fennel, avocado and ginger. Secure lid and blend (from low to high if using a variable speed blender) until smooth.

Gingered Greens

Serves 1

¼ cup	vegetable or chicken broth	50 mL
1 cup	cooked chopped asparagus	250 mL
½ cup	cooked chopped broccoli	125 mL
1 tsp	grated gingerroot	5 mL

1. In a blender, combine broth, asparagus, broccoli and ginger. Secure lid and blend (from low to high if using a variable speed blender) until smooth.

Green Gift

Serves 2

* If you are pregnant, limit your intake of parsley to ½ tsp (2 mL) dried or one sprig fresh per day. Do not take parsley if you are suffering from kidney inflammation.

⅔ cup	steeped green tea, chilled	150 mL
1 cup	chopped kale	250 mL
½ cup	broccoli florets	125 mL
½ cup	green grapes	125 mL
4	sprigs parsley*	4

1. In a blender, combine green tea, kale, broccoli, grapes and parsley. Secure lid and blend (from low to high if using a variable speed blender) until smooth.

Green Gold

Serves 1 or 2

⅔ cup	carrot juice	150 mL
⅓ cup	apple juice	75 mL
½ cup	chopped fresh or frozen spinach	125 mL
½	cucumber, cut into chunks	½
1	apple, quartered	1
2 tsp	chopped fresh basil	10 mL

1. In a blender, combine carrot juice, apple juice, spinach, cucumber, apple and basil. Secure lid and blend (from low to high if using a variable speed blender) until smooth.

Herbed Cauliflower

Serves 3 or 4

1 cup	milk	250 mL
¾ cup	chopped cooked cauliflower	175 mL
¼	onion	¼
¼ cup	shredded Cheddar cheese	50 mL
2 tsp	chopped fresh oregano	10 mL
1 tsp	chopped fresh thyme	5 mL
¼ tsp	salt, or to taste	1 mL

1. In a small saucepan over medium heat, bring milk just to a boil. Pour ½ cup (125 mL) into blender. Reduce heat to low and keep remaining milk warm. Add cauliflower, onion, cheese, oregano and thyme to blender. Secure lid and blend on low for 30 seconds.

2. With blender still running, add remaining milk through opening in center of lid. Blend just until smooth. Season with salt. Serve hot or cold.

Icy Carrot Cooler

Serves 2

½ cup	freshly squeezed orange juice	125 mL
1 tbsp	freshly squeezed lemon juice	15 mL
2	tomatoes, quartered	2
1	carrot, cut into chunks	1
1 tsp	grated gingerroot	5 mL
4	ice cubes	4

1. In a blender, combine orange juice, lemon juice, tomatoes, carrot, ginger and ice. Secure lid and process using the chop or pulse function until smooth.

Leafy Luxury

⅔ cup	freshly squeezed orange or apple juice	150 mL
1 cup	chopped leafy greens (page 111)	250 mL
1	apple, quartered	1
1	pear, quartered	1

1. In a blender, combine orange juice, greens, apple and pear. Secure lid and blend (from low to high if using a variable speed blender) until smooth.

Lima Curry

Tip

Substitute 1 cup (250 mL) cooked lima beans for the canned. Increase the milk by ¼ cup (50 mL).

* If you are pregnant, limit your intake of parsley to ½ tsp (2 mL) dried or one sprig fresh per day. Do not take parsley if you are suffering from kidney inflammation.

1 cup	milk or table (18%) cream	250 mL
1	can (14 or 15 oz/398 or 425 mL) lima beans in water	1
1 tbsp	chopped onion	15 mL
1 tbsp	chopped fresh parsley*	15 mL
2 tsp	molasses or maple syrup, optional	10 mL
½ tsp	curry powder	2 mL
¼ tsp	ground turmeric	1 mL
¼ tsp	salt, or to taste	1 mL

1. In a small saucepan over medium heat, bring milk just to a boil. Reduce heat to low and keep warm.

2. In a blender, combine lima beans with liquid, onion, parsley, molasses, if using, curry powder and turmeric. Blend on low for 30 seconds.

3. With blender still running, add hot milk through opening in center of lid. Blend just until smooth. Season with salt. Serve hot or cold.

Minestrone

* If you are pregnant, limit your intake of parsley to ½ tsp (2 mL) dried or one sprig fresh per day. Do not take parsley if you are suffering from kidney inflammation.

1½ cups	vegetable or chicken broth	375 mL
½	clove garlic	½
1	sprig parsley*	1
½	onion	½
2	stalks celery, cut into chunks	2
1	carrot, cut into chunks	1
2 tbsp	fresh oregano	25 mL
1	tomato, quartered	1
¾ cup	sliced cabbage	175 mL
½ cup	cooked chickpeas, optional	125 mL
¼ tsp	salt, or to taste	1 mL

1. In a blender, combine ½ cup (125 mL) broth, garlic, parsley, onion, celery and carrot. Secure lid and blend on low for 30 seconds. Pour into saucepan; heat over medium heat until vegetables are soft.

2. Meanwhile, in a blender, combine ½ cup (125 mL) vegetable stock, oregano, tomato and cabbage. Secure lid and blend on low for 30 seconds. Add chickpeas if using. Secure lid and blend on high for 30 seconds or until smooth. Add to saucepan. Bring to a boil, reduce heat to low and simmer for 2 to 3 minutes or until heated through.

3. Stir in enough of the remaining stock to make desired consistency. Season with salt. Serve hot or cold with a spoon.

Orange Pepper

Serves 2

1 cup	carrot juice	250 mL
1 tbsp	freshly squeezed lemon juice	15 mL
2	tomatoes, quartered	2
1	red bell pepper, cut into chunks	1
½ cup	pomegranate seeds	125 mL

1. In a blender, combine carrot juice, lemon juice, tomatoes, red pepper and pomegranate seeds. Secure lid and blend (from low to high if using a variable speed blender) until smooth.

Orange Zinger

Serves 1

½ cup	freshly squeezed orange juice	125 mL
1 cup	cooked chopped carrots	250 mL
½ cup	seedless red grapes	125 mL
1	piece (½ inch/1 cm) gingerroot, peeled	1

1. In a blender, combine orange juice, carrots, grapes and gingerroot. Secure lid and blend (from low to high if using a variable speed blender) until smooth.

Parsnip

Serves 1 or 2

⅔ cup	carrot or apple juice	150 mL
1 cup	cooked chopped parsnip	250 mL
½ cup	cooked chopped carrot	125 mL
Pinch	ground nutmeg	Pinch
¼ tsp	salt, or to taste	1 mL

1. In a blender, combine carrot juice, parsnip, carrot and nutmeg. Secure lid and blend (from low to high if using a variable speed blender) until smooth. Season with salt.

Pease Porridge

Serves 4

Tip

Use fresh or frozen peas and spinach for this thick and hearty vegetable smoothie.

* If you are pregnant, limit your intake of parsley to ½ tsp (2 mL) dried or one sprig fresh per day. Do not take parsley if you are suffering from kidney inflammation.

1 cup	vegetable or chicken broth	250 mL
1 cup	peas	250 mL
1	small potato, peeled and chopped	1
1	stalk celery, cut into chunks	1
1	carrot, chopped	1
½ cup	chopped spinach	125 mL
3 tbsp	steel-cut or rolled oats	45 mL
¼ cup	table (18%) cream or milk	50 mL
1 tbsp	chopped fresh parsley*	15 mL
¼ tsp	salt, or to taste	1 mL

1. In a medium saucepan over medium heat, bring broth, peas, potato, celery and carrot just to a boil. Cover, reduce heat to low and simmer for 10 minutes. Stir in spinach and oats; simmer for another 4 to 7 minutes or until vegetables are tender. Pour into blender. Secure lid and blend on low for 30 seconds.

2. With blender still running, add cream and parsley through opening in center of lid. Blend just until smooth. Season with salt. Serve hot or cold with a spoon.

Peas Please

Serves 3 or 4

Tip

You can substitute 1 cup (250 mL) cooked frozen or fresh green peas or sliced green beans for the canned. Add ½ cup (125 mL) chicken or vegetable broth to the recipe.

1	can (14 oz/398 mL) green peas or sliced green beans	1
½ cup	cooked chopped carrots	125 mL
¼ cup	chopped fennel bulb	50 mL
¼ cup	applesauce	50 mL

1. In a blender, combine peas with liquid, carrots, fennel and applesauce. Secure lid and blend (from low to high if using a variable speed blender) until smooth.

Serves 1

Peppered Beet

½ cup	apple juice	125 mL
1 tbsp	freshly squeezed lemon juice	15 mL
½ cup	chopped cooked beets	125 mL
½	red bell pepper, cut into chunks	½
2	ice cubes	2

1. In a blender, combine apple juice, lemon juice, beets, red pepper and ice. Secure lid and process using the chop or pulse function until smooth.

Serves 1

Peppered Potato

* If you are pregnant, limit your intake of parsley to ½ tsp (2 mL) dried or one sprig fresh per day. Do not take parsley if you are suffering from kidney inflammation.

1 cup	vegetable or chicken broth	250 mL
1	potato, peeled and chopped	1
2 tbsp	chopped onion	25 mL
¼ cup	chopped green or red bell pepper	50 mL
1 tbsp	chopped watercress or fresh parsley*	15 mL
½ tsp	chopped fresh thyme	2 mL
½ to 1	chile pepper, chopped, optional	½ to 1

1. In a medium saucepan over high heat, bring broth to a boil. Add potato and onion; reduce heat to low and simmer for 10 to 12 minutes or until vegetables are soft.

2. Pour stock mixture into blender. Add green pepper, watercress, thyme, and chile pepper, if using. Secure lid and blend (from low to high if using a variable speed blender) just until smooth. Serve immediately with a spoon.

Peppery Tomato Cocktail

Serves 2 or 3

½ cup	tomato juice	125 mL
	Juice of ½ lemon	
3	tomatoes, quartered	3
½	red or green bell pepper, cut into chunks	½
¼ cup	chopped fennel bulb	50 mL
1	sprig watercress	1
½	clove garlic	½
¼ tsp	cayenne pepper	1 mL

1. In a blender, combine tomato juice, lemon juice, tomatoes, green pepper, fennel, watercress, garlic and cayenne. Secure lid and blend (from low to high if using a variable speed blender) until smooth.

Pure Tomato

Serves 1

Tip
You can use ¼ cup (50 mL) tomato juice and 3 ice cubes in place of the 4 tomatoes.

4	tomatoes, quartered	4
¼ cup	spaghetti sauce	50 mL
	Juice of ½ lemon	
1 tbsp	chopped fresh coriander	15 mL
	Salt and pepper to taste	

1. Working over a bowl to catch the juices, press tomatoes through a sieve to remove seeds and skins. Discard seeds and skins.

2. In a blender, combine tomatoes, spaghetti sauce, lemon juice and coriander. Secure lid and blend (from low to high if using a variable speed blender) until smooth. Season with salt and pepper.

Quick Vichyssoise

Serves 1

Tip

Vichyssoise is always served chilled, but this thick, smooth soup-drink is just as good right from the blender.

* If you are pregnant, limit your intake of parsley to ½ tsp (2 mL) dried or one sprig fresh per day. Do not take parsley if you are suffering from kidney inflammation.

½ cup	vegetable broth	125 mL
½ cup	milk, table (18%) cream or silken tofu	125 mL
1	green onion, chopped	1
½ cup	cooked chopped potato	125 mL
1 tsp	chopped fresh parsley*	5 mL
	Salt and pepper to taste	

1. In a blender, combine broth, milk, green onion, potato and parsley. Secure lid and blend (from low to high if using a variable speed blender) until smooth. Season with salt and pepper. Serve at room temperature or cold with a spoon.

Red Rocket

Serves 1 or 2

¼ cup	apple juice	50 mL
¼ cup	cranberry juice	50 mL
1 tbsp	freshly squeezed lemon juice	15 mL
½ cup	cooked chopped cabbage	125 mL
½ cup	cooked chopped beets	125 mL
1	stalk celery, cut into chunks	1
1 tsp	chopped fresh thyme	5 mL
1 tsp	rice vinegar	5 mL

1. In a blender, combine apple juice, cranberry juice, lemon juice, cabbage, beets, celery, thyme and vinegar. Secure lid and blend (from low to high if using a variable speed blender) until smooth.

Roasted Eggplant

Tip

Italian plum, or paste, tomatoes stand up to broiling, so use that variety, if available, for this recipe.

Variation

Apples, plums, pears or nectarines may be substituted for the peaches.

- 1 rimmed baking sheet, lightly oiled
- Preheat broiler

1	small eggplant, halved lengthwise	1
1	onion, quartered	1
2 tbsp	olive oil, divided	25 mL
1	clove garlic	1
2	peaches, halved	2
2	tomatoes, quartered	2
½ cup	spaghetti sauce	125 mL
¼ cup	apple juice	50 mL
1 tsp	chopped fresh oregano	5 mL
½ tsp	salt, or to taste	2 mL

1. On prepared baking sheet, arrange eggplant and onion, cut sides down, in a single layer. Drizzle with 1 tbsp (15 mL) olive oil. Broil for 12 minutes, rotating pan once to cook evenly.

2. Remove pan from oven. Turn eggplant and onions; arrange garlic, peaches and tomatoes, cut sides down, on pan. Drizzle with remaining olive oil. Broil, rotating pan once, for 7 to 10 minutes or until vegetables are soft. Let cool enough to handle.

3. In a blender, combine spaghetti sauce and apple juice. Scrape eggplant and tomato flesh into blender and discard skins. Add roasted garlic, peaches and onions, and oregano. Secure lid and blend on low for for 30 seconds. Increase speed to high and blend just until smooth. Season with salt. Serve warm or cold with a spoon.

Rustproofer #1

⅓ cup	carrot juice	75 mL
1 cup	cooked chopped carrots	250 mL
2	tomatoes, quartered	2
1	sprig parsley*	1
1	apple, quartered	1

1. In a blender, combine carrot juice, carrots, tomatoes, parsley and apple. Secure lid and blend (from low to high if using a variable speed blender) until smooth.

Rustproofer #2

½ cup	carrot juice	125 mL
½ cup	cooked yams, squash or pumpkin	125 mL
¼ cup	cooked chopped broccoli	50 mL
4	apricots, quartered	4
1 tbsp	molasses	15 mL
1 tbsp	chopped fresh peppermint	15 mL

1. In a blender, combine carrot juice, yams, broccoli, apricots, molasses and peppermint. Secure lid and blend (from low to high if using a variable speed blender) until smooth.

Serves 1

Spiced Carrot

½ cup	apple juice	125 mL
1 cup	cooked chopped carrots	250 mL
¼ cup	applesauce	50 mL
1	piece (½ inch/1 cm) gingerroot, peeled	1
¼ tsp	ground cinnamon	1 mL
¼ tsp	salt, or to taste	1 mL
⅛ tsp	cayenne pepper, or to taste	0.5 mL

Tip
Substitute 1 can (12 oz/375 mL) diced carrots with liquid for the cooked fresh carrots and apple juice.

1. In a blender, combine apple juice, carrots, applesauce, gingerroot and cinnamon. Secure lid and blend (from low to high if using a variable speed blender) until smooth. Season with salt and cayenne.

Serves 1 or 2

Spinach Salad

½ cup	carrot juice	125 mL
1 tbsp	flax seed oil	15 mL
1 cup	packed spinach	250 mL
1	carrot, cut into chunks	1
1	apple, quartered	1
1	orange, sectioned and seeded	1

1. In a blender, combine carrot juice, flax seed oil, spinach, carrot, apple and orange. Secure lid and blend (from low to high if using a variable speed blender) until smooth.

Spring Celebration

Tip

Substitute 1 can (12 oz/375 g) asparagus tips or spears with liquid for the cooked chopped asparagus when fresh is not in season. Reduce beet juice to ¼ cup (50 mL) if using canned asparagus.

½ cup	beet juice	125 mL
1 cup	cooked chopped asparagus	250 mL
½ cup	cooked diced beets	125 mL
½ cup	chopped spinach	125 mL
2 tbsp	chopped dried or fresh figs or pitted dates	25 mL
1 tsp	maple syrup or sap, optional	5 mL

1. In a blender, combine beet juice, asparagus, beets, spinach, dates, and maple syrup, if using. Secure lid and blend (from low to high if using a variable speed blender) until smooth.

Squash Special

Tip

Substitute an equal quantity of dried apricots in any smoothie recipe if fresh are not available.

½ cup	apple juice	125 mL
1 cup	cooked squash or sweet potato	250 mL
¼ cup	chopped apricots	50 mL
¼ tsp	ground turmeric	1 mL
¼ tsp	cayenne pepper	1 mL
Pinch	ground cumin	Pinch

1. In a blender, combine apple juice, squash, apricots, turmeric, cayenne and cumin. Secure lid and blend (from low to high if using a variable speed blender) until smooth.

Tomato Froth

Serves 1 or 2

¼ cup	plain yogurt	50 mL
1 tbsp	freshly squeezed lime or lemon juice	15 mL
3	tomatoes, quartered	3
1	carrot, shredded	1
½	cucumber, cut into chunks	½

1. In a blender, combine yogurt, lime juice, tomatoes, carrot and cucumber. Secure lid and blend (from low to high if using a variable speed blender) until smooth.

Tomato Juice Cocktail

Serves 3 or 4

¼ cup	tomato juice	50 mL
1	can (14 or 15 oz/398 or 425 mL) diced beets in water	1
1	small zucchini, cut into chunks	1
1 tbsp	chopped fresh basil	15 mL
½	clove garlic	½
⅛ tsp	ground cumin	0.5 mL
⅛ tsp	cayenne pepper	0.5 mL
½ tsp	salt, or to taste	2 mL

1. In a blender, combine tomato juice, beets with liquid, zucchini, basil, garlic, cumin and cayenne. Secure lid and blend (from low to high if using a variable speed blender) until smooth. Season with salt.

Turnip Parsnip Carrot

Serves 4

1 cup	vegetable or chicken broth	250 mL
½ cup	chopped turnip	125 mL
½ cup	chopped parsnip	125 mL
½ cup	chopped carrot	125 mL
½ cup	milk	125 mL
¼ tsp	ground cinnamon	1 mL
¼ tsp	salt, or to taste	1 mL

1. In a medium saucepan over high heat, bring broth just to a boil. Add turnip, parsnip and carrot. Reduce heat to low and simmer for 7 to 10 minutes or until vegetables are tender.

2. Meanwhile, in a small saucepan, heat milk until small bubbles form around the outside of the pan. Pour stock and vegetables into blender. Add cinnamon and hot milk. Secure lid and blend (from low to high if using a variable speed blender) until smooth. Season with salt. Serve hot with a spoon.

Turnip-Tomato Tango

Serves 2 or 3

½ cup	apple or carrot juice	125 mL
6	ice cubes	6
1	small turnip, chopped	1
1	cucumber, cut into chunks	1
1	tomato, quartered	1
1	stalk celery, cut into chunks	1
¼ cup	spaghetti sauce	50 mL
2 tbsp	freshly squeezed lemon juice	25 mL

1. In a blender, combine apple juice, ice, turnip, cucumber, tomato, celery, spaghetti sauce and lemon juice. Secure lid and process using the chop or pulse function until smooth.

Vichyssoise

Serves 2 or 3

* If you are pregnant, limit your intake of parsley to ½ tsp (2 mL) dried or one sprig fresh per day. Do not take parsley if you are suffering from kidney inflammation.

2 cups	vegetable broth	500 mL
1	potato, chopped	1
1	leek (white and light green parts only), chopped	1
2 tbsp	chopped onion	25 mL
1 tbsp	chopped fresh parsley*	15 mL
½ cup	milk or table (18%) cream or silken tofu	125 mL
	Salt and pepper to taste	

1. In a small saucepan over high heat, bring broth to a boil. Add potato, leek and onion. Reduce heat to low and simmer for 12 minutes or until vegetables are soft. Let cool.
2. Pour potato mixture into blender and add parsley. Secure lid and blend on low for 30 seconds.
3. With blender still running, add milk through opening in center of lid. Blend just until smooth. Season with salt and pepper. Serve at room temperature or cold with a spoon.

Watercress

Serves 1 or 2

½ cup	apple or carrot juice	125 mL
2 tbsp	freshly squeezed lemon juice	25 mL
2	sprigs watercress	2
2	radishes, halved	2
1	apple, quartered	1
½	cucumber, cut into chunks	½
1	stalk celery, cut into chunks	1
¼ tsp	salt, or to taste	1 mL

1. In a blender, combine apple juice, lemon juice, watercress, radishes, apple, cucumber and celery. Secure lid and blend (from low to high if using a variable speed blender) until smooth. Season with salt.

Zippy Tomato

Serves 1 or 2

* If you are pregnant, limit your intake of parsley to ½ tsp (2 mL) dried or one sprig fresh per day. Do not take parsley if you are suffering from kidney inflammation.

¼ cup	tomato juice	50 mL
2	tomatoes, quartered	2
1	pear, quartered	1
½	lemon, sectioned and seeded	½
1 tbsp	chopped fresh parsley*	15 mL
1	piece (½ inch/1 cm) gingerroot, peeled	1
½	chile pepper, chopped	½
¼ tsp	ground turmeric	1 mL
¼ tsp	salt, or to taste	1 mL

1. In a blender, combine tomato juice, tomatoes, pear, lemon, parsley, ginger, chile pepper and turmeric. Secure lid and blend (from low to high if using a variable speed blender) until smooth. Season with salt.

Zuke and Cuke

Serves 2 or 3

½ cup	apple or carrot juice	125 mL
2 tbsp	freshly squeezed lemon juice	25 mL
1	small zucchini, cut into chunks	1
½	cucumber, cut into chunks	½
1	stalk celery, cut into chunks	1
¼ tsp	curry powder	1 mL
Pinch	celery salt	Pinch

1. In a blender, combine apple juice, lemon juice, zucchini, cucumber, celery, curry powder and celery salt. Secure lid and blend (from low to high if using a variable speed blender) until smooth.

Healing Herb Smoothies

Using Herbs in Smoothies

Herbs are plants that are often used for medicinal purposes. Like fruits and vegetables, many herbs are high in antioxidants, which counteract the free radicals that can cause cellular damage, aging and susceptibility to cancers. Each medicinal herb has unique active components that offer specific health benefits to humans. In fact, modern drugs were derived from plants, and over half of the drugs prescribed today still have their origins in plants.

For maximum benefit, always use organic herbs. Grow your own or look for fresh, organic herbs in supermarkets and farmer's markets. Use dried herbs in smoothies when fresh are not available.

To substitute dried herbs for fresh in smoothies: Use one-half to one-third less dried herb than the quantity of fresh called for in the recipe. Crush or grind dried herbs to a powder, then add to smoothie ingredients before blending.

Herbal Teas (Infusions)

Medicinal teas made from herbs are called infusions and may be substituted for all or part of the liquid in any smoothie recipe. The issue is whether you like the taste. No one has ever said that all herbal infusions are delicious, but some, such as mint and chamomile, are very pleasant.

When making medicinal teas, most herbalists work with dried herbs because they are widely available and easy to store, transport and use. Purchase small quantities of dried organic herbs from a farm or natural food store (see Sources, page 372) and replace after eight to 10 months. Store dried herbs in a cool, dark, dry place.

To make an herbal tea (infusion): Bring 1 cup (250 mL) pure or filtered water to a boil. Remove the kettle from the heat. Measure 1 tsp (5 mL) — or the amount recommended under Infusion for a specific herb (see Herbs, pages 117 to 145) — into a teapot. Pour the recommended amount of boiling water over top. Place lid on teapot and a cork in the spout to prevent steam from escaping. Steep for 10 to 15 minutes. Let cool before using in smoothies unless a hot drink is desired. Strain and discard bark, seeds or woody stems but blend leaves and flowers into smoothies along with other ingredients.

Tip

For convenience, make 1 to 2 cups (250 to 500 mL) herbal tea and store in a covered jar in the refrigerator for use throughout the day. Medicinal teas should be stored for no longer than one day. Keep them in a container that doesn't leave a large headspace above the liquid, because active ingredients will be lost through oxidation during storage.

Decoctions

When the woody parts (roots, bark and seeds) of herbs are simmered in water, the resulting solution is called a decoction.

To make a decoction: Measure the amount of the ground herb recommended under Decoction for a specific herb (see Herbs, pages 117 to 145) into a small saucepan. Pour the recommended amount of filtered water into the pan and bring to a simmer. Simmer for the recommended amount of time. Use a saucepan made of a nonreactive material, such as glass, enamel or stainless steel and keep the lid on at all times, because some of the active ingredients will be lost if the steam is allowed to escape. Be sure to follow the instructions on the amount to use and the simmering time given for a particular herb.

Tinctures

A tincture is the solution made when herbs are steeped in alcohol and pure water. This technique extracts and preserves their active ingredients, and the resulting solution is so concentrated that only a few drops are required for each dose. Tinctures may be purchased at natural food stores. To take a tincture, drop the amount recommended under Tincture for a specific herb (see Herbs, pages 117 to 145) into water, juice or any fruit or vegetable smoothie or drink.

Allium Antioxidant

Beware: This drink is very strong. Just preparing it will make your eyes water. But for antioxidant and antibacterial power, it can't be beat. Drink it at the first sign of cold or flu. It could upset a flu-ish tummy.

¾ cup	carrot juice	175 mL
1	stalk celery, cut into chunks	1
¼	onion	¼
½	clove garlic	½
1	apple, quartered	1

1. In a blender, combine carrot juice, celery, onion, garlic and apple. Secure lid and blend (from low to high if using a variable speed blender) until smooth.

Anise Anise

Serves 1

* Avoid licorice if you have high blood pressure. The prolonged use of licorice is not recommended under any circumstances.

¼ cup	licorice* decoction (page 133)	50 mL
¼ cup	apple juice	50 mL
1	apple, quartered	1
3 tbsp	chopped fennel bulb	45 mL
1 tsp	crushed fennel seeds	5 mL

1. In a blender, combine licorice decoction, apple juice, apple, chopped fennel and fennel seeds. Secure lid and blend (from low to high if using a variable speed blender) until smooth.

Anti-Depression Tonic

Serves 1

¼ cup	carrot juice	50 mL
¼ cup	lemon balm infusion (page 132)	50 mL
1 tbsp	freshly squeezed lemon juice	15 mL
¼ cup	cooked chopped carrots	50 mL
½	mango	½
2	large fresh basil leaves	2

1. In a blender, combine carrot juice, lemon balm infusion, lemon juice, carrots, mango and basil. Secure lid and blend (from low to high if using a variable speed blender) until smooth.

Aspirin in a Glass

Serves 1

Anti-inflammatory salicylates were originally discovered in meadowsweet, then isolated and chemically duplicated for use in pill form, which was called Aspirin. The name "Aspirin" comes from the old botanical name for meadowsweet, *Spiraea ulmaria* (now known as *Filipendula ulmaria*).

¼ cup	meadowsweet infusion (page 134)	50 mL
¼ cup	cranberry juice	50 mL
¼ cup	pitted cherries	50 mL
¼ cup	chopped mango	50 mL
1 tbsp	chopped fresh alfalfa	15 mL
¼ tsp	fennel seeds	1 mL

1. In a blender, combine meadowsweet infusion, cranberry juice, cherries, mango, alfalfa and fennel seeds. Secure lid and blend (from low to high if using a variable speed blender) until smooth.

Bronchial Aid

Serves 1

Tip

If fresh apricots are not available, use an equal quantity of dried in any smoothie.

* If you are pregnant, limit your intake of parsley to ½ tsp (2 mL) dried or one sprig fresh per day. Do not take parsley if you are suffering from kidney inflammation.

** Avoid licorice if you have high blood pressure. The prolonged use of licorice is not recommended under any circumstances.

¼ cup	hyssop infusion (page 131)	50 mL
¼ cup	marshmallow infusion (page 134)	50 mL
1	pear, quartered	1
2	apricots, halved	2
1	sprig parsley*	1
¼ tsp	ground licorice**	1 mL

1. In a blender, combine hyssop and marshmallow infusions, pear, apricots, parsley and licorice. Secure lid and blend (from low to high if using a variable speed blender) until smooth.

Calming Chamomile

Serves 1 or 2

In Europe, chamomile is a very popular herb. In Germany, for example, there are at least 18 different medicinal preparations that contain chamomile on pharmacy shelves.

½ cup	chamomile or chamomile-ginger tea	125 mL
1	apple, quartered	1
¼	cantaloupe, cubed	¼
1 tbsp	fresh German chamomile flowers or 1 tsp (5 mL) dried	15 mL
2 tbsp	plain yogurt	25 mL
1 tbsp	liquid honey, or to taste	15 mL

1. In a blender, combine chamomile tea, apple, cantaloupe, chamomile flowers, yogurt and honey. Secure lid and blend (from low to high if using a variable speed blender) until smooth.

Serves 1	# Courage	

¼ cup	borage infusion (page 119)	50 mL
¼ cup	freshly squeezed orange juice	50 mL
½ cup	frozen sliced peaches	125 mL
¼ cup	cooked diced beets or frozen raspberries	50 mL

1. In a blender, combine borage infusion, orange juice, peaches and beets. Secure lid and blend (from low to high if using a variable speed blender) until smooth.

Serves 1	# Cramp Crusher	

½ cup	freshly squeezed orange juice	125 mL
2 tbsp	freshly squeezed lemon juice	25 mL
½ cup	blueberries, blackberries or strawberries	125 mL
½ tsp	ground ginger	2 mL
8	drops black cohosh tincture	8

1. In a blender, combine orange juice, lemon juice, blueberries, ginger and black cohosh tincture. Secure lid and blend (from low to high if using a variable speed blender) until smooth.

Day Starter

Serves 1

½ cup	freshly squeezed orange juice	125 mL
3 tbsp	plain yogurt	45 mL
¼ cup	frozen sliced peaches	50 mL
¼ cup	raspberries or strawberries	50 mL
½	banana, cut into chunks	½
15	drops ginseng tincture	15

1. In a blender, combine orange juice, yogurt, peaches, raspberries, banana and ginseng tincture. Secure lid and blend (from low to high if using a variable speed blender) until smooth.

Digestive Drink

Serves 1

¼ tsp	crushed cardamom seeds	1 mL
¼ tsp	ground cinnamon	1 mL
¼ tsp	crushed fennel seeds	1 mL
⅛ tsp	crushed cloves	0.5 mL
1	apple, quartered	1
1	kiwifruit, quartered	1
¼ cup	seedless grapes	50 mL

1. In a teapot, pour ¼ cup (50 mL) boiling water over cardamom seeds, cinnamon, fennel seeds and cloves. Cover and steep for 10 minutes. Strain and discard spices. Let spice infusion cool.

2. In a blender, combine spice infusion, apple, kiwi and grapes. Secure lid and blend (from low to high if using a variable speed blender) until smooth.

Diuretic Tonic

Tip

You can use fresh and frozen fruit interchangeably in most smoothies, although the results will differ. Frozen fruit not only chills a smoothie, it thickens it as well.

* If you are pregnant, limit your intake of parsley to ½ tsp (2 mL) dried or one sprig fresh per day. Do not take parsley if you are suffering from kidney inflammation.

¼ cup	burdock leaf infusion (page 120)	50 mL
¼ cup	dandelion leaf infusion (page 124)	50 mL
¼ cup	frozen blueberries	50 mL
½ cup	chopped cantaloupe	125 mL
1 tbsp	chopped fresh parsley*	15 mL

1. In a blender, combine burdock leaf infusion, dandelion leaf infusion, blueberries, cantaloupe and parsley. Secure lid and blend (from low to high if using a variable speed blender) until smooth.

Flu Fighter #2

Tip

Take this drink at the first sign of cold or flu, before the virus can take hold.

* Avoid licorice if you have high blood pressure. The prolonged use of licorice is not recommended under any circumstances.

¼ cup	pineapple juice	50 mL
¼ cup	echinacea decoction (page 125)	50 mL
2 tbsp	freshly squeezed lemon juice	25 mL
2 tbsp	cranberry sauce	25 mL
1	orange, sectioned and seeded	1
¼ tsp	ground ginger	1 mL
⅛ tsp	ground cinnamon	0.5 mL
⅛ tsp	ground licorice*	0.5 mL

1. In a blender, combine pineapple juice, echinacea decoction, lemon juice, cranberry sauce, orange, ginger, cinnamon and licorice Secure lid and blend (from low to high if using a variable speed blender) until smooth.

Gas Guzzler

Serves 1

Tip

Drink this smoothie one or two hours after eating. To minimize gas, never eat fruit at or immediately after mealtimes.

½ cup	papaya nectar or apple juice	125 mL
1	apple, quartered	1
½ cup	chopped papaya	125 mL
¼ tsp	crushed cumin seeds	1 mL
¼ tsp	crushed fennel seeds	1 mL
⅛ tsp	crushed mustard seeds	0.5 mL
⅛ tsp	ground cinnamon	0.5 mL

1. In a blender, combine papaya nectar, apple, chopped papaya, cumin seeds, fennel seeds, mustard seeds and cinnamon. Secure lid and blend (from low to high if using a variable speed blender) until smooth.

Good Health Elixir

Serves 1

Tip

Alfalfa, humanity's oldest crop, feeds the cells and is safe to use every day.

¼ cup	freshly squeezed orange juice	50 mL
¼ cup	alfalfa infusion (page 117) or carrot juice	50 mL
½	banana, cut into chunks	½
4	frozen strawberries or raspberries	4

1. In a blender, combine orange juice, alfalfa infusion, banana and strawberries. Secure lid and blend (from low to high if using a variable speed blender) until smooth.

Serves 1	# Gout Gone	

¼ cup	burdock root decoction (page 120)	50 mL
¼ cup	raspberry juice	50 mL
¼ cup	frozen strawberries	50 mL
1	banana, cut into chunks	1
1 tbsp	chopped fresh parsley*	15 mL
1 tsp	crushed fennel seeds	5 mL

* If you are pregnant, limit your intake of parsley to ½ tsp (2 mL) dried or one sprig fresh per day. Do not take parsley if you are suffering from kidney inflammation.

1. In a blender, combine burdock root decoction, raspberry juice, strawberries, banana, parsley and fennel seeds. Secure lid and blend (from low to high if using a variable speed blender) until smooth.

Serves 1	# Green Energy	

¾ cup	soy or rice milk	175 mL
¼ cup	chopped dried apricots	50 mL
1 cup	chopped spinach	250 mL
2 tsp	chopped wheat or barley grass	10 mL
1 tbsp	pumpkin seeds	15 mL
1 tsp	dried ginkgo	5 mL

1. In a blender, combine soy milk, apricots, spinach, wheat grass, pumpkin seeds and ginkgo. Secure lid and blend (from low to high if using a variable speed blender) until smooth.

Green Tea Smoothie

Serves 1

* If you are pregnant, limit your intake of parsley to ½ tsp (2 mL) dried or one sprig fresh per day. Do not take parsley if you are suffering from kidney inflammation.

½ cup	green tea infusion (page 130)	125 mL
¼ cup	seedless grapes	50 mL
¼ cup	blueberries	50 mL
1	sprig parsley*	1

1. In a blender, combine green tea infusion, grapes, blueberries and parsley. Secure lid and blend (from low to high if using a variable speed blender) until smooth.

Hangover Remedy

Serves 1

½ cup	apple juice	125 mL
	Juice of 1 lemon	
2	apples, quartered	2
1	banana, cut into chunks	1
1	½-inch (1 cm) piece gingerroot, peeled	1
1 tsp	fresh chamomile flowers or ½ tsp (2 mL) dried	5 mL
½ tsp	slippery elm bark powder	2 mL

1. In a blender, combine apple juice, lemon juice, apples, banana, ginger, chamomile and slippery elm bark powder. Secure lid and blend (from low to high if using a variable speed blender) until smooth.

Healthy Bladder Blitz

Serves 1

Tip
Look for unsweetened cranberry juice, not a "cocktail" or "beverage," which is sweetened and contains very little cranberry.

¼ cup	buchu infusion (page 119)	50 mL
¼ cup	cranberry juice	50 mL
¼ cup	frozen blueberries	50 mL
¼ cup	chopped celery	50 mL

1. In a blender, combine buchu infusion, cranberry juice, blueberries and celery. Secure lid and blend (from low to high if using a variable speed blender) until smooth.

Herb-eze

Tips

Use an equal quantity of dried apricots in smoothie recipes if fresh are not available.

The Chinese call astragalus *huang qi* and add the roots to nourishing soups for the very young and the very old. It is safe to use every day.

¼ cup	carrot juice	50 mL
¼ cup	astragalus decoction (page 118)	50 mL
¼ cup	frozen blueberries	50 mL
¼ cup	chopped apricots	50 mL
Pinch	ground cloves	Pinch

1. In a blender, combine carrot juice, astragalus decoction, blueberries, apricots and cloves. Secure lid and blend (from low to high if using a variable speed blender) until smooth.

Hot Flu Toddy

* Raw elderberries can make some people sick. If in doubt, cook in a small amount of water, cool and drain.

¼ cup	elderberry infusion (page 125)	50 mL
¼ cup	cranberry juice	50 ml
2 tbsp	dried elderberries* or blueberries, optional	25 mL
¼ cup	chopped pineapple	50 mL
4	frozen strawberries	4
¼ cup	frozen raspberries	50 mL
¼ tsp	ground ginger	1 mL
⅛ tsp	ground cinnamon	0.5 mL
⅛ tsp	cayenne pepper	0.5 mL

1. In a blender, combine elderberry infusion, cranberry juice, dried elderberries if using, pineapple, strawberries, raspberries, ginger, cinnamon and cayenne. Secure lid and blend (from low to high if using a variable speed blender) until smooth.

Lavender Smoothie

1 tsp	dried lemon balm	5 mL
¼ tsp	dried lavender flowers and leaves	1 mL
1	plum, quartered	1
2	apricots, quartered	2
¼ cup	seedless grapes	50 mL

1. In a teapot, pour ½ cup (125 mL) boiling water over lemon balm and lavender. Cover and steep for 10 minutes. Let infusion cool (no need to strain).

2. In a blender, combine herb infusion, plum, apricots and grapes. Secure lid and blend (from low to high if using a variable speed blender) until smooth.

Lemon Lemon

Tip

If fresh apricots are not available, use an equal quantity of dried in any smoothie.

1 tsp	dried lemon balm	5 mL
1 tsp	dried lemon verbena	5 mL
1 tsp	dried linden leaves and flowers	5 mL
	Juice of 1 lemon	
¼ cup	chopped pineapple	50 mL
¼ cup	frozen sliced peaches	50 mL
2	apricots, quartered	2

1. In a teapot, pour ½ cup (125 mL) boiling water over lemon balm, lemon verbena and linden. Cover and steep for 10 minutes. Let infusion cool (no need to strain).

2. In a blender, combine herb infusion, lemon juice, pineapple, peaches and apricots. Secure lid and blend (from low to high if using a variable speed blender) until smooth.

Migraine Tonic

* If you are pregnant, limit your intake of parsley to ½ tsp (2 mL) dried or one sprig fresh per day. Do not take parsley if you are suffering from kidney inflammation.

¼ cup	beet juice	50 mL
¼ cup	carrot juice	50 mL
¼ cup	chopped cantaloupe	50 mL
1	stalk celery, cut into chunks	1
1 tbsp	chopped fresh parsley*	15 mL
1	½-inch (1 cm) slice gingerroot, peeled	1
1 tsp	fresh rosemary	5 mL
¼ tsp	cayenne pepper	1 mL
10	drops feverfew tincture	10

1. In a blender, combine beet juice, carrot juice, cantaloupe, celery, parsley, gingerroot, rosemary, cayenne and feverfew tincture. Secure lid and blend (from low to high if using a variable speed blender) until smooth.

Mint Julep

Spearmint is said to repel ants in the home and to keep mice away from the garden.

½ cup	spearmint infusion (page 141)	125 mL
¼ cup	chopped watermelon	50 mL
4	frozen strawberries or raspberries	4
1 tbsp	chopped fresh spearmint	15 mL

1. In a blender, combine spearmint infusion, watermelon, strawberries and spearmint. Secure lid and blend (from low to high if using a variable speed blender) until smooth.

Morning After

* If you are pregnant, limit your intake of parsley to ½ tsp (2 mL) dried or one sprig fresh per day. Do not take parsley if you are suffering from kidney inflammation.

½ cup	freshly squeezed orange juice	125 mL
1	wedge pineapple, cubed	1
2 tbsp	chopped fresh parsley*	25 mL
2 tbsp	freshly squeezed lemon juice	25 mL
1 tbsp	chopped peeled gingerroot	15 mL

1. In a blender, combine orange juice, pineapple, parsley, lemon juice and ginger. Secure lid and blend (from low to high if using a variable speed blender) until smooth.

Muscle Relief

Tip

For the medicinal value of celery seeds, use the seeds from the wild plant, available at health food stores.

½ cup	beet juice	125 mL
¼ cup	chopped celery	50 mL
¼ cup	cooked chopped carrots or beets	50 mL
1 tsp	slippery elm bark powder	5 mL
¼ tsp	crushed medicinal celery seeds (see Tip, left and page 122)	1 mL

1. In a blender, combine beet juice, celery, carrots, slippery elm bark powder and celery seeds. Secure lid and blend (from low to high if using a variable speed blender) until smooth.

Pain Reliever

Tip

Use raw or cooked cabbage in this smoothie. Raw cabbage has more nutrients, but cooked cabbage blends easily and the taste is not as strong.

½ cup	tomato juice	125 mL
2 tbsp	freshly squeezed lemon juice	25 mL
½ cup	shredded cabbage	125 mL
½ tsp	cayenne pepper, or to taste	2 mL
8	drops black cohosh tincture	8

1. In a blender, combine tomato juice, lemon juice, cabbage, cayenne and black cohosh tincture. Secure lid and blend (from low to high if using a variable speed blender) until smooth.

Serves 1	# Pear Basil Raspberry	
¼ cup	raspberry juice	50 mL
¼ cup	Apricot Milk (page 312)	50 mL
1 tsp	balsamic vinegar	5 mL
1 tbsp	chopped fresh basil	15 mL
½ cup	frozen raspberries	125 mL
½ cup	sliced pears	125 mL

1. In a blender, combine raspberry juice, apricot milk, balsamic vinegar, basil, raspberries and pears. Secure lid and blend (from low to high if using a variable speed blender) until smooth.

Serves 1	# Peppermint Aperitif	

This is a pleasing drink that cleanses the palate. When taking fruit drinks, wait a minimum of half an hour before eating a meal, as the fruit can cause gas if followed by other food. Allow one to two hours after meals before taking fruit drinks.

½ cup	peppermint infusion (page 137)	125 mL
4	ice cubes	4
¼ cup	chopped fennel bulb	50 mL
1	kiwifruit, quartered	1
1	apple, quartered	1

1. In a blender, combine peppermint infusion, ice, fennel, kiwi and apple. Secure lid and process using the chop or pulse function until smooth.

Peptic Tonic

Tip

This healing tonic is safe for an everyday breakfast drink if the slippery elm bark powder is eliminated. See Peptic Ulcers, page 78, for other fruits, vegetables and herbs to add to this smoothie.

¼ cup	apple juice	50 mL
¼ cup	calendula infusion (page 120)	50 mL
1	banana, cut into chunks	1
¼ cup	chopped mango	50 mL
¼ cup	chopped papaya	50 mL
1 tsp	slippery elm bark powder	5 mL

1. In a blender, combine apple juice, calendula infusion, banana, mango, papaya and slippery elm bark powder. Secure lid and blend (from low to high if using a variable speed blender) until smooth.

Popeye's Power

Tip

Substitute 1 can (14 oz/ 398 mL) diced beets with liquid for the beet juice and cooked beets when fresh are not available.

½ cup	beet or carrot juice	125 mL
1 cup	cooked diced beets	250 mL
½ cup	chopped spinach	125 mL
½ cup	cooked chopped carrots	125 mL
1	piece (1 inch/2.5 cm) dandelion root, chopped	1
1 tbsp	molasses, optional	15 mL

1. In a blender, combine beet juice, beets, spinach, carrots, dandelion root, and molasses if using. Secure lid and blend (from low to high if using a variable speed blender) until smooth.

Prostate Power

½ cup	freshly squeezed orange juice	125 mL
2 tbsp	freshly squeezed lemon juice	25 mL
1	apple, quartered	1
½	banana, cut into chunks	½
10 to 25	drops saw palmetto liquid extract	10 to 25

1. In a blender, combine orange juice, lemon juice, apple, banana and saw palmetto extract. Secure lid and blend (from low to high if using a variable speed blender) until smooth.

Tip

There is a large range in the amount of saw palmetto extract because people need more or less of it depending on their health, weight, age, the other herbs they are taking and the symptoms they have. Start with the smaller amount of saw palmetto and increase if necessary.

Psoria-Smoothie

½ cup	apricot nectar or carrot juice	125 mL
¼ cup	blueberries	50 mL
¼ cup	chopped cantaloupe	50 mL
2	apricots, halved	2
1 tsp	evening primrose oil	5 mL
½ tsp	crushed fennel seeds	2 mL
20	drops burdock root tincture	20

1. In a blender, combine apricot nectar, blueberries, cantaloupe, apricots, evening primrose oil, fennel seeds and burdock root tincture Secure lid and blend (from low to high if using a variable speed blender) until smooth.

Raspberry Raspberry

Serves 1

Tip

You can use fresh and frozen fruit interchangeably in most smoothies, although the results will differ. Frozen fruit not only chills a smoothie, it thickens it as well.

¼ cup	red raspberry infusion (page 139)	50 mL
¼ cup	raspberry juice	50 mL
2 tbsp	freshly squeezed lemon juice	25 mL
¼ cup	frozen raspberries	50 mL
4	frozen strawberries	4

1. In a blender, combine red raspberry infusion, raspberry juice, lemon juice, raspberries and strawberries. Secure lid and blend (from low to high if using a variable speed blender) until smooth.

Rose Smoothie

Serves 1

¼ cup	fresh rose hip infusion (page 139)	50 mL
¼ cup	apple juice	50 mL
2 tbsp	freshly squeezed lemon juice	25 mL
¼ cup	seedless grapes	50 mL
1	plum, halved	1
4	frozen strawberries	4
1 tbsp	fresh rose petals	15 mL

1. In a blender, combine rose hip infusion, apple juice, lemon juice, grapes, plum, strawberries and rose petals. Secure lid and blend (from low to high if using a variable speed blender) until smooth.

Sage Relief

Tip

Take this drink once a cold or flu has taken hold.

½ cup	beet juice	125 mL
1 tbsp	freshly squeezed lemon juice	15 mL
¼ cup	cooked chopped beets	50 mL
1	apple, quartered	1
½ tsp	chopped fresh sage	2 mL

1. In a blender, combine beet juice, lemon juice, beets, apple and sage. Secure lid and blend (from low to high if using a variable speed blender) until smooth.

Sleepytime Smoothie

Tip

The range in the dosage of valerian reflects individual needs: some people need more than others. Try this first with 20 drops, then increase if required.

* Valerian has an adverse effect on some people.

¼ cup	catnip infusion (page 121)	50 mL
¼ cup	chamomile infusion (page 127)	50 mL
1	apple, quartered	1
½	banana, cut into chunks	½
20 to 40	drops valerian* tincture	20 to 40

1. In a blender, combine catnip infusion, chamomile infusion, apple, banana and valerian tincture. Secure lid and blend (from low to high if using a variable speed blender) until smooth.

Slippery Banana

Serves 1

¼ cup	chamomile infusion (page 127)	50 mL
¼ cup	ginger infusion (page 128)	50 mL
¼ cup	plain yogurt	50 mL
1	banana, cut into chunks	1
1 tsp	slippery elm bark powder	5 mL
¼ tsp	ground nutmeg	1 mL

1. In a blender, combine chamomile and ginger infusions, yogurt, banana, slippery elm bark powder and nutmeg. Secure lid and blend (from low to high if using a variable speed blender) until smooth.

Smart Smoothie

Serves 1

½ cup	freshly squeezed orange juice	125 mL
¼ cup	blueberries	50 mL
¼ cup	seedless red grapes	50 mL
1 cup	chopped spinach	250 mL
1 tsp	dried or fresh ginkgo leaves, optional	5 mL
1 tbsp	flax seeds	15 mL
1 tsp	dried skullcap	5 mL
1 tsp	lecithin	5 mL

1. In a blender, combine orange juice, blueberries, grapes, spinach, ginkgo (if using), flax seeds, skullcap and lecithin. Secure lid and blend (from low to high if using a variable speed blender) until smooth.

Serves 1	# Spa Special	
¼ cup	milk thistle infusion (page 135)	50 mL
¼ cup	silken tofu	50 mL
6	large strawberries	6
½ cup	blueberries	125 mL

1. In a blender, combine milk thistle infusion, tofu, strawberries and blueberries. Secure lid and blend (from low to high if using a variable speed blender) until smooth.

Serves 1	# Teenage Tonic	

Tips

This drink is a cleansing tonic that supports hormone balance and improves skin problems, especially during the teenage years.

Use an equal quantity of dried apricots if fresh are not available.

¼ cup	burdock seed infusion (page 120)	50 mL
¼ cup	calendula infusion (page 120) or carrot juice	50 mL
½	mango	½
¼ cup	chopped cantaloupe	50 mL
2	apricots, halved	2
1 tsp	dandelion root tincture	5 mL

1. In a blender, combine burdock seed infusion, calendula infusion, mango, cantaloupe, apricots and dandelion root tincture. Secure lid and blend (from low to high if using a variable speed blender) until smooth.

Serves 1

The Cool Down

½ cup	carrot juice	125 mL
2	wedges pineapple, cut into chunks	2
1	banana, cut into chunks	1
1 tbsp	chopped fresh lemon balm	15 mL

1. In a blender, combine carrot juice, pineapple, banana and lemon balm. Secure lid and blend (from low to high if using a variable speed blender) until smooth.

Serves 1

The Regular

Tip

Evening primrose oil is sometimes available in small jars but is widely available in gel capsules. If the jars are not available, use a sharp knife to split open capsules, then pour into a measuring spoon and add to smoothies.

½ cup	freshly squeezed orange juice	125 mL
4	large strawberries	4
1	banana, cut into chunks	1
2 tbsp	wheat germ	25 mL
1 tsp	evening primrose oil	5 mL

1. In a blender, combine orange juice, strawberries, banana, wheat germ and evening primrose oil. Secure lid and blend (from low to high if using a variable speed blender) until smooth.

Thyme in a Glass

Serves 1

½ cup	beet juice	125 mL
¼ cup	cooked chopped carrots	50 mL
1	apple, quartered	1
¼ tsp	dried thyme	1 mL
⅛ tsp	dried rosemary	0.5 mL

1. In a blender, combine beet juice, carrots, apple, thyme and rosemary. Secure lid and blend (from low to high if using a variable speed blender) until smooth.

Turmeric Cocktail

Serves 1 or 2

¼ cup	carrot juice	50 mL
¼ cup	tomato juice	50 mL
1	tomato, quartered	1
1	stalk celery, cut into chunks	1
2 tbsp	chopped fennel bulb, optional	25 mL
1 tsp	ground turmeric	5 mL
⅛ tsp	medicinal celery seeds, crushed (see Tip, page 270)	0.5 mL
⅛ tsp	dill seeds, crushed	0.5 mL

1. In a blender, combine carrot juice, tomato juice, chopped tomato, chopped celery, fennel if using, turmeric, celery seeds and dill seeds Secure lid and blend (from low to high if using a variable speed blender) until smooth.

Woman's Smoothie

Serves 1 or 2

Tip
You can use fresh and frozen fruit interchangeably in most smoothies, although the results will differ. Frozen fruit not only chills a smoothie, it thickens it as well.

1 tsp	dried motherwort	5 mL
1 tsp	dried red clover	5 mL
1 tsp	grated gingerroot	5 mL
1/4 cup	freshly squeezed orange juice	50 mL
1/4 cup	frozen blueberries	50 mL
4	frozen strawberries	4

1. In a teapot, pour 1/4 cup (50 mL) boiling water over motherwort, red clover and ginger. Cover and steep for 10 minutes. Let infusion cool (no need to strain).

2. In a blender, combine herb infusion, orange juice, blueberries and strawberries. Secure lid and blend (from low to high if using a variable speed blender) until smooth.

Dairy Smoothies

Using Milk in Smoothies and Shakes

Making smoothies with milk, yogurt, tofu or fortified soy milk is a good way to add bone-building calcium and protein to your diet. As protein and calcium are essential for growth and maintenance of tissue, children, teenagers and many adults, especially postmenopausal women who are at risk of calcium depletion, will benefit from smoothies made with milk and yogurt.

Milk is a source of important nutrients, such as calcium, B vitamins, protein, minerals and vitamin D. This is true not only of whole milk but also of reduced-fat milks (2%, 1% and skim) and chocolate milk. All of the recipes for dairy smoothies may be made with whole or reduced-fat cow's milk, buttermilk, goat's milk, ewe's milk, or regular or low-fat evaporated milk. Milk is perishable, so always buy it and other dairy products that are well within the best-before date printed on the package and keep them refrigerated. Milk may be frozen in ice-cube trays, and the crushed cubes can be used in smoothies.

Other Forms of Milk

- **Buttermilk** is a by-product of the butter-making process. A creamy, rich liquid with a natural bite, it contains no butter and imparts a characteristic flavor. Buttermilk is also available in powdered dried form (see Using Powdered Buttermilk, opposite). Use buttermilk in smoothies to add texture, with less fat than whole milk.
- **Powdered dried skim or whole milk solids** are pasteurized milk crystals made by air-drying milk to remove the water. They are a convenient and economical alternative to fresh milk (see Using Powdered Dried Milk, opposite).
- **Ewe's milk** has about 50% more calcium than cow's or goat's milk. It is high in essential vitamins and minerals and is easily digestible. Although it is used mainly in cheese making, it is sometimes available in specialty-food or natural-food stores.
- **Evaporated milk** is made by evaporating half of the water from fresh whole milk. The heat used to process and can it caramelizes the naturally occurring milk sugars, giving evaporated milk a slightly caramel-like flavor and light brown tint. Evaporated milk makes smoothies thicker and slightly sweeter than those made with regular milk. Do not confuse evaporated milk with sweetened condensed milk, which is very high in sugar. Low-fat evaporated milk is a good choice for smoothies. Cans of evaporated milk are easy to store but need to be refrigerated once they are opened.
- **Goat's milk** is available in most supermarkets and natural-food stores and can be comfortably consumed by many people with lactose intolerance.

Using Powdered Dried Milk

Keep powdered dried milk on the shelf and reconstitute just the amount required with water or add directly to smoothies for thicker, nutrient-enriched drinks. To make 1 cup (250 mL) of milk, whisk 2 to 4 tbsp (25 to 60 mL) with 1 cup (250 mL) water. You can add 2 or 3 tbsp (25 or 45 mL) powdered dried milk directly to a smoothie recipe, but be sure to increase the liquid by 1 or 2 tbsp (15 or 25 mL).

Using Powdered Buttermilk

With a supply of powdered buttermilk in the cupboard, you will always be able to enjoy its rich, tart taste in smoothies. To make 1 cup (250 mL) buttermilk, whisk 3 tbsp (45 mL) powdered dried buttermilk with 1 cup (250 mL) water. You can add 1 or 2 tbsp (15 or 25 mL) powdered dried buttermilk directly to most smoothie recipes, but be sure to add 1 or 2 tbsp (15 or 25 mL) extra liquid or water as well.

Using Yogurt

Yogurt is a fermented milk product that contains a beneficial type of bacteria called lactobacillus, which restores and maintains normal microbial balance in the intestinal tract.

The nutritional value of yogurt is similar to that of milk but it is easier to digest. Check the label to ensure that yogurt contains active bacterial cultures and that it doesn't contain additives, preservatives or colorings.

For smoothies, Greek-style yogurt is popular because it is thick, creamy and sweet. (Strain thin or watery yogurt through cheesecloth before adding to the blender.) Yogurt may be substituted for cream or milk to make thicker, creamier smoothies. Yogurt made from goat's milk is also readily available and may be used wherever regular yogurt is called for.

Dairy Smoothies

Apple Almond Feta

¼ cup	apple juice	50 mL
¼ cup	Almond Milk (page 314) or soy milk	50 mL
2	apples, quartered	2
2	apricots, halved	2
3 tbsp	crumbled feta cheese	45 mL

1. In a blender, combine apple juice, almond milk, apples, apricots and cheese. Secure lid and blend (from low to high if using a variable speed blender) until smooth.

Apricot Cantaloupe

Tip
Dried apricots may be substituted for fresh in any smoothie.

½ cup	freshly squeezed orange juice	125 mL
2 tbsp	freshly squeezed lime juice	25 mL
3	apricots, halved	3
¼	cantaloupe, cubed	¼
¼ cup	cottage cheese	50 mL

1. In a blender, combine orange juice, lime juice, apricots, cantaloupe and cheese. Secure lid and blend (from low to high if using a variable speed blender) until smooth.

Banan-o-rama

Serves 1

½ cup	freshly squeezed orange juice	125 mL
½ cup	banana-flavored yogurt	125 mL
1	banana, cut into chunks	1

1. In a blender, combine orange juice, yogurt and banana. Secure lid and blend (from low to high if using a variable speed blender) until smooth.

Blueberry Banana

Serves 2

2 cups	plain yogurt	500 mL
2 cups	blueberries	500 mL
1	banana, cut into chunks	1
2 tbsp	pure maple syrup, optional	25 mL

1. In a blender, combine yogurt, blueberries, banana, and maple syrup (if using). Secure lid and blend (from low to high if using a variable speed blender) until smooth.

Blue Pear

Serves 1

½ cup	pear nectar or apple juice	125 mL
3	pears, quartered	3
¼ cup	crumbled blue cheese	50 mL
½ tsp	rice vinegar	2 mL
1 tsp	chopped fresh tarragon or basil	5 mL

1. In a blender, combine pear nectar, pears, cheese, vinegar and tarragon. Secure lid and blend (from low to high if using a variable speed blender) until smooth.

	Serves 2	

Breakfast Blitz

Tip

This drink lends itself to any combination of fresh fruit. Add one fresh peach, apple or pear (peel, pit or seed, and chop it before adding to the blender) or ¼ cup (50 mL) chopped seeded peeled melon, orange or grapefruit.

½ cup	milk	125 mL
½ cup	frozen raspberries or strawberries	125 mL
1	banana, cut into chunks	1
2 tbsp	chopped almonds or sunflower seeds	25 mL
2 tbsp	wheat germ	25 mL
2 tsp	ground flax seeds	10 mL
¼ cup	plain yogurt	50 mL
1 tsp	grated fresh ginseng root	5 mL

1. In a blender, combine milk, raspberries, banana, almonds, wheat germ, flax seeds, yogurt and ginseng. Secure lid and blend (from low to high if using a variable speed blender) until smooth.

	Serves 2	

Buttermilk Blush

Tip

You can use powdered buttermilk in this recipe. Substitute ½ cup (125 mL) water and 1 tbsp (15 mL) powdered buttermilk for the buttermilk.

½ cup	buttermilk	125 mL
2	plums, halved	2
1	peach, halved	1
3	frozen strawberries	3

1. In a blender, combine buttermilk, plums, peach and strawberries. Secure lid and blend (from low to high if using a variable speed blender) until smooth.

Serves 2	# Coconut Carob Orange	
¼ cup	Coconut Carob Milk (page 315)	50 mL
¼ cup	freshly squeezed orange juice	50 mL
½ cup	plain yogurt	125 mL
1 tbsp	carob powder	15 mL
1 tsp	grated orange zest, optional	5 mL
3	ice cubes	3

1. In a blender, combine coconut carob milk, orange juice, yogurt, carob powder, orange zest if using, and ice. Secure lid and process using the chop or pulse function until smooth.

Serves 2	# Fruity Splash	
½ cup	milk	125 mL
2	nectarines, halved	2
½ cup	pitted cherries	125 mL
½ cup	raspberries	125 mL

1. In a blender, combine milk, nectarines, cherries and raspberries. Secure lid and blend (from low to high if using a variable speed blender) until smooth.

Serves 1 or 2	# Orange Juniper	
½	can (6 oz/175 mL) frozen orange juice concentrate	½
½ cup	water	125 mL
½ cup	evaporated milk	125 mL
¼ tsp	vanilla	1 mL
4	ice cubes	4

1. In a blender, combine orange juice concentrate, water, milk, vanilla and ice. Secure lid and process using the chop or pulse function until smooth.

Pink Lassi

Serves 1

½ cup	cranberry juice	125 mL
¼ cup	frozen raspberries	50 mL
6	frozen strawberries	6
¼ cup	plain yogurt	50 mL

1. In a blender, combine cranberry juice, raspberries, strawberries and yogurt. Secure lid and blend (from low to high if using a variable speed blender) until smooth.

Very Cherry

Serves 1

1	can (12 oz /375 mL) pitted cherries in juice	1
½ cup	cherry-flavored or plain yogurt	125 mL
¼ cup	frozen raspberries	50 mL
4	frozen yogurt or skim milk cubes (see page 319)	4

1. In a blender, combine cherries with juice, yogurt, raspberries and yogurt cubes. Secure lid and process using the chop or pulse function until smooth.

Green Gift (page 238)

Gazpacho (page 237)

Squash Special (page 250)

Banan-o-rama (page 285)

Pink Lassi (page 288)

Blue Pear (page 285)

Very Cherry (page 288)

Pink Cow (page 297)

Orange Soy (page 308)

Strawberry Soy (page 311)

Mochaccino (page 332)

Smashed Orange (page 352)

Cherry Snowball (page 344)

Peach Parfait (page 350)

Green Cosmo (page 356)

Pink Cosmo (page 359)

Milk Shakes

Serves 2

Banana au Lait

1 cup	milk	250 mL
2 tbsp	instant espresso or coffee granules	25 mL
2 tbsp	chocolate syrup	25 mL
2	bananas, cut into chunks	2
2	scoops banana, chocolate or vanilla ice cream	2

1. In a blender, combine milk, espresso granules, chocolate syrup and bananas. Secure lid and blend (from low to high if using a variable speed blender) until smooth. Add ice cream and process using the chop or pulse function until shake reaches the desired consistency.

Serves 1

Banana Chocolate Shake

1 cup	milk	250 mL
1 tbsp	unsweetened cocoa powder or carob powder	15 mL
1	banana, cut into chunks	1
Pinch	ground nutmeg	Pinch
1	scoop chocolate or vanilla ice cream	1

1. In a blender, combine milk, cocoa powder, banana and nutmeg. Secure lid and blend (from low to high if using a variable speed blender) until smooth. Add ice cream and process using the chop or pulse function until shake reaches the desired consistency.

Berry Shake

½ cup	milk	125 mL
¼ cup	plain yogurt	50 mL
1 tbsp	pure maple syrup or honey	15 mL
¼ cup	frozen blueberries	50 mL
¼ cup	frozen black or red currants or raspberries	50 mL
6	frozen blackberries	6
1	scoop berry-flavored frozen yogurt, optional	1

1. In a blender, combine milk, yogurt and maple syrup. Secure lid and blend (from low to high if using a variable speed blender) until smooth. Add blueberries, currants, blackberries, and frozen yogurt, if using. Process using the chop or pulse function until shake reaches the desired consistency.

Black Cow

1 cup	chocolate milk	250 mL
1 tbsp	unsweetened cocoa powder or carob powder	15 mL
1	banana, cut into chunks	1
1	scoop chocolate ice cream	1

1. In a blender, combine chocolate milk, cocoa powder and banana. Secure lid and blend (from low to high if using a variable speed blender) until smooth. Add ice cream and process using the chop or pulse function until shake reaches the desired consistency.

Blueberry Banana Shake

Serves 1

½ cup	milk	125 mL
½ cup	frozen blueberries	125 mL
1	banana, cut into chunks	1
1 tbsp	chopped pitted dates	15 mL
1	scoop vanilla-flavored frozen yogurt or ice cream	1

1. In a blender, combine milk, blueberries, banana and dates. Secure lid and blend (from low to high if using a variable speed blender) until smooth. Add frozen yogurt and process using the chop or pulse function until shake reaches the desired consistency.

Buttered Banana Shake

Serves 1

¼ cup	milk	50 mL
3 tbsp	butterscotch syrup	45 mL
4	frozen banana chunks	4
2 tbsp	chopped pecans	25 ml
1	scoop vanilla-flavored frozen yogurt or ice cream	1

1. In a blender, combine milk, syrup and bananas. Secure lid and blend (from low to high if using a variable speed blender) until smooth. Add pecans and frozen yogurt. Process using the chop or pulse function until shake reaches the desired consistency.

Serves 1	**Chocolate Malted**	
1 cup	milk	250 mL
2 tbsp	unsweetened cocoa powder or carob powder	25 mL
2 tbsp	malted milk powder (such as Ovaltine)	25 mL
1	scoop chocolate or coffee ice cream	1

1. In a blender, combine milk, cocoa powder and malted milk powder. Secure lid and blend (from low to high if using a variable speed blender) until smooth. Add ice cream and process using the chop or pulse function until shake reaches the desired consistency.

Serves 1	**Chocolate Minted Shake**	
$\frac{1}{2}$ cup	milk	125 mL
1 tbsp	chopped fresh peppermint	15 mL
2	small chocolate-covered peppermint patties	2
1	scoop chocolate ice cream	1

1. In a blender, combine milk, chopped peppermint and peppermint patties. Secure lid and blend (from low to high if using a variable speed blender) until smooth. Add ice cream and process using the chop or pulse function until shake reaches the desired consistency.

Chocolate Orange Shake

Serves 1

¼ cup	chocolate milk	50 mL
2 tbsp	chocolate syrup	25 mL
1 tbsp	grated orange zest	15 mL
1	orange, sectioned and seeded	1
1	scoop chocolate ice cream or orange sorbet	1

1. In a blender, combine milk, syrup, orange zest and sections. Secure lid and blend (from low to high if using a variable speed blender) until smooth. Add ice cream and process using the chop or pulse function until shake reaches the desired consistency.

Chocolate Peanut Butter Banana Slurry

Serves 1

¾ cup	milk or soy milk	175 mL
1	banana, cut into chunks	1
2 tbsp	peanut butter	25 mL
1 tbsp	carob powder or unsweetened cocoa powder	15 mL
1	scoop chocolate ice cream or frozen yogurt	1

1. In a blender, combine milk, banana, peanut butter and carob powder. Secure lid and blend (from low to high if using a variable speed blender) until smooth. Add ice cream and process using the chop or pulse function until shake reaches the desired consistency.

Coco-Choco Shake

Tip

Use canned coconut milk or homemade Coconut Milk (page 315) in this smoothie.

½ cup	milk	125 mL
¼ cup	coconut cream or coconut milk (see Tip, left)	50 mL
2 tbsp	unsweetened cocoa powder	25 mL
1 tbsp	packed brown sugar	15 mL
2	scoops chocolate-flavored frozen yogurt or ice cream	2
2 tbsp	shredded dried or freshly grated coconut, optional	25 mL

1. In a blender, combine milk, coconut cream, cocoa and brown sugar. Secure lid and blend (from low to high if using a variable speed blender) until smooth. Add frozen yogurt, and coconut, if using. Process using the chop or pulse function until shake reaches the desired consistency.

Gingered Cantaloupe Shake

Tip

Try making your own blender ice cream (see recipes, pages 339 to 342) for use in these shakes.

½ cup	coconut milk (see Tip, above)	125 mL
½	cantaloupe, cubed	½
1 tbsp	chopped candied ginger	15 mL
2	scoops vanilla ice cream or frozen yogurt	2

1. In a blender, combine coconut milk, cantaloupe and ginger. Secure lid and blend (from low to high if using a variable speed blender) until smooth. Add ice cream and process using the chop or pulse function until shake reaches the desired consistency.

Mocha Almond Shake

Serves 1 or 2

Variation
Use regular milk or soy or rice milk in place of Almond Milk.

½ cup	Almond Milk (recipe, page 314)	125 mL
4	chocolate-covered coffee beans	4
⅛ tsp	almond extract	0.5 mL
2	scoops chocolate ice cream	2

1. In a blender, combine almond milk, coffee beans and almond extract. Secure lid and blend (from low to high if using a variable speed blender) until smooth. Add ice cream and process using the chop or pulse function until shake reaches the desired consistency.

Nectar Shake

Serves 2

½ cup	milk	125 mL
½ cup	peach or apricot nectar	125 mL
1	peach, halved	1
1	nectarine, halved	1
2	scoops lemon sherbet	2

1. In a blender, combine milk, peach nectar, peach and nectarine. Secure lid and blend (from low to high if using a variable speed blender) until smooth. Add sherbet and process using the chop or pulse function until shake reaches the desired consistency.

Serves 1

Peach Blush

½ cup	milk	125 mL
2 tbsp	raspberry or strawberry syrup	25 mL
1	peach, halved	1
½ cup	halved strawberries	125 mL
1	scoop peach or vanilla ice cream	1

1. In a blender, combine milk, syrup, peach and strawberries. Secure lid and blend (from low to high if using a variable speed blender) until smooth. Add ice cream and process using the chop or pulse function until shake reaches the desired consistency.

Serves 1

Peanut Butter and Jelly Shake

½ cup	milk or soy milk	125 mL
1	container (6 oz/175 g) fruit-on-the-bottom yogurt	1
1	banana, cut into chunks	1
2 tbsp	peanut butter	25 mL
½ cup	vanilla ice cream	125 mL

1. In a blender, combine milk, yogurt, banana and peanut butter. Secure lid and blend (from low to high if using a variable speed blender) until smooth. Add ice cream and process using the chop or pulse function until shake reaches the desired consistency.

Pineapple Colada Shake

Serves 2

Tip
Use canned coconut milk or homemade Coconut Milk (page 315) in this smoothie.

½ cup	coconut milk (see Tip, left)	125 mL
1	can (8 oz/227 mL) crushed pineapple, drained	1
2 tbsp	toasted shredded coconut	25 mL
3	scoops vanilla ice cream	3

1. In a blender, combine coconut milk, pineapple and shredded coconut. Secure lid and blend (from low to high if using a variable speed blender) until smooth. Add ice cream and process using the chop or pulse function until shake reaches the desired consistency.

Pink Cow

Serves 1

1 cup	milk	250 mL
6	frozen strawberries	6
½	frozen banana, cut into chunks	½
1	scoop strawberry ice cream	1

1. In a blender, combine milk, strawberries and banana. Secure lid and blend (from low to high if using a variable speed blender) until smooth. Add ice cream and process using the chop or pulse function until shake reaches the desired consistency.

Serves 2

Plum Bliss

½ cup	milk	125 mL
2 tbsp	raspberry or strawberry syrup	25 mL
3	red or black plums, halved	3
1 cup	raspberries	250 mL
2	scoops vanilla ice cream or frozen yogurt	2

1. In a blender, combine milk, syrup, plums and raspberries. Secure lid and blend (from low to high if using a variable speed blender) until smooth. Add ice cream and process using the chop or pulse function until shake reaches the desired consistency.

Serves 2

Pumpkin Shake

Tip

Canned pumpkin works well in this recipe.

¼ cup	milk	50 mL
½ cup	pumpkin purée (see Tip, left)	125 mL
1	banana, cut into chunks	1
2	pitted dates	2
1 tbsp	packed brown sugar	15 mL
1	scoop vanilla ice cream or frozen yogurt	1
Pinch	ground nutmeg	Pinch

1. In a blender, combine milk, pumpkin purée, banana, dates and brown sugar. Secure lid and blend (from low to high if using a variable speed blender) until smooth. Add ice cream and process using the chop or pulse function until shake reaches the desired consistency. Pour shake into a glass and sprinkle nutmeg over top.

Razzy Chocolate Slush

½ cup	frozen raspberries	125 mL
¼ cup	cranberry-raspberry juice	50 mL
4	frozen chocolate milk cubes (page 319), crushed	4
1	scoop chocolate ice cream	1

1. In a blender, combine raspberries, cranberry-raspberry juice and chocolate milk cubes. Secure lid and blend (from low to high if using a variable speed blender) until smooth. Add ice cream and process using the chop or pulse function until shake reaches the desired consistency.

Summer Strawberry Shake

½ cup	milk	125 mL
1 cup	halved strawberries	250 mL
½ cup	raspberries	125 mL
1	scoop vanilla-flavored frozen yogurt or ice cream	1

1. In a blender, combine milk, strawberries and raspberries. Secure lid and blend (from low to high if using a variable speed blender) until smooth. Add frozen yogurt and process using the chop or pulse function until shake reaches the desired consistency.

Serves 2	**Tropical Shake**	

½ cup	coconut milk	125 mL
1 cup	chopped pineapple	250 mL
3	starfruits, halved	3
½ cup	silken tofu	125 mL
4	frozen banana chunks	4

1. In a blender, combine coconut milk, pineapple, starfruits and tofu. Secure lid and blend (from low to high if using a variable speed blender) until smooth. Add frozen banana chunks and process using the chop or pulse function until shake reaches the desired consistency.

Dairy Alternative Smoothies

Milk Intolerance

A significant number of people have difficulty digesting the sugar in milk, which is called lactose. This condition is called lactose intolerance and is characterized by the appearance of painful symptoms, such as bloating after milk or milk products are consumed. Eliminating milk and dairy products from the diet alleviates this condition. If you are lactose intolerant or allergic to milk, be aware that cream; butter; processed products, such as cereals and baking mixes; and baked goods that contain milk, milk solids, cheese, cheese flavoring, whey, curds or even margarine may trigger digestive problems. Fortunately, a wide variety of nondairy liquids — such as soy milk, rice milk, fruit milks and nut milks, which are usually good sources of protein and calcium — may be used as substitutes for dairy products.

Alternative Sources of Calcium

Commercially produced cow's milk, which can be tainted with hormones and antibiotics fed to cattle, may be an overrated source of calcium. Legumes (dried beans and lentils) are an excellent alternative. For example, 1 cup (250 mL) of 2% milk has 121 g of calcium, but ½ cup (125 mL) canned chickpeas with their canning liquid has 143 g of calcium. Other good sources of calcium are leafy greens, broccoli, nuts and sea herbs (see page 149). Raw sesame seeds contain more calcium than any other food (1 oz/30 g contains 162 g of calcium, compared with 1 oz/30 mL whole milk, which contains 18 g of calcium) and make an excellent addition to your diet.

Soy Milk

People seeking to reduce their saturated fat intake will find soy milk, which is made from soybeans, a versatile and tasty option. It may be substituted for regular milk in all smoothie recipes. Soy milk contains more protein and iron, less fat, fewer calories, no cholesterol and about one-fifth the calcium of cow's milk (for this reason, most soy milk is fortified with extra calcium). Soy milk can be frozen in ice-cube trays for use in smoothies.

Rice Milk

Rice milk, made from brown rice and filtered water, is slightly sweet and, when fortified, provides as much calcium and vitamins A and D as milk. Low in fat, it contains no lactose and is a tasty alternative for people who cannot tolerate dairy products.

Unflavored soy milk or rice milk can be substituted for milk in the recipes in this book.

Fruit Milks

Fruit milk is made by combining chopped dried fruit with boiling water. They are low in fat and cholesterol and can serve as milk substitutes in smoothies. The concentrated natural sugars in dried fruit make fruit milks very sweet.

To make fruit milk: Use unsulfured dried fruit available at alternative/health stores. Figs, dates and apricots are often used for fruit milks, but any dried fruit can be used.

Nut Milks

When blended with water, nuts make a pleasant, thick liquid that can be used in smoothies. Nut milks (see recipes on pages 314 to 316) can be used to cut the sweetness of fruit smoothies. Nut milk make thicker shakes or smoothies than juice or soy milk and can be substituted for these liquids in most recipes.

Nuts contribute protein, vitamin E and fiber to the diet but should be eaten in small amounts because they are high in fat (although the fat in nuts is mostly unsaturated and contains healthful essential fatty acids). Because they are high in fat, nuts go rancid quickly. Purchase them in natural food stores with high turnover and taste them before buying. You can store nuts in the freezer to keep them fresher longer.

To make nut milk: Use unsalted organic nuts with the skins intact. You can also make milk using seeds — sunflower, flax and sesame. Raw sesame seeds are a good choice because they contain more calcium than any other food. Try making milk using half nuts and half sesame seeds.

Coconut Milk

Coconuts are the fruits of the coconut palm tree (*Cocos nucifera*) but are classified as nuts because they have an edible kernel inside a hard, brittle shell. Coconut meat can be eaten fresh or dried, and the thin, watery juice in fresh coconuts is used in cooking and drinks. This juice should not be confused with coconut milk.

Dried coconut meat may be shredded, flaked or compressed into hard cakes. These dried forms are often saturated with sucrose or fructose (sugar) solutions or corn syrup. To make your own Coconut Milk (page 315), use shredded fresh or unsweetened shredded dried coconut (available at natural food stores).

Canned coconut milk is widely available but may contain sugar, water and other additives. Check the label and, if possible, purchase unsweetened coconut milk, which may be substituted for any dairy or nondairy milk or homemade coconut milk in smoothies. Coconut cream is a thicker version of coconut milk.

Caution: Coconuts are high in saturated fat. One ounce (30 g) of sweetened shredded dried coconut contains 10.1 g of fat (8.9 g of which are saturated). One ounce (30 g) of pecans has 20 g of fat, but only 2 g are saturated, making pecans a healthier choice than coconut.

Dairy Alternative Smoothies

Serves 1	**Almond Cherry**	
½ cup	Almond Milk (page 314)	125 mL
½ cup	pitted cherries	125 mL
½ cup	frozen raspberries	125 mL
⅛ tsp	almond extract	0.5 mL

1. In a blender, combine almond milk, cherries, raspberries and almond extract. Secure lid and blend (from low to high if using a variable speed blender) until smooth.

Serves 1	**Almond Raspberry**	
¾ cup	Almond Milk (page 314)	175 mL
½ cup	frozen raspberries	125 mL
2	plums, halved	2
⅛ tsp	almond extract	0.5 mL

1. In a blender, combine almond milk, raspberries, plums and almond extract. Secure lid and blend (from low to high if using a variable speed blender) until smooth.

Serves 1	**Avocado Shake**	
1 cup	soy or rice milk	250 mL
	Juice of ½ lemon	
1	avocado, halved	1
1	grapefruit, sectioned and seeded	1
1 tbsp	molasses	15 mL

1. In a blender, combine soy milk, lemon juice, avocado, grapefruit and molasses. Secure lid and blend (from low to high if using a variable speed blender) until smooth.

Serves 1	# Baklava	
¾ cup	Walnut Milk (page 316)	175 mL
1 tbsp	sesame seeds	15 mL
1 tbsp	liquid honey	15 mL
½ cup	frozen peach slices	125 mL

1. In a blender, combine walnut milk, sesame seeds, honey and peaches. Secure lid and blend (from low to high if using a variable speed blender) until smooth.

Serves 1	# Banana Frappé	
1 cup	Almond Milk (page 314)	250 mL
½ cup	silken tofu	125 mL
4	frozen banana chunks	4
1 tbsp	carob powder or unsweetened cocoa powder	15 mL
⅛ tsp	almond extract, optional	0.5 mL

1. In a blender, combine almond milk, tofu, banana, carob powder, and almond extract (if using). Secure lid and blend (from low to high if using a variable speed blender) until smooth.

Serves 1	# Beta Whiz	
½ cup	Fig Milk (page 313)	125 mL
¼ cup	carrot or freshly squeezed orange juice	50 mL
¼	cantaloupe, cubed	¼
1 tbsp	chopped almonds	15 mL
1 tbsp	buckwheat flakes	15 mL

Tips

This drink is thick and has the refreshing taste of cantaloupe. For a thinner consistency, increase the carrot juice by ¼ cup (50 mL).

Look for buckwheat flakes at alternative/health stores.

1. In a blender, combine fig milk, carrot juice, cantaloupe, almonds and buckwheat flakes. Secure lid and blend (from low to high if using a variable speed blender) until smooth.

Serves 1 or 2

Blueberry Frappé

Tip
Any berries — blueberries, raspberries, strawberries, blackberries or even black currants — work well in this smoothie.

1 cup	Apricot Milk (page 312) or apricot nectar	250 mL
½ cup	silken tofu	125 mL
½ cup	frozen blueberries	125 mL
4	ice cubes	4

1. In a blender, combine apricot milk, tofu, blueberries and ice cubes. Secure lid and process using the chop or pulse function until smooth.

Serves 2

Breakfast in Brazil

¾ cup	soy or rice milk or coconut milk (page 315)	175 mL
¾ cup	frozen strawberries	175 mL
1	banana, cut into chunks	1
2 tbsp	chopped Brazil nuts	25 mL
2 tbsp	wheat germ or steel-cut or rolled oats	25 mL
1 tsp	cod liver oil, optional	5 mL
⅛ tsp	ground cinnamon	0.5 mL

1. In a blender, combine soy milk, strawberries, banana, Brazil nuts, wheat germ, cod liver oil, if using, and cinnamon. Secure lid and blend (from low to high if using a variable speed blender) until smooth.

Caribbean Crush

Serves 1

¾ cup	soy or rice milk or coconut milk (page 315)	175 mL
	Juice of ½ lime	
½	mango	½
1	kiwi, quartered	1

1. In a blender, combine soy milk, lime juice, mango and kiwi. Secure lid and blend (from low to high if using a variable speed blender) until smooth.

Chocolate Pecan

Serves 1

¾ cup	Pecan Milk (page 315)	175 mL
½ cup	frozen peach slices	125 mL
½ cup	chopped pineapple	125 mL
1 tbsp	carob powder or unsweetened cocoa powder	15 mL
4	frozen juice (page 319) or ice cubes	4

1. In a blender, combine pecan milk, peaches, pineapple, carob powder and juice cubes. Secure lid and blend (from low to high if using a variable speed blender) until smooth.

Date and Nut

Serves 1 or 2

Tip
Add 1 tbsp (15 mL) chopped pitted dates to the ingredients if you are using soy milk instead of Date Milk.

1 cup	Date Milk (page 312) or soy or rice milk	250 mL
½ cup	silken tofu	125 mL
2	apples, quartered	2
1 tbsp	chopped almonds	15 mL
Pinch	ground nutmeg	Pinch

1. In a blender, combine date milk, tofu, apples, almonds and nutmeg. Secure lid and blend (from low to high if using a variable speed blender) until smooth.

Gingered Almond

Tip

Using frozen fruit in smoothies thickens and chills the drink. Substitute the same quantity of fresh fruit, if desired.

¾ cup	Almond Milk (page 314)	175 mL
1 tbsp	chopped candied ginger	15 mL
¼ cup	chopped pineapple	50 mL
4	frozen banana chunks	4
⅛ tsp	almond extract	0.5 mL

1. In a blender, combine almond milk, ginger, pineapple, banana and almond extract. Secure lid and blend (from low to high if using a variable speed blender) until smooth.

Just Peachy Almond

¾ cup	Almond Milk (page 314)	175 mL
½ cup	frozen peach slices	125 mL
4	apricots, halved	4
⅛ tsp	almond extract	0.5 mL

1. In a blender, combine almond milk, peaches, apricots and almond extract. Secure lid and blend (from low to high if using a variable speed blender) until smooth.

Orange Soy

½ cup	soy or rice milk	125 mL
2	oranges, sectioned and seeded	2
½ cup	frozen sliced peaches	125 mL
2	ice cubes	2

1. In a blender, combine soy milk, oranges and peaches. Secure lid and blend (from low to high if using a variable speed blender) until smooth. Add ice and process using the chop or pulse function until smoothie reaches the desired consistency.

Serves 2

Peach Coconut

1 cup	canned peaches with juice	250 mL
¼ cup	coconut milk	50 mL
¼ cup	chopped pineapple	50 mL
4	frozen unflavored soy milk cubes (page 319)	4

1. In a blender, combine peaches with juice, coconut milk and pineapple. Secure lid and blend (from low to high if using a variable speed blender) until smooth. Add soy milk cubes and process using the chop or pulse function until smoothie reaches the desired consistency.

Serves 1 or 2

Peach Fuzz

Tip

You can use dried apricots instead of fresh in any smoothie.

½ cup	Fig Milk (page 313) or soy or rice milk	125 mL
¼ cup	peach or apricot nectar or freshly squeezed orange juice	50 mL
¾ cup	frozen peach slices	175 mL
2	apricots, halved	2
4	ice cubes	4

1. In a blender, combine fig milk, peach nectar, frozen peaches and apricots. Secure lid and blend (from low to high if using a variable speed blender) until smooth. Add ice and process using the chop or pulse function until smoothie reaches the desired consistency.

Serves 2 or 3	**Peach Pie**	

Peach Pie

¼ cup	pineapple juice	50 mL
¼ cup	coconut milk	50 mL
1 cup	sliced peaches	250 mL
¼ cup	chopped pineapple	50 mL
2 tbsp	plain or toasted unsweetened shredded coconut	25 mL
½ tsp	pure vanilla extract	2 mL

1. In a blender, combine pineapple juice, coconut milk, peaches, chopped pineapple, shredded coconut and vanilla. Secure lid and blend (from low to high if using a variable speed blender) until smooth.

Piña Colada

Serves 1

¾ cup	coconut milk	175 mL
½ cup	chopped pineapple	125 mL
1	kiwifruit, quartered	1
½ cup	frozen unflavored soy milk cubes (page 319)	125 mL

1. In a blender, combine coconut milk, pineapple and kiwi. Secure lid and blend (from low to high if using a variable speed blender) until smooth. Add soy milk cubes and process using the chop or pulse function until smooth.

Serves 2

Strawberry Soy

½ cup	soy or rice milk	125 mL
12	strawberries	12
½ cup	frozen peach slices	125 mL
2	ice cubes	2

1. In a blender, combine soy milk, strawberries, peaches and ice cubes. Secure lid and process using the chop or pulse function until smooth.

Serves 1

Tropical Tonic

¼ cup	soy or rice milk	50 mL
¼ cup	coconut milk	50 mL
½ cup	chopped pineapple	125 mL
1	banana, cut into chunks	1

1. In a blender, combine soy milk, coconut milk, pineapple and banana. Secure lid and process using the chop or pulse function until smooth.

Apricot Milk

2 cups	boiling water, divided	500 mL
½ cup	chopped dried apricots	125 mL
1 tbsp	chopped vanilla bean	15 mL

Tip

This fruit milk has a unique sweet-tart taste. Use it in any of the fruit shakes or smoothies in this book in place of all or part of the liquid. Look for unsulfured organic dried apricots, to which sulfur dioxide has not been added in the drying process.

1. In a blender, combine 1 cup (250 mL) boiling water, apricots and vanilla bean. Secure lid and blend (from low to high if using a variable speed blender) until smooth.

2. With blender still running, add remaining boiling water through opening in center of lid. Blend until smooth. Check consistency and add up to an additional ½ cup (125 mL) boiling water if desired, blending until smooth. Let cool. Cover and refrigerate for up to 1 week.

Date Milk

½ cup	boiling water	125 mL
¼ cup	chopped pitted dates	50 mL
2 tsp	chopped vanilla bean	10 mL

Tip

Date sugar is commonly used in commercial products as a sweetener. Using date milk is like using sugar (although it provides some fiber and a few nutrients), so use it sparingly.

1. In a blender, combine boiling water, dates and vanilla bean. Secure lid and blend (from low to high if using a variable speed blender) until smooth. Let cool. Cover and refrigerate for up to 1 week.

Fig Milk

Makes ¾ cup (175 mL)

½ cup	boiling water	125 mL
¼ cup	chopped dried figs (or ⅓ cup/75 mL chopped fresh figs)	50 mL
2 tsp	chopped vanilla bean	10 mL

1. In a blender, combine boiling water, figs and vanilla bean. Secure lid and blend (from low to high if using a variable speed blender) until smooth. Let cool. Cover and refrigerate for up to 1 week.

Tip

Figs have antibacterial and cancer-fighting properties and make a sweet milk that can be used with yogurt or tofu in smoothies. Use fresh figs if available. Dried figs are difficult for machines to chop and should be coarsely chopped by hand before processing in the blender.

Almond Milk

2 cups	boiling water, divided	500 mL
1 cup	finely chopped almonds	250 mL
1 tbsp	chopped pitted dates	15 mL
1 tbsp	ground flax seeds	15 mL
1 tbsp	chopped vanilla bean	15 mL

1. In a blender, combine 1 cup (250 mL) boiling water, almonds, dates, flax seeds and vanilla bean. Secure lid and blend (from low to high if using a variable speed blender) until smooth.

2. With blender still running, add remaining boiling water through opening in center of lid. Blend until smooth. Let cool. Cover and refrigerate for up to 3 days.

Cashew Milk

2 cups	boiling water, divided	500 mL
¾ cup	finely chopped cashews	175 mL
1 tbsp	crushed dried dulse	15 mL
1 tbsp	chopped raisins	15 mL
1 tbsp	chopped vanilla bean	15 mL

1. In a blender, combine 1 cup (250 mL) boiling water, cashews, dulse, raisins and vanilla bean. Secure lid and blend (from low to high if using a variable speed blender) until smooth.

2. With blender still running, add remaining boiling water through opening in center of lid. Blend until smooth. Let cool. Cover and refrigerate for up to 3 days.

Coconut Milk

½ cup	boiling water	125 mL
½ cup	shredded fresh coconut (see Tip, left)	125 mL
2 tsp	chopped vanilla bean	10 mL

1. In a blender, combine boiling water, coconut and vanilla bean. Secure lid and blend (from low to high if using a variable speed blender) until smooth. Let cool. Cover and refrigerate for up to 1 week.

Tip

To make this milk, use one fresh coconut and shred the flesh using a regular box grater (freeze any leftovers). If fresh coconut is unavailable, use unsweetened shredded dried coconut, which is available at some alternative/health stores. Use coconut milk in frozen drinks, shakes, puddings and other desserts to replace both sugar and milk.

Variation

Coconut Carob Milk: Coconut is naturally sweet, and when blended with carob, it is even sweeter. For this chocolaty version of coconut milk, add 1 tbsp (15 mL) carob powder to the blender along with the coconut.

Pecan Milk

2 cups	boiling water, divided	500 mL
¾ cup	finely chopped pecans	175 mL
1 tbsp	chopped raisins	15 mL
1 tbsp	chopped vanilla bean	15 mL

1. In a blender, combine 1 cup (250 mL) boiling water, pecans, raisins and vanilla bean. Secure lid and blend (from low to high if using a variable speed blender) until smooth.

2. With blender still running, add remaining boiling water through opening in center of lid. Blend until smooth. Let cool. Cover and refrigerate for up to 3 days.

Walnut Milk

**Makes 2 cups
(500 mL)**

2 cups	boiling water, divided	500 mL
¾ cup	finely chopped walnuts	175 mL
1 tbsp	chopped pitted dates	15 mL
1 tbsp	ground flax seeds	15 mL
1 tbsp	chopped vanilla bean	15 mL

1. In a blender, combine 1 cup (250 mL) boiling water, walnuts, dates, flax seeds and vanilla bean. Secure lid and blend (from low to high if using a variable speed blender) until smooth.

2. With blender still running, add remaining boiling water through opening in center of lid. Blend until smooth. Let cool. Cover and refrigerate for up to 3 days.

Hot and Frozen Smoothies

Hot Smoothies

Comforting and soothing, warm toddies and mulled drinks hark back to earlier times, when thick, syrupy medicinal "robs" were stirred into hot teas and administered to relieve cold symptoms and bronchial problems.

The usual method for making hot smoothies is to add hot liquids (scalded milk, hot broth, herbal tea or boiling water) to the other ingredients before blending. Another technique is to cook the main ingredients before blending and add them to the remaining ingredients while they are still hot. Alternatively, ingredients may be blended while cold or at room temperature, then heated in a saucepan on the stovetop or in the microwave. Adding "hot" herbs, such as ginger, turmeric and cayenne (or other chile peppers), can add a unique warming touch to smoothies.

Heating Milk

When milk or cream is heated for use in smoothies, it is scalded rather than boiled, which can result in scorching.

To scald milk or cream: Measure milk or cream into a small saucepan and heat over low heat, stirring occasionally, just until bubbles form around the edge of the pan. Remove from the heat and use immediately.

Blending Hot Liquids

Place half of any hot liquid in the blender jug with the solid ingredients and blend for 30 seconds. With the blender still running, add the remaining hot liquid gradually through the opening in the center of the lid. This prevents a surge of hot liquid from being forced upward, which might cause the lid to blow off.

Using boiling water: In recipes in which boiling water is required, bring a kettle of water to a boil, remove it from the heat and allow the bubbles to subside before measuring and adding to the ingredients in the blender.

Frozen Smoothies

Thick, cold and refreshing, there is no better way to bring your body temperature down after a workout or during the intense heat of summer than with a frozen blended drink. Consuming nutrients along with water sends energy and food to muscles while rehydrating the system. You can easily turn ordinary fruit smoothies into slushy treats that require a spoon by adding ice, frozen fruit (see page 154 for how to freeze fresh fruit) and/or frozen unsweetened juice concentrates. Ice makes smoothies not only cold but also thicker.

Some liquid (milk, yogurt, juice or nut or fruit milk) is required to make frozen smoothies. This liquid must be added to the jug before the frozen ingredients. Never add ice to the jug and try to process it unless there is some liquid in the bottom. The frozen smoothie recipes are very thick and require a spoon — add more liquid if a thinner drink is desired.

Using Ice in Frozen Smoothies

When adding ice to smoothies, you are actually adding liquid to the drink. If a large quantity of ice is used, the flavor of the smoothie will be diluted. To compensate, reduce the quantity of other liquids. Using undiluted frozen fruit juice concentrates instead of ice is one technique for maintaining flavor intensity while adding that frozen texture.

To facilitate the removal of frozen cubes, let ice-cube trays stand at room temperature for three to five minutes before using. This also makes it easier to chop the cubes.

Liquid Equivalents for Ice

1 ice cube = approximately $1\frac{1}{2}$ tbsp (22 mL) liquid
6 ice cubes = approximately $\frac{1}{2}$ cup (125 mL) liquid

Flavored Ice Cubes

For a concentrated taste, substitute flavored ice cubes for regular in smoothie recipes. Make flavored ice cubes by freezing juice, herbal teas, strong coffee, leftover smoothie mixtures, soy milk, nut or fruit milks, or yogurt in ice-cube trays.

Frozen Milk Cubes

Plain or chocolate milk can be frozen in ice-cube trays to replace ice cream in milk shake recipes. Use six frozen milk cubes to replace one scoop or $\frac{1}{2}$ cup (125 mL) ice cream. To reduce the amount of fat in the drink, use lower fat or skim milk

Frozen Fruit Juice Concentrates

Frozen unsweetened fruit juice concentrates can be added straight from the can when making frozen smoothies. Run the container under hot water and soften just enough so that the contents can be squeezed directly into the blender jug. When only half a can is required, squeeze the remaining half into a resealable plastic freezer bag, label and refreeze immediately.

Frozen Yogurt Cubes

Drain and discard liquid from a 16-oz (500 g) container of unflavored yogurt. Spoon into ice-cube trays and freeze. Use in smoothies where frozen yogurt is called for. Use six frozen yogurt cubes to replace one scoop or $\frac{1}{2}$ cup (125 mL) frozen yogurt.

Serves 2 or 3

Blazing Bullshot

2 cups	beef, chicken or vegetable broth	500 mL
½ to 1	chile pepper, chopped	½ to 1
2	tomatoes, quartered	2
1	stalk celery, cut into chunks	1
1 tbsp	freshly squeezed lemon juice	15 mL
½ tsp	Worcestershire sauce	2 mL
¼ tsp	garam masala, optional	1 mL

1. In a saucepan, heat broth over medium heat just until simmering.

2. In a blender, combine 1 cup (250 mL) of the stock, chile pepper, tomatoes, celery, lemon juice, Worcestershire sauce, and garam masala, if using. Secure lid and blend (from low to high if using a variable speed blender) until smooth.

3. With blender still running, add remaining stock through opening in center of lid. Blend until smooth.

Café au Lait

1 cup	scalded milk (see Tip, left) or soy milk, divided	250 mL
¼ tsp	pure vanilla extract	1 mL
⅛ tsp	ground cinnamon	0.5 mL
1 cup	hot strong brewed coffee	250 mL

1. In a blender, combine ½ cup (125 mL) milk, vanilla and cinnamon. Secure lid and blend (from low to high if using a variable speed blender) until smooth.

2. With blender still running, add remaining hot milk through opening in center of lid. Blend until frothy. To serve, pour hot milk mixture and coffee into mugs at the same time.

Citrus Toddy

1 cup	boiling water, divided	250 mL
2 tbsp	liquid honey, or to taste	25 mL
	Juice of 1 lemon	
1	orange, sectioned and seeded	1
½	grapefruit, sectioned and seeded	½
1	piece (½ inch/1 cm) gingerroot, peeled	1
1 tsp	dried elderflowers, optional	5 mL

1. In a blender, combine ½ cup (125 mL) boiling water, honey, lemon juice, orange, grapefruit, ginger, and elderflowers, if using. Secure lid and blend (from low to high if using a variable speed blender) until smooth.

2. With blender still running, add remaining hot water through opening in center of lid. Blend until smooth.

Serves 2	# Hot Chai	
2 cups	milk or soy milk	500 mL
1	green or black tea bag or 2 tsp (10 mL) loose tea	1
1 tbsp	chopped candied ginger	15 mL
¼ tsp	ground cinnamon	1 mL
3	black peppercorns	3
1	whole clove	1
⅛ tsp	ground cardamom (optional)	0.5 mL
2 tbsp	liquid honey, or to taste	25 mL

1. In a medium saucepan over medium heat, bring milk, tea, ginger, cinnamon, peppercorns, clove, and cardamom, if using, just to a simmer. Remove from heat. Strain and discard tea bags and herbs.

2. In a blender, combine half of the milk mixture with the honey. Secure lid and blend (from low to high if using a variable speed blender) until smooth.

3. With blender still running, add remaining hot milk through opening in center of lid. Blend until smooth.

Hot Chocolate

Serves 2

Tip

To scald milk or cream: Measure milk into a saucepan and heat over low heat, stirring occasionally, just until bubbles form around the edge of the pan. Remove from heat and use immediately.

2 cups	scalded milk (see Tip, left) or table (18%) cream divided	500 mL
1 tbsp	unsweetened cocoa powder or carob powder	15 mL
1 tbsp	granulated sugar	15 mL
1 oz	bittersweet chocolate, chopped	30 g
¼ tsp	pure vanilla extract	1 mL

1. In a blender, combine 1 cup (250 mL) scalded milk, cocoa powder, sugar, chopped chocolate and vanilla. Secure lid and blend (from low to high if using a variable speed blender) until smooth.

2. With blender still running, add remaining hot milk through opening in center of lid. Blend until smooth.

Hot Gingered Apple Cider

Serves 2

1 cup	apple cider or apple juice	250 mL
2 tbsp	liquid honey, or to taste	25 mL
1 tbsp	chopped candied ginger	15 mL
1/8 tsp	ground cinnamon	0.5 mL
1/8 tsp	ground cloves	0.5 mL
Pinch	ground nutmeg	Pinch
1	apple, quartered	1
1 tsp	apple cider vinegar	5 mL

1. In a medium saucepan over medium heat, bring apple cider, honey, ginger, cinnamon, cloves and nutmeg just to a boil.

2. In a blender, combine half of the cider mixture, the apple and cider vinegar. Secure lid and blend (from low to high if using a variable speed blender) until smooth.

3. With blender still running, add remaining hot cider through opening in center of lid. Blend until smooth.

Serves 1	# Hot Spiced Pear	
¾ cup	pear nectar or apple cider	175 mL
1 tsp	balsamic vinegar	5 mL
¼ tsp	ground nutmeg	1 mL
Pinch	ground cloves	Pinch
3	pears, quartered	3
2 tbsp	raisins	25 mL

1. In a medium saucepan over medium heat, bring pear nectar, vinegar, nutmeg and cloves just to a boil.

2. In a blender, combine half of the pear nectar mixture, the pears and raisins. Secure lid and blend (from low to high if using a variable speed blender) until smooth.

3. With blender still running, add remaining hot pear nectar mixture through opening in center of lid. Blend until smooth.

Serves 1	# Mexican Hot Hot Chocolate	

Tip

To scald milk or cream: Measure milk into a saucepan and heat over low heat, stirring occasionally, just until bubbles form around the edge of the pan. Remove from heat and use immediately.

1 cup	scalded milk, divided (see Tip, left)	250 mL
2 tbsp	liquid honey, or to taste	25 mL
1 tbsp	chopped bittersweet chocolate	15 mL
1 tsp	chopped candied ginger	5 mL
¼ tsp	vanilla	1 mL
⅛ tsp	ground cinnamon	0.5 mL
⅛ tsp	hot pepper flakes or cayenne pepper	0.5 mL

1. In a blender, combine ½ cup (125 mL) scalded milk, honey, chocolate, ginger, vanilla, cinnamon and hot pepper flakes. Secure lid and blend (from low to high if using a variable speed blender) until smooth.

2. With blender still running, add remaining hot milk through opening in center of lid. Blend until smooth.

Wassail

Serves 4

- Preheat oven to 375°F (190°C)
- Rimmed baking sheet, lightly greased
- 4 warmed heatproof mugs

4	apples	4
¼ cup	raisins	50 mL
4 tsp	butter	20 mL
¼ cup	liquid honey	50 mL
2 cups	apple cider or apple juice	500 mL
½ tsp	ground cinnamon, divided	2 mL
¼ tsp	ground allspice, divided	1 mL
¼ tsp	ground cloves, divided	1 mL
4	sticks (each 2 inches/5 cm long) cinnamon	4

1. Using a melon baller or spoon, remove apple cores at the tops, making a cavity but leaving bottoms intact. Place, hollow side up, on prepared baking sheet.

2. In a bowl, combine raisins and butter. Divide into 4 equal portions and stuff into the cavity of each apple. Drizzle with honey. Bake in preheated oven for 30 minutes or until tender. Let cool. Remove and discard skins.

3. Meanwhile, in a saucepan over medium-high heat, bring cider to a simmer. Reduce heat to low and keep warm.

4. In a blender, combine 1 cup (250 mL) of the hot cider, ¼ tsp (1 mL) cinnamon, ⅛ tsp (0.5 mL) allspice and ⅛ tsp (0.5 mL) cloves. Blend on low for 30 seconds. Stop blender and add 2 of the baked apples. Secure lid and blend (from low to high if using a variable speed blender) until smooth. Pour into 2 warmed mugs and garnish each with 1 cinnamon stick. Repeat with remaining hot cider, cinnamon, allspice, cloves, baked apples and cinnamon sticks.

Frozen Smoothies

Serves 2

Apricot Ice

1	can (14 or 15 oz/398 or 425 mL) apricots with juice	1
¼ cup	chopped dried apricots	50 mL
⅓ cup	frozen raspberries	75 mL
⅓ cup	frozen strawberries	75 mL
2	ice cubes	2

1. In a blender, combine apricots with juice, dried apricots, raspberries, strawberries and ice cubes. Secure lid and process using the chop or pulse function until smooth.

Serves 2

Chocolate Cherry Chiller

Tip
You can substitute 6 frozen chocolate milk cubes (see page 319) for the frozen yogurt in this smoothie.

1 cup	chocolate milk	250 mL
1 cup	frozen pitted cherries	250 mL
½ cup	chocolate-flavored frozen yogurt	125 mL

1. In a blender, combine chocolate milk, cherries and frozen yogurt. Secure lid and blend (from low to high if using a variable speed blender) until smooth.

Serves 1

Frozen Lemonade

Tip
Make frozen limeade by using frozen limeade concentrate and limes instead of lemons.

¼ cup	frozen lemonade concentrate	50 mL
2	lemons, sectioned and seeded	2
6	ice cubes, divided	6
3 tbsp	liquid honey, or to taste	45 mL

1. In a blender, combine lemonade concentrate, lemons, 3 ice cubes and honey. Secure lid and process using the chop or pulse function until smooth.

2. Add remaining ice cubes, one at a time, and process using the chop or pulse function until smooth. Keep adding ice until desired thickness is achieved. Serve immediately with a spoon.

Serves 2

Frozen Mint Julep

½ cup	chilled brewed green or black tea	125 mL
½ cup	frozen pineapple juice concentrate	125 mL
1 tsp	grated lemon zest	5 mL
1 tbsp	freshly squeezed lemon juice	15 mL
1 tsp	chopped candied ginger	5 mL
1 tbsp	granulated sugar, or to taste	15 mL
1 tbsp	chopped fresh peppermint	15 mL
6	ice cubes, divided	6

1. In a blender, combine tea, pineapple juice concentrate, lemon zest and juice, ginger, sugar, peppermint and 3 ice cubes. Secure lid and process using the chop or pulse function until smooth.

2. Add remaining ice cubes, one at a time, and process using the chop or pulse function until smooth. Keep adding ice until desired thickness is achieved. Serve immediately with a spoon.

Gingered Lemonade

Serves 2 or 3

¾ cup	freshly squeezed lemon juice	175 mL
8	ice cubes, divided	8
1 tbsp	chopped candied ginger	15 mL
2 tbsp	granulated sugar, or to taste	25 mL
1 cup	sparkling mineral water or soda water	250 mL

1. In a blender, combine lemon juice, 4 ice cubes, ginger and sugar. Secure lid and process using the chop or pulse function until smooth.

2. Add remaining ice cubes, one at a time, and process using the chop or pulse function until smooth. Keep adding ice until desired thickness is achieved. Spoon into glasses and top with mineral water. Stir to combine.

Golden Nectar Glacé

Serves 1 or 2

¾ cup	peach nectar	175 mL
¼ cup	frozen orange juice concentrate	50 mL
4	ice cubes	4
¼	cantaloupe, cubed	¼

1. In a blender, combine peach nectar, orange juice concentrate, ice and cantaloupe. Secure lid and process using the chop or pulse function until smooth. Serve immediately with a spoon.

| Serves 2 | **Grapefruit Rosemary Granita** | | |

Grapefruit Rosemary Granita

½ cup	freshly squeezed grapefruit juice	125 mL
3	ice cubes	3
2 cups	lemon sorbet	500 mL
½ tsp	chopped fresh rosemary leaves	2 mL

1. In a blender, combine grapefruit juice, ice, sorbet and rosemary. Secure lid and process using the chop or pulse function until smooth. Serve immediately with a spoon.

| Serves 1 or 2 | **Green Tea on Ice** |

Green Tea on Ice

1 cup	boiling water	250 mL
1 tbsp	green or chai tea leaves	15 mL
2 tbsp	liquid honey, or to taste	25 mL
¼ tsp	ground cinnamon or garam masala	1 mL
6	ice cubes, divided	6

1. In a small teapot, pour boiling water over tea, honey and cinnamon. Cover and steep for 10 minutes. Strain, discarding leaves. Let cool. Chill in refrigerator if time allows.

2. In a blender, combine cooled tea and 3 ice cubes. Secure lid and process using the chop or pulse function until smooth.

3. Add remaining ice cubes, one at a time, and process using the chop or pulse function until smooth. Keep adding ice until desired thickness is achieved. Serve immediately with a spoon.

Iced Citrus Tea

Serves 6

1	lemon	1
1	orange	1
4 cups	boiling water	1 L
3	black or green tea bags	3
2	whole cloves	2
1	stick (2 inches/5 cm long) cinnamon	1
¼ cup	liquid honey, or to taste, divided	50 mL
16	ice cubes, divided	16
6	slices orange or lemon	6

1. Peel lemon and orange; remove and discard bitter pith. Chop rinds and set aside. Seed and chop flesh and set aside separately.

2. In a teapot, pour boiling water over chopped lemon and orange rinds, tea bags, cloves and cinnamon. Cover and steep for 5 minutes. Strain, discarding rind and spices. Chill tea.

3. In a blender, combine half each of the tea, lemon and orange flesh, honey and ice cubes. Secure lid and process using the chop or pulse function until smooth. Pour into 3 glasses and garnish each with 1 lemon or orange slice. Repeat with remaining tea, lemon and orange flesh, honey, ice, and lemon and orange slices.

Lemon Mint Iced Tea

Serves 2

2 cups	chilled strong brewed tea	500 mL
6	ice cubes, divided	6
¼ cup	freshly squeezed lemon juice	50 mL
3 tbsp	liquid honey, or to taste	45 mL
1 tbsp	chopped fresh peppermint	15 mL

1. In a blender, combine tea, 3 ice cubes, lemon juice, honey and peppermint. Secure lid and process using the chop or pulse function until smooth.

2. Add remaining ice cubes, one at a time, and process using the chop or pulse function until smooth. Keep adding ice until desired thickness is achieved. Serve immediately with a spoon.

Lemon Peach Granita

Serves 1 or 2

1 cup	freshly squeezed orange juice	250 mL
1 cup	frozen peach slices	250 mL
1 tbsp	chopped fresh lemon verbena, optional	15 mL
1 tbsp	liquid honey, or to taste	15 mL
4	ice cubes	4

1. In a blender, combine orange juice, peaches, lemon verbena (if using), honey and ice cubes. Secure lid and process using the chop or pulse function until smooth. Serve immediately with a spoon.

Serves 1	**Mochaccino**	
½ cup	chilled espresso or strong coffee	125 mL
⅓ cup	half-and-half (10%) cream or evaporated milk	75 mL
3	chocolate-covered coffee beans	3
1 tbsp	unsweetened cocoa powder or carob powder	15 mL
⅛ tsp	ground cinnamon	0.5 mL
6	frozen skim milk cubes, divided (pages 319)	6

1. In a blender, combine espresso, cream, coffee beans, cocoa powder, cinnamon and 3 skim milk cubes. Secure lid and process using the chop or pulse function until smooth.

2. Add remaining skim milk cubes, one at a time, and process using the chop or pulse function until smooth. Keep adding skim milk cubes until desired thickness is achieved. Serve immediately with a spoon.

Serves 1

Mocha Mint

½ cup	chilled espresso or very strong coffee	125 mL
¼ cup	evaporated partly skimmed milk	50 mL
1 tbsp	chopped fresh peppermint	15 mL
1 tbsp	unsweetened cocoa powder or carob powder	15 mL
1 tbsp	liquid honey, or to taste	15 mL
⅛ tsp	ground cinnamon	0.5 mL
6	frozen chocolate milk cubes, divided (page 319)	6

1. In a blender, combine espresso, evaporated milk, peppermint, cocoa powder, honey, cinnamon and 3 chocolate milk cubes. Secure lid and process using the chop or pulse function until smooth.

2. Add remaining chocolate milk cubes, one at a time, and process using the chop or pulse function until smooth. Keep adding chocolate milk cubes until desired thickness is achieved. Serve immediately with a spoon.

Serves 1

Orange Lavender Ice

Tip

Always use food-grade, organic lavender in recipes.

½ cup	frozen orange juice concentrate	125 mL
1	orange, sectioned and seeded	1
1 tsp	chopped fresh lavender flowers	5 mL
1 tsp	balsamic vinegar	5 mL
6	ice cubes, divided	6

1. In a blender, combine orange juice concentrate, chopped orange, lavender, vinegar and 3 ice cubes. Secure lid and process using the chop or pulse function until smooth.

2. Add remaining ice cubes, one at a time, and process using the chop or pulse function until smooth. Keep adding ice until desired thickness is achieved. Serve immediately with a spoon.

Papaya Citrus Lassi

Serves 2

½ cup	freshly squeezed orange juice	125 mL
3 tbsp	freshly squeezed lemon juice	45 mL
3	scoops lemon sorbet	3
½	papaya	½
6	frozen yogurt cubes, divided (page 319)	6

1. In a blender, combine orange juice, lemon juice, sorbet, papaya and 3 yogurt cubes. Secure lid and process using the chop or pulse function until smooth.

2. Add remaining yogurt cubes, one at a time, and process using the chop or pulse function until smooth. Keep adding yogurt cubes until desired thickness is achieved.

Peach Granita

Serves 1

Tip
If using pure cranberry juice, taste and add liquid honey, brown rice syrup or agave nectar to sweeten.

1 cup	cranberry juice	250 mL
4	ice cubes	4
1 cup	frozen peach slices	250 mL

1. In a blender, combine cranberry juice, ice cubes and peaches. Secure lid and process using the chop or pulse function until smooth. Serve immediately with a spoon.

Pink Lemonade

Serves 4

½ cup	freshly squeezed orange or cranberry juice	125 mL
½ cup	freshly squeezed lemon juice	125 mL
6	ice cubes, divided	6
2 cups	chopped watermelon, divided	500 mL
2 tsp	chopped candied ginger, optional	10 mL
1 tbsp	liquid honey, or to taste	15 mL

1. In a blender, combine orange juice, lemon juice, 3 ice cubes, 1 cup (250 mL) watermelon, and ginger, if using. Secure lid and process using the chop or pulse function until smooth.

2. Add remaining watermelon and ice. Secure lid and process using the chop or pulse function until smooth. Sweeten with honey as required.

Raspberry Flip

Serves 1

⅔ cup	raspberry juice	150 mL
2 tbsp	freshly squeezed lemon juice	25 mL
1 cup	frozen raspberries	250 mL
2 tbsp	granulated sugar, or to taste	25 mL
6	ice cubes, divided	6

1. In a blender, combine raspberry juice, lemon juice, raspberries, sugar and 3 ice cubes. Secure lid and process using the chop or pulse function until smooth.

2. Add remaining ice cubes, one at a time, and process using the chop or pulse function until smooth. Keep adding ice until desired thickness is achieved. Serve immediately with a spoon.

Serves 1 or 2

Triple Chocolate Snowstorm

1 cup	chocolate milk	250 mL
1 tbsp	unsweetened cocoa powder or carob powder	15 mL
1 tbsp	liquid honey	15 mL
1 cup	chocolate-flavored frozen yogurt or ice cream	250 mL

1. In a blender, combine chocolate milk, cocoa powder, honey and frozen yogurt. Secure lid and blend (from low to high if using a variable speed blender) until smooth. Serve immediately with a spoon.

Dessert and Cocktail Smoothies

Using Blender Ice Cream, Frozen Yogurt and Sorbet

Use blender ice cream, frozen yogurt and sorbet in place of commercial products. The blender ice creams and frozen yogurts are very soft and should really be called "ice milks" because most of them do not contain cream. Although cream may be used instead of milk, it is higher in fat. If a more-solid result is desired, freeze the blended mixture in a metal loaf pan for one to two hours. Due to their low sugar content, these frozen mixtures will freeze rock-solid if left in the freezer for longer, so plan to use them within two hours. With a stock of skim and chocolate milk cubes in the freezer, ice cream and frozen yogurt is quick and easy to make. In addition, these treats have the following benefits over their commercial equivalents:

- lower sugar content
- all natural ingredients
- no chemical additives or preservatives
- little (or very low) fat
- no gums or other thickeners and other additives or chemicals used in commercial low-fat frozen products

Adding a Large Number of Ice Cubes to Smoothies

With a Chop or Ice Crush Setting

If using more than five ice cubes in one recipe, add half of the ice cubes and all the other ingredients to the blender jug. Process on chop or ice crush for 30 seconds, then add remaining ice cubes and process on chop or ice crush for 30 seconds more or just until smooth.

Without a Chop or Ice Crush Setting

When making frozen drinks that require more than five ice cubes in a blender without a chop or ice crush setting, the ice cubes must be crushed before you add them to the blender. Place cubes in a resealable plastic freezer bag, remove excess air, seal and place on a cutting board. Smash the cubes with a rolling pin or frying pan until the pieces are the size of quarters. Add half to the ingredients in the blender jug and blend for 10 seconds on medium (or low if you have a two-speed blender). Add more crushed ice and blend until the ice is blended into the drink and it is the desired consistency.

Blender Ice Cream

Almond Banana Ice Cream

¾ cup	Almond Milk (page 314) or vanilla-flavored soy milk	175 mL
2 tbsp	granulated sugar	25 mL
4	frozen banana chunks	4
½ tsp	almond extract	2 mL
8 to 10	frozen skim milk cubes, divided	8 to 10

1. In a blender, combine almond milk, sugar, banana, almond extract and 4 skim milk cubes. Secure lid and process using the chop or pulse function until smooth.

2. Add remaining milk cubes, two at a time, and process using the chop or pulse function until smooth. Keep adding milk cubes until desired thickness is achieved. Use immediately or pour into a metal loaf pan and freeze for up to 2 hours.

Chocolate Frozen Yogurt

½ cup	drained plain yogurt	125 mL
1 tbsp	unsweetened cocoa powder or carob powder	15 mL
2 tbsp	granulated sugar, or to taste	25 mL
12	frozen chocolate milk cubes, divided	12

1. In a blender, combine yogurt, cocoa powder, sugar and 6 chocolate milk cubes. Secure lid and process using the chop or pulse function until smooth.

2. Add remaining milk cubes, two or three at a time, and process using the chop or pulse function until smooth. Keep adding milk cubes until desired thickness is achieved. Use immediately or pour into a metal loaf pan and freeze for up to 2 hours.

Chocolate Ice Cream

½ cup	Date Milk (page 312) or chocolate milk	125 mL
2 tbsp	granulated sugar	25 mL
2 tbsp	unsweetened cocoa powder or carob powder	25 mL
12	frozen milk cubes, divided	12

1. In a blender, combine date milk, sugar, cocoa powder and 6 milk cubes. Secure lid and process using the chop or pulse function until smooth.

2. Add remaining milk cubes, two or three at a time, and process using the chop or pulse function until smooth. Keep adding milk cubes until desired thickness is achieved. Use immediately or pour into a metal loaf pan and freeze for up to 2 hours.

Citrus Sorbet

Tip

You can substitute a lime or an orange for the lemon. Or use the juice of one fruit in place of the whole fruit if desired.

1	lemon	1
¼ cup	freshly squeezed orange juice	50 mL
⅓ cup	granulated sugar, or to taste	75 mL
12	ice cubes, divided	12

1. Grate 1 tsp (5 mL) zest from lemon and set aside. Peel, section and seed lemon.

2. In a blender, combine lemon zest and lemon sections, orange juice, sugar and 6 ice cubes. Secure lid and process using the chop or pulse function until smooth.

3. Add remaining ice cubes, two or three at a time, and process using the chop or pulse function until smooth. Keep adding ice cubes until desired thickness is achieved. Spoon into chilled glasses or dessert cups.

Coffee Ice Cream

Serves 1

½ cup	Coconut Carob Milk (page 315) or chocolate milk	125 mL
2 tbsp	granulated sugar	25 mL
6	frozen espresso or strong coffee cubes, divided	6
3	frozen chocolate milk cubes	3

1. In a blender, combine coconut carob milk, sugar, 3 espresso cubes and chocolate milk cubes. Secure lid and process using the chop or pulse function until smooth.

2. Add remaining espresso cubes, one at a time, and process using the chop or pulse function until smooth. Keep adding espresso cubes until desired thickness is achieved. Use immediately or pour into a metal loaf pan and freeze for up to 2 hours.

Fruit Yogurt Slush

Serves 2

Tip

Use frozen peaches, mangoes, apricots, cherries, raspberries, blueberries or other sweet berries instead of strawberries in this slush. For a change, try it without sugar — it's tart but tasty.

¾ cup	drained plain yogurt	175 mL
¼ cup	evaporated partly skimmed milk	50 mL
12	frozen strawberries	12
2 tbsp	granulated sugar, or to taste	25 mL
6	frozen skim milk cubes, divided	6

1. In a blender, combine yogurt, evaporated milk, strawberries, sugar and 3 skim milk cubes. Secure lid and process using the chop or pulse function until smooth.

2. Add remaining milk cubes, one at a time, and process using the chop or pulse function until smooth. Keep adding milk cubes until desired thickness is achieved. Use immediately or pour into a metal loaf pan and freeze for up to 2 hours.

Serves 2	# Strawberry Ice Cream	
¾ cup	Apricot Milk (page 314) or evaporated milk	175 mL
6	frozen strawberries	6
2 tbsp	granulated sugar, or to taste	25 mL
6	frozen milk cubes, divided	6

1. In a blender, combine apricot milk, strawberries, sugar and 3 milk cubes. Secure lid and process using the chop or pulse function until smooth.

2. Add remaining milk cubes, one at a time, and process using the chop or pulse function until smooth. Keep adding milk cubes until desired thickness is achieved. Use immediately or pour into a metal loaf pan and freeze for up to 2 hours.

Serves 2	# Vanilla Ice Cream	
¾ cup	evaporated milk	175 mL
3 tbsp	granulated sugar	45 mL
½ tsp	pure vanilla extract	2 mL
10	frozen milk cubes, divided	10

1. In a blender, combine evaporated milk, sugar, vanilla and 5 milk cubes. Secure lid and process using the chop or pulse function until smooth.

2. Add remaining milk cubes, one or two at a time, and process using the chop or pulse function until smooth. Keep adding milk cubes until desired thickness is achieved. Use immediately or pour into a metal loaf pan and freeze for up to 2 hours.

Dessert Smoothies

Banana Split

1 cup	chocolate milk	250 mL
4	frozen banana chunks	4
1 cup	chopped pineapple	250 mL
½ cup	frozen strawberries	125 mL
2	scoops vanilla ice cream or frozen yogurt	2

1. In a blender, combine milk, banana, pineapple and strawberries. Secure lid and blend (from low to high if using a variable speed blender) until smooth. Add ice cream and process using the chop or pulse function until drink reaches the desired consistency.

Cherry Cheesecake

Tip

You can replace the canned cherries with 1 ½ cups (375 mL) pitted fresh cherries and ½ cup (125 mL) freshly squeezed orange juice.

1	can (12 oz/375 mL) pitted cherries with juice	1
½ cup	vanilla-flavored frozen yogurt	125 mL
3 tbsp	cream cheese, at room temperature	45 mL

1. In a blender, combine cherries with juice, frozen yogurt and cream cheese. Secure lid and blend (from low to high if using a variable speed blender) until smooth.

Cherry Snowball

Tip
Coconut cream is available canned. It is thicker than coconut milk, which is also available canned or homemade (page 315).

¼ cup	coconut cream or coconut milk (see Tip, left)	50 mL
1 cup	pitted cherries	250 mL
1	scoop vanilla or coconut ice cream	1
1 tbsp	toasted shredded coconut, optional	15 mL

1. In a blender, combine coconut cream and cherries. Secure lid and blend (from low to high if using a variable speed blender) until smooth. Add ice cream, and coconut, if using. Process using the chop or pulse function until drink reaches the desired consistency.

Chocolate Mint

1 cup	chocolate milk	250 mL
2 tbsp	chocolate syrup	25 mL
2	drops peppermint extract	2
2	small chocolate-covered peppermint patties	2
2	scoops mint or chocolate ice cream	2
2 tbsp	grated dark chocolate, optional	25 mL

1. In a blender, combine milk, syrup, peppermint extract and peppermint patties. Secure lid and blend (from low to high if using a variable speed blender) until smooth. Add ice cream and process using the chop or pulse function until drink reaches the desired consistency. Pour into glasses and garnish with grated chocolate, if using.

Choco-Peanut Parfait

Serves 2

¾ cup	chocolate milk	175 mL
2 tbsp	chocolate syrup	25 mL
2 tbsp	smooth peanut butter	25 mL
4	frozen banana chunks	4
2 tbsp	chocolate chips	25 mL
2	scoops chocolate ice cream	2

1. In a blender, combine milk, syrup, peanut butter and frozen banana chunks. Secure lid and blend (from low to high if using a variable speed blender) until smooth. Add chocolate chips and ice cream. Process using the chop or pulse function until drink reaches the desired consistency.

Coconut Cream

Serves 2

1 cup	pineapple juice	250 mL
¼ cup	coconut cream or coconut milk (see Tip, opposite)	50 mL
½ cup	chopped pineapple	125 mL
2	scoops pineapple- or vanilla-flavored frozen yogurt or ice cream	2
2 tbsp	shredded dried or freshly grated coconut, optional	25 mL

1. In a blender, combine pineapple juice, coconut cream and pineapple. Secure lid and blend (from low to high if using a variable speed blender) until smooth. Add frozen yogurt, and coconut, if using. Process using the chop or pulse function until drink reaches the desired consistency.

Coconut Cream Pie

Tip
Use canned coconut milk or homemade Coconut Milk (page 315) in this smoothie.

½ cup	coconut milk (see Tip, left)	125 mL
2	frozen banana chunks	2
¼ cup	cream cheese, at room temperature	50 mL
2 tbsp	toasted shredded coconut	25 mL
1	container (3.5 oz/99 mL) prepared banana pudding	1

1. In a blender, combine coconut milk, banana, cheese, shredded coconut and banana pudding. Secure lid and blend from low to high (if using a variable speed blender) until smooth.

Frozen Berry Slushie

¼ cup	freshly squeezed orange juice	50 mL
1 tbsp	freshly squeezed lemon juice	15 mL
½ cup	sparkling mineral water	125 mL
1 cup	frozen raspberries	250 mL
1 cup	frozen strawberries	250 mL
½ cup	frozen whole açai berries or açai berry pulp, partially thawed	125 mL

1. In a blender, combine orange juice, lemon juice, mineral water, raspberries and strawberries. Secure lid and blend (from low to high if using a variable speed blender) until smooth. Add açai berries and process using the chop or pulse function until drink reaches the desired consistency.

Serves 1

Frozen Fruit Slurry

½ cup	freshly squeezed orange juice	125 mL
4	frozen banana chunks	4
4	frozen strawberries	4
¼ cup	fruit-flavored yogurt	50 mL
4	ice cubes	4

1. In a blender, combine orange juice, banana, strawberries and yogurt. Secure lid and blend (from low to high if using a variable speed blender) until smooth. Add ice cubes and process using the chop or pulse function until drink reaches the desired consistency. Serve with a spoon.

Serves 2

Iced Green Goddess

Tip

Coconut cream is available canned. It is thicker than coconut milk, which is also available canned or homemade (page 315).

½ cup	coconut cream or coconut milk (see Tip, left)	125 mL
	Juice of 1 lime	
2	kiwifruits, quartered	2
3	fresh peppermint leaves	3
2	scoops vanilla ice cream or frozen yogurt	2
	Honey, to taste	

1. In a blender, combine coconut cream, lime juice, kiwis and peppermint. Secure lid and blend (from low to high if using a variable speed blender) until smooth. Add ice cream and process using the chop or pulse function until drink reaches the desired consistency. Taste and add honey, as desired.

Iced Mocha Latte

Serves 2

1 cup	milk or soy milk	250 mL
¼ cup	chocolate syrup	50 mL
1 tbsp	instant espresso or coffee powder	15 mL
2	scoops coffee-flavored frozen yogurt or ice cream	2
2 tbsp	grated dark chocolate, optional	25 mL

1. In a blender, combine milk, syrup and espresso powder. Secure lid and blend (from low to high if using a variable speed blender) until smooth. Add frozen yogurt and process using the chop or pulse function until shake reaches the desired consistency. Pour into glasses and garnish with grated chocolate, if using.

Iced Vanilla Custard

Serves 1 or 2

1 cup	milk	250 mL
1	piece (2 inches/5 cm) vanilla bean or ½ tsp (2 mL) pure vanilla extract	1
1 tbsp	granulated sugar	15 mL
2	egg yolks	2
1	scoop vanilla-flavored frozen yogurt or ice cream	1

1. In a small saucepan over medium heat, heat milk, vanilla bean and sugar until small bubbles form around the edge of the pan. Meanwhile, in a medium bowl, beat egg yolks until pale and thickened.

2. Gradually whisk half of the hot milk mixture into egg yolks. Whisk egg mixture back into saucepan. Reduce heat to low and cook, stirring constantly, for 5 to 7 minutes or until custard is thick enough to coat the back of a spoon. Do not let custard boil. Strain into a small bowl. Place plastic wrap directly on surface and let cool. Chill in refrigerator if time allows.

3. In a blender, combine cooled custard and frozen yogurt. Secure lid and process using the chop or pulse function until smooth. Serve immediately with a spoon.

Neapolitan Sundae

Serves 2

1 cup	chocolate milk	250 mL
2 tbsp	chocolate syrup	25 mL
1 cup	halved strawberries	250 mL
2	scoops vanilla ice cream or frozen yogurt	2

1. In a blender, combine milk, syrup and strawberries. Secure lid and blend (from low to high if using a variable speed blender) until smooth. Add ice cream and process using the chop or pulse function until sundae reaches the desired consistency.

Peach Parfait

Serves 1

$\frac{1}{2}$ cup	peach nectar or freshly squeezed orange juice	125 mL
1 cup	frozen peach slices	250 mL
1	scoop peach-flavored frozen yogurt or ice cream	1

1. In a blender, combine peach nectar and sliced peaches. Secure lid and blend (from low to high if using a variable speed blender) until smooth. Add frozen yogurt and blend (from low to high if using a variable speed blender) until smooth.

Pecan Pie

Serves 2

½ cup	milk	125 mL
2 tbsp	pure maple syrup	25 mL
1 tbsp	liquid honey	15 mL
⅛ tsp	ground cinnamon	0.5 mL
Pinch	ground nutmeg	Pinch
¼ cup	chopped pecans	50 mL
2	scoops butterscotch or pecan ice cream	2

1. In a blender, combine milk, maple syrup, honey, cinnamon and nutmeg. Secure lid and blend (from low to high if using a variable speed blender) until smooth. Add pecans and ice cream. Process using the chop or pulse function until drink reaches the desired consistency.

Raspberry Cheesecake

Serves 1

¼ cup	milk	50 mL
¼ tsp	pure vanilla extract	1 mL
1 cup	frozen raspberries	250 mL
2 tbsp	cream cheese, at room temperature	25 mL
1	scoop raspberry sorbet or vanilla ice cream	1

1. In a blender, combine milk, vanilla, raspberries and cream cheese. Secure lid and blend (from low to high if using a variable speed blender) until smooth. Add sorbet and process using the chop or pulse function until drink reaches the desired consistency.

Smashed Orange

Serves 1

1 tsp	grated orange zest	5 mL
1/4 cup	freshly squeezed orange juice	50 mL
1	orange, sectioned and seeded	1
1	scoop orange sorbet or vanilla ice cream	1

1. In a blender, combine orange zest, orange juice and orange. Secure lid and blend (from low to high if using a variable speed blender) until smooth. Add sorbet and process using the chop or pulse function until drink reaches the desired consistency.

Tropical Storm

Serves 2

Tip
Use canned coconut milk or homemade Coconut Milk (page 315) in this smoothie.

1/2 cup	milk	125 mL
1/4 cup	coconut milk (see Tip, left)	50 mL
1/4 cup	mango juice	50 mL
1	mango, halved	1
4	frozen banana chunks	4
2	scoops vanilla ice cream or frozen yogurt	2

1. In a blender, combine milk, coconut milk, mango juice and mango. Secure lid and blend (from low to high if using a variable speed blender) until smooth. Add frozen banana chunks and ice cream. Process using the chop or pulse function until drink reaches the desired consistency.

Cocktail Smoothies

Serves 2

Blackberry Chiller

¼ cup	cranberry juice	50 mL
1 tbsp	freshly squeezed lemon juice	15 mL
¼ cup	fresh or frozen blackberries	50 mL
4	frozen strawberries	4
2 oz	vodka, optional	50 mL
1 oz	crème de cassis, optional	25 mL

1. In a blender, combine cranberry juice, lemon juice, blackberries and strawberries. Secure lid and process using the chop or pulse function until smooth. Pour into glasses. Divide the vodka and crème de cassis, if using, equally over fruit mixture in glass.

Serves 2

Blackberry Cream

¼ cup	whole milk or table (18%) cream	50 mL
2 oz	crème de cassis	50 mL
1 cup	blackberries	250 mL
1	scoop vanilla ice cream or frozen yogurt	1

1. In a blender, combine milk, crème de cassis and blackberries. Secure lid and blend (from low to high if using a variable speed blender) until smooth. Add ice cream and process using the chop or pulse function until drink reaches the desired consistency.

Black Cherry Mimosa

½ cup	raspberry juice	125 mL
1 cup	pitted black cherries	250 mL
1 cup	champagne or sparkling mineral water	250 mL

1. In a blender, combine raspberry juice and cherries. Secure lid and blend (from low to high if using a variable speed blender) until smooth. Pour into glasses and top each glass with champagne.

Bloody Mary

Tip

Make this a Virgin Mary by omitting the vodka.

½ cup	tomato juice	125 mL
	Juice of 1 lime	
2 tsp	prepared horseradish	10 mL
½ tsp	Worcestershire sauce	2 mL
¼ tsp	hot pepper sauce, or to taste	1 mL
2	tomatoes, quartered	2
2	ice cubes	2
2 oz	vodka	50 mL
	Freshly ground black pepper	
2	celery stalks, optional	2

1. In a blender, combine tomato juice, lime juice, horseradish, Worcestershire sauce, hot pepper sauce and tomatoes. Secure lid and blend (from low to high if using a variable speed blender) until smooth.

2. Add ice cubes and process using the chop or pulse function until drink reaches the desired consistency. Pour into glasses and add an equal amount of vodka to each glass. Grind black pepper over top and garnish with celery stalks, if using.

Bloody Orange Vodka

Serves 2

½ cup	freshly squeezed orange juice	125 mL
1	blood orange, sectioned and seeded	1
½ cup	frozen raspberries or strawberries	125 mL
2	ice cubes	2
2 oz	vodka	50 mL

1. In a blender, combine orange juice, blood orange, raspberries and ice. Secure lid and process using the chop or pulse function until drink reaches the desired consistency. Pour into glasses and add an equal amount of vodka to each glass.

Brandy Alexander

Serves 1

¼ cup	coconut cream or coconut milk	50 mL
2 tbsp	drained plain yogurt	25 mL
1 oz	brandy	25 ml
1 oz	crème de cacao	25 mL
Pinch	ground nutmeg	Pinch

1. In a blender, combine coconut cream, yogurt, brandy and crème de cacao. Secure lid and blend (from low to high if using a variable speed blender) until smooth. Pour into glass and garnish with nutmeg.

Cherry Blossom

Serves 2

¼ cup	cranberry-raspberry juice	50 mL
2 tbsp	drained plain yogurt	25 mL
½ cup	pitted cherries	125 mL
2	ice cubes	2
2 oz	cherry brandy, optional	50 mL

1. In a blender, combine cranberry-raspberry juice, yogurt, cherries and ice cubes. Secure lid and process using the chop or pulse function until drink reaches the desired consistency. Pour into 2 glasses and add an equal amount of cherry brandy, if using, to each glass.

Green Cosmo

Serves 2

2 oz	vodka	50 mL
1 oz	Cointreau	25 mL
¼ cup	freshly squeezed orange juice	50 mL
2 tbsp	freshly squeezed lime juice	25 mL
2	kiwifruits, quartered	2
2	ice cubes	2

1. Pour an equal amount of vodka and Cointreau into 2 glasses. In a blender, combine orange juice, lime juice, kiwis and ice cubes. Secure lid and process using the chop or pulse function until drink reaches the desired consistency. Pour over liquor in glasses.

Mexican Ice

Serves 2

Tip

Chipotle chile peppers are usually available in adobo sauce when commercially canned.

½ cup	crushed ice	125 mL
¼ cup	tomato juice	50 mL
2 tbsp	freshly squeezed lime juice	25 mL
1	plum tomato, quartered	1
1	canned chipotle pepper, or to taste (see Tip, left)	1
2 tbsp	adobo sauce (from chipotle can)	25 mL
1 tbsp	chopped hot green chile pepper, or to taste	15 mL
2 oz	tequila	50 mL
1 tbsp	chopped fresh cilantro, optional	15 mL

1. Spoon an equal amount of ice into 2 glasses. In a blender, combine tomato juice, lime juice, tomato, chipotle chile, adobe sauce, hot green chile and tequila. Secure lid and blend (from low to high if using a variable speed blender) until smooth. Pour over ice in glasses, garnish with cilantro, if using, and serve with a spoon.

Mexican Mudslide

Serves 2

¼ cup	chocolate milk	50 mL
2 oz	coffee liqueur	50 mL
2 oz	Irish cream liqueur	50 mL
1	banana, cut into chunks	1
2	scoops chocolate or vanilla ice cream	2

1. In a blender, combine milk, coffee liqueur, Irish cream liqueur and banana. Secure lid and blend (from low to high if using a variable speed blender) until smooth. Add ice cream and process using the chop or pulse function until drink reaches the desired consistency. Serve with a spoon.

Orange Mimosa

Serves 2

¼ cup	freshly squeezed orange juice	50 mL
2	oranges, sectioned and seeded	2
½ cup	strawberries	125 mL
1 cup	champagne or sparkling mineral water	250 mL

1. In a blender, combine orange juice, oranges and strawberries. Secure lid and blend (from low to high if using a variable speed blender) until smooth. Pour into champagne flutes and top with champagne.

Peach Mimosa

Serves 2

¼ cup	freshly squeezed orange juice	50 mL
2	peaches, quartered	2
½ cup	fresh strawberries	125 mL
1 cup	champagne or sparkling mineral water	250 mL

1. In a blender, combine orange juice, peaches and strawberries. Secure lid and blend (from low to high if using a variable speed blender) until smooth. Pour into champagne flutes and top each with champagne.

Pineapple Daiquiri

Serves 2

⅓ cup	frozen pineapple juice concentrate	75 mL
2	pineapple wedges, cut into cubes	2
2 tbsp	freshly squeezed lemon juice	25 mL
4	ice cubes	4
2 oz	white rum, optional	50 mL

1. In a blender, combine pineapple juice concentrate, pineapple cubes, lemon juice and ice cubes. Secure lid and process using the chop or pulse function until smooth. Pour into glasses and drizzle rum, if using, over fruit mixture. Serve immediately with a spoon.

Serves 2

Pink Cosmo

2 oz	vodka	50 mL
1 oz	grenadine, optional	25 mL
¼ cup	raspberry juice	50 mL
1 tbsp	freshly squeezed lemon juice	15 mL
¼ cup	frozen raspberries	50 mL

1. Divide vodka and grenadine, if using, equally into 2 glasses. In a blender, combine raspberry juice, lemon juice and raspberries. Secure lid and blend (from low to high if using a variable speed blender) until smooth. Pour over liquor in glasses.

Serves 1

Pink Lemon Daiquiri

⅓ cup	frozen lemonade or limeade concentrate	75 mL
6	strawberries	6
4	ice cubes	4
1 oz	rum	25 mL

1. In a blender, combine lemonade concentrate, strawberries and ice. Secure lid and process using the chop or pulse function until smooth. Pour into glass and drizzle rum over top. Serve immediately with a spoon.

Serves 2	# Purple Cosmo	
2 oz	vodka	50 mL
1 oz	grenadine, optional	25 mL
¼ cup	raspberry juice	50 mL
1 tbsp	freshly squeezed lemon juice	15 mL
2	black plums, halved	2

1. Divide vodka and grenadine, if using, equally into 2 glasses. In a blender, combine raspberry juice, lemon juice and black plums. Secure lid and blend (from low to high if using a variable speed blender) until smooth. Pour over liquor in glasses.

Serves 2	# Red Berry Chiller	
¼ cup	cranberry juice	50 mL
1 tbsp	freshly squeezed lime juice	15 mL
¼ cup	frozen raspberries	50 mL
4	frozen strawberries	4
2 oz	vodka, optional	50 mL
1 oz	Cointreau, optional	25 mL

1. In a blender, combine cranberry juice, lime juice, raspberries and strawberries. Secure lid and blend (from low to high if using a variable speed blender) until smooth. Pour or spoon into glasses. Divide vodka and Cointreau, if using, equally over fruit mixture and serve with spoons.

Rose Mimosa

Tip

Always use organic (untreated) rose petals in recipes because they have not been sprayed or treated for color preservation.

¼ cup	cranberry juice	50 mL
½ cup	sliced strawberries	125 mL
½ cup	raspberries	125 mL
1 cup	champagne or sparkling mineral water	250 mL
1 tbsp	untreated red or pink rose petals, optional	15 mL

1. In a blender, combine cranberry juice, strawberries and raspberries. Secure lid and blend (from low to high if using a variable speed blender) until smooth. Pour into champagne flutes and top with champagne. Garnish with rose petals, if using.

Sangria Smoothie

Tip

Try freezing the grapes for a truly frozen sangria smoothie.

⅔ cup	red wine	150 mL
¼ cup	apple juice	50 mL
1 oz	triple sec	25 ml
1	apple, quartered	1
1	orange, sectioned and seeded	1
2	scoops orange or lemon sorbet	2
¼ cup	seedless red grapes	50 mL

1. In a blender, combine red wine, apple juice, triple sec, apple and orange. Secure lid and blend (from low to high if using a variable speed blender) until smooth. Add sorbet and process using the chop or pulse function until drink reaches the desired consistency. Serve in a red wine glass with a spoon and garnish with grapes.

Strawberry Margarita

2 oz	tequila	50 mL
2 oz	triple sec	50 mL
1 tbsp	freshly squeezed lime juice	15 mL
1 cup	halved strawberries	250 mL
2	scoops strawberry sorbet	2

1. In a blender, combine tequila, triple sec, lime juice and strawberries. Secure lid and blend (from low to high if using a variable speed blender) until smooth. Add sorbet and process using the chop or pulse function until drink reaches the desired consistency. Pour into glasses and serve with a spoon.

Strawberry Rhubarb Freeze

⅓ cup	freshly squeezed orange juice	75 mL
½ cup	rhubarb compote (see page 102)	125 mL
6	frozen strawberries	6
2 oz	white rum	50 mL

1. In a blender, combine orange juice, rhubarb and strawberries. Secure lid and blend (from low to high if using a variable speed blender) until smooth. Pour into glasses and top with white rum. Serve with a spoon.

Summer Freezie

2 oz	dark rum	50 mL
1 oz	triple sec	25 mL
2 tbsp	pineapple juice	25 mL
1	orange, sectioned and seeded	1
1	scoop coconut or vanilla ice cream	1

1. In a blender, combine rum, triple sec, pineapple juice and orange. Secure lid and blend (from low to high if using a variable speed blender) until smooth. Add ice cream and process using the chop or pulse function until drink reaches the desired consistency. Pour into glasses and serve with a spoon.

Watermelon Julep

¼ cup	cranberry juice	50 mL
1 tbsp	freshly squeezed lemon juice	15 mL
1 cup	watermelon chunks	250 mL
1	fresh peppermint leaf	1
2 oz	vodka	50 mL

1. In a blender, combine cranberry juice, lemon juice, watermelon and peppermint. Secure lid and blend (from low to high if using a variable speed blender) until smooth. Pour into glass and top with vodka.

Serves 2

Whiskey Sour

¼ cup	cranberry juice	50 mL
3 tbsp	freshly squeezed lemon juice	45 mL
4	frozen strawberries	4
1 tbsp	confectioner's (icing) sugar	15 mL
½ cup	crushed ice	125 mL
2 oz	whiskey	50 mL

1. In a blender, combine cranberry juice, lemon juice, strawberries and sugar. Secure lid and blend (from low to high if using a variable speed blender) until smooth. Spoon crushed ice into glasses. Pour whisky over ice and top with strawberry mixture.

Endnotes

Glossary

Adaptogen: A substance that builds resistance to stress by balancing the functions of the glands and immune response, thus strengthening the immune system, nervous system and glandular system. Adaptogens promote overall vitality. *Examples:* Astragalus and ginseng.

Allylic sulfides: See Organosulfides, page 369.

Alterative: A substance that gradually changes a condition by restoring health.

Amino acid: See Protein, page 369.

Analgesic: A substance that relieves pain by acting as a nervine, antiseptic or counterirritant. *Examples:* German chamomile, meadowsweet and nutmeg.

Anodyne: A substance that relieves pain. *Example:* Clove.

Anthocyanins: See Phenolic compounds, page 369.

Antibiotic: Meaning "against life," an antibiotic is a substance that kills infectious agents, including bacteria and fungi, without endangering health. *Examples:* Garlic, green tea, lavender, sage and thyme.

Anticatarrhal: A substance that reduces the production of mucus. *Examples:* Garlic and marshmallow.

Anti-inflammatory: A substance that controls or reduces swelling, redness, pain and heat, which are normal bodily reactions to injury or infection. *Examples:* German chamomile and St. John's wort.

Antimicrobial: A substance that destroys or inhibits the growth of disease-causing bacteria or other microorganisms.

Antioxidant: A compound that protects cells by preventing polyunsaturated fatty acids (PUFAs) in cell membranes from oxidizing, or breaking down. Antioxidants do this by neutralizing free radicals (see Free radical, page 368). Vitamins C and E and beta-carotene are antioxidant nutrients, and foods high in them have antioxidant properties. *Examples:* Alfalfa, beet greens, dandelion leaf, parsley, garlic, thyme and watercress.

Antipyretic: A substance that reduces fever. *Examples:* German chamomile, sage and yarrow.

Antiseptic: A substance used to prevent or reduce the growth of disease germs in order to prevent infection. *Examples:* Cabbage, calendula, clove, garlic, German chamomile, honey, nutmeg, onion, parsley, peppermint, rosemary, salt, thyme, turmeric and vinegar.

Antispasmodic: A substance that relieves muscle spasms or cramps, including colic. *Examples:* German chamomile, ginger, licorice and peppermint.

Astringent: A drying and contracting substance that reduces secretions from the skin. *Examples:* Cinnamon, lemon, sage and thyme.

Beta-carotene: The natural coloring agent (carotenoid) that gives fruits and vegetables (such as carrots) their deep orange color. It converts in the body to vitamin A. Eating foods high in beta-carotene helps prevent cancer, lowers your risk of heart disease, increases immunity, lowers your risk of cataracts and improves mental function. You can get beta-carotene in squash, carrots, yams, sweet potatoes, pumpkins and red peppers.

Betaine: A phytochemical that nourishes and strengthens the liver and gallbladder. It is found in high concentrations in beets.

Boron: A trace mineral that boosts the estrogen level in the blood, boron is also thought to help prevent calcium loss that leads to osteoporosis and to affect the brain's electrical activity. It is found in legumes, leafy greens and nuts.

Carbohydrates: An important group of plant foods that are composed of carbon, hydrogen and oxygen. A carbohydrate can be a single simple sugar or a combination of simple sugars. The chief sources of carbohydrates in a whole-food diet are grains, vegetables and fruits. Other sources include sugars, natural sweeteners and syrups.

Carminative: A substance that relaxes the stomach muscles and is taken to relieve gas and gripe. *Examples:* Clove, dill, fennel, garlic, ginger, parsley, peppermint, sage and thyme.

Carotenoid: See Beta-carotene, page 366.

Catechins: See Phenolic compounds, page 369.

Cathartic: A substance that has a laxative effect. See also Purgative, page 370. *Examples:* Dandelion, licorice and parsley.

Cellulose: See Fiber, page 368.

Chlorophyll: Found only in plants, chlorophyll has a unique structure that allows it to enhance the body's ability to produce hemoglobin, which, in turn, enhances the delivery of oxygen to cells.

Choline: A phytochemical that researchers believe improves mental function, and is therefore helpful for people with Alzheimer's disease. Good sources of lecithin (which contains choline) are dandelion, fenugreek, ginkgo, sage and stinging nettle.

Cruciferous vegetables: The name given to the Brassica genus of vegetables, which includes broccoli, Brussels sprouts, cabbage, cauliflower, collard greens, kale, bok choy, rutabaga, turnip and mustard greens. The plants in this family were named Cruciferae because their flower petals grow in a cross shape.

Decoction: A solution made by boiling the woody parts of plants (roots, seeds and bark) in water for 10 to 20 minutes.

Demulcent: A soothing substance taken internally to protect damaged tissue. *Examples:* Barley, cucumber, fig, honey, marshmallow and fenugreek.

Diaphoretic: A substance that induces sweating. *Examples:* Cayenne, cinnamon, German chamomile and ginger.

Digestive: A substance that aids digestion.

Diuretic: A substance that increases the flow of urine. These are intended for use in the short term only. *Examples:* Cucumber, burdock (root and leaf), dandelion (leaf and root), fennel seeds, lemon, linden, parsley and pumpkin seeds.

Dysmenorrhea: Menstruation accompanied by cramping pains that may be incapacitating in their intensity.

Elixir: A tonic that invigorates or strengthens the body by stimulating or restoring health.

Ellagic acid: A natural plant phenol (see Phenolic compounds, page 369) thought to have powerful anticancer and antiaging properties. It is found in cherries, grapes, strawberries, and other red, orange or yellow fruits; nuts; seeds; garlic; and onions.

Emetic: A substance taken in large doses to induce vomiting to expel poisons. Small quantities of some emetics, such as salt, nutmeg and mustard, are used often in cooking with no ill effects.

Emmenagogue: A substance that promotes healthy menstruation. *Examples:* Calendula and German chamomile.

Enzymes: The elements found in food that act as the catalysts for chemical reactions within the body, allowing efficient digestion and absorption of food and enabling the metabolic processes that support tissue growth, give you high energy levels and promote good health. Enzymes are destroyed by heat, but using fruits and vegetables raw in smoothies leaves enzymes intact and readily absorbable.

Essential fatty acids (EFAs): Fat is an essential part of a healthy diet — about 20 fatty acids are used by the human body to maintain normal function. Fats are necessary to maintain healthy skin and hair, transport the fat-soluble vitamins (A, D, E and K) and signal the feeling of fullness after meals. The three fatty acids considered the most important, or essential, are omega-6 linoleic, omega-3 linolenic and gamma-linolenic acids. Evidence suggests that increasing the proportion of these fatty acids in the diet may increase immunity and reduce the risks of heart disease, high blood pressure and arthritis. The best vegetable source of omega-3 EFAs in the diet is flax seeds. Other sources of EFAs are hemp (seeds and nuts), nuts, seeds, olives, avocados and oily fish.

Expectorant: A substance that relieves mucus congestion caused by colds and flu. *Examples:* Elder, garlic, ginger, hyssop and thyme.

Fiber: An indigestible carbohydrate. Fiber protects against intestinal problems and bowel disorders. The best sources are raw fruits and vegetables, seeds and whole grains.

Types of fiber include pectin, which reduces the risk of heart disease (by lowering cholesterol) and helps eliminate toxins. It is found mainly in fruits, such as apples, berries and citrus fruits; vegetables; and dried legumes. Cellulose prevents varicose veins, constipation and colitis and plays a role in deflecting colon cancer. Because cellulose is found in the outermost layers of fruits and vegetables, it is important to buy only organic produce and leave the peels on. The hemicellulose in fruits, vegetables and grains aids in weight loss, prevents constipation, lowers the risk of colon cancer and helps remove cancer-forming toxins from the intestinal tract. Lignin, a fiber known to lower cholesterol, prevent gallstone formation and help people with diabetes, is found only in fruits, vegetables and Brazil nuts.

When raw fresh whole fruits or vegetables are used in smoothies, the pulp, or fiber, is still present in the drink and provides all the health benefits listed above.

Flatulence: Release of gas in the stomach and intestine caused by poor digestion. See also Carminative, page 367.

Flavonoids: These phytochemicals (e.g., genistein and quercetin) are antioxidants that have been shown to inhibit cholesterol production. They are found in cruciferous vegetables (see Cruciferous vegetables, page 367), onions and garlic.

Food combining: A disciplined method of eating foods in a specific order or combination (see page 375). It is used as a short-term aid to solve digestive problems and, in simple terms, requires eating fruit alone and never with meals. At mealtime, protein foods are combined with nonstarchy vegetables (leafy greens, asparagus, broccoli, cabbage, celery, cucumbers, onions, peppers, sea herbs, tomatoes and zucchini) only. Grains are also eaten separately and are combined with nonstarchy vegetables. Health conditions that may benefit from food combining are food allergies and intolerances, indigestion, irritable bowel syndrome, flatulence, fatigue and peptic ulcer.

Free radical: A highly unstable compound that attacks cell membranes and causes cell breakdown, aging and a predisposition to some diseases. Free radicals come from the environment as a result of exposure to radiation, ultraviolet (UV) light, smoke, ozone and certain medications. Free radicals are also formed in the body by enzymes and during the conversion of food to energy. See also Antioxidant, page 366.

Glutamic acid: A naturally occurring substance that acts as a flavor enhancer. It is found in mushrooms and tomatoes.

Hemicellulose: See Fiber, left.

Hypotensive: A substance that lowers blood pressure. *Examples:* Garlic, hawthorn, linden flower and yarrow.

Indole: A phytochemical found in cruciferous vegetables (see Cruciferous vegetables, page 367) that may help prevent cancer by detoxifying carcinogens.

Isoflavone: A phytoestrogen, or the plant version of the human hormone estrogen, that is found in nuts, soybeans and legumes. Isoflavones help prevent several types of cancer — including pancreatic, colon, breast and prostate cancers — by preserving vitamin C in the body and acting as antioxidants.

Lactose intolerance: Deficiency of the enzyme lactase, which breaks down lactose, the sugar in both cow's and human milk. If you don't have sufficient lactase, milk sugar will ferment in the large intestine, causing bloating, diarrhea, abdominal pain and gas.

Laxative: A substance that stimulates bowel movements. Laxatives are meant to be used in the short term only. *Examples:*

Dandelion root, licorice root, prune, rhubarb and yellow dock.

Lignin: See Fiber, page 368.

Limonene: A type of limonoid (see Limonoid, below) thought to assist in detoxifying the liver and preventing cancer. It is found in lemons, limes, grapefruits and tangerines.

Limonoid: A subclass of terpenes (see Terpene, page 370) found in citrus fruit rinds.

Lutein: A carotenoid (see Beta-carotene, page 366) found in beet greens; collard greens; mustard greens; and other red, orange and yellow vegetables.

Lycopene: An antioxidant carotenoid (see Beta-carotene, page 366) that's relatively rare in food. High levels are found, however, in tomatoes, pink grapefruits and watermelon. Lycopene is thought to reduce the effects of aging by maintaining physical and mental function and to reduce the risk of some forms of cancer.

Macrobiotic diet: Eating whole food that is seasonal and produced locally. Whole grains, vegetables, fruits (except tropical fruits), legumes, small amounts of fish or organic meat, sea herbs, nuts and seeds are appropriate foods for North Americans who eat macrobiotically.

Metabolism: The rate at which the body produces energy (or burns calories). It is measured by the amount of heat produced by the body, at rest or engaged in various activities, while maintaining its normal temperature.

Milk allergy: Many individuals, especially babies and young children, have allergic reactions to the protein in cow's milk, which causes wheezing, eczema, rashes, mucus buildup and asthma-like symptoms.

Mucilage: A thick, sticky, glue-like substance found in high concentrations in some herbs, which contains and helps spread the active ingredients of those herbs while soothing inflamed surfaces. *Examples:* Marshmallow and slippery elm.

Nervine: A substance that eases anxiety and stress and nourishes the nerves by strengthening nerve fibers. *Examples:* German chamomile, lemon balm, oats, skullcap, St. John's wort, thyme and valerian.

Nonreactive cooking utensils: The acids in foods can react with certain materials and promote the oxidation of some nutrients, as well as discolor the materials themselves. Nonreactive materials suitable for brewing teas are glass, enameled cast iron or enameled stainless steel. While cast-iron pans are recommended for cooking (a meal cooked in unglazed cast iron can provide 20% of the recommended daily intake of iron), and stainless steel is a nonreactive cooking material, neither is recommended for brewing or steeping teas.

Organosulfides: Compounds that have been shown to reduce blood pressure, lower cholesterol levels and reduce blood clotting. *Examples:* Garlic and onion.

Pectin: See Fiber, page 368.

Phenolic compounds: Found in red wine, phenolic compounds, including catechins, anthocyanins, ellagic acid and tannins, can prevent the oxidation of "bad" low-density lipoprotein (LDL) cholesterol, thus reducing the risk of heart disease.

Phytochemicals: Chemicals that come from plants. *Phyto,* from the Greek, means "to bring forth" and is used as a prefix to mean "from a plant."

Protein: The building block of body tissues. Protein is necessary for healthy growth, cell repair, reproduction and protection against infection. Protein consists of 22 parts called amino acids. Eight of the 22 amino acids in protein are especially important because they can not be manufactured by the body. Those eight are called essential amino acids.

A food that contains all eight essential amino acids is said to be a complete protein. Protein from animal products — meat, fish, poultry and dairy products — is complete. The only accepted plant sources of complete protein are soybeans and soy products, but research is establishing new theories that the protein content of legumes may be complete enough to replace animal protein.

A food that contains some, but not all, eight

essential amino acids is called an incomplete protein. Nuts, seeds, legumes, cereals and grains are plant products that provide incomplete proteins. If your meals include foods from two complementary incomplete protein sources, your body will combine the incomplete proteins in the right proportions to make a complete protein. For example, many cultures have a tradition of using legumes and whole grains together in dishes. Scientifically, this combination provides a good amino-acid (complete protein) balance in the diet, because legumes are low in methionine but high in lysine, and whole grains are high in methionine but low in lysine. When eaten together, the body combines them to make complete proteins. Nuts and seeds must be paired with dairy or soy proteins in order to provide complete proteins.

Purgative: A substance that promotes bowel movements and increased intestinal peristalsis. *Example:* Yellow dock.

Quercetin: See Flavonoids, page 368.

Resveratrol: A fungicide that occurs naturally in grapes and has been linked to the prevention of clogged arteries by lowering blood cholesterol levels. Resveratrol is found in red wine and, to a lesser extent, in purple grape juice.

Rhizome: An underground stem that is usually thick and fleshy. *Examples:* Ginger and turmeric.

Rubefacient: A substance that, when applied to the skin, stimulates circulation in that area, bringing a good supply of blood to the skin and increasing heat in the tissue. *Examples:* Cayenne; garlic; ginger; mustard seeds; and oils of rosemary, peppermint and thyme.

Sedative: A substance that has a powerful quieting effect on the nervous system that relieves tension and induces sleep. *Examples:* German chamomile, lettuce, linden, lavender and valerian.

Stimulant: A substance that focuses the mind and increases activity. *Examples:* Basil, cayenne, cinnamon, peppermint and rosemary.

Tannin: A chemical constituent in herbs that causes astringency (see Astringent, page 366) and helps stanch internal bleeding. See also Phenolic compounds, left. *Examples:* Coffee, tea and witch hazel.

Terpene: A class of phytochemicals found in a wide variety of fruits, vegetables and herbs that are potent antioxidants. Ginkgo biloba is a good source of some terpenes. Limonoids (see Limonoid, page 369), which are found in citrus fruit rinds, are a subclass of terpenes.

Tincture: A liquid herbal extract made by soaking an herb in alcohol and pure water to extract the plant's active components. Some herbalists maintain that tinctures are the most effective way to take herbs, because they contain a wide range of the plant's chemical constituents and are easily absorbed.

Tisane: The "official" term used for a solution made by steeping fresh or dried herbs in boiling water. The term is interchangeable with the word *tea* when herbs are used.

Tonic: An infusion of herbs that tones or strengthens the system. Often tonics act as alteratives (see Alterative, page 366). Taken either hot or cold, tonics purify the blood and are nutritive. Tonic herbs support the body's systems in maintaining health. *Examples:* Alfalfa, astragalus, dandelion (root and leaf) and ginseng.

Vasodilator: A substance that relaxes blood vessels, increasing circulation to the arms, hands, legs, feet and brain. *Examples:* Peppermint and sage.

Volatile oil: Essential component found in the aerial parts of an herb. Often extracted to make essential oils, volatile oils are antiseptic and very effective at stimulating the body parts to which they are applied.

Wildcrafting: The practice of gathering herbs from the wild. Many plants today are endangered because of excessive wildcrafting. To avoid contributing to this problem, buy herbs that are organically cultivated.

Bibliography

Bartram, Thomas, *Bartram's Encyclopedia of Herbal Medicine* (Dorset, England: Grace Publishers, 1995), ISBN 0-9515984-1-4.

Brill, Steve, with Evelyn Dean, *Identifying and Harvesting Edible and Medicinal Plants* (New York: Hearst Books, 1994), ISBN 0-688-11425-3.

Carper, Jean, *Food: Your Miracle Medicine* (New York: HarperCollins Publishers, Inc., 1993), ISBN 0-06-018321-7.

Crocker, Pat, *The Healing Herbs Cookbook* (Toronto: Robert Rose, 1996), ISBN 0-7788-0004-0.

Crocker, Pat, *The Juicing Bible Second Edition* (Toronto: Robert Rose, 2008), ISBN 0-7788 0181-0.

Duke, James, Ph.D., *The Green Pharmacy* (Emmaus, PA: Rodale Press, 1997), ISBN 0 312-96648-2.

Foster, Stephen, and James A. Duke, *A Field Guide to Medicinal Plants* (New York: Houghton-Mifflin Company, 1990), ISBN 0-395-46722-5.

Gerras, Charles (editor), *Rodale's Basic Natural Foods Cookbook* (Emmaus, PA: Rodale Press, 1984), ISBN 0 87857-469-7.

Heatherley, Ana Nez, *Healing Plants: A Medicinal Guide to Native North American Plants and Herbs* (Toronto: HarperCollins Publishers, Inc., 1998), ISBN 0-00-638617-2.

Hoffman, David, *The New Holistic Herbal* (Rockport, MA: Element, Inc., 1992), ISBN 1-85230-193-7.

Lad, Vasant, *The Complete Book of Ayurvedic Home Remedies* (New York: Three Rivers Press, 1998), ISBN 0-609-80286-0.

McIntyre, Anne, *The Complete Woman's Herbal* (New York: Henry Holt and Company, 1995), ISBN 0-8050-3537-0.

Mortimer, Denise, *Nutritional Healing* (Boston: Element Books, Inc., 1998), ISBN 1-86204-176-8.

Murray, Michael, N.D., and Joseph Pizzorno, N.D., *Encyclopedia of Natural Medicine* (Rocklin, CA: Prima Publishing, 1991), ISBN 1-55958-091-7.

Pitchford, Paul, *Healing with Whole Foods: Oriental Traditions and Modern Nutrition* (Berkeley, CA: North Atlantic Books, 1993), ISBN 0-938190-64-4.

Turner, Lisa, *Meals that Heal* (Rochester, VT: Healing Arts Press, 1996), ISBN 0-89281-625-2.

Weed, Susun, *Healing Wise* (Woodstock, NY: Ash Tree Publishing, 1989), ISBN 0-9614620-2-7.

Werbach, Melvyn, M.D., *Nutritional Influences on Illness* (Tarzana, CA: Third Line Press, 1996), ISBN 0-9618550-5-3.

Library and Archives Canada Cataloguing in Publication

Crocker, Pat
    The smoothies bible / Pat Crocker. — 2nd ed.

Includes index.
ISBN 978-0-7788-0241-9

1. Smoothies (Beverages). 2. Blenders (Cookery). I. Title.

TX840.B5C76 2010   641.8'75   C2009-906687-4

Sources

Herb and Organic Associations/ Organizations/Information

Canadian Organic Growers (COG)
National Office, 323 Chapel Street
Ottawa, ON K1N 7Z2 Canada
Tel: (613) 216-0741
Web site: www.cog.ca
Canada's national information network for organic farmers, gardeners and consumers.

Herb Society of America (HSA)
9019 Chardon Road
Kirtland, OH 44094 USA
Tel: (440) 256-0514 Fax: (440) 256-0541
Web site: www.herbsociety.org
A well-organized group of herb enthusiasts, with many active local units.

International Herb Association (IHA)
P.O. Box 5667
Jacksonville, FL 32247-5667 USA
Web site: www.iherb.org
A professional organization of herb growers and business owners.

Organic Trade Association (OTA)
P.O. Box 547
Greenfield, MA 01302 USA
Tel: (413) 774-7511 Fax: (413) 774-6432
Web site: www.ota.com
Promotes awareness and understanding of organic farming and provides a unified voice for the industry.

Herb Farms and Herb Mail-Order Sources

Frontier Natural Products Co-op
3021 78th Street P.O. Box 299
Norway, IA 52318
Tel: (800) 669-3275 Fax: (800) 717-4372
Web site: www.frontiercoop.com
Supplier of bulk herbs.

Mountain Rose Herbs
85472 Dilley Lane
Eugene, OR 97405 USA
Tel: (800) 879-3337
Fax: (510) 217-4012
Web site: www.mountainroseherbs.com
Bulk organic herbs, oils, butters, clays and teas available for mail order.

Richters Herbs
357 Highway 47
Goodwood, ON L0C 1A0 Canada
Tel: (905) 640-6677
Fax: (905) 640-6641
Web site: www.richters.com
Herb specialist with over 800 varieties that has been selling herbs since 1969. Mail-order seeds, plants and books. Free color catalogue, seminars and herbal events.

Related Consumer Web Sites

www.organicconsumers.org Activist organization with information and action strategies on organic foods, genetically modified foods, irradiation, mad cow disease and other issues.

www.ofrf.org Organic Farming Research Foundation, which sponsors research related to organic-farming practices.

www.ewg.org The United States–based Environmental Working Group, an activist organization around environmental issues.

www.ocia.org Organic Crop Improvement Association, one of the international organic food certification bodies.

www.biodynamics.com Information about biodynamic gardening and farming.

www.rodaleinstitute.org In the mid-1900s, J.J. Rodale developed an emphasis on health and organic gardening through his publications and the Rodale Family Institute.

www.slowfood.com A member-supported local food, local traditions organization that supports honest foods and food producers.

Appendix A
Food Allergies

Certain foods can trigger or aggravate conditions such as asthma, chronic fatigue syndrome, depression, chronic digestive problems, eczema, headaches, hives, irritable bowel syndrome, migraines, rheumatoid arthritis and ulcerative colitis in adults, and ear infections and epilepsy in children.

Symptoms of food allergies and intolerances can include chronic infections or inflammations, diarrhea, fatigue, anxiety, depression, joint pain, skin rashes, dark circles or puffiness under the eyes, itchy nose or throat, water retention and swollen glands.

In the classic allergic reaction, a trigger (such as nuts) is mistakenly identified as an "enemy" by the immune system, which sets out to get rid of the offending toxin.

Food intolerances or sensitivities differ from "classic" allergies in that reactions do not happen immediately. As a result, allergy tests often cannot detect food intolerances. If you suspect that a food may be causing a chronic problem, the most effective method of identifying the culprit is to use an elimination diet.

Factors in food allergies include digestive system problems and lowered immune system function. While eliminating suspected foods from the diet, work to improve immunity (see Immune Deficiency, page 57) and digestion (see Indigestion, page 60). A key factor in digestion is liver function (see Liver Problems, page 68). Regular daily exercise and stress-reduction activities, such as meditation and yoga, improve immunity.

The most common foods that provoke chronic conditions are dairy products, wheat, corn, caffeine, yeast and citrus fruits. Other common food problems occur with processed and refined foods, artificial food additives and preservatives, eggs, strawberries, pork, tomatoes, peanuts and chocolate. In irritable bowel syndrome, potatoes and onions are also common triggers. Dairy products are the most common trigger for children's chronic ear infections.

Foods that are especially helpful in reducing allergic reactions are:

- antioxidant fruits and vegetables;
- yogurt with active bacterial cultures, which reestablish helpful digestive bacteria;
- flavonoids in the skins of fruits and vegetables;
- essential fatty acids in oily fish (herring, salmon, sardines, mackerel), fish oils, flax seeds and evening primrose oil, which are anti-inflammatory and reduce the severity of allergies; and
- foods that contain vitamin C (broccoli, lemon juice and rose-hip tea are sources that are unlikely to cause allergic reactions).

The Elimination Diet

Preparation

Before starting an elimination diet, consult with your health-care practitioner to eliminate the possibility of a serious disease causing your symptoms. If disease is not evident, ask for (and follow) your health-care practitioner's advice about trying the elimination diet.

Choosing Foods to Eliminate

Eliminate refined and processed foods, which will improve immunity and digestion. Avoid artificial food additives and preservatives, which are common food allergens. If you regularly drink coffee or alcohol and are eliminating them, you may experience headaches. To avoid this side-effect, cut down on them gradually.

You can choose to eliminate one food at a time or multiple foods. It is important that you consume a wide variety of different types of food in your diet. Choose to eliminate dairy products, wheat, corn, caffeine, yeast and citrus fruits first because they are proven to be the most common problem foods. Do not add foods to which you have known allergies.

Steps in the Elimination Diet

1. Start a daily diet diary, noting all the foods you eat each day and the symptoms you experience.
2. Eliminate one food item from your diet for a period of one week. Start with a food that most commonly causes symptoms, especially one that you eat regularly. The food must be completely eliminated. If you are eliminating eggs, avoid cakes, salad dressings and any other foods that may contain eggs. If you are eliminating dairy products, check the ingredient lists of all foods for lactose, lactic acid and whey, which are all dairy. Margarine commonly contains these ingredients.
3. If you have fewer symptoms while eliminating the chosen food or foods, proceed to Step 4 to check each food you have eliminated. If there is no improvement in your symptoms, go back to the Guidelines to Eating Well diet (page 14) while you choose another food to eliminate.
4. Add the suspected food item back to your diet by eating two servings a day for the next three days. If you experience any symptoms, stop eating the food immediately and avoid it for six months while you work on improving your immunity, digestion and liver function.

Reintroducing Foods that Cause Adverse Reactions

After eliminating the food from your diet for six months, it often can be slowly reintroduced to the diet without adverse effects.

Appendix B
Food Combining

Food combining is a disciplined method of eating foods in a specific order or combination. It is used as a short-term aid to digestive problems and, in simple terms, requires eating protein foods, carbohydrate foods and fruits at different times, thus allowing for complete and efficient digestion of each food.

Protein foods — meat, poultry, fish, eggs, nuts, seeds, dairy products, soy products — require the most time and energy for the body to digest.

Carbohydrates are the starches and sugars found in foods that furnish most of the energy needed for the body's activities. Squash, legumes, grains (wheat, oats, rice, rye, etc.), pasta, beets, parsnips, carrots, sweet potatoes and pumpkin are starchy carbohydrate foods that break down faster than protein foods but not as quickly as fruits. Fruits are high-sugar carbohydrate foods that are digested very quickly and are thus considered separately in food combining.

Fruits require the least time and energy for the body to digest and should be eaten before a meal or at least two hours after a meal. When taken this way, fruit acts as a digestive cleanser, promoting digestive function. Fruit taken with a meal causes digestive problems. Melons and bananas should be eaten separately from other fruits.

The best food-combining meals are given below.
- Fruits alone — this is best taken as a variety of fruits at breakfast.
- Proteins with non-starchy vegetables (leafy greens, asparagus, broccoli, cabbage, celery, cucumber, onion, sweet peppers, sea herbs, tomatoes, zucchini).
- Grains with non-starchy vegetables.

Health conditions that may improve with food combining are food allergies and intolerances, indigestion, inflammatory bowel, flatulence, fatigue and peptic ulcer.

Eating Protein and Carbohydrate Foods in the Same Meal

Protein foods need to be in the stomach for three to four hours. Protein requires an acid medium in which to be digested. Pepsin, the enzyme that begins the digestion of protein, is active only in an acid medium.

Starches (elements that break down into sugars) and sugars (honey, sugar and sugar products) pass through the stomach in 20 to 45 minutes and are digested in the small intestine. Starch requires an alkaline medium in which to be digested. The enzyme ptyalin (salivary amylase), which initiates starch breakdown, is active in an alkaline medium only and is destroyed by the hydrochloric acid that the stomach secretes.

When starches and proteins are eaten together, acidic gastric juices destroy the ptyalin and the salivary digestion of starch. Starches cannot pass through the stomach to the small intestine and are left to rot and ferment, causing gas and abdominal pain. The undigested starch in the stomach interferes with the breakdown and absorption of protein, leading to undigested protein in the stool and protein deficiency in the body.

The hydrochloric acid normally produced by a healthy system can neutralize the putrefactive process if it is present in significant amounts. For many people, especially those over age 35 and those with weak secretions, hydrochloric acid is not produced in sufficient amounts.